Material
Cultures
IN CANADA

Cultural Studies Series

Cultural Studies is the multi- and inter-disciplinary study of culture, defined anthropologically as a "way of life," performatively as symbolic practice, and ideologically as the collective product of varied media and cultural industries. Although Cultural Studies is a relative newcomer to the humanities and social sciences, in less than half a century it has taken interdisciplinary scholarship to a new level of sophistication, reinvigorating the liberal arts curriculum with new theories, topics, and forms of intellectual partnership.

Wilfrid Laurier University Press invites submissions of manuscripts concerned with critical discussions on power relations concerning gender, class, sexual preference, ethnicity, and other macro and micro sites of political struggle.

For more information, please contact:

Lisa Quinn
Acquisitions Editor
Wilfrid Laurier University Press
75 University Avenue West
Waterloo, ON N2L 3C5
Canada
Phone: 519-884-0710 ext. 2843
Fax: 519-725-1399
Email: quinn@press.wlu.ca

Material Cultures
IN CANADA

THOMAS ALLEN
and JENNIFER BLAIR, editors

WILFRID LAURIER
UNIVERSITY PRESS

Wilfrid Laurier University Press acknowledges the support of the Canada Council for the Arts for our publishing program. We acknowledge the financial support of the Government of Canada through the Canada Book Fund for our publishing activities. This book was supported by the Research Support Fund.

 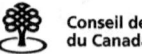 

Library and Archives Canada Cataloguing in Publication

    Material cultures in Canada / Thomas Allen and Jennifer Blair, editors.

(Cultural studies series)
Includes bibliographical references and index.
Issued in print and electronic formats.
ISBN 978-1-77112-014-2 (pbk.).—ISBN 978-1-77112-015-9 (pdf).—
ISBN 978-1-77112-016-6 (epub)

    1. Material culture—Canada. I. Blair, Jennifer, 1975–, editor II. Allen, Thomas M., 1967–, author, editor III. Series: Cultural studies series (Waterloo, Ont.)

FC95.M39 2015   306.4'60971   C2015-900231-1
                                                                                C2015-900232-X

Front-cover photograph: *Container Ports #8, Racine Port, Montreal, Quebec*, by Edward Burtynsky. Copyright © Edward Burtynsky. Courtesy Nicholas Metivier Gallery, Toronto. Cover design by hwtstudio.com. Text design by Angela Booth Malleau.

© 2015 Wilfrid Laurier University Press
Waterloo, Ontario, Canada
www.wlupress.wlu.ca

Every reasonable effort has been made to acquire permission for copyright material used in this text, and to acknowledge all such indebtedness accurately. Any errors and omissions called to the publisher's attention will be corrected in future printings.

No part of this publication may be reproduced, stored in a retrieval system, or transmitted, in any form or by any means, without the prior written consent of the publisher or a licence from the Canadian Copyright Licensing Agency (Access Copyright). For an Access Copyright licence, visit http://www.accesscopyright.ca or call toll free to 1-800-893-5777.

CONTENTS

Acknowledgements	vii
Introduction Material Cultures in Canada, Material Cultures Now *Thomas Allen and Jennifer Blair*	1

PART I   MATERIALITIES

1	The Work of the Beaver *Jody Berland*	25
2	Night in a Box Anne Carson's *Nox* and the Materiality of Elegy *Tanis MacDonald*	51
3	Maxims and Contraries Notes from a Project in Process *Alison Calder*	65
4	The Geranium in the Window One Plant's Literary Hardiness in the Canadian Imagination *Shelley Boyd*	83
5	Is It Still a Cinch? The Transformational Properties of Objects in Guy Vanderhaeghe's *The Last Crossing* *Susan Birkwood*	107

PART II   IMMATERIALITIES

6	Obama's Playlist Materializing Transnational Desire at the CBC *Mark Simpson*	131

	7	Grinning Things Object Lessons in Violent Labour Michael Epp	155
	8	Moses Cotsworth and the Authenticity of Time Thomas Allen	171
	9	Materializing Climate Change Images of Exposure, States of Exception Nicole Shukin	189
	10	Waters as Potential Paths to Peace Rita Wong	209
PART III		MATERIALS OF AND FOR SPACES	
	11	The Biotopographies of Seth's *George Sprott (1894–1975)* Candida Rifkind	225
	12	Woodrow Memory and Nostalgia at Play Jessa Alston-O'Connor	247
	13	Plaques and Persons Commemorating Canada's Authors Carole Gerson	265
	14	Archaeological Detritus and the Bulging Archive The Staging of *He Named Her Amber* at the Art Gallery of Ontario May Chew	283
	15	Poetry and Globalized Cities A Material Poetics of Canadian Urban Space Jeff Derksen	301
Afterword		Endless Material The Future of Things in Canada Thomas Allen and Jennifer Blair	323
		Contributors	333
		Index	339

Acknowledgements

A grant from the Social Sciences and Humanities Research Council of Canada helped make possible the Material Cultures conference, where the work that appears in this book was first presented. The conference was held at the University of Ottawa in 2011 (it was the Canadian Literature Symposium for that year), and we would also like to acknowledge the Department of English, the Faculty of Arts, and the Research Development Program for their generous support of the event. We are especially grateful to all of the conference participants for the lively and rigorous conversations that inspired much of the thinking that is represented here, and that crystallized a sense of what material culture studies in Canada is today.

The conference would not have been as successful as it was without the tremendous help of our research assistant, Tania Aguila-Way, and we would like to thank her for all of the hard work that she put into planning and facilitating the event. From organizing conference matters to taking care of so many administrative details leading up to the publication of this book, Nadine Mayhew was indispensible; we feel lucky to work with her, especially for her skill, wit, and patience. Several of our fellow professors in the Department of English have contributed to our thinking about material cultures scholarship within various areas of literary and cultural studies and we would like to thank them for their ongoing support and inspiration, especially Lauren Gillingham, Craig Gordon, Anne Raine, and Robert Stacey. We would also like to thank the editorial and production staff at Wilfrid Laurier University Press for all that they did to bring this book to fruition, along with the anonymous reviewers, whose comments made this a stronger publication. Finally, we are grateful to Edward Burtynsky for permission to use his compelling photograph on the book's cover.

INTRODUCTION

Material Cultures in Canada, Material Cultures Now

Thomas Allen and Jennifer Blair

When we set out to create a collection of chapters showcasing the current state of the field of material culture studies in Canada, we found ourselves attempting to situate something elusive in time and space. The essays we received in response to our call for papers conjured a plethora of problems of definition. The phrase "material culture," which has had so much influence on scholarship in the humanities over the past decade, sometimes refers to a field and sometimes to an approach, sometimes to a method of analysis and sometimes to the objects of analysis. How does this rather loose concept fit within the national framework of an already protean field such as "Canadian studies," or the even more capacious "studies in Canada"? And what does it mean to try to define the state of a field at a particular moment, when that field is so various and leads in so many different directions?

If this book succeeds in offering a snapshot of material culture studies in Canada at this time—and we hope that it does—then the picture is emergent, issuing from the confluence of the work of scholars with quite different approaches and interests. Nevertheless, there is a commonality to these chapters in which can be recognized major elements of the history of material culture studies in the humanities. Addressing topics as various as comic books and climate change, the CBC and the YMCA, these chapters exemplify the way that a material culture approach can illuminate crucial issues in a variety of fields by revealing connections between history and the present, between the immaterial and the material, and between Canada and the rest of the world. The chapters presented here also highlight the value of this approach to efforts to understand the relationships between, on the one hand, identity and autonomy in certain contexts (individual and collective, human and non-human), and the ever-shifting economic and political structures that inform how people locate themselves and engage with the world on the other. In these respects, these chapters reflect the best potential of material culture studies, an often diffuse field whose remarkable growth over the past thirty years has been propelled by a series of influential scholarly engagements with pressing political, economic, and environmental problems.

The interdisciplinary field of material culture studies as we now know it developed fairly recently and rapidly. Before the 1980s, the phrase material culture usually designated sub-fields of work within social scientific disciplines such as archaeology, anthropology, and social history. These fields typically defined themselves with reference to empirical methodologies derived from the sciences. The material world was a privileged category in such fields precisely because it promised a kind of empirical certainty that meshed well with scientific positivism. In the humanities, on the other hand, material culture played a minor role through studies of topics such as book history, artistic production, and provenance, but the scholarly approach to these subjects was primarily antiquarian and un-theorized.

This situation changed dramatically with the 1986 publication of Arjun Appadurai's revolutionary collection of essays on *The Social Life of Things: Commodities in Cultural Perspective*. Appadurai brought theory to bear on the material world in ways that transcended disciplinary boundaries and opened up possibilities of analysis for cultural theorists from a variety of different fields, including the humanities. Over the ensuing years, these theorists recognized that material culture studies was no longer a carefully policed set of practices within mature, quasi-scientific disciplines, but an insurgent field that promised new insights into areas of study from cultural history to literature and philosophy.

As Appadurai's subtitle suggests, his collection focused on the status of objects as commodities, a term critical to theory and philosophy in the Marxian tradition. This emphasis is unsurprising, given that Appadurai's remarkable intervention came at a time when the humanities were being reshaped by the powerful influence of a number of major works of neo-Marxism, such as Fredric Jameson's *The Political Unconscious* (1981) and Marshall Berman's *All That Is Solid Melts into Air* (1982). This was also the decade in which a number of important European philosophers influenced by Marxism became required reading in humanities departments in the English-speaking world, including Georg Lukács, Walter Benjamin, Antonio Gramsci, and Louis Althusser. Due in large part to this broader context, the first wave of overtly theorized material culture scholarship in the anglophone world was essentially a version of historical materialism, in which objects were understood primarily as aspects of nature transformed into commodities, and as sites bringing to visibility the contradictions of ideology and the misperceptions of reification. For Appadurai and the other scholars whose work was included in his collection, the "life" of things was a function of their circulation as commodities through human activities of exchange and consumption. This "life" was an aspect of ideology, reality misperceived in politically important ways, rather than an essential attribute of the non-human world.

Fifteen years later, in 2001, Bill Brown issued a call for a "new materialism" that redirected our attention away from commodities and toward *things* that precede and exist independently of people.[1] As Brown put it in the introduction to the landmark special issue of *Critical Inquiry* on "Things": "As they circulate through our lives, we look *through* objects (to see what they disclose about history, society, nature, or culture—above all, what they disclose about *us*), but we only catch a glimpse of things" (4). Brown's "thing theory" shifted the focus of analysis away from a Marxist concern with how human beings transform nature into useful objects and toward a consideration of how the material world shapes us. Similarly, the recent work of Jane Bennett and other "new vitalists" has sought to give voice to the agency of the non-human world, to recognize the non-human as autonomous and valuable in its own right. These interventions mark a trajectory away from an anthropocentric view of the material world and toward an effort to acknowledge "the thing itself," a Kantian phrase from Wallace Stevens that is cited repeatedly in material culture theory.

This interest in the agency of the non-human world is connected to the sense of ethical urgency that underlies much of the recent materialist theory. The new materialism of today responds to economic and environmental crises that demand a profound rethinking of the human relationship to the non-human world. As Diana Coole and Samantha Frost write in the introduction to the important collection of essays entitled *New Materialisms: Ontology, Agency, and Politics* (2010), "In terms of theory itself ... we are summoning a new materialism in response to a sense that the radicalism of the dominant discourses which have flourished under the cultural turn is now more or less exhausted. We share the feeling current among many researchers that the dominant constructivist orientation to social analysis is inadequate for thinking about matter, materiality, and politics in ways that do justice to the contemporary context of biopolitics and global political economy" (6). Like other recent new materialist work, the collection edited by Coole and Frost reveals not only the way that new materialism differentiates itself from older historical materialism, but also the way it defines itself in opposition to cultural constructivism. Both Marxism and the "cultural turn" posit a world whose important features are all products of human activity. For the most part, new materialists see their work as predicated upon a recognition of the other, not in the epistemological form of cultural or historical difference or even the economic form of class difference, but in the ontological forms of differences between species, between animate and inanimate, between matter and energy. Such recognition requires an acknowledgement of the reality of a world outside of culture. From this perspective, the "life" of things is not ideological or metaphorical, but rather the essence of that reality.

This perspective draws inspiration from philosophers such as Bruno Latour and Michel Callon, whose actor-network theory accounts for the agency of non-human "actors" involved in patterns of activity with human beings, and from other contemporary studies of science and technology. New materialists have investigated the human relationship to machines and the built environment, as well as the kinds of distributed agency emerging from large-scale assemblages such as electrical grids and computer networks. In terms of life sciences, new materialists have addressed the human relationship to animals, plants, and bacteria, not only in light of environmental concerns but also with an eye toward rethinking our sense of our embodied selves as autonomous and unitary. For many, these issues are tied together. As Bennett writes, what we habitually think of as the individual person is in fact an *"array of bodies"* in which the microbes far outnumber the human cells (112); Bennett wonders whether "if we were more attentive to the indispensable foreignness that we are, would we continue to produce and consume in the same violently reckless ways?" (113). Noting that the foods we eat and the bacteria that inhabit us can shape our behaviour in complex ways, Bennett argues that we must understand ourselves as parts of "biochemical-social systems" (112) where the doctrines of rights and ethics derived from Enlightenment humanism seem ill-equipped to enable us to confront the ecological and political challenges of the moment.

Nevertheless, the new materialists have remained deeply aware of the difficulty of ever seeing the material world as other than an object world, as long as the human subject is the source of perception, and thus material culture studies has wrestled again and again with the trouble of escaping what Daniel Miller calls "the simplistic duality of subjects and objects" (10). For scholars in the humanities, then, much of the attraction of material culture studies resides in the questions the field raises about perception, knowledge, and representation, topics that have always been central to literary, philosophical, and art historical inquiry. In this respect, the "picture theory" of

W. J. T. Mitchell (who asks, "What do pictures want?") and the studies of miniatures and collections by Susan Stewart can be seen as branches of material culture studies. This kind of work in the humanities begs us to consider how our perceptions of the world redound within networks of subject and object relations in which the boundaries between human and non-human are frequently transgressed. In *Persons and Things* (2008), literary critic and theorist Barbara Johnson identifies four tropes that condition our relations to the non-human world: apostrophe, prosopopeia, anthropomorphism, and personification. Johnson's work enables us to see that our connections to the non-human world, the world of objects, materials, and things, are both enabled and limited by our propensity to make sense of things through the very rhetorical strategies we employ to interpret literary narratives or painterly scenes. That these rhetorical terms would be so central to our relationship to the material world suggests the central role the humanities have to play in material culture studies, especially at this moment when the distinction between subject and object has become the central question of the field.

The recently published *Oxford Handbook of Material Culture Studies* (2010), edited by Dan Hicks and Mary C. Beaudry, reveals how these changes have come full circle. Almost all of the contributions to that volume come from archaeology, anthropology, and geography, three of the more scientific disciplines that have now, as the essays collected in the *Handbook* amply illustrate, adopted many of the theoretical perspectives on material culture that have come back to them through the humanities. In his contribution to the volume, Hicks, an archaeologist, acknowledges the impact of Latour and other theorists on his own field: "Things can matter, we might suggest, even when people do not say that they matter. The human significance of meaningful 'material culture' is, of course, a crucial element of accounting for the material world: but the physicality of things calls into question the idea of 'material culture' as an excessively anthropocentric definition of the field of inquiry: delimited by those moments in which things are meaningful or filled with cultural significance" (75). Hicks proposes that we understand both things and theories as "events" and "effects" unfolding within and productive of time, just like human beings, and thus that we recognize archaeological fieldwork as "constituted by moments of permeability between fieldworker, place, things, and people" (89). Scholars in the humanities will immediately be struck by the way that Hicks's terminology and approach evoke recent efforts by cultural theorists to make sense of the relationships between observers, images, and texts.

In a complementary movement, some recent work in the humanities has reached back to older concepts of historical materialism and to interdisciplinary concepts from the social sciences in order to understand how the material world functions in relation to imperialism and globalization. Both *The Ideas in Things: Fugitive Meaning in the Victorian Novel* (2006), by Elaine Freedgood, and *Portable Property: Victorian Culture on the Move* (2008), by John Plotz, make use of notions of commodity fetishism and cultural "life" in order to analyze the meaning of objects circulating through the nineteenth-century British Empire. In both cases, this somewhat traditional Marxist analysis is juxtaposed with rhetorical insights akin to those developed by Johnson, and an attention to the autonomy of things derived from Brown. For Freedgood, the key to unlocking "fugitive meaning" is a strong metonymic reading, which "involves taking a novelistic thing materially and literally and then following it beyond the covers of the text" so that "the object is investigated in terms of its own properties and history and then refigured alongside and athwart the novel's manifest or dominant narrative— the one that concerns its subjects" (12). Freedgood's metonymic reading thus enables her to acknowledge the autonomy of objects while still tracing the role those objects play in the culture and politics of a global empire. For Plotz, "portable property" serves as a "third term" between Appadurai's fetishized commodities and Brown's autonomous things. Plotz employs anthropological theory about gift-giving and exchange to develop his argument that the sentiments invested in objects circulating across the Victorian world were neither atavistic remnants of a pre-capitalist age nor merely projections of a middle-class ideology, but rather embodiments of English culture "in its most particularist and nonteleological sense" (21). Eschewing the teleology of Marxist theory, Plotz employs social scientific perspectives to revise Appadurai's interpretation of the commodity. For both Freedgood and Plotz, the concepts of other eras and fields provide resources with which to continue to develop new perspectives in material culture studies in the humanities.

Just as the question of what constitutes material culture studies today elicits a wide-ranging and continually shifting set of responses, the question of what a particularly "Canadian" version of such an endeavour might be complicates matters further still. As a number of our contributors note, the nation persisted through globalization much more solidly than expected, and this book reflects this persistence in terms of the objects it studies and the categories of analysis it pursues.[2] This is not to say that our contributors grant some sort of citizenship status to things. Nor do they seek to ascribe to them some sort of identity or legitimacy by affiliating them with a national entity. In fact, the focus of this book, as our title indicates, is *Material Cultures in Canada*, rather than Canadian materials. In their varied objects of study, the chapters presented here illustrate how the nation informs the ways in which we think and conduct scholarly work without limiting the scope of that work to the confines of a national border.

Perhaps it is no surprise to find that this complex relationship between national identity and transnational inquiry comes to the fore in that most inevitable of Canadian icons, the beaver. As Jody Berland reveals, the beaver (at least as it appears in various material and representational contexts) sustains its nationalist affiliation by erasing from popular national consciousness the troubling aspects of Canada's social and environment history. In this way, the beaver embodies the historical nature of the Canadian border and Canada's necessary relationship with the world beyond. The powerful yet provisional nature of bounded national identity is also brought to light in chapters about things like the CBC's playlist of Canadian music for Barack Obama (assembled so that the president could acquire an appreciation of Canadian culture upon his inauguration), Mary Maxim sweaters, and geraniums. These things, as well as many of the others discussed in this book, all have explicit Canadian affiliations, but they are also fundamentally transnational. The beaver became famous only because Europeans wanted felt hats. The playlist is an example of Canada's renewed post-Bush eagerness for American recognition that, as Mark Simpson argues, ultimately speaks to "the vexed histories of Canadian content." The Mary Maxim sweater also arises out of a set of different national affiliations. It may have been dubbed "the cardigan that says Canadian,"[3] as Alison Calder notes in her chapter in this volume, but its overall concept and some of its decorative designs were taken from the sweaters knit by members of the Cowichan First Nation. The transnational movement of the sweater does not stop there, however, since, as Calder explains, "the Cowichan knitters re-appropriated and continued to adapt the Mary Maxim patterns that had been based on their own work to begin with." The geranium, meanwhile, is one of the plants most commonly found on Canadian windowsills (in winter) and window boxes (in summer). But these ordinary, container-bound annuals demonstrate Canadians' desire to cultivate large and colourful blooms in a climate that is inhospitable to the African plant.

Like geraniums, many of the things in this book have their roots, or their reasons for being, elsewhere. They have travelled across geographical, national, and cultural borders, or they are meant to travel beyond the location in which they were produced. Although not all of them are commodities, they call to mind Appadurai's claim that "it is the things-in-motion that illuminate their human and social context" (5). More specifically, these things accrue their status as objects, and their social and material value, by virtue of this border crossing (or even the mere potential for such border-crossing). This emphasis on migrant objects is also a feature of a material culture approach, which is more often than not transnational at its core. A case in point is Brown's 1996 book *The Material Unconscious*; in the introduction to this study of Stephen Crane's writing and "American amusement," Brown recalls that Association football "developed only after a team from McGill University had introduced rugby at Harvard in 1874" (2). When the aim of Brown's study is to show "how the material past inhabited a determinate but not wholly determinant ideology or symbology" (18), in this early example Brown highlights the transnational past of a sport that is most often viewed as representing the national uniformity of the United States. This book exhibits the various ways in which even those objects that have the most nationalist of aspirations tend to find these aspirations compromised by the connections they inevitably maintain to other nations and to modes of located-ness or identification that are not nationalist in their configuration.

Simpson's chapter in this volume points to the fact that things can alert us to "national identification and disidentification all at once." As Simpson has argued elsewhere, resisting the pull of nationalism does not always amount to a progressive move. Writing on the culture of object exchange in early-twentieth-century Alberta, Simpson notes how hunters, taxidermists, and wildlife museum curators "could consign the 49th parallel to myth and memory because of a faith not so much in U.S. American superiority as in transnational racial community" ("Immaculate" 79). He goes on to point out that the wildlife-carcass object providers he cites were "passionate nationalists," but only when this passion worked "to secure the common health of the white body along the lines of commerce" (97). Political borders, then, can function in the service of a racism that strives to transcend borders when doing so furthers its campaign. What's more, it is dangerous to assume that the nation continues to function as it has historically—that is, as a self-determining and self-regulating entity primarily committed to maintaining its borders. In his chapter in this volume, Simpson points out that "the nation, in its very resurgence, has not simply reverted to its twentieth-century form" but "materializes instead in deregulatory guise, as a kind of geopolitical switch-point requisite to the tendencies of neoliberal capitalism."

In a somewhat different take on objects and their affiliation with nations, Michael Epp's chapter in this collection assesses a 1921 war manual called *Entertaining the American Army* for its treatment of the smile as an object of war. If this object does rest in a twentieth-century moment, Epp suggests that it forecasts the emotional labour of war in more recent contexts, including the rock band Glass Tiger's visit to Afghanistan to entertain Canadian soldiers and "show them that Canada still cares." The most lethal border-crossing object considered in this book is a workman's belt, which, as Susan Birkwood explains, precipitates gender and class-affiliated violence in Guy Vanderhaeghe's *The Last Crossing*. In that novel, a wealthy Englishman travelling in Canada murders a young girl with the belt that the gamekeeper on his home estate gave him when he was a boy. The gamekeeper initially intended the belt to be used on the boy himself, assuming that he would need to be whipped when he went off to school. Once the boy grows up, however, he finds that in colonial Canada he can turn this violence against others more vulnerable than himself.

As Birkwood's chapter points out, things can come to act and signify differently as they move across national borders. As with other scholarly communities organized within national boundaries, materialist criticism in Canada has a unique history and position within the larger global field. In his "Manifesto for Materialism," the introduction to the "Materializing Canada" 1999 Special Issue of *Essays on Canadian Writing*, Szeman explained that his impetus for the issue was his desire "to draw attention to how marginalized materialist criticism has always been in Canada—to be more specific, how marginalized it has always been in English Canadian criticism" (11). Rereading this introduction in 2015 serves as a reminder of how far materialist criticism has come in English Canadian scholarship. No longer does Canadian criticism seem, as Szeman put it in his polemic, "to be happy to contemplate even contemporary writing as if nothing really significant has happened in the world" (13). Szeman insisted that critical attention to context alone did not amount to a materialist approach, and he sought to separate a materialist method from New Historicism's "cultural materialism," arguing that the "aim of materialist criticism" was "to effect a fundamental reorientation of our approach to texts that challenges this very way of understanding culture" (2). Still, Szeman did not propose a definite model for what material culture studies in Canada should be. Instead, he drew from Peter Hitchcock's use of the term "oscillation" to describe the "permanent, productive critical vacillation" that informs materialist thinking, and insisted that materialist criticism maintain this constant motion and indeterminacy as it gained momentum in Canadian contexts (6).

Since 1999 the study of culture as part of literary analysis, as part of what we do with texts, has become almost the norm in Canadian scholarship. The idea that analyses of culture can usefully inform literary criticism (and that cultural studies can be situated, in some cases, within literature departments) is now relatively standard. It is a testament to the work of Szeman and other material culture scholars that the introduction to "Materializing Canada" now reads as an artifact of a different era of literary studies. It has become commonplace to examine how various material aspects of texts contribute to the ways in which they are read and affect the world, and also to our methods for analyzing them and understanding ourselves in relation to them—as critics, educators, political subjects, and consumers, and as embodied social and material beings. In fact the rich interdisciplinarity of material culture studies has become commonplace as well, so much so that Szeman's elaboration upon the explanation of the "aims of materialist criticism," quoted below, now seems curiously devoted to textual studies alone:

> In other words, to undertake materialist criticism is to try to understand the processes of literary and cultural transubstantiation: the processes by which an *object* composed of glue, paper, and ink, the product of printing presses, literary circles, and social machines of influence and reputation, all organized in particular ways given the social, historical, and political weightiness of every epoch, is mystically transformed from a state of material solidity into the *spirit* of the text with which criticism has alone typically wanted to commune. (3)

But has materialist criticism, or its descendant, material culture studies, come into its own in the past dozen years or so in Canada? In comparison with the United States and the United Kingdom, Canada lacks a consolidated group of researchers working in literary and cultural studies domains who identify themselves as doing work on "material culture."[4] While those familiar with the material culture approach in American and British contexts may decry the absence of such an identifiable group, it may be more in keeping with Szeman's oscillation metaphor that academics working within Canada, or writing about it, remain somewhat disparate. These scholars do exist, of course. It does not take a lot of searching to come up with some examples of scholarship conducted by academics working in Canada that can be located within this oscillating field of material culture studies. Consider Misao Dean's recent monograph on the canoe, or Pauline Wakeham's on taxidermy. Nicole Shukin, one of our contributors, also made an important contribution to materialist criticism in the context of animal studies with her book *Animal Capital: Rendering Life in Biopolitical Times* (2009).

Not to go unmentioned here is the book history component of material culture studies, which has risen in critical popularity in Canada in the past decade. The History of the Book in Canada Project, a major collaborative research initiative that took place from 2000 to 2007, galvanized the field of book history within Canadian contexts. The scholars involved in this project conducted a kind of materialist criticism of books, perhaps not quite of the explicitly political and polemical sort that Szeman envisioned, but one that does respond, in general, to his insistence upon new ways of working with texts that are attentive to the conditions of their production and their material life thereafter. Extraordinarily productive, the History of the Book in Canada Project published a six-volume book series, constructed a number of databases, and organized several conferences. Another of our contributors, Carole Gerson, was one of the editors of the third volume of the book series. Her chapter in this collection shifts its critical gaze away from "the book"—away, even, from print culture—to focus instead on the historical plaque as its material object of analysis. In this move, the stationary plaque supplants the mobile book, emphasizing fixity over circulation. This move also reflects a turn in material culture studies to an emphasis on the spatial arrangement of things in specific locations, or what Nigel Thrift calls their "worlding" (638).[5]

Notwithstanding this work being conducted by literature and cultural studies scholars, it appears that, by and large, Canadian research on material culture still tends to be located within the fields of anthropology, archaeology, and museum studies. The *Material Culture Review*, now housed at Cape Breton University, reflects this disciplinary focus insofar as many of its contributors hold positions with museums rather than in universities. The journal is also affiliated with the Canada Science and Technology Museum in Ottawa, which was once its publisher under the title *Material History Review*. When the journal was first established in the 1970s as the *Material History Bulletin*, it was a co-production of the National Museum of Man (now the Canadian Museum of History) and what was then called the National Museum of Science and Technology. The *Material History Bulletin* was initially launched to provide a forum for research on the increasingly large number of historical artifacts that Canadian museums had been amassing. As the former editor Gerald Pocius explains, the journal was "largely the creation of historians, mostly working in museum contexts" and it was part of a broader scholarly effort to "discover the material past of ordinary people" (5). Pocius also points out that the journal's founders felt that "Canadians should not be burdened with the problems that Americans faced by using the term 'culture'. Culture was a much-debated and ill-defined term, and therefore would be avoided" (5). The term "culture" made its appearance only in the third (and current) version of the title in 2006, when the journal moved to Cape Breton University, its first academic home. The editorial board felt the title change reflected the "kinds of scholarship the journal publishes" as well as "the intellectual changes in our study of artifacts within the Canadian context" (8). This self-conscious attention to the methodological utility of the concept of culture recalls Szeman's emphasis on the term, specifically when he cites Fredric Jameson's argument that "in postmodernity culture can no longer be understood separately from other spheres of social life, because it has expanded 'throughout the social realm, to the point at which everything in our social life ... can be said to have become "cultural" in some original yet untheorized sense'" (Szeman 12; Jameson, *Postmodernism* 48). While much of material culture studies engages the wide-ranging but also increasingly pressing question of what constitutes matter, objects, and the human and social environments in which these objects dwell, both Szeman and Pocius point out that "culture" is also a variable that has different significances in different times and contexts.[6]

The *Material Culture Review*'s current editor, Richard MacKinnon, a specialist in Atlantic Canadian culture, also holds a Canada Research Chair in "Intangible Cultural Heritage."[7] This combination of the material and the intangible seems paradoxical, but it in fact speaks to the questions arising out of the contradictions that material culture studies currently faces. After all, even before the "new materialist" turn, materialist criticism had typically questioned static distinctions between the material and the non-material. Since then, it has evolved into a field that highlights, in Pocius's words, "how inseparable are ideas and objects, knowledge and artifacts, the tangible and the intangible" (9). In fact, many of the objects discussed in this book might more readily classify as "immaterial" rather than "material." Several chapters address the absent and the fleeting: the loss of venerated authors, of an estranged brother, of Arctic ice. Then there is Epp's chapter, which alerts readers to the problems that can occur when certain things are not quite as fleeting as they should be. Epp's object is the smile, specifically the smiles that World War I soldiers were meant to sport on their faces as they attacked enemy lines. This tactic is outlined in Epp's focus text, the YMCA's *Entertaining the American Army: The American Stage and Lyceum in the World War*. Even though the smiles were initially intended to make the soldiers able to fight more successfully, Epp points out that they had to be wiped off upon returning from the violence of the battlefield so as to require the managerial apparatus of the war effort to cheer the soldiers up again.

A smile might not at first seem like an "object." Is a facial expression a thing? Smiles may have a disturbing persistence to them in Epp's wartime example, but in other instances they are transitory, they are not very palpable, they might be exchanged, but not quite as commodities are exchanged (with the exception of the trafficking of smiles that takes place in the advertising, entertainment, and dental industries). As well, even though they occur on the body, they occupy the body only slightly, through the motion of the lips and other facial muscles, and so they do not quite have the same substantial, fleshy quality to them that one thinks of when one considers "the body" within material culture studies. Smiles might be just a bit too human to qualify as "material culture." But, in fact, many of the things that are featured in this book do not at first seem to possess the obvious "thingness" that would make them readily available to a traditional material culture analysis. Such an expansion of our notion of the thing is also part of the current ferment of material culture studies.

Ice. Water. Playlist. Belt. Calendars. Sweaters. Cities. An accordion-shaped book. A miniature sculptural rendition of an actual town in Saskatchewan (animated with mechanized puppets and stop-motion film). A miniature cardboard rendition of an imagined town depicted in an oversized graphic narrative. Plaques. Waxen fake artifacts. The geranium. Beavers. Smiles. The handcrafted here trumps the machine-made, and things that are not created by people at all feature quite prominently. Note as well the emphasis on collaborative creation, and on piecework. Seth's cardboard constructions realize a whole town. Built out of discarded cardboard boxes and not initially intended for show, they have an irreverent quality to them, rather than any aspiration to the monumentalism of architecture. Similarly, Patterson's sculptures that comprise *Woodrow* (based on the town of Woodrow, Saskatchewan) are "counter-monuments" in Jessa Alston-O'Connor's reading, which incorporate both truth and fiction, rather than seeking to authentically memorialize the past. Furthering the already varied contents of the artwork, the viewer "is inspired to remember his or her own associations with rural pasts, and to bring those memories and understandings into the viewing experience of Patterson's miniature town." Even Ann Carson's *Nox*, as Tanis MacDonald explains, is more of a private "scrapbook" or "collage journal" than a singular work made for public consumption, and it went through several hands before coming to fruition in its current form as a marketable book.

As is apparent in these examples, the things in this volume reflect Latour's return to "thing" or "ding" as an "old word" that "designated originally a certain type of archaic assembly" ("From Realpolitik to Dingpolitik" 22). Latour here also recalls Heidegger's emphasis on the definition of "thing" as a "gathering." In a somewhat similar vein Epp, in his chapter in this volume, recalls that the first definition of "thing" in the *OED* is "meeting." In some cases, actual meetings between people are integral to the things discussed here: the plaques are the product of elections, and the destruction of waterways has inspired the organization of several activist groups. The playlist is the result of the collective participation of CBC listeners rather than an individual's selection and careful crafting, but the work that this virtual assembly accomplished counters that which Latour celebrates in his invocation of the term. Simpson highlights the potential for assemblies to function in markedly different ways when he points out that we live in a "moment when participation in a virtual public sphere contributes in increasingly consequential ways to the manufacture of hegemony." Latour's thing that is a meeting, assembly, or gathering, understands matter as a site or field informed by difference rather than by singularity and internal cohesion. And as Latour also notes, the root for the word "democracy" is "to divide."

All in all, for Latour, the "point of reviving this old etymology is that we don't assemble because we agree, look alike, feel good, are socially compatible or wish to fuse together but because we are brought by divisive matters of concern into some neutral, isolated place in order to come to some sort of provisional makeshift (dis)agreement" ("From Realpolitik to Dingpolitik" 23). Isabelle Stengers makes a similar argument when she observes that *ensemble* in French means "set" (as in a mathematical set) and "togetherness." As she explains, the "mathematical set can be defined from the outside; all its members are interchangeable from the point of view of this definition and, as such, may be counted. But those who participate 'together' in a minority group cannot be counted, as participating is not sharing a common feature but entering into a process of connections" ("Including Nonhumans in Political Theory" 14). The arguments made by Latour and Stengers reflect the new critical interest in linking material culture studies with political theory.[8] As Bruce Braun and Sarah J. Whatmore write in their recent collection, *Political Matter: Technoscience, Democracy, and Public Life*, "to become political" means "to interrogate, contest, and engage with the force of things" (xii). Latour has gone so far as to offer up new "political slogans" for constituent material culture scholars—rallying cries, in a sense, declaring that "Public matters!" and urging a return "Back to Things!" With these slogans, Latour is "not trying to go back to the old materialism of *Realpolitik*, because *matter itself* is up for grabs as well" ("From Realpolitik to Dingpolitik" 24). Matter, however, is not the only thing up for grabs; what counts as public involvement, what counts as politics, is similarly undergoing some significant change. As Thrift has declared, "things are producing a politics that had been little thought of or practised before" (641). Or as Rita Wong writes in her chapter in this book assessing the "participatory ethics" of water, it "is not merely a political struggle, but a paradigm shift that is at work, one that expresses a reverence for local waters, and a long-term understanding of their role in both the local ecosystem and human communities." The political stakes of the chapters in this book are more explicit in some cases and less so in others. However, this continual reconfiguration of what is the matter of study in material culture studies and how this reconfigures the political is perhaps what best characterizes the scholarship presented here.

In an effort to emphasize the ways in which our contributors highlight the dynamism and indeterminate nature of material culture studies today, we have organized the chapters gathered here into three categories: the persistently material, the immaterial, and materials of and for spaces. The first two sections work in concert insofar as they sort the chapters on a spectrum determined by, at one end, the amount in which a thing might qualify as more material than other things, and, at the other end, the amount that a thing's immateriality best characterizes its constitution and affectivity in a given context. The things that we have associated with the former—a belt, the geranium, sweaters, beavers, and *Nox*—are things that have a palpable presence. They are hard, long-lasting (think of the stiff stem and fleshy leaves of the geranium, or the indefatigability of the beaver—the actual animal and the national symbol). On the whole, however, the things in this first section are more stable in the physical consistency of their material properties than the things we have allocated to the "immaterial" section. This does not make them necessarily more amenable to material culture studies, however. In fact, given Latour's claim that "critique was useless against objects of some solidity" ("Why Has Critique" 242), this section displays some remarkable scholarly inventiveness from our authors. Of course, science tells us that even the most solid of things are always in flux, and so the distinctions we make here between the "material" things and the things we put in the "immaterialities" section—smiles, the playlist, calendars, ice, and water—are somewhat arbitrary. Take, for example, Wong's comment that "the same water keeps circulating for millennia, for eons; what we drink might have flowed through the bladders of woolly mammoths, or might end up eventually dousing one of the Fukushima nuclear reactors." Could any other thing be this enduring? Meanwhile, MacDonald, whose chapter appears in the "materialities" section, identifies a related sort of categorical dilemma when it comes to distinguishing between the materiality and immateriality of things when she describes *Nox* as "durably ephemeral and sturdily fragile."

Ultimately, we would prefer that the interchangeability between the objects we've located in parts I and II remain pronounced for our readers, rather than muted. All of the things in this book qualify more as assemblages of components than as singular objects, and even the things in Part I (the belt-cum-weapon included) recall Latour's point that "things that gather cannot be thrown at you like objects" ("Why Has Critique" 237). By organizing this book according to a somewhat arbitrary scale of materiality, we hope to make ever more apparent the tendency to associate a kind of stability to matter that is not there in most cases: materiality shapes perceptions and conceptualizations of the world in powerful, if not always scientifically rationalized, ways.

If objects that are "persistently material" are assumed to be unchanging, those that qualify as "immaterial" are thought to be much more in flux. Thus, temporal contingency becomes especially prominent in considerations of immaterial things. Water moves, freezes, and melts again. The playlist was a work that took time and input from many different people, but its use could only be anticipated, not confirmed: Even if Obama did listen to the music, what would his reaction be? While the purpose of calendars is to regulate time into distinct days, months, and years, they too are riddled with idiosyncrasies that are rooted in the fundamentally immaterial nature of time. These idiosyncrasies were the basis for Moses Cosworth's influential campaign to standardize the calendar by authenticating time through material objects. Smiles, even though they last too long and are considered weapon-like in Epp's chapter, have found their place here in the "immaterial" category as well, largely because they are event-based things rather than objects. It's the temporal irregularity of the smiles that interests us here, whether this irregularity expresses itself in their fleeting quality or in their disturbing persistence. Shukin's chapter highlights how different representations of the effects of climate change in the North "are underpinned by a biopolitics that involves stark differences in the duration and intensity of a body's or population's exposure to the most punishing effects of global warming." Her concern is with those that foster a crisis mentality that mobilizes an "ecological state of exception" approach to climate change, one that is led largely by people in the global South and that combines Western knowledge systems with imperial modes of agency and governance. Looking specifically at the 2010 documentary by Zacharias Kunuk and Ian Mauro, *Qapirangajuq: Inuit Knowledge and Climate Change*, and a 2005 photographic "ice slides" series by Heather Ackroyd and Dan Harvey, Shukin argues that "while territory, or space, matters in relation to the Arctic expedition that launches in the south, time will emerge as even more crucial to the ecological state of exception that it passionately pronounces."

Much of the current scholarship attending to the dynamism of things, to their changeability in time, tends to portray this changeability as an effect of things' material composition and structure. But of course things also change because of the way that the other things situated around them behave: things that are time-sensitive are also, of course, action-sensitive as well. How things become affected depends upon time and also upon where they are located spatially. Recognizing that things are not discrete entities, that they exist in environments with other things, means that located-ness and relative proximity become crucial considerations in material culture studies. For Thrift, "[t]hings have now become a key part of worlds." In this geographer's view, material culture studies today looks to "the production of environments ... that can catch and modulate affect" (643).[9] This attention to the affective environments in which things dwell inspires our Part III: "Materials of and for Spaces." The chapters in this section discuss historical plaques, faux-artifacts encased in wax globules, graphic novelist Seth's oversized "picture novella" *George Sprott (1894–1975)*, Graeme Patterson's sculptural miniatures and animated puppets that represent Woodrow, Saskatchewan, and, finally, the city in the context of neoliberalism.

Interestingly, while the chapters in this third group all deal at some level with textual material, the book-as-object, or other forms of representation, text is not the end point of an affective chain of events (and consequently the moment at which analysis intervenes). Instead, texts are and give rise to the materials that are the subjects of the analyses presented here. Gerson, for example, discusses plaques devoted to Canadian authors or, as in the case of the Anne of Green Gables site in Cavendish, Prince Edward Island, devoted to a particular fictional character. Candida Rifkind considers the series of cardboard buildings that Seth made of his invented city of Dominion, in which part of *George Sprott 1894–1975* is set, alongside the images of these buildings (drawn and photographed) within the book itself. Rifkind argues that there is a "shared conceptual core between the form of the comic book and the form of the cardboard city" insofar as the two "merge to demand the work of contemplation and regard ... that slows down time and mediates between present and past, distance and proximity."

In the case of both Gerson's and Rifkind's analyses, the material object's construction within and of space, which instantiates a kind of layering of spatial, temporal, and material components, can cause alterations in the direction and consistency of time's progression. Derksen explores the potential of this particular layering to explicate, if not also circumvent, the current "neoliberal urban regime of a city." Drawing from the work of Henri Lefebvre who, in Derksen's words, pointed out that "social space is also laced into social time" and that "both are understood as social practices," Dersken considers critical and poetic practices that identify the "new complexities of scale" that inflect urban environments as they shift with and against globalization. In this respect, Derksen's chapter offers perhaps another version of Latour's "assembly" and Stengers's "togetherness," arguing that it is the poetic attempt to express the complex multiplicity of scales that mobilizes a new version of

Lefebvre's "right to the city"—one that is attuned to neoliberal dynamic processes and their effects on social conditions and aesthetic practices. Derksen sees poetry as a medium and an act of creation that "could assist us in getting at the very dynamism of urbanization, understood as a process that is as filled with the moments and events of everyday life, the life of the streets, and the deep levels of affect and engagement of the city, as it is fettered with neoliberal urban governmentality and its new spatial regime." In fact, the chapter itself embodies a kind of layering of space and time by drawing spatial analyses associated with an earlier version of materialist criticism together with contemporary literary and critical perspectives on urbanism.

With his insistence that neoliberal governmentality does not entirely quash the dynamism of the urban or our capacity to engage with it, Derksen highlights another of the key arguments in these chapters that deal with the relationship between things and spaces, which is that the latter—even the most institutional of spaces like a public art gallery—can never subsume the things in them into a particular program or set of investments in which that institution is involved. May Chew reveals this potential in her critique of Iris Haüssler's *He Named Her Amber* staged archaeological site art installation at The Grange, a historic house that is part of the Art Gallery of Ontario. Haüssler made mysterious wax objects and attributed them to a character she invented—Mary O'Shea, a woman who supposedly worked in the house in the 1820s. Much of Chew's discussion emphasizes the ways in which the work fell "easily in line with liberal-multiculturalist tropes" perpetuated by "institutions eager to revision and rebrand themselves as post-colonial," but she also points out how allowing "for the very *thingness* of Mary's artifacts ... means recognizing that they exist somewhat beyond archival seizure, ever slipping between the fractures and fissures of an all-consuming hegemonic architecture." In a similar vein, the plaques that Gerson discusses, once installed in a particular location, have the capacity to make that location newly and differently meaningful. "Few objects," she writes, "can have a stronger material presence than an historic plaque: a solid brass rectangle, fixed to a building or a sturdy stone cairn, whose words and images will endure through time and weather in a meeting of national and cultural interests that transforms undifferentiated landscapes into places with specific stories to tell."

While the distinctiveness of this section dealing with space might seem somewhat more definite than that of parts I and II, again it is important to note that all of the chapters in this book engage with the issue of space to the extent that they deal with things in particular environments that are subject to time and to various sorts of affect. The notion of thing-as-assembly is perhaps more explicit in these "materials of and for spaces," and perhaps they make Latour's notion of democracy-as-division more apparent in a material culture context, but the new politics of material culture studies is very much present in the chapters that consider the traditionally object-like things, like the belt, the sweater, and the geranium, as well. Objects though they may be, these things are situated in various affective environments, among different people and different things. They are private and public, and they may be affiliated with humans, animals, and other non-humans in the course of their meaningful existence. These things also mark time having passed, and they anticipate the future: the belt marks the change in Custis's body weight in *The Last Crossing*, and the sweaters on display in the Vancouver Original Costume Museum are "still on the needles as if waiting for a knitter to pick them up again."

When the weightiness of objects—their substantiality, their palpability, their *materialism*—no longer holds as their most effective feature (even if this quality still functions to confound certain dominant modes of analytical thinking in important ways), it is the situatedness of things in proximity to one another that makes environments, that recreates politics and scholarship into the unique assemblages that they embody today. Things are not fully formed and discrete objects, but components of varying physical consistencies that are, no matter how solid or immaterial, always in the process of being made. The conditions of this making are key for our authors. Drawing from David Gauntlett, Calder notes that "'everyday creativity' of the kind embodied in common knitted items is a political act" (Gauntlett 19). Derksen also invokes everyday experiences of and responses to the city, particularly those enacted through poetry, as a potential alternative to the city's uptake of neoliberal ideals. But questions regarding who and what can count as an agent in this making, and what this sort of agency might look like in its most effective composition, continue to be the topics of theoretical debate. In this book human agency remains prominent, even while several of the chapters contend with the increasing recognition and significance of non-human actors. The chapters by Shukin, Wong, and others, however, seek to clarify what sorts of human involvements in current dilemmas are more useful than others, particularly when non-human matters are important factors. Shukin cites Inusiq Nashalik's commentary on climate change in the North as an example that does "revive the lively powers of non-humans," but that "can also serve to temper the new surge of interest in nonhuman agency." On the whole, the chapters here begin to address the difficulties that can attend the calls for an assemblage-based politics, insofar as they ask questions about agency, and about what sorts of ethical positions of action individuals can assume when they have the power to do so. These chapters also highlight contradiction and disagreement, and they acknowledge the inaction that can arise out of these disjunctures as much as they celebrate the productivity (however indeterminate in its ends) that such gatherings of disparate components can enable. In this respect, they anticipate important discussions still to come about the value and position of agency within a field that also makes an important case for a politics based in vitalist conceptions of matter.

NOTES

1. Brown also employed the phrase "new materialism" in his 1996 book *The Material Unconscious*. However, it was in the later introduction to the edited collection *Things* that he elevated "new materialism" into a call for methodological change throughout the field.
2. Mark Simpson, for example, refers to Eric Cazdyn and Imre Szeman's recent discussion of this phenomenon in their book *After Globalization* (2011).
3. Calder takes this quotation from an article in the *Globe and Mail* called "Mary Maxim Sweaters: More Canadian than a Beer Commercial" (see Zolkewich L4).
4. While this book is centred largely within literary studies, and modes of cultural analysis that have been housed within or otherwise quite closely affiliated with English departments, its objects of analysis more often than not stray significantly from the literary. While this tendency may be taken as an indication that "the literary" is an unstable category, it also speaks to the staying power of national literary traditions through and beyond various attempts to reconfigure "literary studies."
5. Other considerations of the materiality of the book in Canada include Robert Lecker's reflection on the "material factors" that limit the selection of texts for anthologies. Drawing from the Australian critic Katherine Bode, Lecker argues that an "emphasis on quantitative methods" is necessary in an assessment of national anthologies because it "stresses the importance of using a materialist methodology to examine both canon and nation" (30). Carrying out such an analysis, Lecker explains that many of the inclusions in his recent anthology *Open Country: Canadian Literature in English* were informed by their length and by the cost of permissions. He also laments the "crasser material factors at work," such as the actual physical weight and shape of the book, which caused him to feel as though he "needed to create the Weight-Watcher's version of a national literary canon" (38).
6. In terms of material culture scholarship undertaken in the area of museum studies, Ruth Phillips, a Canada Research Chair in modern culture and professor of art history at Carleton University, is another influential scholar in Canada who bears mention here (although of course there are several curators and museologists who have had a tremendous impact on material culture studies within the context of Canadian museums). Formerly the director of the University of British Columbia Museum of Anthropology, Phillips has authored numerous works on Indigenous North American art and culture. Recently, she co-edited, along with Chris Gosden and Elizabeth Edwards, the collection *Sensible Objects: Colonialism, Museums and Material Culture* (2006). From museum studies and art history to the related fields of architecture, fine art, and design, it may be so self-evident that one's research focuses on "material culture" that it is unnecessary to explicitly claim any association with this area. A scholar who does declare a "material culture" focus is Rhona Richman-Kenneally, a professor of design and computation arts at Concordia University. In addition to her research on food and architecture, Richman-Kenneally studies the role of material

cultures in the construction of Canadian and Irish-Canadian identity. Along with Johanne Sloan, she recently co-edited the book *Expo 67: Not Just a Souvenir* (2010). There is also a notable interdisciplinary Material Culture Institute at the University of Alberta, which is affiliated with the Department of Human Ecology, the Faculty of Agricultural, Life, and Environmental Sciences, and the Faculty of Arts. This institute hosts an annual symposium, and the topic for 2012 was "Materiality & Independence: Disability, Ability & the Built Environment."

7 According to MacKinnon's web page at the Centre for Cape Breton Studies: "Intangible cultural heritage encompasses folklore, oral traditions, performing arts, social practices, rituals and craftsmanship" ("Introduction").

8 See also "Comparison as a Matter of Concern" in which Stengers charts a methodology that recognizes difference or, in her term, "divergence," for undertaking the sort of comparative work that a material culture approach requires. Adapting William James's notion of "pluriverse," Stengers advocates for a practice in which "[c]onnections are in the making, breaking indifference but bringing no encompassing unity. Plurality means divergences that communicate, but partially, always partially" (60-61). As the title suggests, the essay also draws significantly from Latour's work.

9 While Thrift's scholarship specifically focuses on "things" in a contemporary material cultures context, his emphasis on the connection between material environments and affect builds from a long-standing tradition in cultural geography that harkens back to Georg Simmel's "The Metropolis and Mental Life" (1903) and beyond to Simmel's earlier Marxist influences.

WORKS CITED

Appadurai, Arjun, ed. *The Social Life of Things: Commodities in Cultural Perspective*. Cambridge: Cambridge UP, 1986. Print.

Bennett, Jane. *Vibrant Matter: A Political Ecology of Things*. Durham: Duke UP, 2010. Print.

Berman, Marshall. *All That Is Solid Melts into Air*. New York: Simon and Schuster, 1982. Print.

Braun, Bruce, and Sarah J. Whatmore, eds. *Political Science: Technoscience, Democracy, and Everyday Life*. Minneapolis: U of Minnesota P, 2010. Print.

Brown, Bill. *The Material Unconscious: American Amusement, Stephen Crane, and the Economies of Play*. Cambridge: Harvard UP, 1996. Print.

Brown, Bill, ed. *Things*. Chicago: U of Chicago P, 2004. Print.

Cazdyn, Eric M., and Imre Szeman. *After Globalization*. Hoboken, NJ: John Wiley & Sons, 2011. Print.

Coole, Diana, and Samantha Frost. *New Materialisms: Ontology, Agency, and Politics*. Durham: Duke UP, 2010. Print.

Edwards, Elizabeth, Chris Gosden, and Ruth B. Phillips, eds. *Sensible Objects: Colonialism, Museums, and Material Culture*. Oxford: Berg, 2006. Print.

Freedgood, Elaine. *The Ideas in Things: Fugitive Meaning in the Victorian Novel*. Chicago: U of Chicago P, 2006. Print.

Gauntlett, David. *Making Is Connecting: The Social Meaning of Creativity, from DIY and Knitting to Youtube and Web 2.0*. Cambridge: Polity, 2011. Print.

Hicks, Dan, and Mary C. Beaudry, eds. *The Oxford Handbook of Material Culture Studies*. Oxford: Oxford UP, 2010. Print.

Jameson, Fredric. *The Political Unconscious: Narrative as a Socially Symbolic Act.* Ithaca: Cornell UP, 1981.
———. *Postmodernism: Or the Cultural Logic of Late Capitalism.* Durham: Duke UP, 1991. Print.
Johnson, Barbara. *Persons and Things.* Cambridge: Harvard UP, 2008. Print.
Kenneally, Rhona Richman, and Johanne Sloan, eds. *Expo 67: Not Just a Souvenir.* Toronto: U of Toronto P, 2010. Print.
Latour, Bruno. "From Realpolitik to Dingpolitik: or How to Make Things Public." Introduction. *Making Things Public.* Ed. Bruno Latour and Peter Weibel. Cambridge, MA: MIT P, 2005. 14-41. Print.
———. "Why Has Critique Run Out of Steam? From Matters of Fact to Matters of Concern." *The Future of Criticism.* Spec. issue of *Critical Inquiry* 30.2 (Winter 2004): 225-48. Print.
Lecker, Robert. "Materializing Canada: National Literature Anthologies and the Making of a Canon." *Australasian Canadian Studies* 26.1 (2008): 23-41. Print.
MacKinnon, Richard. "Introduction." *Centre for Cape Breton Studies.* Web. 7 Jan. 2013. <http://culture.cbu.ca/ccbs /rmk/introduction.html>.
Miller, Daniel, ed. *Materiality.* Durham: Duke UP, 2005. Print.
Mitchell, W. J. T. *Picture Theory: Essays on Verbal and Visual Representation.* Chicago: U of Chicago P, 1995. Print.
———. *What Do Pictures Want? The Lives and Loves of Images.* Chicago: U of Chicago P, 2006. Print.
Plotz, John. *Portable Property: Victorian Culture on the Move.* Princeton: Princeton UP, 2008. Print.
Pocius, Gerald. "A New Name, New Home, and New Directions/Nouveau nom, nouveau domicile, nouvelles orientations." *Material Culture Review/Revue de la culture matérielle* 63 (2006): 3-11. Print.
Shukin, Nicole. *Animal Capital: Rendering Capital in Biopolitical Times.* Minneapolis: U of Minnesota P, 2009. Print.
Simpson, Mark. "Immaculate Trophies." *Materializing Canada.* Spec. issue of *Essays on Canadian Writing* 68 (1999): 77-106. Print.
Stengers, Isabelle. "Including Nonhumans in Political Theory: Opening Pandora's Box?" Braun and Whatmore 3-33. Print.
———. "Comparison as a Matter of Concern." *Common Knowledge* 17.1 (Winter 2011): 48-63.
Stewart, Susan. *On Longing: Narratives of the Miniature, the Gigantic, the Souvenir, the Collection.* Durham: Duke UP, 1993. Print.
Szeman, Imre. "Introduction: A Manifesto for Materialism." *Materializing Canada.* Spec. issue of *Essays on Canadian Writing* 68 (Summer 1999): 1-18. Print.
Thrift, Nigel. "Afterword: Fings Aint Wot They Used T'Be: Thinking Through Material Thinking as Placing and Arrangement." Hicks and Beaudry 634-45. Print.
Zolkewich, Shel. "Mary Maxim Sweaters: More Canadian Than a Beer Commercial." *Globe and Mail* 18 Feb. 2006: L4. Print.

PART I
Materialities

CHAPTER 1

The Work of the Beaver

Jody Berland

In Margaret Atwood's early novel *Surfacing*, the male protagonist, David, makes a comment that has become one of the most widely circulated citations in Canadian literature. "Canada was built on dead beavers," he says; indeed, "the beaver is to this country what the black man is to the United States" (Atwood 39-40). An online Google search finds at least ten non-redundant pages listing sources where this emblematic citation has appeared. The observation appears on forty websites and blogs devoted to famous quotations in Canada and beyond, including great-quotes.com, thinkquotes.com, famousquotes.com, brainyquote, and animalquotes, among others. It also appears in a number of books that collect "great Canadian quotes" or "great literary quotes," and in one or two academic essays. Almost none of these listings reference the source of the quotation; its frequent appearance without reference conveys the strong impression that collections of popular quotes are not invitations to read books.[1] This recurrence without context or commentary makes the abstraction of dead beavers from their literary context as symptomatic of national forgetting as the abstraction of beaver images from their historical and environmental context, as I show in the following pages.

The floating inscription of Atwood as author onto beaver as sacrificial subject produces a blend of melancholy and irony so characteristic as to make the imprint seem inevitable. Through the frequent citation of this remark in digital and literary archives, the association between Canada and dead beavers acquires its own life, forming an uneasy undertow to the popular iconography of the Canadian as the bustling busy beaver. The direction of the undertow is undecidable: is David's (Atwood's) claim literal or metaphorical? We killed beavers to build Canada. Are we also (or perhaps just some of us) like dead beavers ourselves? If we identify collectively with the beaver as our nation's totem, are we slaves or smart amphibious subjects? But then, who is "we?" Atwood's fiction explores this same brainy ambivalence. Simultaneously awakening and imploding popular imperialist nostalgia, one step removed from the story while undermining that very distance, and introducing a bad conscience into the mix, Atwood's words obviously strike a chord.

This study addresses the conditions of the beaver's appearance, its special historical status as material and semiotic object, and the tensions that arise when reading its material and symbolic forms in relation to one another in the context of contemporary cultural and animal theory. While this line of questioning owes a great deal to changing understandings of animality and materiality, it is also immanent in the object—that is to say, the complex materiality of the animal itself. The image of the beaver is in constant circulation in and about Canada. It is as though the amphibious body whose smooth head rises to the surface as it swims across a body of water has a doppelgänger in the semiotic body that so fluidly displays and hides this animal. Reiterated and renewed throughout colonial and postcolonial history, the cumulative image of the beaver has doubled back upon itself in a striking trajectory of visual abstraction that is joined with an almost compulsive search for meaning to confirm the validity of the culture—Canada—that identifies itself through that same imagery. This tension between animality and abstraction from animality has been profoundly formative in contemporary culture.

In the case of the beaver, this same tension is also a residue of colonial history that haunts contemporary research on the social and geographical contexts of human-animal relations. Unravelling these threads is part of a larger search for a progressive politics for the twenty-first century, which depends not only on the redress of colonial violence but also on reassessing the roles of animals in spatial ecology and identity construction (Wolch and Emel xvi-xvii). First Nations peoples have made visible and sought to remedy the colonial appropriation of their lands and land rights. Given the constancy of beavers in our visual and symbolic landscapes, one might assume that the animal's obvious political significance has been understood precisely in this way. But this is not so. The way the image has served to condense and obscure the animal's own history corresponds closely to Roland Barthes's description of myth as "depoliticized speech" (142).[2] His concept assumes that not all signifiers are words, and that behind their explicit meanings are intentional connotations that evacuate the object's historical context. As

Barthes suggests and as the beaver exemplifies, the discursive absence of the past is not accidental, nor is it incidental to the sign's appearance.

The case of the beaver also demonstrates the cogency of the argument that Western man has sought to suppress or demolish animality in a "schema of purification" justifying his supremacy on the basis of uniquely moral and rational behaviour (Derrida, "Before the Law" 194). Placing others inside or outside that schema, through myth and/or violence, determines who and what has rights, and on what grounds. Post-humanist thought has been important to realizing more diverse accounts of human subjects and objects, but Foucault's biopolitics find their limit with non-human animals. This problem is not just conceptual and analytical, Nicole Shukin argues, but deeply material, involving not just the semiotic currency of animal signs but also "the carnal traffic in animal substances" (7).[3] Today, then, animals need to be accounted for as both subjects and objects in any attempt to address the material circulation of society.

In her recent book *The Beaver Manifesto*, Glynnis Hood insists that "Beavers truly are the shapers of the physical and ecological landscapes of North America.... They and these landscapes have evolved together for millennia and much of our natural environment has really only known a world that has beavers in it.... Without them, one can imagine the ecological desert left behind" (6). Hood addresses her *Manifesto* to readers whose ambidextrous commitment to modern wilderness aesthetics and modern individual property rights (in other contexts, these might not be so cordially joined) lead them to decry beavers' destruction of their trees and rivers. This individualized assertion of control over the landscape obscures the larger significance of beavers: they shape the flow of rivers to lakes, trees to dams, water to us. Decrying their work pushes aside the ways we ourselves act destructively within this milieu.

We know from modern anthropology and cultural studies that there are deep cultural biases at work in our estimation of human social value. Western colonial cultures classify some people as less human by attributing to them closer metaphorical or physical relations with nature. Their reasoning is that if humans are close to animals, they must also be like them—that is to say, behaving in reactive instinctual ways rather than as thinking subjects. This association requires that we also downplay purpose and agency in animals' interactions with their environments. As research in bio-semiotics and animal studies has shown, however, animals' activities and interaction involve some of the meanings and skills we accord to our own purposeful behaviour.[4] The light from today's iconic beaver casts our look backward, then, on a history of visibility and invisibility that illuminates both the animal and the trappers and traders who turned them into commodities in the New World.

In her recent study of whiteness and indigeneity and their semantically unstable expression in Canada's national symbols, Margot Francis argues that

> On the one hand, we have banal national emblems: the hard-working beaver, the enterprising railway, the majestic mountains—all of which present the values, technologies, and landscapes of white enterprise and manly accomplishment. On the other hand, we have a national literature and popular discourse that suggest we couldn't possibly be associated with the more rapacious aspects of imperialist adventure because the Canadian character is best expressed by anti-heroes absorbed in a struggle for survival. Might these seemingly oppositional images express the state of play between the renewed respectability of an innocent white Anglo-Canadian identity versus our fear of annihilation? And is the outcome of this tension a sense of Canadianness so riven by contradiction as to be a blank and formless void? (xx)

In *North of Empire* I situate this semantic oscillation as a function of Canada's status as a Second World empire that has both colonized and been colonized throughout its history. The beaver, as a particularly visible symbol, invites our attention to this history of dual colonization that produced Canada as an ambivalent modern nation. Indeed the "blank and formless void" Francis describes could be understood psychoanalytically as the product of a suppressed consciousness of our rapacious possession of a country "built on dead beavers." This same void, Derrida suggests, drives the compulsion to selectively collect images and to create an archive or container for an identity that threatens to disperse (*Archive Fever* 11-12).

The hard-working beaver is both symbolic and more than symbol; while the animal has not chosen to be our symbol any more than it chose to be hunted for body parts, we need its animality—together with its de-animalization—to convince us that there is something certain in our shared citizenship. If we choose living entities like beavers or polar bears for our collective symbols, according to the totemic thinking that postcolonial cultures congratulate themselves for having left behind, then the nation congregated under its sign is equally vital, natural, and distinct. While pop culture loves to comment satirically on the oddity of this particular selection, and to overlook the "strategic absences" (Francis) that surround its meanings, the desire to identify collectively (via) an animal totem is not unique. As Steve Baker has discussed in *Picturing the Beast*, the circulation of animal images has helped to build a comparable iconography in many countries.

Indeed, modern nation-states have created a fascinating zoological inventory of animal symbols—kangaroo, bear, lion, tiger, elephant, parrot, bison, flamingo—many of which are, like the beaver, at risk of extinction through extensive hunting and habitat loss. While their images circulate and mutate through political, cultural, and commercial networks, their physical habitats, kinship structures, and species viability are being destroyed. To reconnect these iconic images with living entities requires the constitution of a new kind of archive that situates these images of animals in a more politically and ecologically reflexive context.

SKINS AND OTHER SIGNS

From federal law to social media, from postage stamp to parody, the beaver is an iconographic figure standing unmistakably for the nation.[5] Its status as totem of Canadian identity has been advanced through various aspects of material culture, from corporate logos to T-shirts to government insignia to natural history magazines. Most recently, its appearance as a corporate symbol advertising Bell Media, a telecommunications giant, coincided roughly with Parks Canada's official adoption of the beaver as its mascot and corporate emblem. Both organizations released parodic oversized figures of beavers into urban centres to promote Canada's technological friendliness and its famous wilderness, as though to cement, so to speak, the triumphal reconciliation of the two. At the same time, the parodic beaver tells us, the beaver image doesn't need to mean anything once that childish spark of recognition has occurred. The schematized figures of the national beaver and the Bell beaver echo one another in a ghostly reiteration of the doppelgänger maps of the fur trade and the new dominion I describe below.

This dance between semiotic recurrence and meaninglessness has a history, so much so that the Government of Canada passed a federal act in 1975 naming the beaver the official national animal. The beaver was already a popular symbol of the country, locating Canada's prehistory in early colonial trade relations between the New World and the old, and it already signified diverse ideas about busyness, cheerful industriousness, building, global trade, wilderness, domestic life, and the masculine accumulation of wealth and sex. The accomplishment of this official state conscription was to enhance and reconcile its dual status as populist icon and friendly mascot of corporate globalization. Like other animals populating the virtual menagerie, Canada's beaver imagery is successful precisely because it remains indeterminate in its meanings and effects. If, as Baker argues, animal symbolism has lost its connection with animals, and thus its semiotic reliability, the beaver symbol apparently does not mind; it continues to be busy and productive (47).

In any case, the popularity of the Atwood citation does not simply confirm the slipperiness of the animal's semiotic ground or the semantic resilience that we like to attribute to Canadian writers and readers. It suggests that when we transmit the notion that Canada was built on dead beavers, we are at least half-conscious of the country's historical dependence on a sacrificial economy of animal and human lives. This is a complicated half-recognition given our own association with the beaver; popular identification with the iconographic animal rubs up against the polis's amnesia about (and indifference to) the violence through which country and animal emerged together as a representational system. Through the indeterminate totemic fusion wrought by this figure, we are simultaneously progeny of the fur trade and its dead remains.

A live beaver is an amphibious rodent; a dead beaver is a pelt. There is an equally significant distinction between beavers with fur (live or dead) and beavers without fur (skinned or symbolically disembodied). In the case of the former, the animal is capitalized in the form of the fur it is forced to relinquish through violent death. In the case of the latter, the commodity transformation has already occurred. Then the beaver is a body without a skin, a fur without a body, or perhaps an animal-like image graphically released from the mortality of the animal body. A fur without a body, the necessary cause and effect of the animal's death, becomes a hat or coat. Initially, the oil of the anal glands, used in some perfumes and also as a food additive, was a by-product of this same process. A body without a fur is either the corpse of the beaver with its fur removed or more recently the pared down, hairless, digitally e-animalized image proliferating in the contemporary mediascape.[6] Both are outcomes of the transformation of animal body into commodity. The rendition of one to the other is never shown, no matter how often the beaver appears in a drawing or on a map, screen, stamp, coin, toy, or logo. Extraction haunts the symbolic landscape by its absence.

In this process, the beaver has been severed from its essential hydrological activities. While traditional images showed beavers swimming through water, commercial graphics now largely depict beavers on land or context-free. And yet the renowned quality of the animal's fur is related directly to the animal's amphibious capabilities. Uniquely among fur trade historians, Harold Innis explains the beaver fur's value in relation to its activities in water. As an amphibious mammal, its pelt is fine and thick, with two layers of hair; "examined through a microscope," Innis comments, "the fur has numerous small barbs. It was these barbs which made it unusually suitable for the manufacture of felt and of felt hats" (4). Protected by this special fur, the beaver moves easily between land and water, collecting wood to build strong dams, which create new bodies of clean water, and then, below the surface of this water, it builds lodges of solid and complex construction. Having constructed such well-crafted homes, the beaver has no inclination to travel; he moves in and raises his family. "In the language of the economists," Innis observes, as though this is not his language, "the heavy fixed capital of the beaver became a serious handicap with the improved technique of Indian hunting methods, incidental to the borrowing of iron from the Europeans" (5). That is to say, the amphibious beaver is a profitable resource for Europeans, and European technologies make it easier to kill beavers, which (my Word program won't let me say "who") are less mobile, less inclined to travel than the Europeans.

Citing an undated journal by David Thompson, Innis explains:

> when the arrival of the White People had changed all their weapons from stone to iron and steel and added the fatal Gun, every animal fell before the Indian ... the Beaver became a desirable animal for food and clothing, and the fur a valuable article of trade, and as the Beaver is a stationary animal, it could be attacked at any convenient time in all seasons, and thus their numbers soon became reduced. (6)

Thus the beaver's aquatic habitat, the value of its fur, the seasonal nature of hunting, the solidity of the beaver's home, the Indigenous familiarity with the animal's habitat, the success of traditional practices of trapping and hunting, the expansion of colonists ever further north and west, the building of settlements and stores allowing trappers to trade the valuable furs and glandular secretions for goods brought from Europe by the same boats bringing traders and weapons, and the Indigenous adaptation to new goods such as guns and blankets, all form part of the human-land-animal assemblage through which the beaver enters history. Through Innis's account of the beaver, political economy meets assemblage theory half a century before the latter's declared arrival.

But this history did not start in Canada. Because of the quality of their fur, beavers have been hunted since the ninth century. By 1240, in areas of what is now Ukraine, the supply of fur-bearing animals was already exhausted. As Clive Ponting records in *The New Green History of the World*, the decline of fur imports into London was evident by the early fifteenth century. "By the sixteenth century," Ponting writes, "the beaver trade from Southern Europe had collapsed and only low quality skins such as rabbit were available" (156). European merchants expanded into Siberia, using both Russian and Native trappers. By the end of the eighteenth century, the trade in what had been a plentiful population of friendly animals had "denuded" the habitat of these animals. Writing of the European settlement of North America, Ponting argues that "the search for [beaver] furs was one of the driving forces behind trade and expansion across the continent" (157). This is where Innis's account of the fur trade begins.

The devastation of the species in these waves of hunting and settlement in North America involved not only the depletion of the animal population, but also an alteration of its habitus through the colonial management of lands by both the French and the English. As Alice Outwater has noted, the animal was in fact extinct for some years in parts of the United States. When the population of beavers dropped, their ecological activity was also reduced. The absence of beavers and their effect on the land is considered desirable for some frustrated humans whose territorial pleasures and investments have been marred by the work of living beavers. In this respect, the un-warlike beaver establishes its kinship with the bear, the tiger, the elephant, and other species whose semiosis on behalf of modern nation-states and various commodities and companies obscures the inter-species fight for territory and resources that so destructively alters the lands, habitats, and possibilities of the animal lives there represented. By clothing ourselves in the skins and scents of these symbolically empowered species, and by indexing our collective identity through their images, humans announce their conquest of nature and of time as well as space. Animals are both the impetus for and the symbol of colonial conquest.

While the animal, the pelt, the fashionable hat, the stamp, the coin, the perfume, and the popular image of the beaver are materially different, they are part of one history and continue to act as important instruments in a changing discursive regime. Canada was built on a territorially charted interdependency between fur and trapper, Hudson's Bay Company (HBC) and Royal Charter, Indigenous lands and colonial conquest. The territory, the animal, and the Indigenous person became part of a racialized history that was transformed in the process. The HBC was formed by a Royal Charter from Prince Rupert in 1670. Almost exactly three hundred years later, a federal act declared the beaver the country's national animal. The period between 1670 and 1975 was characterized by a close partnership between the HBC and the "mother country" whose progeny was the Dominion of Canada, to the extent that their territories emerged as cartographically almost indistinguishable. The interdependency between Crown corporation and colonial dominion is visible in maps of HBC territory between colonial initiation and the consolidation of the nation-state. As Innis points out in *The Fur Trade in Canada*,

> The Northwest Company and its successor the Hudson's Bay Company established a centralized organization which covered the northern half of North America from the Atlantic to the Pacific.... It is no mere accident that the present Dominion coincides roughly with the fur-trading areas of northern North America. The bases of supplies for the trade in Quebec, in western Ontario, and in British Columbia represent the agricultural areas of the present Dominion. The Northwest Company was the forerunner of the present confederation. (392)

It was the beaver that brought the Northwest Company (NWC) to the northern part of the continent, and fur traders for the NWC and the HBC who created the outlines and travel routes for the new dominion. "The pursuit of beaver allowed access to even the most remote areas of what was to become Canada," Hood explains. "At profits of 1000 to 2000 per cent during the most successful years of the trade, it was a lucrative means to claim a country. It is amazing that the beaver survived at all" (39). In geopolitical terms, the valuable and thus vulnerable beaver was a crucial mediator between the old geography and the new, between Indians and whites, between the old hunting cultures and the new organization of international trade.

This mediation is visible not only in terms of the territory charted by these maps, but also in terms of how their language changes. Early maps of European exploration were commonly illustrated with animal figures, ranging from sea monsters to beavers, illustrating the exotic nature of the new lands and the brave exploits of the explorers. With the fur trade's more instrumental approach to mapping territory, fanciful animal symbols were eliminated from the cartographic text. The theme of heroic exploration of exotic lands was displaced by a detached rhetoric of spatial administration showing which land belonged to whom. The newer maps identified by name and place the location of fur-bearing animals and the tribes that trapped them. They were used to negotiate and govern trapping rights and rules of exchange and to represent colonial relations or agreements with Indigenous peoples in a language that confirmed their own presumed cultural and scientific superiority over the people on whom they depended to fulfill these goals. Their intent to organize land in terms of property rights, trade relations with local tribes, and the rational culling of the beaver population is realized in the design and circulation of the new maps.

The explorer's maps and journals form an important layer in the production of a colonial *topos*,[7] a concept that allows us to see place as a spatial and textual archive of colonial (and other) inscriptions. Maps, journals, and company records are not only archives but also topographical inscriptions.

The management of land, resources, and bodies accomplished through such topographic inscription was the precondition for both corporate success and national sovereignty. On the basis of such sovereignty, as Foucault has famously argued, governance enters into the era of biopolitics, which involves the management of life as well as death.[8] We see this era emerging in the correspondence and records of the Northwest Company and HBC through how they address the ecological health of the beaver population. Their assessment of animal well-being obviously differs from the ways this topic is taken up in twenty-first-century critical animal studies, which aim to trouble human-centred uses and assumptions. The fur traders release beavers into an area, they measure their progress through the sizes of beaver dens, they wait until the population is sufficiently developed, and then they (or their trappers) trap beavers, skin them, and sell the pelts. As modern entrepreneurs they are careful not to exhaust the population of their prey; they assure that life lives, even if it is a quantitative assurance. Just as their maps mark boundaries between landowners rather than animal habitats, so their correspondence refers to "pelts," never "beavers" or "muskrats." As the beaver is being counted and measured, its body symptomatically disappears from view. It leaves traces, however, both of the body and of its modes of disappearance.

THE INDIGENOUS ANIMAL

"The fur trade," Innis writes "was a phase of a cultural disturbance incidental to the meeting of two civilizations with different cultural traits" (42). Note his use of "incidental"; it does not mean unimportant, but rather, an event arising from the meeting point of two histories, a logic of change, a "disturbance" to the entities that through colliding reconstitute one another and themselves. The rhetorical shift in how the land is represented reminds us that the fur trade was part of a larger process of global modernization in which sending back maps, accounts, and reports of Indigenous behaviour was crucial to legitimating the explorers' travels, expenses, and authority.[9] We could speculate that the erasure of the animal from the explorers' documentation expressed some ambivalence about the large-scale killing of animals. This would be anachronistic, however, for the concept of the animal as subject to suffering had not yet entered the vocabulary of European thought.[10] Indeed, the impetus of early modern thought was to enact a clear division between nature and culture, to purge the human from the non-human and the non-human from the human, as Latour has argued, in order to establish who was eligible to live within the community of the state. In the colonial context, this process had to be reconciled with the establishment of successful managerial relations with both animal and human resources in the context of the fur trade. The injustice of such relations was critiqued in their own time, and on precisely these terms.

The erasure of "human" attributes from the beaver is not hard to discern. More complicated is the understanding of human communities that were endowed with both human and animal characteristics. As representatives of the Northwest Company and the HBC mapped, counted, measured, and recorded, they asserted epistemological as well as economic and military superiority over an Indigenous culture that (in their perception) survived with the ingenuity of an animal. The corporate coats of arms for the HBC and the Northwest Company include stylized figures of deer, bears, and beavers, all animals hunted by Indigenous peoples who sometimes appear with them in maps and other such logos as if interchangeable with the non-human species selected to identify the place. Through the visual proximity between Indian and animal emphasized by colonial observers, the Indigenous person was configured as somewhere between human and animal, symbolically defined and diminished by the bond between trapper and animal. Through natural history museums, this idea was extended into the twentieth century with the placement of costumed replicas of Indigenous peoples in close proximity to taxidermy displays of animals of the region.

Like some of the national iconic animals such as the bald eagle, the snow leopard, or the bear, the beaver was hunted to near extinction with the assistance of local Indigenous populations. But the beaver lacks the heroic carnivorous qualities of these other animals, which ostensibly transfer from the animal to the nation in support of military or industrial prowess. This anomaly was made explicit in 2011, when a Conservative member of Canada's Senate, Nicole Eaton, proposed that Canada replace the beaver, a "dentally defective rat," with the more aggressive polar bear as its official animal (qtd. in Chase). The beaver icon is the relic of a time of plunder, as Atwood's David makes clear, and it was not beavers doing the plundering. In Eaton's view, Canadians embraced the beaver symbol as a pusillanimous residue, untouched by the powerful semantic tensions between beaver as sacrificial animal, as fur, as builder, as family-oriented mammal who must chew trees or die, as troubled index of colonial power, as national totem, stuffed animal, icon, Boy Scout, finally as a toothy, glossy, ironically expressive, and peculiarly loved and disdained symbol set adrift in the static decontextualized multiples of imagery today. She got nowhere with her plan.

Perhaps, though, her campaign speaks to the absence of representations of the beaver as an entity deserving of respect. During my visit to the HBC Archives I found many early photographs of Indigenous peoples posing for the camera with beavers, but very few of whites with (uncrated) live beavers. The photographs of Grey Owl with his pet beavers are a famous and deliberate exception to the rule. When white settlers came to face the camera, they modelled the perceived interdependency of beaver and Native hunter not by posing with the animals but rather through mimetic rituals in which they draped themselves in furs and masqueraded as Indians. Clad in the furs that had become their property, their ethnic drag enacts the connection between Indigenous and animal entities over and because of which they sartorially declare their supremacy. This performance presupposes both closeness between the colonizer and the colonized, and absolute distinction, predicated in part on the Indigenous peoples' assumed closeness to the world of animals.[11]

In the symbolic triangulation of Indigenous communities, wild animals, and colonial conquest, and in the ontological environment of purification already mentioned, the beaver could not appear as a living animal capable of suffering. The semi-consciousness of a sacrificial economy of animal lives that Atwood evokes in *Surfacing* has been successfully managed by a colonial account of history, reiterated in museums and schoolbooks, wherein the beaver and the Indian are so othered and so closely associated that the meaning of each entity relies on its connection to the other. Rather than affirming the achievements of Indigenous peoples in the area, the beaver figures as part of a discursive milieu in which animality "naturalizes" our conquest of them. Re-examination of the beaver archive makes it possible to trace the creation of this interdependency. It provides testimony to the manner in which the beaver became both site and alibi for the same abjection of indigeneity that has more broadly been projected onto alterity through the trope of animality.[12]

At the HBC Archives I asked to see a book published in 1703 entitled *New Voyages to North America* by Baron de Lahontan. I discovered a hand-illustrated report, bound in a leather cover, which offers close and respectful accounts of Indigenous practices and beliefs.[13] Lahontan's Canadian journals drew on ethnographic and personal studies to contrast Christian injustice against the justice and freedom of Native peoples.[14] His willingness to observe, study, and translate Indigenous knowledge for an English-speaking audience needs to be read in light of Lewis Saum's general observation, in *The Fur Trader and the Indian*, that traders oriented their correspondence and reports around the debate as to whether or not Indians were noble savages. Who did they more closely resemble, the traders speculated, the beaver or the white man? Lahontan describes an intelligent and effective Indigenous culture whose transmission included detailed knowledge of beaver habitats and habits. Innis cites him in his history of the fur trade for this reason. According to Samuel Hearne of the HBC, the beaver had been greatly over-endowed with organizational ability, sagacity, and ingenuity (see Saum 91). It was the savages, of course, who committed this error. As traders who often relied on Indigenous trappers, the white commercial representatives of the NWC and the HBC perceived naiveté in the Indigenous estimation of the animal. With little interest in the sagacity of beavers or trappers, this trader readily believed himself to be superior to both, deserving to be master of the fur trade.

It was the association of Indigenous peoples with animality that produced the colonizer's claim to power.[15] In this cultural production of the non-Western person as not fully human, beavers and Indigenous peoples are linked in the historical imagination not only because beaver pelts were trapped and traded by Indigenous peoples, but also because traders observed and described Indigenous peoples as though they were a different species from themselves, as close to the animals they hunted as to the humans with whom they traded. Were Indians really projecting too much sagacity onto the animal, we wonder, or were white men projecting this perceived pathology, i.e., primitiveness or animality, onto their Indigenous contacts, assuming that long-established observation of the animal was a symptom of their lack of reason? This is not just a textual problem of course, and while understanding this discourse's inscription onto territory and land use is crucial, it is outside the scope of what I can do here.

Traders less enlightened than Lahontan, Saum argues, cast the Indigenous traders as primitive and animalistic. As Alexander Ross wrote, when a "red man" took up the white man's ways, his happiness vanished: "like a wild animal in a cage, his luster is gone" (qtd. in Saum 203). In other words, colonial observers unenlightened by Lahontan's way of thinking saw beavers and Indigenous communities as linked and parallel subjects of a natural(ized) history in which white traders were necessary agents of progress. They believed that the Native, ingenious but not intelligent, was incapable of mastering his natural environment, of modernizing, of progress. Indigenous knowledge is contained by the concept of the machinic animal, adaptive but not reflexive and defined, as postcolonial critics have argued, outside of history.[16] This is the rhetorical structure Grey Owl set out to sabotage two centuries later when he withdrew from trapping, married an Indigenous woman, and began to write about the interdependent lives of humans and animals in the North. Writing just before Innis first published *The Fur Trade in Canada*, Grey Owl was eager to demonstrate the beaver's ingenuity and the complex spiritual and ecological relationship between trapper and prey.

The narrative of the Indigene as living outside of history has less to do with actual trade encounters, during which Native and colonial inhabitants were often connected through trade, friendship, marriage, and mutual aid, than with fixed ideas about Western civilization in which Indigenous peoples and animals, linked by proximity and similarity, had no place. White commentators prejudicially underestimated the sagacity of the beaver and its trappers, and assumed, as Laura Peers argues, an unrealistically limited role for Indigenous communities in the fur trade, according to which Native peoples trapped animals, prepared the pelts, and brought them to fur trade sites, but never contributed food, building materials, or other objects or knowledges. Indigenous peoples are discursively marginalized and contained by their links to animals and plants and by their perceived reluctance to transform their environments. This marginalization is comparable to the beaver's, who ostensibly cannot change, but who nevertheless sagaciously transforms the environment and does some good hydrological cleansing in the process. Like the beaver, the Indian is always already in a failed transitive mode in this narrative, always already both busy and dead. Unlike the beaver, First Nations peoples continue to articulate and enact a critical anti-colonial response.

THE BEAVER ARCHIVE

As Peers has noted, "fur trade history has always been closely connected to public history sites" (101). Writing of reconstructed fur trade posts built in the 1960s and 1970s, Peers observes that such sites have been contentious because they failed to take Native perspectives and memories into account. "It seems simplistic and misleading," she argues, "to represent the complexity of the fur trade by an insistently repetitive set of artifacts consisting of a blanket, a beaver hide on a stretcher, some beads, and a musket." Peers suggests that the repetitive display of these few visible tokens "connote[s] the still-popular assumption that Native people became dependent on European trade goods; and they thus affirm the underlying assumption that European cultures have always been superior to those of 'Others'" (105-6).

Such displays reinforce the symbiotic association between Native person and animal entity already embedded in colonial culture. But the "insistently repetitive" quality of such displays has a more general force; it enacts the impulse or "desire" that Derrida describes in *Archive Fever: A Freudian Impression* (1996). Insisting that the archive arises from an active process of inscription, rather than a simple process of collection, Derrida suggests that one can find in the genealogy of the term both "commencement" and "commandment." Through the display of evidence, the curator authorizes the telling of a particular story based on the inclusion ("commencement") of specific memories and the abandonment of others. Underlying this drive to collect and display, Derrida suggests, is the felt lack of a fully authoritative space of identity. The individual or communal subject seeks to reconstitute its identity, to separate it from that which it is not, through memory, i.e., through keeping together the contents of its archive. Derrida's understanding of the archive parallels and draws from Freud's understanding of the subject whose individual constitution through memory relies on the evacuation of what is to be forgotten. "Nothing is less reliable, nothing is less clear than the word 'archive,'" Derrida writes:

> The *trouble d'archive* stems from a *mal d'archive*.... It is to turn with a passion. It is never to rest, interminably, from searching for the archive right where it slips away. It is to run for the archive, even if there is too much of it, right where something in it anarchives itself. It is to have a compulsive, repetitive, and nostalgic desire for the archive, an irrepressible desire to return to the most archaic place of absolute commencement. (91)

Commencement: the fur trade. As if nothing was there before. Absolute desire: museum, logo, symbol, legislation. Slipping away; the endless receding of history, context, embodiment, animality. Accumulating more variations of a theme enhances the authority of collective governance, but can inhibit new ways of understanding the memories. As the space of collective memory spills out into newer technological spaces, the inscription of memory becomes a greater challenge and an even stronger compulsion. Through this compulsion the archive seeks to demolish the gap between public record and private psyche. The beaver performatively attaches national subjects to their common destiny within a permitted range of rhetorical and affective strategies. But the compulsion for thematic closure informing this archive is undermined in contemporary culture by the detachment from meaning that occurs in the vortex of information. This process too can be said to begin with the beaver, whose representation, following Derrida, marks both commencement (the story of Canada's origin) and return (as the beaver pops up in one form or another). If this proliferation of signs might compulsively reassure and entertain anxious citizens, it also succumbs to and secures the cool and differently comforting meaninglessness of the corporate logo.

The beaver at the centre of this archive is a commandment to remember and to forget. And yet, at the same time, the beaver is a lively animal, and won't stand still. It swims from natural history (beaver as architect, builder, and chewer of wood) to cultural anthropology (The beaver is so ingenious! It plans and builds houses much as humans do!)[17] to material resource in economic history. The beaver is token of colonial rights in the New World, signature on coins and maps, symbol of achievement on Boy Scouts' brands and badges, logo of the nation-state, and natural ally of woman. It doubles back on itself in a process of increasing stylization and abstraction to provide commercial logos and populist symbols, indexing diverse realms of the social through commodity fetishism, animal justice activism, advertisements, Canadian studies, contemporary art, political metaphors and cartoons, the latter stripped of any explicit evidence of the animal or its anthropological history, which is at once evoked and dismissed.

The compulsion to multiply beaver images has tended to produce a lexicon of familiarities, as though a database of likenesses is the best we can do.[18] But this would be a misinterpretation of what we see. In "Archive Fever and Twentieth-Century Critical Theory," Rachel Price writes that "The archive requires imagination. Its prosthetic capacity is insufficient, for it is always a collection of interruptions: more like a container of history, it consists of a few digressive fragments of information which only suggest what was omitted" (Price 5, cited in Funcke 47). Having reviewed important presences and absences in the beaver archive, it is time to consider the interruptions it contains. Note Price's use of the word "container" with its multiple meanings: it holds history, contains it from spilling, allows it to speak, contains it from speaking. What does it mean to find a "collection of interruptions" played out in archival containers? How might we make such interruptions productive in the reconstitution of psyches, territories, and relations?

Let us briefly review recent contributions to the archive to help address these questions. Jim Cameron's 1991 richly illustrated book *The Canadian Beaver Book: Fact, Fiction, and Fantasy* offers an enthusiastic collector's documentation of the beaver as popular visual symbol. This richly illustrated historical resource contains hundreds of images of the beaver drawn from popular, political, and corporate iconography over a hundred years. It contains no reference to natural history. Chantal Nadeau's adventurous 2001 book *Fur Nation* has much to say about intimate relations between fur, masculine power, feminine sexuality, performativity, and photography, but nothing to say about trapping or beavers. In *The Sexual Politics of Fur*, Julia Emberley writes with pointed eloquence about the fur trade's devastating effects on North America's Indigenous peoples and about the "abject animalization" of fur-clad women, but the word "beaver" rarely appears, and then only when annexed to the word "fur" (93). Margot Francis's *Creative Subversions*, an eloquent study of the heritage of white-Indigenous relations, attends to the beaver as symbol, but not as animal; there is no sense of a shared biosphere from which the symbol emerges and upon which it continues to act. Hood's *Beaver Manifesto* builds on Hood's work with Parks Canada and her "long and interesting acquaintanceship" with the Canadian beaver (2). Her more recent contribution fills in much of the absence where the beaver itself is concerned, marking a shift from sexual and racial to environmental politics.

Hood's "manifesto" registers two important shifts or interruptions in the production of the beaver archive. First, as this quick summary suggests, the inescapably masculine inflection of earlier writing on the fur trade (with its emphasis on conquest, purification, economy, and adventure) has given way to the publication of studies by women that attend more closely to culture and power. Second, this literature is beginning to retrieve and incorporate the history and the question of the animal itself. It constitutes its subject as beaver, not just pelt or fur. Given that fur coats enact a long-standing relationship between money and sex, and that the name of the beaver has a long-standing *double-entendre* relating to women's privates, it is not surprising that animal meaning and metaphor have also shifted in another direction in twentieth-century women's writing and in lesbian and feminist culture, where "beaver" stands metonymically for women's genitals. From works like *The Cultural Politics of Fur*, *Fur Nation*, and *Creative Subversions* to popular discourse, the beaver performs a work of double substitution wherein the animal is subsumed and remediated by mainly white women as part of the act of repossessing their own sexual bodies.

This brief review opens a window to a more purposeful approach to the "collection of interruptions" found in the beaver archive. First, the political contest between Canada's founding narratives and the counter-narratives of the First Nations foreground the colonization of Indigenous lands and cultures and expose the sacrifice of animal and human bodies. By reminding us of this history, beaver imagery plays an important role in the production of postcolonial and anti-colonial pleasures. Second, growing animal awareness reminds us that however much the beaver indexes and entertains the nation-state, this same state does not permit the non-human animal to assert its own right to rights. While provincial laws vary, in general one needs a permit or process of consultation to destroy a beaver dam because of potential damage to property or wildlife downstream, but not to trap or kill a beaver.[19] Given the tension between the animal's symbolic and legal status, the beaver poses a challenge to law as well as to history and culture. Acknowledging this tension challenges the complacency of our feelings when we glimpse the beaver's familiar shape. Third, feminism and environmental activism have challenged the conventional relationship between the bodies of the fur-bearing animal and the fur-wearing woman. As fur returns to the fashion mainstream, how do we interrupt the elision between animal, sex, and power without undermining the traditional cultures and values of

Indigenous hunters? Feminism and animal rights activism find their way into the archive through oppositional texts and image productions. Fourth, the hybrid animal-human figuration of this archive poses questions about human, animal, and shared habitat. We have barely begun to consider ourselves in relation to species diversity or ecological risk, or what such thinking does for our understanding of animal subjects. Timothy Morton poses this challenge when he asks, "Does the beaver phenotype stop at the end of its whiskers or at the end of a beaver's dam?" (34).

My review of recent contributions to the beaver archive suggests that we have a lot to learn to better materialize the important role that animals play in spatial ecology and identity construction (in the words of Wolch and Emel, cited above). Our relationship with the beaver reiterates the territorial battles that human enterprises are now waging with species as diverse as bees, elephants, tigers, slender-snouted crocodiles, Atlantic cod, and various species of dolphins and whales. To urban postcolonial subjects, they are all equally remote, if not equally charismatic. How we think about these issues matters in every sense of the term. "Now more than ever," Guattari insists in *The Three Ecologies*, "nature cannot be separated from culture; in order to comprehend the interactions between ecosystems, the mechanosphere and the social and individual Universes of transference, we must learn to think 'transversally'" (43). In other words, as these interruptions remind us, we need new mapping strategies that situate the beaver in the violent histories that include them. We need beaver figurations that acknowledge colonial history, the land reserves set aside for Indigenous populations, beaver natures, and the rivers now polluted beyond recognition.

The fifth interruption we want to make productive, then, concerns our territorial competition with non-human animals and our actions and effects as animals ourselves. While water experts like Outwater call beavers "nature's hydrologists" and emphasize their ecological importance to continental waterways, land-owning Westerners do not know how to share rivers or trees with them. And yet the risk of separating water from its natural symbiots has never been more urgent than it is today. Perhaps better strategic collaboration with beavers could help ensure the sustainability of water, lakes, and rivers. But the beavers' inscriptions of rivers don't show up on *our* maps. If there's going to be any interference in our aqueous territories, we proclaim as we define beavers as pests, it will be *our* interference.

Finally, then, this story of human interaction with the beaver can be told through a history of images, but such a telling is not sufficient. Restoring animality and agency to the beaver challenges us to confront this fragmentary archive from a material and ecological perspective. Comprised of so many kinds of matter, the beaver archive travels energetically between art and life, allowing us to forget that what is at stake is life itself, the object of biopolitics, which produces both life and death and regulates the process in which these occur. Just as the beaver's life was strategically sustained in order for it to die to be circulated as fur, oil, and tribute laid before the visiting Crown, so its newer forms of reproduction (which do not displace the older ones) are sustained and managed in the system of signs. These relations are embedded in violence and spatial politics where the animal enacts and symbolizes new management. But the animal itself is never just commodity. We know that elephants and bees are traumatized by their oppression, but we know nothing of beavers' states in response to urban sprawl. It is a rodent, now, not an architect.

THE BEAVER SMILES

These archival "interruptions" show that the beaver's phantom use value derives from its claim to a shared human-animal history and from its sagacious respect for the water it calls home, both of which have something important to teach us. Both values are negatively indexed in the cumulative loss of fur in current symbolic renderings. Through stylistic abstraction, the paradigm of work—the beaver as architect, the trapper as provider—has given way to what Baudrillard calls a "paradigm of control" in the ongoing commodification of life itself (102).[20] Such control is enacted visually through abstraction, repetition, digitization, and affect management. Just as animal imagery has played a key role in the development of new representational technologies,[21] so the work of the animal and of its image are central to the biopolitics of late capitalism. The beavers put to work in the contemporary knowledge economy are stylized graphic images that resemble the animal just enough to be recognizable in a glimpse. Through such imagery the design environment of corporate capitalism easily dominates the archive. Alan Liu's critique of the knowledge economy and the production of "cool" usefully supplements this critique of the symbolic abstraction, regulation, and "dematerialization" of animals as historical projects.

In his study of aesthetics in the knowledge economy, Liu defines "cool" as "information designed to resist information [or] the incest of information." It has "everything to do with the mythopoetic landscapes of work," he writes, "leading from filmic deserts to screensaverlike digital highways and seas: the mainstream is identified with the pure milieu, ambience or texture of challenge, with style emptied of agents and agency to become a world sufficient unto itself" (103). This is what makes these latest beaver simulations so extreme and yet so weirdly anticlimactic. Their denial of violence and the infantilization of affect suppresses both animality and meaning. For Liu, the culture of cool arises from the creative knowledge workers' need to balance their self-concept as autonomously creative people against the material constraints of their training and employment in the knowledge economy. Forced to distance themselves from their highly regulated milieu, they participate in a design vocabulary that articulates and exacerbates their ambivalent relationships with their objects. Cool is ironic, inarticulate, narrow-minded, self-centred, and sometimes cruel. It is strongly invested in the meaninglessness of things. Unlike the destructive actions of the Reformation or the Nazis, Liu writes, we do not destroy our archives but rather render them meaningless, non-sense. We could not find a better description of the annoying de-furred beavers promoting Bell phones and Canada Parks in their campaigns. These beavers are cool in a bad way. Their pallid irony licenses indifference and cruelty. As Liu concludes, it is our task as educators to show that cool is an historical condition, to help advance understanding of this condition and to consider how its circumstances might be overcome. The growth of empathy toward living creatures is a necessary step in this direction.

So much is at stake in this virtual archive of the beaver: colonial history, animal bodies, water, money, the fur trade, maps and correspondences, inequitable encounters between settler and Indigenous cultures, ideas about nature and land, the so-called dematerialization of the global economy, the source of "natural" and "artificial" flavours, fetishism, post-humanism, fashion, sexuality, water, deindustrialization, the aesthetics of cute, the dominance of cool, the biopolitics of colonialism, and the corporatization of national identity are all present in the beaver archive. The beaver "contains" all this, along with traces of diverse interests acting to make other meanings productive in the contending histories of the present. Unravelling these threads is important to revisiting what is remembered and what is forgotten in the inscription of Canada.

In *A Fair Country*, John Ralston Saul claims that our society has become dysfunctional and that we need to rethink its history. For Saul, imaging ourselves differently means letting go of European hierarchies and rationalities and recognizing the degree to which Canada's values and modes of connection are shaped by the influence of Indigenous cultures with which we have interacted from the start. "We have to learn how to express that reality," Saul writes, "the reality of our history. I am not talking about a passive projection of our past, but rather about all of us learning how to imagine ourselves differently" (35). There is something touching and problematic in the royal "we" that Saul invokes in "all of us." But let's go there. What might this imagining bring to our depiction of beavers, humans, and natural resources? To alter our shared political trajectory we need to relearn this history and what its different players know and don't know about water, ecology, land, culture, and species. We need to appreciate the artistry of beavers, as well as our own, and think differently about maps, the ones that got us here and the ones we might remake. The work of the beaver is to live and rebuild the landscape. That is our job as well.

NOTES

This research was funded by a SSHRC Insight Grant. Sincere thanks also to HBC Archives, Winnipeg, and to Sabine Lebel and Ryan Murphy for their able assistance with this research.

1. See <http://en.wikiquote.org/wiki/Talk:Margaret_Atwood>.
2. Notable exceptions to this tendency to ignore the political import of the beaver in history include Keith Thomas, *Man and the Natural World* (1983), Clive Ponting, *The New Green History of the World* (2007), and *The New Green History of the World* (2011).
3. See also Wolfe's quotation of Shukin's phrase and discussion of her argument in *Before the Law*, 51-52.
4. Von Uexküll presents some of this evidence in *A Foray into the Worlds of Animals and Humans*. However, he also offers a caution: "We comfort ourselves all too easily with the illusion that the relations of another kind of subject to the things of its environment play out in the same space and time as the relations that link us to the things of our human environment. This illusion is fed by the belief in the existence of one and only one world, in which all living beings are encased. From this arises the widely held conviction that there must be one and only one space and time for all living beings" (54).
5. In Argentina and Belgium, on the other hand, the animal is largely represented as a pest wreaking devastation onto the land. There is no historic or symbolic value attached to its presence.
6. For an important discussion of the concept of "rendering" of the animal's body in the production of culture, see Nicole Shukin, *Animal Capital*.
7. The idea of the *topos* offers a geopolitical extension of Derrida's notion of the archive, used to analyze the layering of texts, imprints, and spatial politics of the New World. See Belton, *Orinoco Flow*, and Berland, *North of Empire*, for a fuller discussion of this idea.
8. See, for example, Foucault's lectures collected in *Security, Territory, Population*.
9. For an analysis of this process in the writings of seventeenth-century Jesuit missionary Le Jeune, as well as in twentieth-century interpretations of his work, see McKegney.
10. Such consideration for beavers appeared only in the twentieth century with the publication of books by trapper-turned-writer Grey Owl, who adopted beavers as pets, described them as "Little People," and endowed them with endearing qualities. His writing was a deliberate intervention into the anthropocentrism and indifference of the entrepreneurs of the fur trade, for whom the animal was a serviceable tool for and index of their own imperial prowess over the territories they mapped and the bodies they encountered.
11. My use of this concept is indebted to correspondence with Pauline Greenhill.
12. See, for example, Midgley, "Beasts, Brutes, and Monsters," and Wolfe, *Before the Law*.
13. Innis cites Lahontan's work in his own research on the fur trade, with reference to the debate in fur trade literature about whether Indians are closer to the beaver or the white man.

14 For an overview of Lahontan's career, see Payne (n. pag.).
15 A detailed examination of this process in seventeenth-century political philosophy can be found in Craig McFarlane, "Early Modern Speculative Anthropology," unpublished PhD dissertation (2014), Department of Sociology, York University.
16 See Fabian, *Time and the Other*, and Sioui, *For an Amerindian Autohistory*, on othering through concepts of time. For further discussion of colonial discourse and its reliance on a Western view of the mastery of nature, see Berland, "Weathering the North" in *North of Empire*.
17 In his 1868 book *The American Beaver and His Works*, "[Lewis Henry] Morgan felt that the thinking principle was *not* unique to humanity. To the contrary, he believed that the Creator had endowed *all* animal species, and not mankind alone, with a mind as well as a body. If anything convinced him of this, it was his observations of the technical accomplishments of the Beaver" (Ingold 87).
18 For more on the production of seriality and abstraction in the virtual menagerie, see Berland, "Visitor's Guide to the Virtual Menagerie" (2014).
19 Ministry of Environment, Conservation Species Act, Beavers: <http://www.env.gov.bc.ca/cos/info/wildlife_human_interaction/docs/nuisance_fauna.html>
20 In *For a Critique of the Political Economy of the Sign*, Baudrillard writes that "Stylization always signifies the elision of muscular energy and of work. All the processes of elision of primary functions to the profit of the secondary functions of relation and calculation, or of the elision of the drives to the profit of culture (*culturalité*) have for a practical and historical mediation at the level of objects the fundamental elision of the gestures of effort (*gestuel d'effort*), the passage from a *universal gestural paradigm of work* to a *universal gestural paradigm of control*. It is there that a millenarian status of objects, their anthropomorphic status, definitely comes to an end; in the abstraction of the sources of energy" (102).
21 See, for example, Jonathan Burt's *Animals in Film* for a discussion of this phenomenon.

WORKS CITED

Atwood, Margaret. *Surfacing*. Toronto: McClelland and Stewart, 1972. Print.

Baker, Steve. *Picturing the Beast: Animals, Identity, and Representation*. Manchester: Manchester UP, 1993. Print.

Barthes, Roland. *Mythologies*. Trans. Annette Lavers. New York: Hill and Wang, 1972. Print.

Baudrillard, Jean. *For a Critique of the Political Economy of the Sign*. St. Louis: Telos, 1981. Print.

Belton, Benjamin Keith. *Orinoco Flow: Culture, Narrative, and the Political Economy of Information*. Lanham: Scarecrow, 2003. Print.

Berland, Jody. "Animal and/as Medium: Symbolic Work in Communicative Regimes." *Global South* 3.1 (Spring 2009): 42-65. Print.

———. *North of Empire: Essays on the Cultural Technologies of Space*. Durham: Duke UP, 2009. Print.

———. "A Visitor's Guide to the Virtual Menagerie." *Virtual Animals. Antennae: Journal of Nature in Visual Culture* 30 (2014): 55-73. Web. http://www.antennae.org.uk. 21 Dec. 2014.

Burt, Jonathan. *Animals in Film*. London: Reaktion, 2004. Print.

Cameron, James McIntyre. *The Canadian Beaver Book: Fact, Fiction, and Fantasy*. Burnstown: General Store, 1991. Print.

Canada. *Government of Canada Response to Report of Standing Committee on Aboriginal Affairs and Northern Development: The Fur Issue: Cultural Continuity and Economic Opportunity*. Ottawa: Indian and Northern Affairs Canada, 1987. Print.

Chase, Steven. "Beavers Can't Cut It as National Emblem, But Polar Bears Can, Senator Says." *Globe and Mail*. 27 Oct. 2011. Web. 20 Aug. 2014.

Derrida, Jacques. *Archive Fever: A Freudian Impression*. Trans. Eric Prenowitz. Chicago: U of Chicago P, 1996. Print.

———. "Before the Law." Trans. Avital Ronell. *Acts of Literature*. Ed. Derek Attridge. New York: Routledge, 1992. Print.

Dugmore, Arthur Radclyffe. *The Romance of the Beaver: Being the History of the Beaver in the Western Hemisphere*. Philadelphia: J. B. Lippincott, 1914. Print.

Emberley, Julia. *The Cultural Politics of Fur*. Ithaca: Cornell UP, 1997. Print.

Fabian, Johannes. *Time and the Other: How Anthropology Makes Its Object*. New York: Columbia UP, 1983. Print.

Fiamengo, Janice. "Postcolonial Guilt in Margaret Atwood's *Surfacing*." *American Review of Canadian Studies* 29.1 (1999): 141-63. Print.

Fleming, Marnie. *Beaver Tales*. Curated by Reid Diamond and Marnie Fleming. Oakville, ON: Oakville Galleries, 2000. Catalogue of an exhibition held 20 May to 16 July 2000. Print.

Foucault, Michel. *Security, Territory, Population: Lectures at the Collège de France 1977–1978*. Paris: Editions du Seuil/Gallimard, 2004. Trans. Graham Burchill. New York: Picador, 2007. Print.

Francis, Margot. *Creative Subversions: Whiteness, Indigeneity, and the National Imaginary*. Vancouver: UBC P, 2011. Print.

Fudge, Erica. "A Left-handed Blow: Writing the History of Animals." *Representing Animals*. Ed. Nigel Rothfels. Bloomington: Indiana UP, 2000. 3-18. Print.

Funcke, Bettina. *Pop or Populus: Art Between High and Low*. Berlin: Sternberg, 2009. Print.

Gagnon, François-Marc. *Images du castor canadien, XVIe-XVIIIe siècles*. Sillery, Québec: Septentrion, 1994. (Les Nouveaux cahiers du CÉLAT; 7). Print.

Grey Owl. *The Collected Works of Grey Owl: Three Complete and Unabridged Canadian Classics*. Toronto: Discovery, 1999. Print.

Guattari, Felix. *The Three Ecologies*. Trans. Paul Sutton and Ian Pindar. London: Athlone, 2000. Print.

Harvey, David. *Justice, Nature, and the Geography of Difference*. Cambridge: Blackwell, 1996. Print.

Hood, Glynnis. *The Beaver Manifesto*. Victoria: Rocky Mountain, 2011. Print.

Howell, James. *Thērologia, the parly of beasts, or, morphandra, queen of the inchanted iland wherein men were found, who being transmuted to beasts, though proffer'd to be dis-inchanted, and to becom men again, yet, in regard of the crying sins and rebellious humors of the times, they prefer the life of a brute animal before that of a rational creture ...: With reflexes upon the present state of most countries in christendom. Divided into a XI sections*. London: W. Wilson for William Palmer, 1660. *Early English Books Online*. Web. 25 June 2014.

Hutcheon, Linda. *The Canadian Postmodern: A Study of Contemporary English-Canadian Fiction*. Toronto: Oxford UP, 1988. Print.

Ingold, Tim, ed. *What Is an Animal?* London: Unwin Hyman, 1988. Print.
Innis, Harold. *The Fur Trade in Canada: An Introduction to Canadian Economic History*. Rev. ed. Toronto: U of Toronto P, 1962. Print.
Krech, Shepard K. III, ed. *Indians, Animals, and the Fur Trade: A Critique of Keepers of the Game*. Athens: U of Georgia P, 1981. Print.
Kroeber, Alfred Louis. *The Nature of Culture*. Chicago: U of Chicago P, 1952. Print.
Lahontan, Louis-Armand de Lom d'Arce, Baron de. *New Voyages to North America: Containing an Account of the Several Nations of That Vast Continent, Their Customs, Commerce, and Way of Navigation*. Vol. 2. London: H. Bonwicke, T. Goodwin, M. Wotton, B. Tooke, and S. Manship, 1703. Print.
Latour, Bruno. *Politics of Nature: How to Bring the Sciences into Democracy*. Cambridge: Harvard UP, 2004. Print.
———. *We Have Never Been Modern*. Trans. Catherine Porter. Cambridge: Harvard UP, 1993. Print.
Levi-Strauss, Claude. *Totemism*. Trans. Rodney Needham. Boston: Beacon, 1971. Print.
Liu, Alan. *The Laws of Cool: Knowledge Work and the Culture of Information*. Chicago: U of Chicago P, 2004. Print.
MacKay, Douglas. *The Honourable Company: A History of the Hudson's Bay Company*. Indianapolis: Bobbs-Merrill Co., 1936. Print.
Martin, Calvin. *Keepers of the Game: Indian-Animal Relationships and the Fur Trade*. Berkeley: U of California P, 1978. Print.
McKegney, Sam W. "Second-hand Shaman: Imag(in)ing Indigeneity from Le Jeune to Pratt, Moore and Beresford." *TOPIA: Canadian Journal of Cultural Studies* 12 (2004): 25-40. Print.
Midgley, Mary. *Animals and Why They Matter*. Athens: U of Georgia P, 1983. Print.
———. "Beasts, Brutes, and Monsters." Ingold 35-46. Print.
Morgan, Lewis H. *The American Beaver and His Works*. Philadelphia: Lippincott, 1868. Print.
Morton, Timothy. *The Ecological Thought*. Cambridge: Harvard UP, 2010. Print.
Nadeau, Chantal. *Fur Nation: From the Beaver to Brigitte Bardot*. London: Routledge, 2001. Print.
Outwater, Alice B. *Water: A Natural History*. New York: Basic, 1996. Print.
Payne, David. "Lom d'Arce de Lahontan, Louis-Armand De, Baron de Lahontan." *Dictionary of Canadian Biography*. Vol. 2. U of Toronto/U Laval, 1969. N. pag. Web. 29 July 2014. <http://www.biographi.ca/en/bio.php?id_nbr=956>
Peers, Laura. "'Fur Trade History, Native History, Public History: Communication and Miscommunication." *New Faces of the Fur Trade: Selected Papers of the Seventh North American Fur Trade Conference*. Ed. Jo-Anne Fiske, Susan Sleeper-Smith, and William Wicken. Halifax, NS, 1995. Proceedings. East Lansing: Michigan State UP, 1998. 101-20. Print.
Ponting, Clive. *A New Green History of the World: The Environment and the Collapse of Great Civilizations*. Rev. ed. New York: Penguin, 2007. Print.
Price, Rachel. "Archive Fever and Twentieth-Century Critical Theory." MS. Duke U, Durham, 2001. Print.

Saul, John Ralston. *A Fair Country: Telling Truths about Canada*. Toronto: Viking Canada, 2008. Print.

Saum, Lewis O. *The Fur Trader and the Indian*. Seattle: U of Washington P, 1965. Print.

Shukin, Nicole. *Animal Capital: Rendering Life in Biopolitical Times*. Minneapolis: U of Minnesota P, 2009. Print.

Sioui, Georges E. *For an Amerindian Autohistory: An Essay on the Foundations of a Social Ethic*. Montreal: McGill-Queen's UP, 1992. Print.

Thomas, Keith. *Man and the Natural World: Changing Attitudes in England 1500-1800*. London: Allen Lane, 1983. Print.

Uexküll, Jakob von. *A Foray into the Worlds of Animals and Humans: With a Theory of Meaning*. Trans. Joseph D. O'Neil. Minneapolis: U of Minnesota P, 2010. Print.

Wolch, Jennifer, and Jody Emel, eds. *Animal Geographies: Place, Politics, and Identity in the Nature-Culture Borderlands*. London: Verso, 1998. Print.

Wolfe, Carey. *Before the Law: Humans and Others in a Biopolitical Frame*. Chicago: U of Chicago P, 2012. Print.

CHAPTER 2

Night in a Box
Anne Carson's *Nox* and the Materiality of Elegy

Tanis MacDonald

> The process of reproducing the original journal is a story unto itself. The book is not really a book of poetry, though that's how it's labeled. Carson says it was her editor's idea to call it poetry. The book [*Nox*] is an extraordinary object to behold, and more extraordinary to read, but it's hardly accurate to even call it a "book." It's perhaps 10 feet of paper, folded accordion-like, displaying as near a reproduction of Carson's original collage journal as is possible. The whole thing is folded and packed into a beautiful gray box.... The result is breathtaking, evidence of visionary publishing at a moment when the book business is increasingly cynical.
> —Craig Morgan Teicher, *Publisher's Weekly*

> history can be at once concrete and indecipherable
> —Anne Carson, *Nox*

In his March 2010 review in *Publisher's Weekly* hailing the publication of Anne Carson's *Nox*, a book-length elegy for her brother, Craig Morgan Teicher notes that the text is "evidence of visionary publishing" in an "increasingly cynical" literary market. Similar kinds of cynicism could be said to lurk in some branches of literary studies as we head into the second decade of the twenty-first century, with special critical asperity and claims of visionary originality reserved for the texts of Anne Carson. Her prolific literary output, and her swift ascendance to the ranks of must-read authors, have marked Carson as a writer about whom everyone has an opinion, with Michael Ondaatje on one side praising her "huge range of intellect and wit and emotion" on the back cover of *Men in the Off Hours* and David Solway on the other side saying that the "Carson phenomenon" is a "gigantic pyramid scheme" (Solway 25). The bifurcated reception of Carson's work is perhaps best expressed by poet Fraser Sutherland's assessment: "People either hate her or think she's the Second Coming" (qtd. in Heer). Scholarly work has begun to address Carson as a literary phenomenon, with Ian Rae noting that each one of her texts is marked by her trademark fascination with "the anomalous, the erratic, the inimitable" (254) and Kevin McNeilly asserting that in Carson's work, inquiry and instability are key: "What we take for fixity, for self-evidence, is only another way to frame a question" (McNeilly 9). This kind of attention to reception is not unheard of in Canadian literary studies, but it is surprisingly quick in the case of a writer who published her first literary work less than twenty years ago. Suffice it to say that Carson has become a lightning-rod figure in Canadian poetic criticism, largely because she refuses to justify her choices, to capitulate to criticisms of her eclectic mash-ups of contemporary and classical references, or to discuss her work under terms other than those that she brings to the text. Her readership outside the academy is remarkably broad for a writer who is often accused of being too intellectually esoteric, so it should come as no surprise that the publication of a new book by Carson creates considerable ripples in the reading world, and that *Nox* received early reviews that challenged cynicism about the literary market through Carson's experimentation with form.

Teicher's effusive review—representative of the kind of breathless praise reviewers have lavished upon the physical appearance and tactility of *Nox*—is attentive to the striking material features of the text and emphasizes its origins in a "collage journal" that Carson compiled over a series of years. The subject of the collage journal was the absence of her brother from her life since 1978: a twenty-two-year absence punctuated by only five phone calls, the final call in 2000 coming only a few months before Michael Carson's death. The reception of *Nox* as an object of aesthetic beauty in reviews such as Teicher's brings to mind Bill Brown's excellent question about the collection and organization of objects: "Do we collect things in order to keep the past proximate, to incorporate the past into our daily lives, or in order to make the past distant, to objectify it (as an idea in a thing) in the effort to arrest its spectral power?" (Brown 12). *Nox* sustains and sharpens Carson's use of elegiac convention even as the text manipulates the perceived intimacy of the book's material properties—so deliberately connotative of a scrapbook's privacy, yet so self-consciously reproduced to function as a public object. Carson's own admonition in *Nox* that "history can be at once concrete and indecipherable" (1.3) suggests her own view of the past as a conundrum as it exists in the collection of objects that make up this elegiac interrogation: Is *Nox* an epitaph or an elegy? Using Brown's terms, we could say that as an epitaph, *Nox* functions to keep the past proximate through tactile materials, and as an elegy, *Nox* arrests the spectral power of the past and draws our attention to the insoluble problem of "telling a life" that resists narrative. In *Plainwater*, Carson writes "the poet's task, Kafka said, is to lead the isolated human being into the infinite life, the contingent into the lawful" (12). In *Nox*, Michael Carson is the "isolated human being," and his sister as collector and rearranger of objects moves him from the isolation he chose in 1978 into the "infinite life" of the elegy, and from the contingency of death and disappearance back into the lawful space of the family.

Carson has contributed to the controversy surrounding her place in Canadian literature with her constantly shifting, hybrid-sensitive method of generic expansion and exploration in which her subjects remain constant while her modes of address fluctuate. Such an approach to form is deliberate, even when it is made in frustration or desperation, as Carson suggests in her 2001 interview with Mary Gannon: "I think the forms are in chaos. I seize upon these generic names like essay or opera in despair as I'm sinking under the waves of possible naming for any event that I come up with" (Carson 31). But Kevin McNeilly discusses this chaotic approach as part of the Carsonian appeal, affirming that the author is aware that "poetry consists in the fact of getting caught, often by mistake, emblematized in the everyday presence of human bodies that won't, that can't, be written off" (7). Ian Rae discusses her similarity to Michael Ondaatje in her "mixed-media approach" in which "the defining genre ... is absent except as a trace in the writing" (227). Part of Carson's ongoing project of exploring the expansive quality of various forms has also led her to invite other artists to engage with her texts in a variety of performance genres. A portion of Carson's opera "Decreation" was performed by students at the College of Saint Benedict and Saint John's University in Minnesota in 2001. A number of dance pieces based on *Nox* have been posted on YouTube. Carson herself illustrated *Autobiography of Red* with her own painting of a volcano.

Carson's interests in book as artifact, as well as her pursuit of the intersections between poetry and visual art, are evident throughout *Nox*. At once a book-length elegy and a meta-text about the ephemerality of text, narrative, and memory itself, *Nox* is a Carsonian object par excellence: an artifact that both preserves affect and shreds it. Her use of the terms "elegy" and "epitaph" in reference to *Nox* should not be construed as a conflation of the terms, but rather as evidence of the text's dual purpose: the elegy as an inquiry "fill[ed] with light of all kinds" (*Nox* 1.0) and the epitaph as a "way of praising him," as Carson says during her interview with Eleanor Wachtel for CBC Radio's *Writers and Company*. The distance between inquiry and praise, or between elegy and epitaph, describes the psychological distance between text and material. On the back cover of *Nox*, Carson notes: "When my brother died I made an epitaph for him in the form of a book. This is a replica of it, as close as we could get."

To clarify these terms, an elegy is a poem that takes as its subject matter the scope and inquiry of mourning ritual. The elegy longs after that which is lost, most often a human being who has died, as in John Milton's "Lycidas" or Percy Bysshe Shelley's "Adonais," but also may mourn the loss of states of being or vanished worlds: "the knell of parting day" as in Thomas Gray's "Elegy Written in a Country Churchyard." Most importantly, the elegy purports to position the lost beloved as the subject, but in reality it offers the elegizing self as the true centre of the elegy. An epitaph, in contrast, is a short verse or aphorism usually composed for a person's gravestone; in a larger sense, it is indicative of the deceased person's philosophical or relational legacy. An epitaph is usually sombre, sometimes comic, and often the subject of witty or despairing speculation while the person is still alive. The two genres, then, serve different needs. An elegy, even in contemporary poetry, questions the parameters and scope of self-conscious mourning in dialogue with the culture, while the epitaph has a starker purpose and may speak volumes, as Toni Morrison suggests in *Beloved*. While the two terms may intersect on occasion, they are not interchangeable.

However, *Nox* enacts its own paradox by offering itself as an epitaph not only for Michael Carson, but also for the idea of the book itself. The anxiety of disappearance is inextricably linked to the object of the collage journal that was the basis for *Nox*, and when New Directions launched *Nox* in the spring of 2010, the marketing emphasis on the book as a survivor of the circumstances of its own production echoed the "breathtaking" rhetoric of its immediate reception. The story that Carson and New Directions tell about the journal's transition into a marketable book is a narrative of fateful adventure, beginning with Carson's creation of an "unpublishable" book made of letters, envelopes, drawings, poems, a translation of Catullus's Poem 101, scraps of poetry, and entries from a Latin dictionary. Carson created this elegiac object with the understanding that the scrapbook would be an artifact that could not be reproduced: a "book" to be sure, but not a book that was commercially marketable. However, the force of the Carson phenomenon was stronger than mere concerns with genre or publishing techniques. When a German publisher of art books offered to publish the scrapbook, Carson mailed it to Germany, only to hear after a silence of several years that the proposed publisher had lost the scrapbook. Some years later, the material was returned to her anonymously and unceremoniously in a FedEx package (Sehgal). Robert Currie of New Directions then convinced Carson that he could design and reproduce her scrapbook in a form that would preserve the aesthetic of the original; *Nox* is the result of that collaboration.

Certainly many manuscripts undergo harrowing escapes and just-in-time interventions in the process of becoming books. The melancholia of *Nox* as an object has been enhanced by its separate narrative as an imperilled object. The story of the publication of *Nox* is notable because of the slippage between book and body that is promoted by this narrative of disappearance, miraculous recovery, and artistic transcendence of difficulty that describes both Michael Carson's life and the book as epitaph. The public reception of the book, of which Teicher's review is the exemplar, has been quick to honour those parallels as quasi-mythological in scope. But when read as an elegy, the materiality of *Nox* suggests a more complicated relationship with the ineffable, as well as a rigorous discourse about the essential invisible that is at the core of elegy studies. The physical text of *Nox* is offered as sublime elegiac material precisely because it defies the durable technology of a regular, sturdily bound book.

W. David Shaw posits in his foundational study *Elegy and Paradox* that the modern elegy necessarily incorporates a "paradox of veridiction" as a constitutive element of the elegiac mode: that an elegy claims to tell the truth because of, not despite, the manipulation of the lost beloved's biography by the elegist. This paradox of veridiction is most acute in its disavowal, for "even in denying a truth-claim we presume to make one" (Shaw 147). While Carson writes that in "prowling the history of a person" she has discovered that there is "no use expecting a flood of light. Human words have no main switch" (*Nox* 7.1), the form of the scrapbook suggests a tone of veridiction. *Nox* offers the apparently private *veritas* of the scrapbook as a material truth-claim that has been faithfully reproduced by Robert Currie at New Directions, but the refusal of a complete narrative arc complicates the notion of a personal history offering itself up to confession or examination. The letters and photos that *Nox* contains are, in fact, uncontainable according to Carson's notion of history as inquiry; as she writes with weary recognition in *Nox*, "Always comforting to assume there is a secret behind what torments you" (5.4).

Much of the texture of this paradox of veridiction may be read through Carson's work with the scrapbook materials and through the decision of New Directions to market *Nox* as both epitaph and elegy: an object of melancholy beauty and an inquiry into the power of memory. The drama of the text's production plays out in the space between the materiality of the text's production and the ephemerality of its subject, and these dynamics position *Nox* as a book whose "thingness" was established through a series of fateful accidents, happy and unhappy. This ecstatic emphasis on the material melancholia of *Nox* sometimes threatens to spill over into bathos; the reception of *Nox*'s faux-tactile surface is reminiscent of no other book so much as it resembles the 1991 publishing sensation *Griffin and Sabine*, in which West Coast visual artist Nick Bantock reimagined the epistolary novel to include actual letters in actual envelopes, complete with beautiful stamps, within the book. While Bantock's book was entirely fictional, *Griffin and Sabine* and its two sequels were marketed on the voyeuristic thrill of opening a letter addressed to someone else, and on the physical beauty of the text itself as an object that contained a secret that would yield itself up to manipulation of the text. Certainly, comparisons between Bantock's book and Carson's are ridiculous in one way, but it is hard to get away from the fact that, like *Griffin and Sabine*, it is the thingness of *Nox* that fascinates and may in turn frustrate the reader. There is certainly irony to be read in this marketing strategy, for *Nox* in its protective box is very durable and bulky. The carapace of the cover offers a book-like appearance, and lends the object a stiffness that shores up the accordioned pages inside the box.

Carson and New Directions offer *Nox* as book/body, positioning the artifact of the book itself as an oxymoron: durably ephemeral and sturdily fragile. Teicher's description of the material presence of *Nox* is accurate as far as it goes, and in addition, the book is, like many objects of beauty, difficult to hold. Its accordioned pages cannot quite be turned as book pages are turned; after a certain point, the pages bend easily under the weight of all the other pages behind them. But in her interview with Parul Sehgal in *The Irish Times*, Carson riffs whimsically on the book's durability in a way that is strikingly at odds with the book's material reality. She suggests that readers who have "a long staircase" at their disposal ought to place the text at the top of the stairs, then "Drop it down and watch it unfold," adding "I did" (Sehgal). The book is, realistically, far too fragile for such rough treatment, playful though the suggestion may be. If handled with care, the accordioned pages of *Nox* have a fragile kinetic quality, like a flipbook that must be delicately handled. How much Carson's claim to have treated her copy of *Nox* with such ludic roughness is a kind of writer's bravado, and how much a material version of what Rae calls "concealment drama" (251), in which she adopts a self-conscious flippancy to offset the melancholic reception of the book, a verbal casualness with the precious *objet d'art*, remains a puzzle. But either way, Carson's admonitions to handle the text as roughly as one pleases do not end there; she also suggests that the back of the accordioned pages are blank so that readers may "make their own book there" (Sehgal). The implication is, undoubtedly, that one grief will awaken another: that elegies will beget elegies so that the "books" generated by this single book are potentially infinite. All books composed on the back of *Nox* will be inevitably part of *Nox*: informed by its style, influenced by its propinquity, and folded into the proliferations of *Nox*.

The elegy as a Slinky; the elegy as usefully recyclable. These seemingly irreverent suggestions for the material text imply that though *Nox* takes as its core subject Carson's contemplation of her brother's life, in its brief history as a book it has operated, in part, as an elegy for elegies. When she asserts that "history and elegy are akin," Carson also offers the insight that "autopsy" is the historian's term for "eyewitnessing" that connotes "a mode of authorial power" (1.2). But the body under autopsy in *Nox* is not the body of Michael Carson, although he is most definitely the lost beloved of this elegy; the body undergoing autopsy here is the body of the book itself. There is a dialogic movement between reading *Nox* as an aestheticized object reproduced from the "affect object" of the journal, and reading *Nox* as "night in a box," an object that exposes itself as an elegiac apostrophe of personal history. As a book made to fit snugly into a box, *Nox* forces a kind of tactile revelation in the voyeuristic examination of its unfolding. The book's first page displays the declaration "NOX FRATER NOX" in bold capitals on a strip of paper superimposed over a vertical row of six holographic iterations of the name Michael. The title and organizational spine of the text—and its elegiac tone—is established through Carson's use of Catullus's Poem 101, an ancient fraternal elegy that she uses as a translational intertext, offering a smudged but still readable Latin text of Poem 101 in a yellowed rectangle of paper seemingly glued to the second page of *Nox*. The fourth page brings Carson's statement of her difficulty with writing in the elegiac mode: "No matter how I try to evoke the starry lad he was, it remains a plain, odd history. So I began to think about history" (1.1). The rest of the text's defiantly unnumbered pages offer slices of photos, letters, postage stamps, drawings, graffiti-like doodles, distressed fragments of documents, and messages revealed through pencil rubbings. English definitions of each of the Latin words appear in the sequence that they appear in the poem throughout *Nox*, giving the reader with little or no Latin a chance to contemplate Carson's and Catullus's fraternal elegies in tandem. Marked as section 2.2, a paragraph that details Michael's disappearance from his sister's life, his travels, and his infrequent communication is repeated four times. The single letter that Michael Carson wrote to his mother is reproduced several times from a variety of angles and eventually a number of textures—folded, scrunched, ink-smeared, partially in focus, torn into fragments—as a material demonstration of the ways Michael's "muteness ... resists" his sister's attempts to write him as history: a "transactional order," in Carson's terms. She additionally cites the "overtakelessness" of history or the ephemerality that "facts lack" and that defy anyone who "collects facts" (*Nox* 1.3) as the forces against which she cannot compete to write her brother's narrative.

While the inclusion of photographs in a text has become fairly common in the past fifteen years, holographic pictures of letters are a bit more unusual. Of course, the presence of pictures of letters does suggest that what is being reproduced in the text is a version of the epistolary novel with the added frisson of veridiction, all the more fraught because such promises of a consciously manipulated "truth-telling" are inevitably partial. The attraction of the thingness of *Nox*, with its artifacts of a life lovingly reproduced, is on display in a YouTube video that focuses upon "beautiful books" posted by DIESEL Books on 30 August 2010, in which the host, Thomas Bailey, discusses how Carson offers the text as a "tangible puzzle" that attempts to "piece her brother together" while he pages through *Nox*, displaying its striking physical features. What may have been intended to be an elegiac moment becomes hyperbolic, or even darkly humorous, when the camera pulls back from the speaker's contemplation of the text to reveal that he is sitting in a cemetery. Comparisons of the box to a headstone have been noted in several reviews, but whose headstone is the text meant to be? While the cover of the box shows a slice of a photograph of Michael at the age of nine wearing swimming trunks and goggles, the name that appears so starkly above the photograph, and apparently "on" the headstone, is that of the author.

Musing aloud on *Writers and Company* that composing *Nox* made her brother's history "more storied but not more complete," Carson herself rejects the notion that the scrapbook was ever meant to be read as pieces of a puzzle and insists on the opposite: the text is a site in which she could replace her brother's apparent presence in photographs with the more familiar "vanishing," right down to representing her brother as shadows or splices in the family photographs. More than halfway through *Nox*, Carson questions, "Why do we blush before death?" (7.1) and then pages later, advises "If you are writing an elegy begin with the blush" (7.2). This advice—if advice it is—comes closer to the end of the text than the beginning, providing that the reader is paging through the text and not watching it roll down a staircase. But the location of this statement in the text is important. Carson begins *Nox* by noting the perpetually unmet desire of elegists: "I wanted to fill my elegy with light of all kinds. But death makes us stingy.... No matter how I try to evoke the starry lad he was, it remains a plain, odd history." Carson's dual assertion that history is "the strangest thing that humans do" (1.3) and that "history and elegy are akin" (1.1) suggests that *Nox* is not a reproduction that strives to offer authenticity but, rather, that *Nox* is a meta-reproduction, a gesture to the original scrapbook that was itself a gesture to her brother's seemingly perpetual absence. What this box of text offers is a copy of a memory constructed to comment on the elegy as an artifact of mourning that attends to the materiality of loss even as loss defies both speech and material evidence. *Nox* is a simulacrum that foregrounds its own ephemerality by displaying the inherent contradictions at work in the project of collection. Any self-admonishment to "begin with the blush" is necessarily an afterthought: advice that has been discovered through the experience of doing the opposite.

Carson has positioned herself as a family elegist at least since the early nineties, when she devoted a large portion of "The Anthropology of Water" in her 1995 book, *Plainwater*, to rewriting her father's illness and death. She has also used the photograph as the elegiac ekphrasis since *Men in the Off Hours*, in which a photo of the author as a child with her mother appears on the very last page of the text, as an accompaniment to the collection's final prose poem, "Appendix to Ordinary Time." The photo shows a woman and a girl of perhaps three reclining on chairs ingeniously suspended over a lake, dangling their feet in the water. The woman wears sunglasses and the child a sunhat; both are in bathing suits. The words "Margaret Carson 1913-1997" with the Latin "Eclipsis est pro dolore" appear below the photo, caption-like (*Men* 167). In "Appendix to Ordinary Time," Carson begins by writing that her mother has died and that on the day after her mother's funeral, she "was turning over the pages" of Virginia Woolf's diaries and wondering at the strange comfort she finds in the final entries, including the fact that in 1941, in the days before her suicide, Woolf wrote the phrase "How vanished everyone is" in several letters to friends. Carson goes on to wonder about the liminal position of two crossed-out phrases in a diary entry that Woolf wrote about a month before her death. The phrases are "She did not sufficiently. She had no grasp" (*Men* 166). The subject of these phrases in Woolf's diary is ambiguous; it could be Woolf herself, but that conclusion is complicated by the fact that Woolf has just used the first-person singular in the previous sentence. For Carson, the phrase has a certain status as that which has been written and refused, but still exists *sous rature* as a wordly haunting with which to be reckoned. And the subject for Carson is less ambiguous, though inevitably doubled by the context in which she offers it in "Appendix to Ordinary Time." The stroking out of the phrases suggests that Carson's mother, as the elegiac object, may be the referent, even as Carson as daughter figure and elegist struggles with her own sufficiency: "Crossouts are something you rarely see in published texts. They are like death: by a simple stroke—all is lost, yet still there. For death *although utterly unlike life* shares a skin with it" (*Men* 166; italics in original). That "shared skin" is both visually evident and textually coded in the photograph on the facing page: the vulnerable bodies of mother and child hovering over the lake, their relaxed postures, the photo's deceptive casualness. A simple translation of the Latin phrase below the photo of woman and daughter would be "It is painful to be eclipsed," but in an open translation like Carson's own, Sophie Mayer translates it as "It is crossed out in the face of sorrow" (Mayer 113), emphasizing the anglicized meaning of dolour as sorrow rather than pain. Mayer's translation aligns the Latin with Carson's statement: "Crossouts sustain me now. I search out and cherish them like old photographs of my mother in happier times…. Now I too am someone who knows marks" (*Men* 166). Mayer also notes that this caption takes an "epitaphic position" in that it is not the mother who has been "crossed out" because the photo offers such clear evidence of her presence. Rather, Mayer asserts that the caption refers to "death itself, the great crosser-out—eclipsed by photography, as the line survives underneath the crossing through, as the daughter also depicted survives the mother" (113).

A similar photograph of Margaret Carson appears in *Nox*, this time showing Margaret on a towel on a dock on the lake, clad in another bathing suit and accompanied by her son rather than her daughter. From the declaration in "Appendix to Ordinary Time" that "Death lines every moment of ordinary time. Death hides right inside every shining sentence we grasped and had no grasp of" (*Men* 166) to the italicized caption below the photo in *Nox* of "*I make a guess. I make a guess*" (2.1), these family elegies show a visual dialectic between the hidden and the apparent, and the repetition of both "grasp" and "guess" shows the tenuous state of the elegiac object as both "lost" and perpetually present. *Nox*—in the works for years, at least since Michael Carson's death in 2000—offers in good elegiac fashion the eclipse not of the dead person, but of death itself, by working and reworking the "dolore" of the maternal elegy into an examination of her brother's estrangement from the family, a subject Carson broached first in "The Wishing Jewel" and "Water Margins," the final two sections of 1995's long prose poem "The Anthropology of Water."

Carson, by her own admission, fires her imagination by daring to "break rules or change categories or go outside where they say the line is" (di Michele 10), and in order to do so, she is always seeking to redefine the genres she explores. Carson often employs what Ian Rae has called a "mixed-media approach to writing" in which genre (even when it can be defined, and Carson is the first to acknowledge that sometimes it cannot) is manifest only "as a trace in the writing" (Rae 227). Rae also points out that in her work, the combination of ancient source material and contemporary poetics "are meant to function as collage," something Carson herself noted long before she published *Nox* (Rae 226). If we want to think about *Nox* as an elegy, we could do worse than consider its use of what Carson has called "volcano time" in *Autobiography of Red* (144), which Rae calls "the sudden eruption of the past and the future into the poem's present tense" (246). Carson's own comments about the text include her assertion that *Nox* "is not about grief. It's about understanding other people and their histories as though we are all separate languages.... Exploring grief would have made it a book about me, and I didn't want that" (Sehgal). Carson is right to note that elegies are inevitably about the elegist, that the lost beloved is the elegiac object and not the elegiac subject. But to say that there is no exploration of grief in *Nox* seems disingenuous, or perhaps it is just Carson's way of sidestepping the elegist's conundrum of the need to keep the private personal, especially when the lines between the private and public are as blurred as they are in this text, where what is arguably authentic—the artifact of the scrapbook—is displayed in so self-conscious a form.

One of *Nox*'s most elegiac components can be seen in its return to the motif of the lost beloved as a drowned body, a convention in the elegiac mode at least as old as Milton's "Lycidas" (1638). This connection is particularly striking as Carson notes that her brother died "(unexpectedly)" (6.1) but, like Catullus, she does not disclose the cause of the brother's death in the text of *Nox*, though she does reveal in her *Writers and Company* interview that Michael Carson died of a sudden aneurism. But passages of the shared lives of brother and sister are full of watery references to swimming and sailing and, eventually, to tears. A passage noting that her brother's widow scattered his ashes in the sea near Helsinore in Denmark is followed, with the enervated joy so characteristic of the elegy, by the author's metaphor of the siblings as sailors who loved speed but could not manage the rituals of sailing: "we couldn't get anything to work, again and again we gave up frustrated, threw the victims into the sea. Kept sailing" (*Nox* 9.1). When she defines the Latin word *aequora*—a term for "a smooth or level surface" as either a flat plain of ground or a calm sea—Carson ends with the example "*tibi rident aequora ponti*: the waters of the sea laugh up at you" (*Nox* 1.3). Even more disturbingly, in her translation of Catullus's fraternal elegy, she translates the word *manantia* as "tears" (rather than the more literal "flow"), stressing that the word refers to leakage, and emphasizing this seepage in her sample sentence "*omne supervacuum pleno de pectore manat*" when she translates the sentence not as the literal and already poetic "All flows full away from the breast," but more plangently—and elegiacally—as "the whole pointless night seeps out of the heart" (*Nox* 9.1).

But just as Carson offers up these metaphors soaked in hyperbolic tears, she also makes it clear that the elegy is heartbreaking because it cannot help but point out its own limitations. Late in the text, quoting Herodotus, she writes a stark acknowledgement of what it means to "go as far as [one] can go in explaining an historical event" and then stop for lack of information or understanding, leaving the inquiry to be resolved by other minds: "Let anyone who finds such things make credible use of them" (*Nox* 10.1). *Nox* is a book that is amazed at the capaciousness of the concrete objects that it is dedicated to fracturing, as well as a record of multiple fragments that it reproduces. The book's strength comes not from its authenticity, but from its challenge to rigid veridiction and its tacit distrust in the storytelling capacity of objects. In *A Sense of Things*, Bill Brown notes that fragmenting an object like a photo or a letter "enables them to achieve a formulism that obfuscates any exchange or use value the objects may have" (Brown 9). Carson, in her exploration of the abiding strangeness of narrative history, stands amazed, not at the amassing of memory as puzzle pieces, but at a kind of archival reproduction and reorganization that speaks to the "overtakelessness" of memory abutted against the "muteness" of history. After noting that "history and elegy are akin," Carson reminds readers that "the word 'history' comes from the ancient Greek verb meaning 'to ask'" (*Nox* 1.1). If history and elegy are indeed akin, it is not because Carson has opened her scrapbook to the world, but because she has inquired into the narrative insufficiencies of prose description, memoir, and even poetry to substantiate a life.

Nox ends without a revelation about the history or the memory of Michael Carson's life. The fragments that Carson has gathered and re-fragmented in *Nox* establish the book itself as a ruin, the reproduction of the long night of mourning—that folded and translated *Nox*—into an elegiac box. Carson is no stranger to the poetic challenge of reading fragments, a project with which she has been fascinated since her earliest encounter with Sappho as a teenager. In the introduction to *If Not, Winter: Fragments of Sappho*, Carson calls these fragments "acts of deterrence" that "carry their own kind of thrill—at the inside edge where [Sappho's] words go missing, a poem of antipoem that condenses everything you ever wanted her to write" (xiii). The force of elegy meets the thrill of fragment in *Nox*, when Carson writes "We want other people to have a centre, a history, an account that makes sense. We want to be able to say This is what he did and Here's why.

It forms a lock against oblivion. Does it?" (3.3). What, then, is on display in *Nox*, this more tactile, but still infinitely slippery, collection? What happens when Carson shifts from working with fragments of phrases to rearranging fragments of objects?

In her 2001 essay, "Foam: (Essay with Rhapsody) On the Sublime in Longinus and Antonioni," Carson describes her fascination with objects, her refusal to succumb to the sweep of the completed narrative, and her reasons for "skating" back and forth between perspectives:

> you are crossing back and forth on the frame of facts, skating from document to document, while retaining your own point of view—which is called "objective" because you make the facts into objects by viewing them this way. You are not so swept along by the facts as to forget your own viewing, as you would be in the middle of a story or poem or dramatic film. Instead you insist on seeing the edge of the frame wherever you look … the facts spill over the frame, then spill again. ("Foam" 96)

The image of *Nox* proceeding Slinky-like down a staircase haunts this reading of the text, and Carson's metaphor of facts that "spill" is just different enough from the poststructuralist "slip" of language. The difference between slipping and spilling is the difference between subjectivity and objectivity: the subject slips, but objects spill. The thingness of *Nox* not only shows Carson as a mourner skating from frame to frame in her memories of her brother, but also as someone who acknowledges—and wonders about—the composition of frames.

WORKS CITED

Bantock, Nick. *Griffin and Sabine*. San Francisco: Chronicle Books, 1991. Print.
Brown, Bill. *A Sense of Things: The Object Matter of American Literature*. Chicago: U of Chicago P, 2003. Print.
Carson, Anne. *Autobiography of Red*. Toronto: Random House, 1999. Print.
———. "Foam: (Essay with Rhapsody) On the Sublime in Longinus and Antonioni." *Conjunctions* 31 (2001): 96-104. Print.
———. *Decreation: Poetry, Opera, Essays*. New York: Knopf, 2005. Print.
———. Interview by Eleanor Wachtel. *Writers and Company*. CBC Radio. 18 Sept. 2011. Web. <www.cbc.ca>.
———. "Introduction." *If Not, Winter: Fragments of Sappho*. Trans. Anne Carson. Toronto: Vintage Canada, 2003. ix-xiv. Print.
———. *Men in the Off Hours*. New York: Knopf, 2001. Print.
———. *Nox*. New York: New Directions, 2010. Print.
———. *Plainwater*. New York: Vintage, 1995. Print.
di Michele, Mary. "The Matrix Interview (with Anne Carson)." *Matrix* 49 (1997): 10-17. Print.

Gannon, Mary. "Anne Carson: Beauty Prefers an Edge." Interview with Anne Carson. *Poets & Writers* 29.2 (2001): 26-33. Print.

Heer, Jeet. "Anne Carson's Disputed Laurels." *National Post* (Toronto) 31 Jan. 2002. Web. <www.jeetheer.com/culture/carson>.

MacDonald, Tanis. "The Pilgrim and the Riddle: Father-Daughter Kinship in Anne Carson's 'The Anthropology of Water.'" *Canadian Literature* 176 (2003): 67-83. Print.

Mayer, Sophie. "Picture Theory: On Photographic Intimacy in Nicole Brossard and Anne Carson." *Studies in Canadian Literature* 33.1 (2008): 97-117. Print.

McNeilly, Kevin. "Five Fairly Short Talks on Anne Carson." *Canadian Literature* 176 (2003): 6-10. Print.

Rae, Ian. *From Cohen to Carson: The Poet's Novel in Canada*. Montreal and Kingston: McGill-Queen's UP, 2008. Print.

Sehgal, Parul. "Evoking the Starry Lad Her Brother Was." *Irish Times* 19 March 2011. Web. <www.irishtimes.com>.

Shaw, W. David. *Elegy and Paradox: Testing the Conventions*. Baltimore: Johns Hopkins UP, 1994. Print.

Solway, David. "The Trouble with Annie." *Books in Canada* 30.1 (2011): 24-26. Print.

Teicher, Craig Morgan. "A Classical Poet, Redux: *Publisher's Weekly* Profiles Anne Carson." *Publisher's Weekly* 29 March 2010. Web. <www.publishersweekly.com>.

Upton, Lee. *Defensive Measures: The Poetry of Niedecker, Bishop, Glück, and Carson*. Lewisburg: Bucknell UP, 2005. Print.

CHAPTER 3

Maxims and Contraries
Notes from a Project in Process

Alison Calder

What says "I am Canadian" more than a beer commercial? A Mary Maxim hand-knit sweater, of course. It's the cardigan that says Canadian.

—Shel Zolkewich, *Globe and Mail*

Almost everyone who has grown up in Canada since the 1950s is familiar with Mary Maxim sweaters: bulky, heavy, knit cardigans that feature images of geese, bears, hunters, or trucks, and which have become thoroughly associated with the sport of curling in many people's minds. Often confused with Cowichan or Siwash sweaters,[1] to which they are closely and problematically related, Mary Maxim sweaters represent a uniquely Canadian expression of vernacular fashion. My creative critical project, "Maxims and Contraries," combines poetry and knitting with conventional academic inquiry to explore the ways in which these sweaters continue to resonate. As textile and text, these sweaters participate in and create a nationalist rhetoric that both celebrates and effaces its appropriation of Aboriginal and ethnic cultural markers. As material objects familiar to many Canadians, they have also become repositories of powerful emotions that complicate any straightforward academic analysis of their meaning and impact. Since I am a scholar who is also a poet and knitter, it became important to me to engage with these sweaters on multiple levels, in an effort to acknowledge both the potentially troubling effects of their iconography and the genuine creative energy and skilled crafting that went into making them. In other words, when looking at Mary Maxim sweaters, I found that it was not enough just to talk about the pictures on them, but that I also had to recognize the object for what it is: a sweater hand-knit by an individual, made to be worn. As David Gauntlett points out in *Making Is Connecting*, "everyday creativity" (19) of the kind embodied in common knitted items is a political act.[2] But what exactly can we say about the politics of these loved and reviled sweaters? My simultaneously ironic and sincere display of these sweaters in "Maxims and Contraries" suggests both their iconic power, and the possibility of subverting that power through creative intervention. In this chapter, I describe the history of the sweaters, unravel some of the strands of meaning that they embody, and suggest ways in which their commemorative values can be mobilized as cultural critique.

PART ONE: THE CONTEXT

The Mary Maxim company is embedded in Manitoba cultural and industrial history. As Sharon Reilly points out, together with other small industries, Mary Maxim "represented a self-reliant, diversified rural economy that characterized the early period of settlement in the region and demonstrated the process of industrialization and deindustrialization" (78). The company originated in a woollen mill called Sifton Wool Products, which was located in Sifton, Manitoba, and owned by the railway station agent, Willard McPhedrain, and his wife, Olive ("Our History"). It produced wool blankets and socks. Sometime in the mid-1940s, McPhedrain was struck by the possibilities presented by the hand-knitting market, which had expanded with wartime charity efforts. In response to this active knitting population, the company moved into producing patterns and yarn, rather than pre-made woollen items. In 1947, wanting to personalize the company, McPhedrain "borrowed" the name of Mary Maximchuck, who was his housekeeper. He chopped off the "chuck," and Mary Maxim was born. The anglicized "Mary Maxim" persona proved very popular, with "Mary" "receiv[ing] numerous love letters and valentines along with orders for the patterns and yarn" (Graff). By 1951, McPhedrain had decided to take the suggestion of one of his department store buyers to emulate the Cowichan sweaters that were proving popular on the West Coast. He purchased several sweaters to use as models, and employed a designer. As Anne L. Macdonald points out in *No Idle Hands*, her social history of knitting in America, World War II had produced a huge knitting population, whose efforts had been largely focused on knitting fine-gauge items like socks and balaclavas for soldiers. These items, knitted on small needles with fine wool, would have taken considerable time and effort to make, as knitters would have had to knit at a gauge between eight and nine stitches to the inch. It is not difficult to imagine the relief with which these fatigued knitters greeted Mary Maxim's large-scale patterns, which required only three stitches per inch. "Knit half a sweater in an evening" was one company tagline, playing both to ideas of wartime efficiency and to the desire of the knitter to achieve a finished product quickly. The company's first bulky pattern, "Reindeer," was quickly followed by many others, and it would not be an overstatement to say that Mary Maxim dominated the Canadian hand-knitting market during the 1950s. One of the company's lead designers, Barry Gibson, is credited with inventing the graph style of pattern, which allowed designers to represent the designs visually, rather than writing out line-by-line instructions. In other words, instead of writing out a pattern as "knit 2 black, knit 2 white" and so on, the pattern was shown as a picture, with the squares of a grid indicating which colour to use for particular stitches. This innovation meant that knitters could really see what they were doing—and could also see ways to change the design. This move also meant that Mary Maxim patterns could travel internationally, as language was no longer a barrier for non-English-speaking knitters (Graff). The patterns circulated widely, and as they did, they conveyed and reproduced particular ideas of Canadian-ness, especially in relation to race, nordicity, gender, relation to the environment, and progress and modernity. As Richard Rutt points out, while the designs were at their peak of popularity in Canada in the late 1950s, "in Britain the vogue of Mary Maxim sweaters was at its height in 1961-3" (208), suggesting that the rhetorical impact of these "Canadian" designs happened at different times in different places.[3]

Vintage Mary Maxim designs fall into several categories. The best-known designs focus on the outdoors, wilderness, and nature, with hunting and fishing featuring prominently (see Figure 3.1). Sporting events and "healthy" Canadian pastimes, like playing hockey or football, figure skating, or riding horses, make up a second category. A third strand of designs represents Canada in terms of images of progress and technology, ranging from airplanes, tractors, and oil rigs, to successful farming displays as seen in prize cattle. The fourth large category, distant from the ideas of technology but very much linked to the outdoors and wilderness, appropriates Aboriginal imagery from across North America, either in terms of geometric patterns drawn mainly (though not exclusively) from Cowichan sweaters, or in children's sweaters sporting cartoon-like figures representing "Cowboys" and "Indians." These images were all absorbed into a pan-Canadian ideal that extended even to the name of the yarn: Northland (see Figure 3.2).

All of these patterns also very much reinforced the idea of the nuclear family, which was achieving new prominence in the postwar baby boom. One marketing strategy that the Mary Maxim company used to great effect was

Figure 3.1 Advertisement from 1959 showing typical sweater designs. Used with permission of Mary Maxim Inc.

to make a base pattern, then introduce versions that would be appropriate for every member of the family. Thus, a single pattern like "Reindeer" would be produced in variations for men, women, and children, so that the entire family could be outfitted in matching designs. This marketing strategy put the nuclear family on show, where knitters created and reinforced family identity through their handwork. In addition, many Mary Maxim designs were strongly gendered in their marketing: bunnies and majorettes for girls, and trucks and toy soldiers for boys.

Mary Maxim sweaters, tremendously popular in their day, are currently enjoying a renaissance, this time as ironic, retro national icons. Their recent popularity also fits into the rise of a "weary nostalgia" identified by Kristen Williams, which may be accompanied by "a politics of resistant self-sufficiency and a do-it-yourself ethos relative to the service economies associated with late capitalism" (305). The thrift-shop aesthetic of original Mary Maxim sweaters, coupled with the fact that they were knitted by hand and not commercially manufactured, allows them to enter a larger mainstream cultural discourse that privileges "traditional folkways" (305) and celebrates "sustainability, thrift, and self-sufficiency" (306).[4] As their ugly-chic nature

Figure 3.2 Canadian Beaver pattern. Used with permission of Mary Maxim Inc.

makes them a hipster favourite, they have also become increasingly powerful symbols of national sentiment, as indicated in a 2006 article from the *Globe and Mail* about how and why to buy vintage sweaters. With her own combination of irony and sincerity, Shel Zolkewich describes them as "emblazoned with enthusiastic cowboys or majestic white-tailed deer," and suggests that if you "sort through old photographs [...] you're sure to find friends and family wrapped in pheasants, reindeer, and fish." Other sweaters feature "iconic Canuck wardrobe staple[s]" including "hockey players, snowflakes, beavers, and Indian heads," presenting the national image as a seemingly unproblematic mix of athleticism, environment, and Aboriginality. The disjunction between the new audience/wearers for the sweaters and the iconography represented on the sweaters is highlighted in the author's suggestion that readers should look for the sweaters in thrift shops in downtown urban centres or on ebay.com. She concludes:

> If you're not a knitting aficionado, there's really no way to tell if you're getting a vintage sweater crafted from a Mary Maxim pattern and co-ordinating yarn. The sweaters were never made commercially, rather they were

> handcrafted by knitters across the country eager to outfit their clans with warm and fashionable cool-weather gear.
>
> Fact is, it doesn't much matter if it's a true Mary Maxim or not. It's about the spirit of the sweater. So next time you're feeling particularly patriotic, go hunting for pheasants, geese and moose without the gun. Take your wallet instead. (Zolkewich)

This article clearly speaks to the transformation of Mary Maxim sweaters from Canadian sweaters into Canadiana. It draws on the idea of the authenticity of their production ("handcrafted by knitters" rather than "made commercially"), but then argues somewhat paradoxically that their material authenticity is irrelevant, as long as the sweater (of whatever origin) conveys the right patriotic "spirit." The importance of the sweater lies in the connection it establishes between its wearer and other "Canadians." As Anna-Mari Raunio argues in her study of the memories that people invest in handmade clothes,

> handcrafted clothes stretch beyond the material items.... Here the clothes themselves and the images they have created are sometimes less important than the ways that they represent a relationship with people who are or have been connected with them. In this case the clothes are worn and cherished for the purpose of symbolizing identity in relation to other people. (70)

Raunio is speaking specifically about clothes made by one family member for another, but her statement is also relevant when applied to the idea of inclusion in a national "family" through shared clothing. For the *Globe and Mail's* urban and technologically savvy readers, the sweaters function both ironically and sincerely as national symbols. While a wearer may sport the sweater with an "it's so ugly that it's cool" vibe, this attitude does not cancel out the notion that the wearer may also be wearing it because of its association with ideas of the nation, as both Raunio and Zolkewich suggest. Wilson points out that

> while contemporary urban homesteaders and craftivists may traditionally align themselves with the political Left, it should still be noted that the source materials they use (such as discourses and practices of tradition and "craft" that relies on individualized production) are essentially culturally conservative insofar as they aim to preserve or recapture the "lost" or devalued practices, ethics, and artifacts of the past. (307)

This tendency toward conservatism within notions of crafting may explain the persistence of questionable iconography in second-hand Mary Maxim sweaters that would not be acceptable were they to be mass-produced today. It is hard to imagine that someone could pull off wearing a sweater decorated with Indian heads no matter how ironic his or her stance, unless he or she was Aboriginal in the first place, which would introduce a whole new layer of performance and self-consciousness.

The status of Mary Maxim sweaters as national icons is confirmed in the official decision to use Mary Maxim-style sweaters, provided by HBC, to clothe the Canadian Olympic team at the 2010 Winter Olympics in Vancouver. This decision was immediately criticized by members of the Cowichan First Nation, who saw it as an appropriation of their art ("First Nation Alleges Olympic Ripoff"). HBC responded with a statement that "'our premium hand-knit sweater is not a Cowichan sweater' but rather is a contemporary design that 'nods towards this icon of Canadian fashion,'" a declaration that moves the Cowichan design into the context of the nation-state, rather than maintaining its particular Cowichan provenance (Hume). The controversy surrounding this Olympic clothing decision shows that far from being an irrelevant footnote, vernacular fashion remains a powerful vehicle for ideology. While the controversy was based on the idea that HBC had appropriated the traditional designs used by Cowichan knitters,[5] the styling, colours, and gauge of the HBC sweaters leads me to think that they are actually appropriating Mary Maxim patterns—which appropriated the Cowichan designs in the first place.[6] Thus, HBC is actually engaging in second-generation appropriation, with the original appropriative act having become so naturalized into nationalist iconography that the Cowichan source remains hidden or sublimated, though it is explicitly on public display. Interestingly, when the Cowichan planned to protest the Olympic Torch run, their means of protest was "a show of sweaters": they would simply stand along the torch route wearing their traditional sweaters (Hume). This is one example in which the sweaters are very clearly invested with political meaning. It also highlights the fact that if a particular style can be appropriated by HBC and Mary Maxim, it can also be used as a means of resistance.[7]

Further consideration of Cowichan sweaters sheds light on the ideas of authenticity, originality, appropriation, and nation that swirl around the Mary Maxim sweaters. As the cultural products of an Aboriginal community, Cowichan sweaters are heavily invested with the purchaser's desire for authenticity, which is to say that sweater purchasers generally want what they perceive as traditional designs that may be rooted in Aboriginal stories, clan signs, or craft motifs. A recent article in the *Globe and Mail* describing

Cowichan knitter May Sam as practising an "ancient craft" is typical, and the designs themselves are seen as representing genuine Aboriginal experience: "the incorporation of traditional motifs—deer, whale, eagle—make the sweaters immediately recognizable as a product of this landscape" (Hawthorne). An article by Bethany Lyttle in *Interweave Knits*, a leading North American magazine for knitters that features patterns as well as articles on knitting history, designers, and techniques, echoes that description. Speaking from the perspective of a non-Aboriginal Cowichan sweater wearer, Lyttle asks:

> How many of us understood that the arc of a jumping salmon motif was a symbol of the provider of life? Passed down within families, individual motifs and the design arrangements they became part of were a rich blend of artistry and metaphor: many representational motifs (clam, eagle, deer, and elk are just a few among many) had deep-rooted meanings, and even elements such as wave-shaped borders were references to the sea and rivers that were crucial to tribal life, rather than the simple striking designs we saw them as. (Lyttle 28)

However, as Margaret Meikle points out in *Cowichan Indian Knitting*, the history of Cowichan sweater knitting is complicated. The Cowichan people did not originally knit; knitting was introduced to the community at Catholic and Anglican missions in the 1850s. The geometric motifs now associated with Cowichan sweaters started to be used in the early 1900s, when Fair Isle and Shetland knitting became popular globally; the technique of stranded knitting was likely introduced to the Cowichan knitters by Scottish immigrants or British sailors.[8] Meikle describes the sources of the large motifs favoured by the Cowichan knitters as follows:

> Embroidery and crochet patterns, a child's pinwheel, tablecloths, linoleum, labels, a kerchief, a tea box, lace curtains, and oak leaves. Many designs, however, are aboriginal in origin, taken from traditional Salish basketry and weaving motifs. Some families have proprietary designs, although this is relatively rare. Designs are incorporated only for their artistic appeal; there is no meaning or implication to them. (17)

Of particular interest to my project are Meikle's remarks about the Cowichan knitters' response to the Mary Maxim company's appropriation of their designs in the 1940s: "Ironically, the knitters soon began to collect and use these charts and the wide variety of Indian sweater patterns available today" (18). This complicates the understanding of these designs and their impact considerably, as the Cowichan knitters reappropriated and continued to adapt the Mary Maxim patterns that had been based on their own work to begin with. Meikle suggests that Mary Maxim hand-knitting patterns did not pose a serious economic problem to Cowichan knitters, since the production was on such a small scale and the materials used were considerably different. Sylvia Olsen, in *Working with Wool*, a study of Cowichan knitting and weaving practices, agrees that the Mary Maxim patterns presented no real economic threat to the Cowichan knitters:

> Mary Maxim acts as a melting pot of international knitting traditions and styles, ultimately producing its own conventional and conservative style. Some Cowichan knitters may have believed that Mary Maxim infringed on a market that should have been reserved for Cowichan sweaters, but few took that position seriously. The home-knitting kits probably had no negative effect on the Cowichan sweater industry. There was no mistaking a Mary Maxim home knit for a Cowichan sweater, and it may well be that the widespread distribution of Mary Maxim's lighter weight, more colourful home knits helped popularize the Cowichan look. (284)

Instead of a clear division between the "authentic" and the "commercial," between the "traditional" and the "mass-produced," or even between the "original" and the "copy," we see potential overlap at a number of points. Such overlap is seen as both expected and natural in knitting circles. Olsen describes it as "a fundamental reality of knitting: if it's good, other knitters will copy it" (282). She adds,

> That's how Cowichan sweaters became what they were in the first place. Coast Salish women eagerly adopted exciting new ways to work with wool, adapting, amending, and reproducing what interested them. Once Cowichan sweaters became a popular icon, there was no way to stop the cross-pollination of their design in wool fashion. (283)

Such cross-pollination points to the need to pay attention to the particular history of material practices, and to be cautious when applying ideas like appropriation of voice that developed in one particular literary or scholarly arena, to other arenas like textiles and fashion. This is not to say, of course, that issues of appropriation do not hang over the Mary Maxim company's use of Cowichan-inspired designs, but rather to assert that these issues may be differently nuanced and require a different kind of theorization. The cross-pollination Olsen identifies also points to the value of considering craft as a repository of cultural history. In this particular case, the Cowichan sweaters reveal and embody a history of negotiation between cultures in a colonial setting, for good and bad, as Cowichan design is absorbed to a pan-Canadian nationalist discourse through its appropriation by the Mary Maxim and HBC companies, while at the same time also maintaining its own distinctive cultural and regional importance.[9]

PART TWO: MY PROJECT

"Maxims and Contraries" draws on Mary Maxim sweaters as a source of insight into cultural production and popular imaginaries in Canada in a number of ways. Responding to them critically has been challenging because, as material objects, they make different demands and require different readings than do conventional texts. As Julia Bryan-Wilson writes, "Craft is a wedge that reveals stark distinctions within ideologies of taste and value. Craft polarizes and collapses theoretical positions about what making means today. Craft is contemporary because it is the pivot between art and commerce, between work and leisure, between the past and the future" (10). Although I originally imagined that my research into Mary Maxim designs would result in a scholarly essay, I found the knitted sweaters themselves so fascinating that I also needed to engage with them on the levels of knitting process and finished knitted object. As well, I wanted to make my research accessible to different audiences, and to allow those audiences to participate in the project. In fact, audiences began to involve themselves in the project whether I wanted them to or not: when I told people about my project, they started telling me the stories of their own sweaters. I began to realize the value of creative artistic practice in analyzing these objects. Part of the power of the Mary Maxim sweaters, and of the nostalgia they engender in many viewers/wearers, is that they are able to engage memory and imagination, and so incorporating creative research into my scholarship seemed a way to address that imaginative power. The project has thus become four linked projects: a scholarly essay, a collection of poems, a collection of sweater designs, and finally a collection of four knit sweaters.

You are reading the essay component of this project. Another strand of the project involves the writing of a poetry manuscript, a written text, that uses both the actual history of the Mary Maxim company and also imagined scenes to produce a collision of voices: factory owner and housekeeper, textile worker and designer, artisan and industrialist. Other poems are based on patterns, advertising copy, and the language of knitting itself. Knitted fabric functions as a metaphor for the historical record: while the fabric seems solid, it is made of a series of spaces, and it is these historical gaps that the poetry seeks to explore. Poetry is the ideal medium for this project because it engages so directly with language; like knitting, it is both process and product. The repetitive structures underlying and creating poetic language parallel the repeating nature of knitted stitches, and both pattern and metaphoric language gesture to something outside themselves.

Another strand of the project relates to the designs themselves, and to the sweaters as objects. In November 2010 I travelled to Vancouver to visit the Vancouver Original Costume Museum, which houses a collection of approximately 150 original sweaters, plus various ephemera associated with the Mary Maxim company. At the time I visited, the museum was located in several small attic rooms in Hycroft, a heritage building. Space restrictions presented some challenges, but I was able to lay out and examine dozens of Mary Maxim sweaters made by individual knitters over several decades. The majority were completed sweaters, but a few were only partially knit, still on the needles as if waiting for a knitter to pick them up again. What I discovered in my survey was that while many knitters had reproduced the original patterns without changing them very much, there were a significant number of sweaters that used designs that the knitters had clearly invented or modified themselves: these are unique and idiosyncratic designs. Further, many of these original designs had a kind of commemorative or monumental function, such as one marking the anniversary of the College of Medicine at the University of Saskatchewan. They were meant to celebrate something, but as a material artifact of this celebration with a vernacular sort of historical record. Such personalization also shows the ability of knitters to subvert expectations, as these patterns, intended to produce a series of identical products, ended up facilitating individual expression and entering, intentionally or not, into general conversations about personal and national identity. Raunio comments on this opportunity of "interrupting the process" that handmade items present, writing that "designing and making is not only about getting new clothes but also contemplating and negotiating with the sense of self" (67). Most of the modifications were relatively minor: knitters were not so much asserting a counter-narrative to the pattern's iconography as they were personalizing it by changing the colours or including the name of a particular sports team. Some of the modifications were accidental. One sweater was designed to commemorate Alberta's semi-centennial celebrations, with a large provincial crest on the back and the dates "1905" and "1955" on the two front pockets. However, the numbers in the dates on the pockets were reversed, so that the numbers appear in the form of a mirror-image. The knitter had somehow flipped the charts—possibly by reading them from left to right as he or she knit, rather than from right to left, which would have produced the correct image. My questions about how this reverse image happened, twice, and why the knitter chose not to correct it, reminded me that these sweaters were not mass-produced, but knit by individuals with their unique desires, priorities, and skills. The kind of imaginative engagement that these sweaters generated speaks to the affective power that Raunio alludes to when she writes that "handcrafted items always hint of familiarity even if you are hopeless at making things yourself" (63).

The discovery that some knitters had modified Mary Maxim patterns right from the start gave my "Maxims and Contraries" project a genealogy. I came to recognize the agency of individual knitters, whom I had formerly imagined as relatively passive consumers, and also to see my own design interventions as part of a continuum rather than as an abrupt departure. I am now creating new colourwork charts that engage with traditional Mary Maxim icons. In a sense, the poems and the charts are translations of the same source materials, but the differing media present different representational possibilities. By incorporating both poetry and charts, my project examines the implications of the new concepts introduced by Gibson's invention of graphed knitting language, which also moved between written language and images. My new images draw on the power of Mary Maxim's visual archive and also critique it. Traditional Mary Maxim designs speak about the nation in terms of a pan-Canadian-ness that is rooted in generalized concepts of progress, the natural world, and Aboriginality. The new charts use contemporary urban icons rooted in Winnipeg to suggest an alternate vision of prairie space that challenges the images of progress, wilderness, and ethnic assimilation found in traditional Mary Maxim iconography. My decision to focus the design project on Winnipeg was motivated by several factors. First, Winnipeg is now my home, a place that I feel I have enough experience of to address artistically, and given the Mary Maxim company's location in Manitoba, it seems a logical place to base the project.[10] In a scholarly sense, situating the project in an urban centre on the prairie allowed me to engage with critical notions of regionality that continue to construct prairie identity as largely rural, white, and male. Some critics have argued that we are now "post-prairie," that traditional ideas of the region are obsolete, but I argue that prairie culture continues to be informed by the colonial ideologies that created this space in the first place, though those ideologies now veil themselves in different ways.[11] The sweater project, which links both tradition and innovation, represents and suggests the importance of seeing these connections between past and present ways of thinking. Other artists, of course, are also addressing the transformation of the prairie: the collection *Scratching the Surface: The Post-Prairie Landscape* records the work of twenty visual artists and seven writers who address the issue of prairie landscape and identity from diverse perspectives. It is also particularly appropriate to situate a project about urban prairie identity in Winnipeg because Winnipeg has such a strong tradition of artistic self-scrutiny and self-display. Guy Maddin's 2007 film *My Winnipeg* is probably the best-known example of this kind of self-examination, but it is a widespread practice, and more so after Maddin's film. In 2008, Shawna Dempsey and Lorri Millan curated "Subconscious City," an extensive visual art exhibition that focused on Winnipeg. In the exhibition catalogue, they write that "more than any other city in Canada, the history of colonization lives here, not in beautifully preserved forts and historic buildings, but in its people and its ruins" (104-5). Making new designs for Mary Maxim sweaters is a way to engage with the history of both city and sweater, while also commenting on the ways in which those histories remain active in the present in this particular place.

What might a new chart for a cardigan represent, using the sweater's three main surfaces (two front panels and a back panel)?[12] A number of Mary Maxim designs feature iconic "cowboys" and/or "Indians," in different configurations. My new design uses the construction of the sweater to bring these images into conflict: a "cowboy" on one front panel, an "Indian" on the other, and a gritty scene of Winnipeg's Main Street across the back. The sweater thus works to bring out powerful and problematic assumptions rooted in the traditional patterns, while also suggesting the troubled real-world outcome of such colonizing imaginings (see Figure 3.3). Other sweater designs toy with ideas of neighbourhood or civic identity, asking viewers to consider the implications of popular Winnipeg touchstones: a sweater with "7-11" motifs asks what, for example, it means to live in a city where civic pride and identity depends on annual rates of Slurpee consumption. Instead of familiar scenes of duck or pheasant hunts, burning dumpsters and graffiti stencils could ring a sweater, suggesting urban poverty and violence. Likewise, where traditional sweaters conveyed ideas of progress and environmental mastery through stylized images of oil rigs and crawler tractors, the new image of a flooded city could remind viewers of their own fraught relationship with the prairie environment. While a reconsideration of our relationship to the environment is happening across Canada, these new urban icons emphasize a local vernacular, rather than a pan-Canadianism, and offer a reading of the complicated relationship between icon and culture. Sweaters are, after all, comforting: in Winnipeg's self-imaginings, who is being comforted, and who is left out in the cold?

A further creative dimension of the project is the knitting of the sweaters themselves. I am knitting four sweaters that use these new charts, so that the project is literally made material. The audience will simultaneously recognize and be disquieted by the sweaters: the ubiquity of the Mary Maxim

Figure 3.3 Inner City sweater design.

style makes the sweaters instantly familiar, while the unexpected patterning provokes confusion and questions. Knitting these sweaters will allow me to see how the charts work on fabric and on moving bodies. It is important to me that the sweaters actually be knit. Vernacular handwork has traditionally been devalued as a feminine occupation not worthy of sustained attention. Knitting the sweaters myself acknowledges the skilled labour of the thousands of women who knit the original Mary Maxim patterns, and recognizes the value of their time. Knitting the sweaters is thus an important part of the project's politics. In fact, I'm finding that the actual knitting of the sweaters is the most challenging aspect of the project. As my Great-Aunt Ethel, age ninety-six, said when I suggested that Mary Maxim sweaters had been easy for her to knit because of their large gauge: "Yes, but we had to knit so many!"

PART THREE: TOWARD CONCLUSIONS

Raunio writes that "craft is in a sense an extreme way of producing clothes; to some extent, craft is always a territory unexplored, including the possibility of hazard in the context of emotional experience. Memories and experiences of handcrafted clothes indicate that they make 'sharp edges' in the landscape of memories" (71). While this project-in-progress has had many challenges, one of the most rewarding aspects of it has been the responses of listeners/viewers, many of whom immediately want to participate in some way by sharing with me their ideas for sweater images. Others will reminisce, usually fondly, about Mary Maxim sweaters that someone knit for them when they were little. These audience responses, sometimes quite emotional, testify to the power of material objects to carry complicated and sometimes conflicting ideas about family, politics, and aesthetics. Comments like "of course they're racist, but I kind of love them anyway" demonstrate these emotional and ideological complexities. Other people have voiced regret at not valuing the sweater that someone else (usually a mother or grandmother) knit for them: they now see the sweater as an expression of love and wish that they had it back, or they now value the amount of work that went into the sweater and wish they could properly thank the knitter. In this project in particular, audience responses speak to the continuing impact of the Mary Maxim sweater designs on Canadian self-imaginings: while an individual viewer may not think about the message that the individual sweater image is imparting, all viewers identify the sweater as "the cardigan that says Canadian" (Zolkewich). Choosing to wear a Mary Maxim sweater now means choosing to engage in a performance of national identity in way that is both sincere and ironic, both an homage and a subversion. When my designs are eventually displayed in a gallery, I will include graph paper and coloured pencils, so that viewers can negotiate their own relations to these icons of national and personal identity, and contribute their own designs to the archive.

NOTES

Funding from the University of Manitoba Creative Works Program made the travel for this project possible. I am especially grateful to the director of Vancouver's Original Costume Museum, Ivan Sayers, for letting me look at the museum's Mary Maxim collection.

1. Wikipedia asserts incorrectly that "Cowichan sweater," "Siwash sweater," and "Mary Maxim sweater" are variant names for the same thing.
2. For a discussion of crafting, particularly knitting, as political action ("craftivism"), see Newmeyer (2008), Williams (2011), Kelly (2014), and Corbett and Housley (2011). Kelly discusses the role of intention in craftivism at length; this political intention separates my own creative interpretations of Mary Maxim designs from the modifications found in the sweaters I observed in the Vancouver Original Costume Museum. While my sweater design project is inspired by craftivist projects, it remains mediated by institutional constraints and lacks the direct action element of yarn bombing, for example.
3. The international appeal of these sweaters continues. Now collectors' items, the original sweaters have become particularly popular with Japanese enthusiasts, and an informal survey of Ravelry.com, the social networking and pattern database site

for knitters, shows that most new Cowichan sweater knock-off patterns come from Japanese pattern books.
4   Williams notes that "most contemporary chroniclers of the craftivist movement have documented a renewed dedication to traditional folkways ranging from subsistence farming to blacksmithing and welding, hand-sewing and other needlework, knitting and crocheting, and darkroom photography" (306). These traditional practices may be applied to what are "often considered 'low' or 'middle-brow' cultures," but they may also appear in "'fine arts' venues like performance art, live theatre, and gallery showcases" (306).
5   HBC had not actually appropriated Cowichan clan or basketry designs; the motif they chose, of two deer heads, is not traditional. However, the symmetry of the design and the placements of the motifs are obviously rooted in Cowichan practice.
6   Sylvia Olsen also identifies the reindeer motif on the Olympic sweaters as being derived from Mary Maxim designs (311).
7   For a report on the controversy's resolution, see "Cowichan Tribes Reach Olympic Sweater Deal."
8   A recent article in *The Knitter* credits Jeremina Colvin, who emigrated to British Columbia from Shetland in 1885, as introducing Shetland motifs to Cowichan knitters. The article stresses that the development of what are now recognized as Cowichan sweaters was collaborative, as Colvin and several Cowichan women, particularly Mary Edwards and Sophia Percy, worked to refine stranding techniques and to invent an innovative collar structure (Brown).
9   In November 2014, Mary Maxim and Roots launched a collaborative sweater line. As a newspaper article describes it, the project is "a new line of curling sweaters, a term synonymous with those itchy, unevenly knit and ugly—but much loved—sweaters that have woven a place in this country's fabric. They'll be stitched with images of polar bears, maple leaves, hockey players and reindeer" (Henry n. pag.).
10 In one sense, the designs are related to the "Wolseley" section of my poetry collection *Wolf Tree*, which addresses my home neighbourhood and which actually deals with some of the same issues, such as gentrification.
11 See Jon Paul Fiorentino's introduction to the poetry anthology *Post-Prairie*, and my thoughts on it in "The Importance of Place; or, Why We're Not Post-Prairie," in *Place and Replace: Essays on Western Canada*.
12 A cardigan actually has five main surfaces, if one includes the sleeves (which usually carry identical designs).

WORKS CITED

"Air Canada Stands by Winnipeg Hotel Move Reasons." CBC.ca 5 Oct 2011. Web. 22 Apr. 2012.
Brown, Barb. "Jeremina's Story." *The Knitter* 71 (2014): 56-57. Print.
Bryan-Wilson, Julia. "Eleven Propositions in Response to the Question: 'What Is Contemporary about Craft?'" *Journal of Modern Craft* 6.1 (2013): 7-10. Print.
Calder, Alison. "The Importance of Place; or, Why We're Not Post-Prairie." *Place and Replace: Essays on Western Canada*. Ed. Leah Morton, Esyllt Jones, and Adele Perry. Winnipeg: U of Manitoba P, 2013. 169-78. Print.
———. *Wolf Tree*. Regina: Coteau, 2007. Print.
Corbett, Sarah, and Sarah Housley. "The Craftivist Collective Guide to Craftivism." *Utopian Studies* 22.2 (2011): 344-51. Print.

"Cowichan Tribes Reach Olympic Sweater Deal." CBC.ca. 28 Oct. 2009. Web. 13 Oct. 2011.

Dempsey, Shawna, and Lorri Millan. "Subconscious City." *Subconscious City*. Ed. Shawna Dempsey and Lorri Millan. Winnipeg: Winnipeg Art Gallery, 2008. 101-15. Print.

Fiorentino, Jon Paul, and Robert Kroetsch. "Post-Prairie Poetics: A Dialogue." Introduction. *Post-Prairie: An Anthology of New Poetry*. Ed. Jon Paul Fiorintino and Robert Kroetsch. Vancouver: Talonbooks, 2005. 9-13. Print.

"First Nation Alleges Olympic Ripoff." CBC.ca 7 Oct. 2009. Web. 13 Oct. 2011.

Gauntlett, David. *Making Is Connecting: The Social Meaning of Creativity, From DIY and Knitting to YouTube and Web 2.0*. Cambridge: Polity, 2011. Print.

Graff, Tom. "'Mary,' the Iconic Canadian." *Vancouver Observer*, 29 Mar. 2009. Web. 13 Oct. 2011.

Hawthorne, Tom. "Cowichan Sweaters: From Raw Wool to Cherished Keepsake." *Globe and Mail*, 26 Mar. 2012. Web. 21 Apr. 2012.

Henry, Michele. "Roots, Mary Maxim Collaborate on Iconic Curling Sweaters." *Toronto Star*, 10 Sept. 2014. Web. 16 Sept. 2014.

Hume, Mark. "The Bay, Cowichan Leaders Hope to Settle Sweater Row." *Globe and Mail*, 27 Oct. 2009. A8. Print.

Kelly, Maura. "Knitting as Feminist Project?" *Women's Studies International Forum* 44 (2014): 133-44. Print.

Lyttle, Bethany. "Cowichan Sweaters: Durable and Enduring." *Interweave Knits* 13.3 (Fall 2008): 24-28. Print.

Macdonald, Anne L. *No Idle Hands: The Social History of American Knitting*. New York: Ballantine, 1988. Print.

Matijcio, Steven, ed. *Scratching the Surface: The Post-Prairie Landscape*. Winnipeg: Plug-In Institute of Contemporary Art, 2008. Print.

Meikle, Margaret. *Cowichan Indian Knitting*. Vancouver: UBC Museum of Anthropology, 1987. Print.

Newmeyer, Trent S. "Knit One, Stitch Two, Protest Three! Examining the Historical and Contemporary Politics of Crafting." *Leisure/Loisir* 32.2 (2008): 437-60. Print.

Olsen, Sylvia. *Working with Wool: A Coast Salish Legacy and the Cowichan Sweater*. Winlaw, BC: Sono Nis, 2010. Print.

"Our History." *Mary Maxim Retail Canada*. n.d. Web. 13 Oct. 2011.

Raunio, Anna-Mari. "Clothed Landscape of Memories." *Design Journal* 10.2 (2007): 62-72. Print.

Reilly, Sharon. "Deindustrialization as Public History: An Exhibition at the Manitoba Museum." *Urban History Review* 35.2 (Spring 2007): 77-83. Print.

Rutt, Richard. *A History of Hand Knitting*. London: B. T. Batsford, 1987. Print.

Siamandas, George. "The Tale of the Wolseley Elm." *Winnipeg Time Machine*. 21 Apr. 2009. Web. 21 Apr. 2012.

Williams, Kristen A. "'Old Time Mem'ry': Contemporary Urban Craftivism and the Politics of Doing-It-Yourself in Postindustrial America." *Utopian Studies* 22.2 (2011): 303-20. Print.

Zolkewich, Shel. "Mary Maxim Sweaters: More Canadian Than a Beer Commercial." *Globe and Mail*, 18 Feb. 2006. L4. Print.

CHAPTER 4

The Geranium in the Window
One Plant's Literary Hardiness in the Canadian Imagination

Shelley Boyd

In L. M. Montgomery's classic *Anne of Green Gables* (1908), Anne Shirley enters Marilla Cuthbert's kitchen on her first morning and names the apple-scented geranium situated in the window "Bonny." When Marilla questions "the sense of naming a geranium," Anne replies, "'Oh I like things to have handles even if they are only geraniums. It makes them seem more like people. How do you know but that it hurts a geranium's feelings just to be called a geranium and nothing else? You wouldn't like to be called nothing but a woman all the time'" (38). In naming "Bonny," Anne attempts to take possession of her not-yet-confirmed home. Her ordering of Marilla's kitchen is reminiscent of what social anthropologist Sophie Chevalier describes as a domestic process of "appropriation" in which individuals "personalize their material environment, rather than succumbing to a world of objects that are resistant to their influence" (849). Gendering the potted plant, Anne lays claim to her own suitability for an adopted life with Marilla and Matthew, populating their home with additional feminine presences even though she is not the useful boy whom the Cuthberts had anticipated and desired. Ultimately, Anne's comments reveal, as Chevalier contends, that within domestic environs, "relationships between people and their community [are] mediated by the world of objects" (851), but in this case, the object is not inanimate, but rather a living plant, which further complicates the situation, as Anne's chastisement of Marilla reveals. While it is unlikely that "Bonny" feels slighted by her prior namelessness,

Anne implores Marilla to see the world from the overlooked plant's perspective, and thus to realize that a generic naming and simple negation are far from sufficient. Just as Marilla is more than simply a woman, and Anne is more than not-a-boy, Bonny is so much more than just a geranium. Ultimately, Anne's personification of the flower implies that plants have a material cultural presence in the home and a capacity to attract attention, influencing their human custodians, including their authors and especially (but not exclusively) women writers who focus on the domestic sphere. As it happens, Montgomery's fictional depiction of "Bonny" was inspired by her own experience potting and naming geraniums.[1] Her fondness for the flower, along with Anne's and Marilla's, is not out of the ordinary, as the potted geranium is one of the most ubiquitous plants in Canadian letters. While the flower's horticultural history and physical properties provide insight into the reasons why this botanical inclination exists, Canadian authors are, of course, not the only ones who have created a literary life for the geranium.[2] Nevertheless, the Canadian colonial condition and climate have facilitated the geranium's recurrence in our homes and subsequently in our texts. Ultimately, this domesticated exotic's material endurance and versatility—its potential for thriving in new contexts and its cultural significance with respect to aspirations of belonging and social status—translate to a kind of literary hardiness: the geranium continually appears across a range of temporal periods and regional traditions of Canadian literature. In fact, the potted geranium is a plant that has been so successfully propagated in our texts that it functions as a botanical gauge of the material and social conditions that shape both the geranium's experience and, by association, its human custodian's.

In her discussion of the ways in which social identities are constructed through the domestic realm and its material furnishings, Chevalier notes that inherited objects or gifts "present the self through an exhibition of our relationships both to the living and the dead. By appropriating an inherited item or gift, we recognize our links to others and agree to maintain them" (851). The same premise holds true for living plants, according to Chris Tilley's material study of the garden, as the giving of plants is "a valuable way of maintaining social networks" (186). This is certainly true of the geranium, whose horticultural and colonial history provides a partial explanation for its prominence on Canadian windowsills, both real and literary. As an "inherited" houseplant, the geranium carried with it sociocultural ties across the Atlantic that many early Canadian gardeners sought to maintain. Studying the history of potted plants, Catherine Horwood reveals that geraniums, which are actually pelargoniums, originated in the Cape of Good Hope, South Africa, from where they were introduced to Europe (by the Dutch) and then to Britain in the seventeenth century, and despite a correction being made to their classification in the eighteenth century (by a French botanist), they have retained their popular misnomer to this day (45).[3] During the early 1700s, the British aristocracy's interest in collecting and methodically crossing this exotic promoted its status while also showcasing its diverse beauty, which appealed to a range of aesthetic preferences. One such esteemed plant collector, Mary Capel Somerset, Duchess of Beaufort, cultivated some of the first pelargonium imports: "In 1701 she introduced *P. peltatum*, the first ivy-leafed geranium, now seen in a million window-boxes every summer" (Horwood 36), and in 1704, the ever-popular Zonals (Horwood 93).[4] Today, geraniums are known for being colourful, prolific bloomers that require little care, and with "nearly 2000 varieties" of the common zonal geraniums taking their place in gardens and on windowsills, present-day gardeners have an abundance of choice (Wetherbee).

But while illustrious plant collectors and versatile beauty initially secured the geranium's foothold in British society, what truly ensured this exotic's cultural longevity was its relationship with the lower classes, as facilitated by the plant's other material properties. The flower's ease of propagation through the cutting and planting of slips and its capacity to survive indoors (in pots) meant affordability and suitability to the middle and working classes who may otherwise lack the property or financial means for a garden. Horwood notes that according to the well-known nineteenth-century garden writer Shirley Hibberd (1825-90), England experienced "a mania for raising scarlet pelargoniums" (93) between 1840 and 1855, and "[b]y the end of the Industrial Revolution ... [this plant was] an integral part of ... British domestic interiors" (94), as the plants thrived in pots and could tolerate the "atmospheres of Victorian homes" (93). This same premise held true for geraniums growing in nineteenth-century Canadian homes that either lacked sufficient light or the privilege of a conservatory.[5] When wintertime arrived, these flowers were omnipresent because of their hardiness, surviving indoors in pots on a cool windowsill. Canadian garden historian Eileen Woodhead notes that a variety of geraniums, including scented ones, were advertised in the earliest known Toronto nursery catalogue from 1827, which explicitly promoted the fact that these plants "thrive in a comfortable sitting room during winter" (32). Garden columnists from the period promoted houseplants as a way to counteract the cold Canadian climate "when all nature seems dead," and listed geraniums first, highlighting the plant's popularity: "Conspicuous among the flowers that adorn our rooms and cheer our eyes in winter is the Geranium. It flourishes and blooms in the midst of much ill-usage and neglect, a hardy and beautiful house plant" ("Winter Flowers" 377). The necessity of hardiness, even for indoor cultivation, cannot be underestimated in a Canadian context, as nineteenth-century homes were often cold and frosty during winter nights. In an 1869 letter, Juliana Horatia Ewing describes carrying hyacinth pots up to bed in her New Brunswick home, "put[ting] them round the stove—& bury[ing] them in dressing gowns ... but the poor things were frozen & thawed—over & over again!!" (225). Tellingly, Ewing praises the window gardens of a green-thumbed friend who, over the winter months, successfully grows "variegated sweet geraniums—kept very dwarf in pots" (226).

Because of its hardiness and availability, the exotic geranium transformed into a common houseplant both in England and, in turn, in a young Canada, which inherited this horticultural tradition. As Horwood acknowledges in the context of nineteenth-century England, the geranium was "so widely propagated and available that soon even the poorest of homes sported [one] on its window-sill" (93-94). Just as these popular flowers were sold at major London nurseries and by "[p]edlars called 'botany bens' [who] knocked on servants' doors offering cheap 'geraniums' for sale" (Horwood 93), scarlet scented geraniums were sold as inexpensive buttonhole bouquets by street flower girls to passersby in North American cities, as recounted in an 1872 issue of *The Canada Farmer* ("Street Flower Girls"). Their showy, affordable beauty meant geraniums were in demand by gardening-consumers of all walks of life living in either country. This adaptable plant attributed a cultivated, homey nature to those who tended it; tellingly, even floral lexicons from the period decipher geraniums as signifying "gentility" (Waterman 87). With respect to the plant's popularity in England, Horwood concludes, "If there is one plant that sums up the attitude of Victorian sentimentalists towards the unfortunate working class in the nineteenth century, it is the forlorn red 'geranium' sitting on a cottage window-sill. Hundreds of artists used this as a symbol of aspirations to respectability" (138). But while the geranium was pervasive in nineteenth-century British culture, it was not viewed as synonymous with England; that national symbolism is reserved for the rose, which leads to an interesting cultural distinction between the two plants.

In *The Botany of Desire: A Plant's-Eye View of the World*, Michael Pollan argues that there are a handful of exceptional flowers that have successfully infiltrated human culture: "There are flowers, and then there are flowers: flowers ... around which whole cultures have sprung up, flowers with an empire's worth of history behind them, flowers whose form and color and scent, whose very genes carry reflections of people's ideas and desires through time like great books" (77). Pollan's list of what he terms "canonical flowers" (78) includes the rose, tulip, peony, orchid, and lily, and most of these evoke national cultures and identities, such as England's Tudor Rose, Holland's tulip mania of the seventeenth century, or France's fleur-de-lys. In contrast to these elite plants' aristocratic associations, the geranium's popular cultural life as tied to the middle and working classes does not garner it esteemed "national" status; nevertheless, the geranium is undeniably a part of an "empire's worth of history" with respect to colonization: that is, the expropriation and alteration of foreign lands along with the incorporation of exotic plants into domestic terrain as part of the material, and in this case botanical, spoils of conquest. Plants that appeal to an imperial nation for aesthetic, economic, and pragmatic reasons subsequently experience an expansion of their geographical range, cultural meaning, and influence. But while Pollan stresses beauty as a flower's "path to world domination" (79)— and the vibrantly coloured geranium certainly possesses this attribute—the geranium reveals that other factors also facilitate a flower's canonical status, as this flower's physical hardiness and affordability translate to particular cultural uses and significance that have also led to its (often criticized) pre-eminence in human culture across time and space. Because the geranium became almost too popular and too common in the nineteenth century, the plant was met with derision by garden writers on both sides of the Atlantic who longed for variety, something other than the ever-predictable geranium.[6] The fact that numerous geraniums, many of which are described with disdain, appear not only within Canadian horticultural texts but also within our literature suggests that some writers have either succumbed to the supposed banality of Canada's colonial culture, producing an uninspired literature, or alternatively, have employed the flower as a means of critiquing the unappealing aspects of a society hankering after an illustrious British predecessor.

When the geranium was transplanted to Canada, this popular exotic afforded a sense of botanical, socio-cultural continuity with Britain even as its English-Canadian cultivators addressed the unnatural placement of this plant in an inhospitable northern climate.[7] One of the most famous backwoods gardeners, Catharine Parr Traill, writes about her scarlet geraniums, grown from slips over the winter, being killed by a late spring frost ("To Ellen Dunlop"). Although she admires the household uses of the native species of the Wood Geranium, or Cranes-Bill, which she promotes in *Canadian Wild Flowers* (1868), Traill's gardening preference for zonals remains steadfast, undoubtedly through the flower's association with her original home in England.[8] In contrast to Traill, who perseveres, in 1839 Henrietta

Prescott, the daughter of the then governor of Newfoundland, situates the dying flower as tragically out of place in her poem "Lines to a Fading Geranium," which she published in her book *Poems Written in Newfoundland*. In this excessively sentimental poem, Prescott laments the transplanting of the geranium as the flower fades, rather than thrives, in this formidable environment, where British-defined notions of beauty and cultured society seem impossible. Following a "wintry tempest's breath," the speaker grieves the sudden death of her geranium, which she describes as a "Child of a gayer land, / And milder clime than this" (256). The speaker readily associates the flower with Africa through references to the acacia tree and with her previous life in England as the flower is a "record of the past," bringing with it its humble, homey associations: "Thy modest garb I've seen / Cheering the humble cot, / Or dwelling in some bower green / Unnoticed and forgot" (260). Overwhelmed by homesickness, Prescott mourns the loss of her flower's vitality and lustre; indeed, she even notes on the first page of her poem that the geranium can be "the emblem of a melancholy spirit" (256).[9]

The geranium's incongruous presence in North America later enters the works of twentieth-century Canadian writers who also take a critical look at the supposed transatlantic cultural continuity fostered by this flower, which in its new context seems a sad, colonial derivative of its former British glory. In Earle Birney's 1942 poem "Anglosaxon Street," the slogan "There'll Always Be an England" declares itself across the cracked windowpane of a home in a Toronto slum, and "enhances geraniums" (15) that occupy the nearby windowsill. Just as Prescott's transplanted geranium fades in an inhospitable Newfoundland setting, Birney's geraniums require a verbal declaration of British allegiance in the form of a window sign in order to "enhance" flowers that should, in effect, be able to speak for themselves because of their imperial past and long-established association with homely attachments. Birney's reference to the plant evokes its English working-class history, but this ironic poem is decidedly unsentimental in its depiction of some of the most unappealing, racist aspects of the Toronto ghetto. The beleaguered community attempts to align itself with an illustrious past through its present status as a British ally during the ongoing conflict of World War II, but the "cultivating" presence of the geranium as a symbol of refinement and care is undermined by a populace mired in drudgery, disease, and pollution. Even their achievements are questionable, as the "V's for victory" are implicated merely in "vanquish[ing] the housefly," no doubt through the geranium keeping flies at bay (16). In the context of Birney's poem, this exotic as an inherited domestic item evokes, to use Chevalier's phrase, "constraining social links" (852), since the well-established but poorly replicated British cultural history, as objectified by the flower, is ridiculously out of place in Canada, and seemingly precludes the formation of independent Canadian identities, communal cohesion, and homegrown triumphs.

While the geranium fails to enhance its custodians in Birney's "Anglosaxon Street," reflecting instead the banality and derivativeness of Canadian society, the frequent use of the flower nonetheless reveals its cultural transportability and its openness to reinterpretation within new contexts of Canadian literary culture. The plant's long imperial history, which includes ties to trade routes and botanical discovery as well as to social categorization, means that it is well situated to aid in investigations of the complex colonial heritage and the socially mixed populace of Canadian society. This out-of-place plant inspires one writer, Ronald Everson, to reflect on material inequalities and racial injustices that result from an imperial past when he highlights the zonal geranium's African origins and adoption into Canadian homes under the guise of "esteemed" British culture. In *The Oxford Companion to Canadian Literature,* David Staines describes Everson primarily as a poet with an ability "to find a sudden analogy that captures a person or an incident" (242). This use of analogy, and specifically a botanical one, carries over into Everson's short story "Geranium," published in an October 1931 issue of *Maclean's.* In this Halloween narrative, racial stereotypes direct the characterization of the protagonist, a six-year-old black boy named "Geranium," who is identified in the subtitle as a "penniless pickaninny" (9). The character conforms to the racist caricature: clothed in "daringly tattered hand-me-downs," the half-naked Geranium lives in poverty and without parental supervision beneath the "Gas Fittings' smokestacks" among the "nigger shanties" (9). The protagonist's name draws attention to his transplanted status: both as someone of African descent living in North America, and as a shantytown resident who literally crosses the railway tracks into the affluent white neighbourhood on Halloween night, where "[u]nder the pruned trees of the clean-swept, lighted streets, the thinly romantic, carefully sun-tanned, medically-examined children of the secure pla[y] at danger" (9). Despite Everson's racist portrayal of the "half savage" Geranium (9), a satirization of the white neighbourhood is also apparent in his depiction of it as excessively regimented and exclusive. Wandering alone, cold, and hungry on the sidewalk, Geranium is eventually swept up by a group of white children on their way to attend a party, all of them outfitted in costumes and painted faces that "burlesqu[e] the races of the earth" (9). Upon entering the mansion surrounded by children dressed as pickaninnies and "chinamen," Geranium is greeted by the hostess of the party who believes him to be an extraordinarily well-costumed Master Charles

Polgrain-Titterton, the son of an affluent family. This "pseudo Charles" (73) soon experiences the privileges of this "precarious paradise" (9) since normally his skin colour would automatically exclude him: the hostess's friend flashes him a smile "devised to express a love for all tiny tots—that is to say, for all tiny tots who belonged" (73), and one of the McGill twins takes the black Geranium by the arm and leads him into the dining room with the white, "snowy tablecloth" and the promise of a meal (73). Geranium's acceptance occurs only because the adults misidentify him as possessing an illustrious "nature"—that is, belonging to a desirable family of Anglo-Saxon stock. In this world of "false faces" (9), the treatment of Geranium draws attention to the white adults' racist engagement with the other. Like the pelargonium flower that was misclassified as a plant from the Northern rather than Southern hemisphere, Geranium's actual identity and background are subsumed to the dominating white society's preferences and vision, but this erasure sadly occurs at all levels of the story, as Geranium never moves beyond his pseudo-Charles identity, or his original presentation as a pickaninny. While Everson writes primarily to entertain *Maclean's* readership, the story provocatively highlights the social inequalities of a modern, urban Canada and especially an elite segment of the population whose privilege is founded upon an imperial past tied to the slave trade. Everson creates an embodiment of difference through this personified black Geranium, yet simultaneously and ironically exposes an instance where the physical self fails to be recognized, subsequently shifting the flower's "cultivating" social role toward a mode of costuming. The denial of Geranium's racial identity subtly reveals, therefore, a superficially maintained, removed white neighbourhood, contentedly oblivious to the harsh realities of the world around them and their own exploitative role within it.

As a transplant precariously out of place, the geranium (plant or human) serves Traill, Prescott, Birney, and particularly Everson in highlighting Canada's colonial history: its role as either a "lesser" version of England, or as a society perpetuating the power structures intrinsic to imperialism and its objectives of expropriation and material wealth. Other authorial custodians of the geranium's fertile literary life build upon these associations by using the physical endurance of this exotic-turned-common plant to reflect the inter-relationship between materiality and socio-cultural experiences of daily life in a sometimes inhospitable and unfamiliar Canadian context. Specifically, the plant's portability (surviving as a slip and especially being moved around in a pot) confirms its suitability to itinerant Canadian populations of different regions and periods that are participating in either rural settlement or modern urban expansion. As the most transient plant in Canadian letters, the potted geranium is the ideal botanical companion for rootless characters actively confronting social dislocation as they seek alternative homes, communities, and modes of existence. For instance, it is perhaps not surprising that this transportable and especially hardy plant frequently appears in the context of the western prairies with this region's extreme climate and adopted agrarian economy. In the article "The Greening of the West: One Geranium at a Time," Elizabeth Blight examines photographs of Manitoban businesses and homes around the year 1912 to demonstrate how indoor gardening was a "private" initiative "in the rapid spread of horticulture across the prairie provinces" (n. pag.). With her "magnifying glass in hand," Blight examines plants in windowsills and speculates that the homeowners' desire was twofold: first, to have "the passing public view them," and second, to "demonstrate the care given to decorating the home" amid rather "bleak surroundings" (n. pag.). In his material study of the garden, Tilley similarly suggests that the act of gardening in one's dwelling space is not only "a means of creating both a personal and social identity through a vegetative medium" (178), but also a way of laying claim to "territory, time, and resources" (184). In the context of Blight's photographic survey as well as literary treatments of prairie-based geraniums, colourful window displays of exotic flowers undoubtedly facilitated the material expression of European settlement and property ownership in the West, but gardens can also, as Clarissa T. Kimber aptly contends, tell an additional story of "the acculturation that immigrant groups have undergone" (272) even as they lay claim to a new space. Gabrielle Roy's depiction of the prairies during the 1920s in *Street of Riches* (originally published in French as *Rue Deschambault*, 1955) reveals, for example, that geraniums foster a sense of accomplishment and belonging for newly arrived settlers insecure in their adopted home. In the story "The Well of Dunrea," the Russian colonists of Dunrea, Saskatchewan, plant red geraniums in windows and "along the paths ... from the houses to the little privies" (76) in order to establish ownership of their homesteads. The protagonist's French-Canadian father, who works for the Ministry of Colonization, believes that when settlers display flowers it is a "sure sign of success, of happiness" (75-76), yet he also "laugh[s] at this excess of adornment" as he views cultivation primarily in terms of economics and believes the "first concern was to look after the crops" (76). With the Ministry having an opinion about the significance of flower gardening, the Russian settlers use the widely known geranium as a means of demonstrating their aptitude as prairie farmers and materially objectifying their social integration despite being ethnically diverse newcomers. The sheer quantity of geraniums throughout Dunrea suggests these flowers were not tended gradually from slips, but likely purchased, a significant factor since gardening is not always about personal expression, but rather social image and public perception, as Tilley acknowledges: "Status emulation, impressing others by the manner in which the garden is maintained ..., and the conspicuous consumption entailed by growing fashionable plants" are of concern when a garden is within public view (185). Geraniums may not be "fashionable," but they are certainly commonplace, a factor that aids the Russian settlers in communicating their desire to be an accepted part of quotidian prairie life and its larger pioneer farming community.

Projecting desired social identities outward, for public view, through the material presence of a geranium framed by a window creates a kind of legible self-portrait that Roy's Dunrea settlers are by no means alone in pursuing.[10] Because the geranium serves as a public display of the transient, rootless self's desire for social approval, integration, and even status, the flower is clearly tied to communal values—related primarily to home and belonging—that should, ideally, be attainable for all members of Canadian society no matter their circumstances. Sadly though, for some, even a single geranium in the window is a dream out of reach, and when its demise or absence is noted in our literature, it becomes a subtle indication of social and economic circumstances that undermine these commonly held beliefs in modest material comfort and domestic happiness. Therefore, as much as a garden can serve, in Tilley's view, as a "transitional space" through its private-public mediation and outward projection of the "social standing of the gardener" (185), the geranium in the window can also assume an inverse role: reflecting back on members of the community who view the flower from the outside. In these instances, a neighbour's geranium serves as a critical mirror, not simply of the gardener, but of other citizens' remoteness or even exclusion from realizing these basic social goals, or modest ideals, in their own lives. In Gabrielle Roy's *The Tin Flute* (originally published in French as *Bonheur d'occasion*, 1945), for example, the homely aspirations of urban migrants, previously uprooted from the Quebec countryside, are undermined by the environmental and working-class conditions of the French ghetto of Saint Henri. The impoverished Rose-Anna Lacasse wanders the Montreal neighbourhood in search of affordable housing for her family, dreaming of an abode where sunlight streams in "the kitchen doorway ... land[ing] on the geraniums in their clay pots ... [and] brighten[ing] the face of a little girl sitting in her high chair" (100). Rose-Anna's daydream is in keeping with gardening as a hopeful, future-oriented practice; unfortunately, this imagined geranium is from the past, as the daydream recalls the home she had as a twenty-year-old newlywed.[11] In contrast to the remembered abode, Rose-Anna's present urban surroundings are like "a tomb": grey brick homes with soot-covered windows from the pollution of the surrounding factories and trains (97). Here, women, "thin and sad, [stand] in evil-smelling doorways, astonished by the sunlight" (97) and set not flowers, but "their babies on the windowsill" (97) for the benefit of some precious rays. Few flowers are to be found here, and those that are serve only to underscore Montreal's economic inequalities, such as when Rose-Anna ventures onto a middle-class street and spies "on the inside sill of a window, robust plants that had more air and space ... than the children she'd just glimpsed on St. Ferdinand Street" (98). This windowsill "oasis" (98) is beyond the financial reach of the Lacasse family, and Rose-Anna's humble pastoral dream is lost. The unending drudgery of her existence means springtime no longer signifies physical and emotional renewal through the process of settling one's family in a new place (and starting a garden), but rather a season that dictates the time to uproot and move to a dingier, cheaper apartment with no place for a geranium.

Another example where the geranium projects not only the identity of its owner, but also, and perhaps more importantly, the dire social conditions of those who view the plant from outside on the street is Duncan Campbell Scott's *In the Village of Viger* (1896). In this short-story cycle, the geranium participates in what Klay Dyer identifies as the recurring "motif of failed gardens" in a text deeply ambivalent about the passage of time and a modernizing world (101). The geranium—which is transported to the village by Mademoiselle Viau, the milliner who moves from the city—meets its demise in this town so averse to the future and to progress. The mysterious, entrepreneurial milliner is a rootless figure whose origins are unknown despite the villagers' persistent questioning. Her sudden presence is signalled by the appearance of a potted geranium, which is spotted one morning "standing on the sill" of the new home (5). Although Mademoiselle Viau seems domestic-minded—feeding the birds, hanging curtains, and "watering ... the geranium, which was just going to flower" (7)—the suspicious villagers' unwelcoming attitude and violent intrusions into her private space contribute to her eventual departure. Significantly, the geranium, which "only had one blossom all the time it was alive" (13-14), as if to reflect the vulnerability of the single, young woman, no longer travels with its owner, but is left unaided on the windowsill, where it dies. The milliner's original impulse to foster a sense of home and build her business is absolutely undermined by the villagers' dislike of all things urban and their resistance to change. In the end, the "dry stick" sticking out of the pot (14), which remains on the windowsill for three years in full view of the main street, becomes reflective not of the absent milliner, but of the villagers themselves: their close-minded, detrimental influence on the future growth of their community. Whereas in *The Tin Flute*, poverty prevents Rose-Anna from "planting" a comforting future (as envisioned in her geranium daydream) for her ever-transient, down-and-out family, in Scott's cycle, the villagers' maladaptive attitude toward modernity and urbanization alienates the gentle, industrious newcomer who abandons her houseplant, which stood initially as a symbol of her new life in the village. Ironically, then, the modest dream of "home" and the value of care associated with the geranium are sabotaged for all involved, even though the ailing villagers of Viger see themselves as protecting the health and future of their community through their alienation of outsiders. In the end, both Roy and Scott use either the absence or death of a geranium as a form of critical, botanically inspired commentary on the intolerable conditions of Saint Henri and the failures of Viger where, in both places, the realization of a sense of home seems almost impossible.

Evidently the geranium plays a key public role in communicating visibly a rootless individual's longing for social acceptance and domestic achievement, but what happens when readers shift perspective from the external view of the home (which Blight pursues through her photographs) to the private, indoor cultural life of the geranium? In less common photographs of early-twentieth-century domestic interiors, such as the photograph taken of a kitchen buffet in a Saskatchewan farmhouse (circa 1919), the wintering geranium suns itself inconspicuously off to the side of the frame (see Figure 4.1). The primary reason it is easy to overlook the geranium as an inconsequential part of domestic interiors is precisely because it is part of a domestic practice. For instance, when Margaret Atwood sets the scene of an ordinary day at home, apparently without drama, in her short prose piece "Bad News" from *Good Bones* (1992), the banal geranium begins the first line: "The red geraniums fluorescing on the terrace, the wind swaying the daisies, the baby's milk-fed eyes focusing for the first time on a double row of beloved teeth—what is there to report?" (9). The geranium bathing in sunlight hardly seems newsworthy in a world hungering for drama and destruction, yet, paradoxically, the very act of acknowledging the plant's domestic presence potentially substantiates the daily work and lives of those who may otherwise go unnoticed and undervalued. The flower's quotidian, material presence translates, therefore, to a robust literary life, as the plant that is there, that is visible, is the plant that inspires. To demonstrate this point, Russell Hitchings argues in his article "People, Plants, and Performance" that according to proponents of actor network theory, "people, objects, plants, animals and ideas all jostle against each other, and it is through these

Figure 4.1 Kitchen geraniums wintering indoors on a homestead near Vanguard, Saskatchewan, circa 1919. Photograph courtesy of the collection of Carol Miller.

interactions that society takes shape and our understandings of this society find form" (100). In this relational model, Hitchings focuses on domestic gardens and, specifically, plant materiality, discovering that while initially gardeners describe themselves as artists controlling their terrain, when the discussion shifts to the plants' perspective, gardeners view themselves, instead, as facilitators, "plantperson[s]' working with a lively and dynamic set of non-human companions" who are an influential part of this material culture and space (107). In a literary context, the sight of a common geranium struggling to survive in a pot leads many female characters, who are tasked with the flower's maintenance, to reflect on their own endurance within their domestic lives and roles, particularly when others take these women's presence and daily contributions for granted. Therefore, just as Anne Shirley, the unwanted orphan, identifies with the overlooked "Bonny" in *Anne of Green Gables*, Daisy Goodwill Flett in Carol Shields's *The Stone Diaries* (1993) considers the geranium a supportive witness to the quotidian, as evidenced by a fan letter she receives for her "Mrs. Green Thumb" column: "Your tribute to geraniums touched the middle of my heart. These sturdy, stout-hearted darlings have kept me company for the fifty years of my married life, sitting on the window sill and cheering me on while I peeled the supper spuds" (220). Out of this close alignment, or relational model, of the geranium and the "domesticated" feminine subject develops the recurring trope of the woman-as-potted-plant, which represents a central paradox of the geranium's literary significance. This supposedly transient, highly portable exotic also serves in communicating experiences of confinement: lives embedded in the domestic and curtailed by limited social and personal mobility. Exemplary in this particular use of the geranium is Gabrielle Roy, who connects the seasonal indoor-outdoor planting of the geranium to her female characters' predictable experiences and deferential positions within their housebound existences. In *Street of Riches*, Christine's Aunt Thérésina pursues a "real passion ... for geraniums" (100) despite her debilitating asthma, the foreshortened growing season in Manitoba, and her husband's unfulfilled promise to move to California for a more temperate home and garden. Confined indoors for most of the year because of her health, Aunt Thérésina tends her potted red geraniums, doing for these plants what no one will do for her: "She would dust them ... with the tip of her finger, delicately cleaning off their leaves, and she would say, 'You must not leave dust on the leaves of plants; plants breathe through their leaves; plants need good air'" (100). In her depictions of these daily struggles, Roy drew upon her own Manitoban childhood, as her autobiography, *Enchantment and Sorrow* (originally published in French as *La détresse et l'enchantement*, 1984), recounts her mother "drop[ping] everything to gather up the geraniums and fuchsias that had spent the winter on the windowsills and plant[ing] them in the earth around the house" (31). By the end of a homemaker's work-filled day, these flowers, which first suggested renewed maternal fortitude, come full circle and communicate exhaustion. In *Street of Riches*, Christine sees a parallel between her own depleted mother and the flowers drooping in the twilight hours, "so sadly hang[ing] their heads" (143).

Among the numerous examples in Canadian literature of the woman-as-potted-geranium, the most famous are undoubtedly those of poet Dorothy Livesay as she reflects on the everyday, material circumstances of her gendered subjects. In the introduction to Livesay's collection *The Self-Completing Tree* (1986), Linda Rogers notes the pre-eminence of the garden as "linked to the notion of renewal," with Livesay's "recurring geranium," in particular, "struggl[ing] toward the window and the light" (vii). In a similar vein as Roy's fictional portrayals of women's seasonal domestic work, Livesay's geranium-related poems—including "'Geranus.'... Crane," "Green Rain," and "Bartok and the Geranium"—place gender and its relation to life cycles of decline and renewal at the forefront. With respect to the latter poem, Livesay's most anthologized, critical discussions of "Bartok and the Geranium" (1952) position it primarily as an investigation of male-female binaries and the particular challenges of the woman artist.[12] Livesay's reputation as a poet of "proletarian verse" (Rogers iv) means, however, that it is equally important to keep in mind how the class-related, material culture of this flower subtly works in combination with the feminine floral subject at the centre of the poem in order to capture both the vulnerability and endurance of those individuals most associated with, or defined by, the limitations of physical circumstance. "Bartok and the Geranium" contrasts the modesty of the geranium, who is dressed to communicate quiet aspirations to gentility (with her "furbelows" and "bustling boughs"), with the boundless ambition and elite artistry of Bartok (213). Readers surmise that unlike her musical counterpart, the potted geranium is "content with this small room" (213) and the humble, daily experiences it affords: the light, the rain, "[w]hatever falls" (213). Bartok, on the other hand, is a figure of entitlement, even greed: he "Wrench[es] from the stars their momentary notes / Steal[s] music from the moon" (213). Refusing to be confined even to the sky, this Bartok is reminiscent of the Miltonic Lucifer, who fails to usurp heaven's supposed tyranny and is eventually hurled "From heaven's height" (214). In contrast to Bartok's disembodied performance of sound, violent ambition, and momentary transcendence, the hardy but silent geranium "preens herself in light" (214). Surviving by virtue of being a grounded figure, rooted in and attentive to her physical conditions, this potted houseplant reveals the quiet, tangible illuminations that quotidian life affords. In light of the geranium's cultural history as a "common" houseplant, the flower becomes emblematic of Livesay's gendered and working-class artistic vision, a vision that she celebrated explicitly in "Without Benefit of Tape" (1967), a poem written at a later point in her career and in response to the poetic innovations of Vancouver's Tish group.[13] Although initially inspired by Tish, Livesay ultimately described the group in a 1978 interview as "writing from an ivory tower" and being too focused on performance in a way that made them "rootless" in their craft (Twigg n. pag.). Alternatively, Livesay praised poets who as "working people … really felt the pulse of the country" (Beardsley and Sullivan n. pag.). In "Without Benefit of Tape," which Livesay once acknowledged as a kind of poetic manifesto, she invokes her own poem "Bartok and the Geranium," when the speaker declares, "The real poems are being written in outports / on backwoods farms / in passageways where pantries still exist / or where geraniums / nail light to the window" (203; emphasis added).[14] In much the same way as Livesay's famous geranium models expression realized through the physical-cultural self and related environment, rather than through Bartok's discarnate music that transcends into the heavens, the poem "Without Benefit of Tape" celebrates voices heard, not through a tape-recorder (such as the Tish performances Livesay recorded), but in the context of daily working life: "shouted out / by men and women leaving railway lines" or

"Hallooed / across the counter, in a corner store" (203). Ultimately, Livesay's humble, feminine geranium stands as a profound, embodied form of artistry that not only gives material existence its due, but endures precisely because of this sensibility. As Livesay herself once reflected, "Some poems have meaning now and some poems have meaning for always. A poem like 'Bartok and the Geranium' might have meaning for always. It's a male/ female poem, but it's also about art and nature" (Twigg n. pag.). In this, perhaps the most famous hardy geranium of Canadian poetry, Livesay muses upon and questions the legitimacy of this last binary by way of a domesticated cultured flower whose very artistry is realized through her physical form and rootedness in a circumscribed environment.

The geranium's association with women's domestic lives and expression is hardly unexpected because it is in keeping with conventional (but not uncomplicated) pairings of the feminine with nature, beauty, and containment; there are texts, however, that situate this flower more ambiguously with respect to gender when examining power politics within the home. In Timothy Findley's short story "Losers, Finders, Strangers at the Door" from his collection *Dinner Along the Amazon* (1984), the wealthy protagonist Daisy McCabe repeatedly curses her hanging cages of geraniums, flowers that reflect her own entrapment within her unfulfilled marriage and her acquiescence to her husband: "Damn them. So high up, she said aloud, all of them so unwatered: wanting. Expecting me to do it. Me to always do it for them. Why can't they do it for themselves? she bellowed, filling the house with sound at last. And then, as well, with laughter. How could geraniums possibly water themselves. It was perfect. Madness" (190). Beholden to care for both her geraniums and her husband, Daisy exhibits an intense need to maintain her social status as part of an esteemed couple. With Daisy's public reputation at stake, Findley exposes the necessarily private negotiations that occur within the family home (and marriage) in order to maintain respectable appearances by keeping the marital union, at least visibly, intact. As the story progresses, readers learn that Daisy is waiting for the arrival of a "package, person, parcel—in her husband's absence" (190), this euphemistically termed "parcel" being a young man who is coming to reside with the McCabes in order to fulfill Arnold McCabe's sadomasochistic desire to be beaten.[15] When the young man, Caleb, arrives, Daisy performs her (limited) power and authority through dramatic gestures that equate Caleb and his male sex, not herself, with the flower:[16]

> Were you aware, she asks, that flowers are the genitalia of plants....
> She reaches up and plucks the nearest dangling head.

I just castrated that geranium. You see? And, there's a theory, also ... (she twirls the scarlet head between her fingers, rolling it back and forth) that if we only had microphones sensitive enough—the picking and cutting of flowers would produce an unbearable scream. (She pauses.) Fascinating. Yes?
No answer.
Suddenly, Daisy throws the genitalia across the room, where they land—if only approximately—in Caleb's lap. (195)

By the end of the story, Daisy successfully negotiates her position as "head" of the household (in the absence of her husband), and finds in Caleb someone who will maintain her household, her marriage, and, thereby, her social standing, as he is finally tasked with the watering of her geraniums. Daisy may be confined by, and begrudge, her feminine role of always facilitating the needs of others (whether husband or plant), yet she exerts some measure of control within her domestic world by using her indoor gardening as a means of communication, objectifying Caleb's now-precarious function as sexual interloper. Purposely castrating the geranium to enact a physical threat, Daisy underscores her position relative to Caleb's, as this homosexual male "servant" is now associated with the lower-class houseplant. In contrast, the still-contained Daisy distances herself from the caged flowers, acting instead as both complicit "witness" to Arnold's clandestine activities and contentious supervisor to her husband's hired help.[17]

Colonial history, immigration and settlement, socio-economic inequalities and aspirations, gender politics, and domestic culture are all part of the potted geranium's Canadian literary history. While the geranium's popularity may reside with older generations (such as the 1950s homemakers of Shields's fiction), its cultural demise seems unlikely since writers celebrate this flower precisely because of its endurance. Indeed, the geranium's seasonal indoor-outdoor planting operates as a trope in contemporary Canadian literature, a ritual that evokes this humble plant's survival despite the passage of time and challenging circumstances. John Pass's Governor General's award-winning collection *Stumbling in the Bloom* (2005) contains the poem "Depleted Geranium," in which the speaker addresses a lone plant surviving in a cold frame: "You are a geranium, vivid and vital / as lucky accident, tenacious / as lingering illness" (61-62). Pass concludes his poem singing the sickly geranium's praises, recognizing its endurance as "we live through, live through, live through ..." (62). Patrick Lane expresses a comparable sentiment in his unpublished poem "The Last Geranium," of which several drafts are archived in the Patrick Lane fonds at the University of

Regina. In the poem, dedicated to Lorna Crozier, the speaker watches his lover unearth the last geranium from the fall garden, a plant whose ancestor was "brought from Wales" a century ago: "a cutting / from a cutting, a rooted slip of green that holds / in its sap all she knows of history." With winter approaching, the geranium's leaves are "ready to hang in the false air, ready to fall, /... / But it will survive," and at the same time, the speaker contemplates his and his lover's own vulnerability to life's seasonal decline. But perhaps the most powerful evidence of the geranium's continued literary hardiness is its capacity to exert its presence even in its absence, suggesting that this flower has firmly rooted itself in the imaginations of Canadian writers, touching on something central to their artistic visions, especially when they address the physicality of human experience. Lane captures this complex material interplay between life and death, creation and disintegration, through the image of the geranium in his essay "Counting the Bones" from the edited collection *Addicted: Notes from the Belly of the Beast* (2001). Bringing into focus his own struggle with alcoholism, Lane describes an experience of retching into a toilet bowl and spying a garden of his own making as tied to his body:

> Three more surges and the first blood comes, a few drops that splash into the snot-skewed water. They drop and flower there like the lost blossoms of a geranium, a heavy red, bright with oxygen. They are like the blossoms that grow on the fists of a man who strikes a cement wall so he can feel something, anything, himself. It is blood from an artery.... There is in my mind a kind of grim amusement at this flowering.... The next spasm brings more, a tablespoon of blood that drowns the delicate flowers that shimmered there a moment before. I am somehow sorry to see them go. (4)

Even in this moment of despair and self-destruction, there is a longing for sensation, for life, and the bloody, dissipating geranium reflects the human subject's own precarious vitality.[18] Forcing readers to see this supposedly ordinary flower in a new and provocative light, Lane contemplates physicality as a fundamental component of the human experience and one's awareness of self.

Through Lane's expelled, brutally embodied red geranium, as well as through the many other diverse portrayals of this plant in alternative periods and contexts of Canadian literature, readers come to appreciate its status as an exceptional flower, carrying, as Michael Pollan suggests, centuries' worth of human culture and expression: "It's a lot to ask of a plant, ... and this may explain why only a small handful of them have proven themselves supple and willing enough for the task" (77). With its long colonial history and ability to survive in a Northern climate as a houseplant, the geranium has secured a cultural foothold in Canada precisely because it is an out-of-place plant that endures. In some ways, it is not surprising that the supposedly banal geranium has become a canonical flower in Canadian literature, a tradition that has itself typically been met with disparaging assessments or dismissals. By appearing, however, in a range of literary windowsills, in characters' daydreams and memories, and in unexpected personified formulations (such as a boy walking down a sidewalk on a cold Halloween night), the hardy geranium has proven its cultural longevity and versatility: relating tangible experiences of survival, belonging, poverty, race, alienation, gender, and sexuality. This flower accompanies historical figures and writers through time and space, growing and dying in homes and in texts.

NOTES

I am grateful to Patrick Lane for permission to quote from his unpublished poem "The Last Geranium." Copyright © Patrick Lane.

1 In *The Annotated Anne of Green Gables*, Margaret Anne Doody writes, "Anne ... sees trees and flowers not as emblems but as friends. Her desire to give names to growing things was shared by her author," who wrote about a similar experience as a girl (438). In the 21 September 1889 entry of her journal, a young Montgomery describes "repotting all [her] geraniums" that originated from the "matronly old geranium called 'Bonny,'" which was given to her two or three years earlier as a slip: "And it blooms as if it meant it. I believe that old geranium has a soul!" (Montgomery, *The Selected Journals* 1).
2 In American literature, Flannery O'Connor and Theodore Roethke have produced much lauded treatments of the flower in the short story "The Geranium" and the poem "The Geranium," respectively. O'Connor and Roethke focus on the geranium's association with transplanted figures and with gender; however, they do not examine either the plant's colonial heritage, or its ability to winter indoors—two key aspects of the geranium's material cultural significance in Canadian literature.
3 In *Potted History: The Story of Plants in the Home*, Horwood documents that the *Pelargonium triste* appears to be the first variety of geranium cultivated indoors in England as early as 1631 (190). Regarding the issue of misclassification, present-day gardeners continue to seek clarification. In one popular online gardening publication, Dr. Allan Armitage, professor of horticulture at the University of Georgia, advises that both geraniums and pelargoniums come from the same family (*Geraniaceae*) and share many botanical features, which likely led to the conflation: "Another reason that pelargoniums may have been lumped under the same common name is that true geraniums ... —native from Europe to Asia to North America—were likely in commerce in Europe before the annual pelargoniums were introduced from South Africa. Over time, the annual pelargonium became more popular than its look-alike cousin as a showy bedding plant, and became much more widely known as the 'geranium'" ("Geranium vs. Pelargonium"). For the purposes of my paper, I will use the common misnomer, which is frequently used by Canadian writers when referring to pelargoniums.
4 "Zonal" refers to the "dark purple zone on the leaves" of many geraniums, and although "many are not zoned (for example, the scented forms) ... deep zonation

has long been an objective of breeders of the annual bedding geranium" ("Geranium vs. Pelargonium").

5   Writing a report on indoor floral culture for the Montreal Horticultural Society in 1879, Mrs. Symmes chastises women gardeners for trying to grow delicate plants "behind a curtain in the 'dim religious light' of a conventionally darkened room" (233). Symmes adds that while these ladies "can have little idea of the natural conditions of plant life, or, indeed, of human life," the common geranium is one plant capable of surviving such neglect: these "will exist in semi-darkness, probably because they are scantily watered and have stored up some vitality out of doors in summer; but mere existence is hardly an object to those who take the trouble to start and pot plants from the house" (233). Ironically, while Symmes dismisses "mere existence" as a gardening objective, this is one factor of many that account for the geranium's longevity and multi-faceted role in Canadian literature, as the flower's very struggle to live amid dire conditions leads writers to address the significance of physicality in human experience and cultural life.

6   On this point, Horwood quotes Shirley Hibberd, who "had no patience with gardeners who were not prepared to be adventurous in their choice of plants.... 'It is simply to tax one's patience ... to pass from a blaze of geraniums in the parterre to another blaze of geraniums in the conservatory ... a rabbit cooked a hundred different ways is tiresome, and the cooking must be very tiresome to the rabbit'" (qtd. in Horwood 126). In *Garden Voices: Two Centuries of Canadian Garden Writing*, one selection reveals the excessive use of geraniums in the colony. Louisa Aylmer, wife of the governor of Lower Canada, writes in 1831 of planting "200 Geraniums" in her flower garden at the couple's country home in Sorel near Quebec City (38).

7   I have been unable to determine the exact date when geraniums were brought to Canada; however, according to the National Garden Bureau in the United States, these flowers were introduced in the late eighteenth century: "In 1760 seeds of pelargoniums were sent to John Bertram of Philadelphia, marking the arrival in America, and plants were brought back from France by Thomas Jefferson in the '70s and '80s" ("Geranium Fact Sheet").

8   In *Canadian Wildflowers* (1868), Traill notes that herbalists are aware of the Wood Geranium's properties as an astringent: it is used as "a styptic for wounds," "a gargle for sore throats and ulcerated mouth," and a laxative for "young children to correct a lax state of the system" (42). This native species is evidently not popular in Upper Canadian gardens because Traill works diligently to counter its dismissal because of gardeners' tastes for more fashionable plants. The "Wood Geraniums" in Traill's text are the true geraniums, not the popular exotics properly classified as pelargoniums.

9   Melancholy and grief are also attributed to the geranium's lexicon. For example, Duncan Campbell Scott's elegiac poem "The Leaf" describes a geranium at a headstone: "This silver-edged geranium leaf / Is one sign of a bitter grief" (167). "The Leaf" appears in *Lundy's Lane and Other Poems* (1916), a book that Scott dedicated to the memory of his daughter, Elizabeth Duncan Scott, who died at the age of twelve. Contemporary writers continue to evoke these sentiments through the geranium. See Laura Best's short story "The Red Geranium" (2000), in which a geranium is placed at a gravesite in memory of a dead child.

10 See also Sinclair Ross's *As for Me and My House* (1941), which features Mrs. Bentley, the minister's wife, maintaining the pretense of a fertile domestic life by growing geraniums in the windows of her new home in the Saskatchewan town of Horizon during the Great Depression. While Mrs. Bentley is overly preoccupied with her social standing in the town, other Canadian literary characters, such as Flo's cousin Billy Pope in Alice Munro's *Who Do You Think You Are?* (1978), project more genuine,

humble aspirations. Readers are told that Billy Pope once grew "geraniums in old tobacco cans, on the thick cement windowsill" of the slaughterhouse rooms in which he once lived, with the narrator surmising from Billy's makeshift garden that he "must have had a home-loving nature" despite the smell of pig entrails that surrounded him (63).

11 See Tilley's discussion of time's relationship to the material practice of gardening, as "the gardener always views his or her garden through the prism of time: how it is now and how it used to be, and how in their dreams it might be in the future" (188).

12 Tanya Butler argues that "No other poem emphasises the disparate natures of man and woman so clearly" as the geranium, dressed in her "feminine costume," is associated with nature, silence, and passivity (n. pag.). With a similar equation between nature and the feminine, Nadine McInnis situates "Bartok and the Geranium" within a larger discussion of Livesay's focus on the "creative conflict of the woman artist who desires to communicate within a literary tradition that does not fully recognize her experiences and perceptions" (27), resulting in numerous "metaphors of language and silence" (28). McInnis concludes that Livesay's decision to close her famous poem "with the dominance of one force over the other is part of the pessimism of many of the poems written during her years of active maternity" (45).

13 Peter Stevens writes that upon returning to Canada in the 1960s after living in Zambia, Livesay reacted to the poetry of Vancouver's Tish group with its "emphasis on the oral" (65). In "Without Benefit of Tape," she "readdress[ed] the poetic concerns she had in the 1930s," which was her "interest in finding a poetry for the people, a poetry that is proletarian yet does not have political connotations" (66).

14 In addition to using the image of the geranium in the window in "Without Benefit of Tape" as an example of what a "real poem" accomplishes, Livesay also chose to group this anti-Tish poem with her earlier piece "Bartok and the Geranium" in her collection *The Self-Completing Tree*. This arrangement undoubtedly informs the reading of the flower in "Bartok and the Geranium" as engaging simultaneously with gender, class, and artistic concerns. According to Butler, "the reading of a poem can be deeply affected by its bibliographic context" and "the selection, grouping, and ordering of the poems in *The Self-Completing Tree* represent something of an active artistic creation in itself" (n. pag.).

15 Heather Sanderson notes that when Daisy tells a "circuitous tale" of a friend's husband and his unusual desire to be beaten, she is "clearly describing herself and the cause of the current situation" (84).

16 Sanderson notes that Findley also wrote "Losers, Finders, Strangers at the Door" as a play, with the story "illustrat[ing] the closeness of drama and fiction in his writing" (75). Daisy's role-playing is central to creating this theatrical effect, as is the fact that the story continually highlights the home's windows (and the view from outside) through the epigraphs, one of which, Sanderson explains, "evokes a window as frame for the action" through which the private lives of others may be observed (81). Findley's story, which focuses on the performance of private lives for public consumption (as mediated by windows), brings the geranium and its windowsill culture of display into the fray of the McCabe household and its many actors.

17 Daisy's floral name is significant not only because it distinguishes her from the geranium (unlike Everson's African "pickaninny," who is named after the exotic), but also because it plays on the meaning "day's eye," suggestive of Daisy's clear, open-eyed perception of the extramarital sexual relationships and power dynamics taking place within her home (Waterman 74).

18 Lane's poem "China White" also uses images of geraniums, whose blossoms appear "as close to blood / as any flower is," to describe a drug addict's reflections on his

past and present circumstances (71). This association of the scarlet geranium with human blood (and even a syringe) at moments when life hangs in the balance may be related to the geranium's symbolism of grief and consolation. For another example of blood-red geraniums, see Barbara Folkart's poem, "Old Woman Beside a Geranium Bush," in which the "hemorrhaging" growth of a "towering" flower drains the life of the elderly gardener (82).

WORKS CITED

Atwood, Margaret. "Bad News." *Good Bones*. 1992. Toronto: McClelland and Stewart, 1997. 9-10. Print.

Aylmer, Louisa A. "From 'Some Notes on Architecture, Interiors, and Gardens in Quebec 1831,' in *APT Bulletin*." *Garden Voices: Two Centuries of Canadian Garden Writing*. Ed. Edwinna von Baeyer and Pleasance Crawford. Toronto: Vintage, 1997. 37-38. Print.

Beardsley, Doug, and Rosemary Sullivan. "An Interview with Dorothy Livesay." *Canadian Poetry* 3 (1978): 87-97. Web. n. pag. 1 Apr. 2011. <http://www.uwo.ca/english/canadianpoetry/cpjrn/vol03/sullivan.htm>.

Best, Laura. "The Red Geranium." *Antigonish Review* 1226 (2000): 21-26. Print.

Blight, Elizabeth. "The Greening of the West: One Geranium at a Time." *Manitoba History* 31 (Spring 1996): n. pag. Manitoba Historical Society. Web. 17 May 2009.

Birney, Earle. "Anglosaxon Street." 1942. *Canadian Literature in English: Texts and Contexts*. Vol. 2. Ed. Laura Moss and Cynthia Sugars. Toronto: Pearson, 2009. 114-16. Print.

Butler, Tanya. "Dorothy Livesay's Poetic Re/vision: Reading Binaries, Lesbian Love, and Androgyny in *The Self-Completing Tree*." *Canadian Poetry* 50 (2002): 32-50. Web. n. pag. 11 Apr. 2011. <http://www.canadianpoetry.ca/cpjrn/vol50/butler.htm>.

Chevalier, Sophie. "The Cultural Construction of Domestic Space in France and Great Britain." *Signs* 27.3 (Spring 2002): 847-56. Print.

Doody, Margaret Anne. "Gardens and Plants." *The Annotated Anne of Green Gables*. Ed. Wendy E. Barry, Margaret Anne Doody, and Mary E. Doody Jones. New York: Oxford UP, 1997. 434-38. Print.

Dyer, Klay. "Passing Time and Present Absence: Looking to the Future in *In the Village of Viger*." *Canadian Literature* 141 (Summer 1994): 86-106. Print.

Everson, Ronald. "Geranium." *Maclean's* 15 Oct. 1931. 9, 73.

Ewing, Juliana Horatia. "Letter 76, in *Canada Home: Juliana Horatia Ewing's Fredericton Letters, 1867-1869*." *Garden Voices: Two Centuries of Canadian Garden Writing*. Ed. Edwinna von Baeyer and Pleasance Crawford. Toronto: Vintage, 1997. 224-28. Print.

Findley, Timothy. "Losers, Finders, Strangers at the Door." *Dinner Along the Amazon*. Markham: Penguin, 1984. 189-203. Print.

Folkart, Barbara. "Old Woman Beside a Geranium Bush." *Antigonish Review* 96 (1994): 82. Print.

"Geranium Fact Sheet." National Garden Bureau. Northern Gardening. Web. 15 Sept. 2011.

"Geranium vs. Pelargonium." *Fine Gardening* 59 (2011): 14. *Fine Gardening*. Taunton. Web. 28 Sept. 2011.

Hitchings, Russell. "People, Plants, and Performance: On Actor Network Theory and the Material Pleasures of the Private Garden." *Social & Cultural Geography* 4.1 (2003): 99-113. Print.

Horwood, Catherine. *Potted History: The Story of Plants in the Home*. London: Frances Lincoln, 2007. Print.

Kimber, Clarissa T. "Gardens and Dwelling: People in Vernacular Gardens." *Geographical Review* 94.3 (2004): 263-83. *Jstor* 7 June 2012. <http://www.jstor.org/stable/30034274>.

Lane, Patrick. "China White." *Witness: Selected Poems 1962-2010*. Madeira Park, BC: Harbour, 2010. 71. Print.

———. "Counting the Bones." *Addicted: Notes from the Belly of the Beast*. Ed. Lorna Crozier and Patrick Lane. Vancouver: Greystone, 2001. 1-15. Print.

———. "The Last Geranium." Patrick Lane Fonds. MS Accession 90-102. Box 17. File 581. U of Regina, Regina.

Livesay, Dorothy. "Bartok and the Geranium." 1952. *The Self-Completing Tree*. Vancouver: Beach Holme, 1999. 213-14. Print.

———. "Without Benefit of Tape." 1967. *The Self-Completing Tree*. Vancouver: Beach Holme, 1999. 203. Print.

McInnis, Nadine. *Dorothy Livesay's Poetics of Desire*. Winnipeg: Turnstone, 1994. Print.

Montgomery, L. M. *Anne of Green Gables*. 1908. Toronto: McGraw-Hill Ryerson, 1968. Print.

———. *The Selected Journals of L. M. Montgomery*. Vol. 1. Ed. Mary Rubio and Elizabeth Waterston. Toronto: Oxford UP, 1985. Print.

Munro, Alice. *Who Do You Think You Are?* 1978. Toronto: Penguin, 1991. Print.

Pass, John. *Stumbling in the Bloom*. Lantzville, BC: Oolichan, 2005. Print.

Pollan, Michael. *The Botany of Desire: A Plant's-Eye View of the World*. New York: Random House, 2002. Print.

Prescott, Henrietta. "Lines to a Fading Geranium." *Poems Written in Newfoundland*. London: W. Clowes, 1839. 256-61. *Early Canadiana Online*. Web. 26 May 2011.

Rogers, Linda. "The Poet Lovely as a Tree." *The Self-Completing Tree*. Vancouver: Beach Holme, 1999. i-ix. Print.

Ross, Sinclair. *As for Me and My House*. 1941. Toronto: McClelland and Stewart, 1989. Print.

Roy, Gabrielle. *Enchantment and Sorrow*. Trans. Patricia Claxton. Toronto: Lester and Orpen Dennys, 1987. Print.

———. *Street of Riches*. 1957. Trans. Henry Binsse. Toronto: McClelland and Stewart, 1991. Print.

———. *The Tin Flute*. 1980. Trans. Alan Brown. Toronto: McClelland and Stewart, 1989. Print.

Sanderson, Heather. "'What Is There Left to Say?': Speech and Silence in Timothy Findley's *Dinner Along the Amazon*." *Journal of Canadian Studies* 33.4 (Winter 1998/1999): 75-88. *CBCA Complete*. Web. 20 June 2011.

Scott, Duncan Campbell. *In the Village of Viger.* 1896. Toronto: McClelland and Stewart, 1996. Print.

———. "The Leaf." *Lundy's Lane and Other Poems.* Toronto: McClelland, Goodchild and Stewart, 167. Print.

Shields, Carol. *The Stone Diaries.* Toronto: Random House, 1993. Print.

Staines, David. "Everson, R. G." *The Oxford Companion to Canadian Literature.* Ed. William Toye. Toronto: Oxford UP, 1983. 242. Print.

Stevens, Peter. *Dorothy Livesay: Patterns in a Poetic Life.* Toronto: ECW, 1992. Print.

"Street Flower Girls." *The Canada Farmer* New series. 15 Apr. 1872. 146-47. *Early Canadiana Online.* 26 May 2009.

Symmes, Mrs. "From 'Flower Culture,' in *Report of the Montreal Horticultural Society and Fruit Growers' Association for the Year of 1879.*" *Garden Voices: Two Centuries of Canadian Garden Writing.* Ed. Edwinna von Baeyer and Pleasance Crawford. Toronto: Vintage, 1997. 232-34. Print.

Tilley, Chris. "What Gardens Mean." *Material Culture and Technology in Everyday Life: Ethnographic Approaches.* Ed. Phillip Vannini. New York: Peter Lang, 2009. 171-92. Print.

Traill, Catharine Parr. "To Ellen Dunlop." 23 May 1860. Letter 38. *I Bless You in My Heart: Selected Correspondence of Catharine Parr Traill.* Ed. Carl Ballstadt, Elizabeth Hopkins, and Michael Peterman. Toronto: U of Toronto P, 1996. 145-47. Print.

———. *Canadian Wildflowers.* 1868. Classic Reprint Series. Almonte: Algrove, 2003. Print.

Twigg, Alan. "Interview: Dorothy Livesay." 1978. *ABC Bookworld* 6 June 2011. <http://ABCBookWorld.webarchive>.

Waterman, Catharine H. *Flora's Lexicon: The Language of Flowers.* 1860. Ottawa: Algrove, 2001. Print.

Wetherbee, Kris. "The Potted Geranium." *Country Living* 22.9 (Sept. 1999): 53. *Canadian Periodical Index.* Web. 26 May 2009.

"Winter Flowers." *Farming* 13.6 (Feb. 1896): 377-78. *Early Canadiana Online.* Web. 26 May 2009.

Woodhead, Eileen. *Early Canadian Gardening: An 1827 Nursery Catalogue.* Montreal and Kingston: McGill-Queen's UP, 1998. Print.

CHAPTER 5

Is It Still a Cinch?
The Transformational Properties of Objects in Guy Vanderhaeghe's *The Last Crossing*

Susan Birkwood

In his review of Guy Vanderhaeghe's latest novel, *A Good Man*, Michael Bryson observes that Vanderhaeghe "has been demystifying 'the Western' for some time now." In *The Last Crossing*, the second of three novels set in the frontier region ranging from Fort Edmonton to Fort Benton (Montana), Vanderhaeghe revises and subverts a number of the generic conventions of the Western. He also crafts a work of "speculative" historical fiction, to use Herb Wyile's term for novels that "prob[e] the gaps ... of received history" (13) and strive "to come to terms with both the present and the past" (*Speculative Fictions* xi).[1] In *The Last Crossing*, the imagined relationships not just between people but between people and things reflect Vanderhaeghe's view that "the historical novel is always about contemporary issues in disguise" ("Making History" 26). Clothing is often an essential element of material disguise, and Vanderhaeghe scripts part of a "dialogue between older, more conventional notions of masculinity and newer, more contemporary ideas of what it means to be male" through those items that conceal, reveal, or fashion identity in the novel ("Making History" 47). To quote Ann Jones and Peter Stallybrass's study of Renaissance fashion: "Clothing is a worn world: a world of social relations put upon the wearer's body" (3). In the anarchic world of Fort Benton, a man's leather cinch is transformed through an act of violence into a weapon, but proves a misleading, if central, clue to the identity of the perpetrator, detached as it is from its wearer and anyone who knows its history. Nevertheless, in the possession of a new caretaker, it becomes a potent "metonymic contact point"—to borrow a term from Jeffrey David Feldman (256)—standing for the trauma and death of the female victim at the hands of a male aggressor, and, by extension, social relations predicated upon notions of male superiority that promote violent competition and domination. Crossing geographical and class borders, the belt facilitates the "dialogue" regarding the codes of masculinity typically celebrated in the Western, and its fate signals the potential for social and cultural change.

As Mary Lea Bandy and Kevin Stoehr note, "The death of a loved one often drives the plot of the early Western" (28), and Vanderhaeghe draws upon this convention as his two main narrative lines set in the 1870s begin with the disappearance of a British man and with the murder of an American girl, respectively. These events draw together an unlikely group of travellers, and a brief overview of the group may bring to mind the cross-section of society found in John Ford's *Stagecoach* (1939), a film that is in part about "overcoming social conflicts, such as those resulting from class-based prejudice" (Bandy and Stoehr 97); however, this work of Canadian historical fiction is no apology for manifest destiny as so many classical Hollywood Westerns are. The matters of sexual orientation and female agency—not to mention the detailed representation of Blackfoot and Crow histories, along with the portrayal of the devastating effects of colonialism and of the American whisky trade, in particular—signal the revisionist nature of the novel. Simon Gaunt has journeyed to North America with Reverend Obadiah Witherspoon of the Church of Christian Israel on a conversion mission. Simon barely survives when he is caught in a blizzard, but he is found by Talks Different, a Two Spirit and holy being of the Crow. Because Simon never sends word of his whereabouts, though, he is deemed missing and presumed dead, prompting his father to send Simon's twin Charles and older brother Addington to Montana to look for him. There they assemble a search party, which includes the historical figure Bear Child (1840-96), better known by his English name Jerry Potts. The grisly murder of fourteen-year-old Marjorie Dray after the arrival of the Gaunt brothers in Fort Benton sets her sister Lucy Stoveall on a quest to find Titus and Joel Kelso, the men she assumes are the murderers. Concealing her true intentions, she joins the Gaunts' search party as cook in order to travel with them. Custis Straw, a Civil War veteran and local rancher, follows her, for as he puts it, "'It's a dangerous business for a woman out there, shepherded by English bumblers'" (Vanderhaeghe, *The Last Crossing* 119). Following Custis is Irish immigrant Aloysius Dooley, saloon-keeper and Custis's faithful friend. Through this microcosm of frontier society, Vanderhaeghe's novel examines the barriers separating people of different genders, classes, and ethnicities, highlighting the exchanges and accommodations made across national and social borders and eschewing the Western's typical valorization of "rugged individualism" (Schatz 50). Human agency may be central to such exchanges; however, the novel also recognizes the role of material agency in social interactions.

Vanderhaeghe dedicates the novel "to all those local historians who keep the particulars of our past alive," and the specifics of material culture contribute to a sense of authenticity in this work of historical fiction. Alessandro Manzoni has observed that readers want the historical novelist "'to put the flesh back on the skeleton that is history'" (qtd. in de Groot 3), and Vanderhaeghe credits local historians with "supply[ing] a lot of texture" ("Making History" 42) through their collections. The apparent life of objects in the novel such as Simon Gaunt's collected buttons, Lucy Stoveall's dowsing wand, or Bear Child's medicine bundle goes beyond mere "texture." The belt that becomes both murder weapon and clue encircles and circulates over the course of the narrative, finally finding its way into Custis Straw's hands, where as a "metonymic contact point," it possesses the power of a fetish object. The cinch acts upon Custis, signifying a type of material agency in a network of relations that forms part of the novel's commentary on personal and social responsibility and "what it means to be male." Jones and Stallybrass argue that "clothes are detachable ...[;] they can move from body to body. That is precisely their danger and their value: they are bearers of identity, ritual, and social memory, even as they confuse social categories" (5). This "danger" and this "value" are evident in the history of the belt, as in the novel's other explorations of social border crossing.

This belt may become detached from the clothing and person who originally owned it, but its function cannot be divorced from that of clothes in general as markers and concealers of identity. Again, to quote Jones and Stallybrass, "[w]e need to understand the animatedness of clothes, their ability to 'pick up' subjects, to mold and shape them both physically and socially, to constitute subjects through their power as material memories. Memories of subordination ... memories of collegiality ... memories of love ... memories of identity itself" (2). The three Gaunt brothers' personalities vary as markedly as their clothing choices while in England, and the transition to North America not only brings out their differences, painting them on a much larger canvas, but also aligns Simon and Addington with the religious and military forces of imperialism. There is an obvious allegorical dimension to the narrative portraits of the brothers, with Addington as the military explorer and sportsman, Simon as the missionary, and Charles as the artist and poet. Of note is the fact that in a novel that employs four first-person narrators along with a third-person perspective, Charles is the only Gaunt allowed to give his version of events, and he is the only brother to return to England, his sense of filial duty calling him away from a love affair with Lucy. In his "[l]ounge jacket, fawn waistcoat, Shepherd's plaid trousers, [and] low-crowned bowler, cocked jauntily to the side of his head" (94), Charles is dismissed as "a genuine English toff" (94) by Custis, but Charles's attention to fashion is not simply a mark of vanity or superiority in wealth and class. He is the one Gaunt who does his best to conform to Victorian notions of what constitutes a true gentleman. In Charles's words to Simon, "'I cannot be a saint, so I shall endeavour to be a gentleman'" (113). Consequently, his brothers' occasional eccentricities of dress are matters of concern for him.

In England, Simon, the emotionally and spiritually sensitive brother, wears the "'hat of antique shape, and cloak of grey'" of Matthew Arnold's "Scholar-Gipsy" (Arnold qtd. in Vanderhaeghe 153). At Oxford, according to Charles, "Simon had fallen under the spell of Matthew Arnold's elegiac poetry.... [H]e had caught the disease of romanticism" (153). Simon goes to a second-hand shop in order to buy what is literally old-fashioned clothing: "a worsted cloak fashionable at the turn of the [previous] century" and "a shapeless, felt hat" (152-53). As a result, he is in danger of being perceived as a pauper or a poacher (153). The notion of romance takes on a potentially twofold meaning when Simon befriends Oronhyatekha (Burning Cloud [1841-1907], another historical figure), a Mohawk man from Six Nations who attends Oxford. Under Reverend Witherspoon's influence, Simon's emulation of the literary ideal celebrated in Arnold's poem of the impoverished Oxford student who goes to learn the gypsy lore turns into something more troubling when Simon's "*one* aim, *one* business, *one* desire" (Arnold, "The Scholar-Gipsy" 152) is to follow Witherspoon on a mission to convert the "Red Indians" (Vanderhaeghe 213). Charles may attempt to "inoculate him against the mysticism of Blake" (199), but he is powerless to stop Simon seeking the "Hidden Holy Land" in North America (213).

Addington may have been forced to resign from the army after leading a brutal attack on rioters in Ireland (160); however, he holds the rank of captain, and both his military bearing and fashion sense lend themselves to a romanticized perception of him as a chivalric hero on the part of the women in his social circle in England. Miss Venables, one of the Toxophilites attending an event on the Gaunt estate, for example, looks at Addington and sees "Sir Tristram's visor lift" (20). This, though, is not Malory's Tristram, but Tennyson's Sir Tristram of "The Last Tournament" (Vanderhaeghe 19) published in 1871 in *Contemporary Review*. Miss Venables wishes to see only the courageous champion, rather than the cynical adulterer who wins "The Tournament of the Dead Innocence" (Tennyson 136). Of course, there may be something attractive about a knight who says, "We are not angels here" (Tennyson 693), even if for Tennyson, Tristram's adultery is a "sign of the pervasive decay throughout [Arthur's] realm" (Staines 103). Robert L. Patten comments that "innocence is as dead at court as the 'maiden babe'" (271) for whom the tournament is named. Addington's façade masks a morally transgressive character and a syphilitic body. As Wyile has already argued, "Vanderhaeghe exposes the corruption and stifling social stratification of Victorian patriarchy," and Addington "symbolizes the hypocrisy and decay beneath the veneer of Victorian moral and sexual propriety." In the open frontier country, Addington revels in the new role of "intrepid British explorer" (30) and for a time enjoys a respite from the symptoms of his illness.[2] Inside the confines of Rowand's Folly—the chief factor's home in Fort Edmonton—where men of authority "see themselves as exemplars of everything British" (282), however, Addington's behaviour becomes erratic, and his diseased perception of the world is made manifest in a dramatic parody of the knight in shining armour when Charles witnesses his brother covered in the mercury that is the treatment for syphilis. In Charles's words, "[t]he flame of the lantern completely burnishes his torso and arms with an armorial, chivalric, silvery brightness. He looks as if he has donned a chain-mail shirt" (293).

Simon and Addington both possess objects while still in England that are imbued with a significance beyond utility, raising thoughts of animism and fetishism. Charles characterizes his brothers' relationship to these objects as a symptom of what he calls the "disease of the Gaunts—superstition," which he defines as "believing in something that isn't there" (358). Simon collects buttons as a child, treating them with "reverence" (374). Charles recalls sensing the life of Simon's collection, but refuses to accept the animist implications, for he claims to be the only one of his family "untouched" (358) by superstition:

> Buttons, buttons, ordinary buttons. He [Simon] spent hours tracing their shapes with his fingers, staring at them, sometimes even popping them in his mouth and sucking them as avidly as he would lemon drops.
> One afternoon in the library, he lifted a button of blue glass to the summer light cascading through the tall windows. I heard him murmur two words, "How bright!" and, as he did, a spot of celestial fire winked on his face as he waggled his button in the sunshine.
> I edged closer. Simon exchanged a bone button for the glass one. Squeezing it tightly, he exclaimed ecstatically, "How warm it is!" and passed it to me. I felt an animal heat burn in my palm, felt that old, dry piece of

bone pulse with living blood and marrow. I hurled the button to the carpet, frightened by Simon's powers of suggestion. (34-35)

Charles, unwilling to consider these ordinary objects as possessing light, warmth, and lifeblood, attributes the experience to his brother's agency. "His spirit affected all of us in a mysterious fashion," recalls Charles (33), which may account in part for Simon's attraction to Arnold's "gipsy-crew, / [who] had arts to rule as they desired / The workings of men's brains" (44-46).

Simon's compulsion to experience the buttons with all of his senses brings to mind Walter Benjamin's observation that a collector has "inside him … spirits, or at least little genii, which have seen to it that … ownership is the most intimate relationship that one can have with objects" (67). However, whereas Benjamin suggests that the collector "lives in" the objects, Simon's buttons seem to have lives of their own. Simon's openness to an animist view of things explains, perhaps, why Simon deems the life of the Crow people "precious" (357) and refuses to leave Talks Different and his new family in the Lodge of the Sun—that and his sexual orientation. (Simon's presence in the Crow community proves disruptive, nevertheless, as he converts Talks Different to Christianity and insists on a monogamous relationship with the bote [347].) Charles takes a rather dim view of Simon's eccentricity, wondering if even as a child reading *Robinson Crusoe*, Simon had "fantasized a life in some barren waste, an existence shared with a primitive incapable of pronouncing judgment on his oddities" (374). As Andrew Jones and Nicole Boivin point out, "[e]thnographic concepts of animism and fetishism … both have been the subject of derogatory comment by Western observers of non-Western societies. The belief in the agency of things seen to be 'self-evidently' inanimate … was considered to be a category error to which 'primitive' societies were especially prone" (342-43). Charles voices the common, dismissive view of animism and fetishism, though as Barbara Johnson illustrates in *Persons and Things*, dismissal of such agency does not necessarily preclude a longing to find "in the sensual enjoyment of the material something divine" and to adore "[a] figure that is a thing in the world … [that] can itself contain the heightened aliveness it gives access to" (139). When Simon asks his brother, "'Do you not desire to love and be loved …?'" Charles claims that he does but will "'settle for affection'" (113) in the same way that he says, "'I cannot comprehend metaphysics and theology, so I shall place my faith in reason and logic'" (113). Given Charles's yearning for the love his father feels only for Simon, the allegiance to "reason and logic" seems as much a protective stance as an embracing of Victorian empiricism. Charles may resist his button-collecting brother's "powers of suggestion," but he later accepts Simon's opinion that his paintings "'scratch no deeper than the surface of things'" (203). They have no fire or pulse.

Addington is something of a collector, too, but his predilections fall under the category of erotic fetishism, which Valerie Steele explains is "not only 'about' sexuality; it is also very much about power and perception" (5). Addington collects trophies as he hunts both game and women. He has a hunter's conventional "collection of animal skins and heads" (14); his illicit acquisitions are "purloin[ed]" (15) gentleladies' items, such as handkerchiefs or gloves, items he holds "to his nose at the moment of climax" (27) when he has sex with servants and prostitutes. His ritual is a perverse version of the knight taking a lady's favour into a competition or battle. The items are only of use to him, though, while the woman's scent, or "spoor," as he thinks of it, remains on the items (15), suggesting that while each item may cross class boundaries, it is not the thing so much as the smell of the absent body that is of value. In many cases, Addington layers the scents of the different classes of women, as well as that of licit and illicit activities: "How many lace handkerchiefs, embroidered gloves, muffs, had he posted anonymously to their virgin owners after using them to sop up the juices from Pearl's [his favourite prostitute's] mott …?" (27).

The object that ends up traversing the ocean and changing owners is not a lady's favour, but the workman's belt that Addington prizes. Originally a gift from Caitlin, the Gaunts' gamekeeper, the belt moves across class lines as a memento, and the exchange is perhaps suggestive of Andrew Jones's claim that "remembrance is a bodily activity as much as a cognitive one" (*Memory* 31). Charles recalls:

> As a child, Addington adored our gamekeeper, old Caitlin…. When the time came for Addington to be sent away to school, he begged the gamekeeper for a memento, something to take away with him to remember the old man by. Do you know what he gave him? His belt. He took it off and said, 'There you go, young master. If I know ye, like as not ye'll be in and out of trouble at school. When time comes to tan your arse, ask them to use this on you. That'll recall your old friend Caitlin well enough, bring him to mind. My own boys certain do remember me by it.' (358)

Added to the crossing of class lines from "old Caitlin" to the "young master" is the layering of adoration and corporal punishment. The lower-class gamekeeper imagines an ongoing relationship between subject and object—the tanning of Addington's wealthy arse—in the process of remembering.

But a relevant and perversely formative moment for Addington comes much earlier, before the twins are born, an event that dramatically illustrates the confluence of Addington's hatred of his father, whose lust he blames for his mother's death (she died giving birth to the twins), his love for his mother, and his fondness for Caitlin, which looks ahead to the man's transgressive activities. Addington recalls walking on the English estate with his mother, who "speaks kindly to him of a recent misdemeanour" (308). Having heard his father speak to his mother "unkindly," the boy had cast his father's gift of lead soldiers into the fire (308). What causes his mother's mouth to "pucker with revulsion" (309), however, is the sight of "[a] grey, weathered outhouse ... covered with the corpses of scavengers and predators, rooks, crows, owls," a macabre collection assembled by the gamekeeper and the young master. "Caitlin ... whom Addington admires more than anyone but Mother, shoots offenders and nails them up on the wall.... Addington had passed Caitlin the spikes the day he had crucified the menagerie" (309). Such a display may not have been unusual for an English estate, for Richard Jefferies describes a gamekeeper's shed "ornamented with rows of dead and dried vermin, furred and feathered, impaled for their misdeeds" (5) in his 1878 publication *The Gamekeeper at Home*. Eunice's distress, however, leads to her dutiful son's attempts to remove the cause of her revulsion. Addington pulls down one of the bodies, and his hands are immediately covered in "feathers, maggots, and putrefying meat" (309). The boy is torn between his allegiance to his lower-class surrogate father and his arguably Oedipal love for his mother and is literally marked by his complicity in the punishment of non-human offenders. The scene ends with his mother wiping the "carrion stench" from him with "her skirts" and telling him he is "brave" and "kind" (310). Addington spends the rest of his life trying to rid himself of that stench, a stench later associated with his syphilis. The adult Addington never has sex with women of his social circle, but, as already mentioned, he holds their stolen garments to his face as he commits acts of sexual violence with prostitutes and servants. (He thinks his father should have left his mother alone and pursued sex with lower-class women.) As a captain in the British army, he tramples and slaughters Irish protesters without compassion or compunction, and is eventually forced to resign his position. Back on his father's estate, he becomes a poacher, seeking to hurt the man who "poisoned his life" (24) and to subvert his father's authority as landowner, an authority hard-won by the railway man whose own father had been a "builder of gimcrack houses" (11).

Charles, who knows nothing of his brother's criminal activities, does contemplate the "'idea'" of the belt, admitting that "'what intrigued [him] about it was what it meant to Addington'" (359). He also comments on the lack of propriety it signified: "'When Addington came to manhood, he wore Caitlin's belt on sporting occasions, riding to hounds, shooting. Quite incongruous since my brother was a bit of a dandy among the sporting set. To wear the belt of a servant hardly seemed proper. But Addington believed it brought him success in the field'" (358-59). Given that belts were not commonly worn by fashionable men in the 1860s and 1870s—waistcoats covered braces (suspenders)—the gamekeeper's belt would be particularly conspicuous.[3]

The "incongruous" and "hardly ... proper" "workman's belt" (358-59) becomes part of Addington's night-poaching attire. He dons only trousers and the belt, wearing the memento of the gamekeeper, while engaging in the criminal activities of the poacher, activities that he finds sexually arousing; "the blood reminds him of the smell of a woman on his fingers. Sexual congress" (25). As part of his ritual, Addington leaves pieces of a deer haunch as "his gift for the foxes, the ravens" (25); he remembers both the predatory animals who are potential "offenders" to the gamekeeper and the gamekeeper himself.

Henry Gaunt assumes that poachers are "killing his deer, selling his venison in London game shops" (14), and there is reason to think so, given what D. J. V. Jones calls "an extensive network of dealing in these goods [which] had developed to meet the spiralling demand for cheap meat for the urban working classes and for game from the middle and upper classes" (832); however, not all poaching was about money. According to Christopher Holdenby's *Folk of the Furrow* (1913), it was also about "'doing' a person in a better position ... the suggestion of a just reprisal'" (qtd. in D. J. V. Jones 828). Such a "reprisal" was fraught with danger, for during the Victorian period those caught poaching at night could be subject to fines, imprisonment, or even transportation. D. J. V. Jones observes that for some the risk was exciting, and poaching "had the compulsive attraction of 'drug-taking'" (835). In retrospect, Addington sees the "business at Sythe Grange, stealing into the night with a longbow, dodging the gamekeeper and his minions, risking mantraps and spring guns" as "an invalid's attempt to combat torpor, to stir sluggish blood with a dose of artificial danger. The red deer a sacrifice to propitiate the savage gods of his malady" (159-60). The belt he wears connects him not only to his surrogate father but to the notions of masculinity linked to the figure of the gamekeeper in general. Of the gamekeeper, Richard Jeffries writes: "freedom and constant contact with nature have made him every inch a man; and here in this nineteenth century of civilised effeminacy may be seen some relic of what men were in the old feudal days when they dwelt practically in the woods" (12). Given that Addington is troubled by the effects of the treatments for his syphilis, finding that the doctor's prescriptions only make him "*womanish*" (159), he may well want the connection to such a "relic." Jeffries also calls the gamekeeper "[a] keen, shrewd judge of horseflesh" (12).

Addington looks at women with "a discriminating horse-dealer's eye" (16) when he is not sizing them up as prey.

The belt leaves Addington's body in North America. By the time Charles notices that the belt is missing from Addington's possessions—after Addington's death by grizzly, near the end of the novel—it is pretty clear to readers that Addington's belt is in fact the murder weapon introduced in the opening chapters when fourteen-year-old Marjorie Dray is found raped and murdered.

Custis Straw, one of the first-person narrators, is introduced in the novel when he is accused of the murder. When shown the body, he responds:

> Jesus Christ Almighty. Poor little Marjorie Dray in a homespun dress, sorrel hair fanned out, bits of dried grass and twigs tangled in her curls, a belt pulled tight around her throat. She's bitten her bottom lip clean through.
> I have to steady myself against the sight....
> ... There's streaks of rusty blood, blisters of dried spunk on her thin thighs.... I have to shut my eyes.... (42)

For readers looking for clues, the description of Madge's hair as "sorrel" and the fact that her body is covered with a saddle blanket (57) are of note, since Addington, who is notoriously hard on horses, rides a sorrel both in his recurring dream of the attack on Irish rioters and on the journey to find Simon. With respect to the belt, here it is "pulled tight"; however, Addington earlier "cinches" the belt around his waist (25), and Custis uses the nouns "cinch" and "girdle" at various points for the belt. As a noun, "cinch" usually refers to a saddle girth, and the verb "to cinch" can mean to "girdle" ("cinch"). The murderer seems to have felt as much compassion for Madge as he does horses whose legs he "smashe[s]" (8)—that is, none at all. Back in England, when Addington's reckless riding results in serious injury to a horse, the gamekeeper "deliver[s] the coup de grâce" (8); there is nothing merciful about Addington's silencing of the young girl with the gamekeeper's belt.

What spurs Custis into action after his initial viewing of the body is Sheriff Hinckey and Justice Daniels's refusal to remove the belt from the girl's throat; Custis takes it off himself, in spite of the fact that he is tampering with evidence. He can no longer bear to witness the spectacle of male violence. He at once distances himself from the act of aggression by proclaiming himself a "'suspenders man'" (44), but Justice Daniels orders him to try the belt on. It clearly does not fit, yet it attaches itself to Custis nevertheless.

Herb Wyile asserts that Custis is a "chivalric foil" ("Doing the Honourable Thing") to the Gaunt brothers, and I would say to Addington in particular, given the relationship between chivalric knight and Western hero as defined by Bandy and Stoehr. "As the symbolic embodiment of passion as well as *com*passion, the traditional cowboy hero may be compared with the medieval knight who undertakes self-transforming journeys and adventures, adhering to some code of chivalry. In many cases each gains a sense of moral self-improvement through his love of a beautiful maiden whom he wants to serve" (21). Whereas Addington embodies moral degradation as he murders a young girl and embarks on a self-interested quest for fame and a trophy grizzly, Custis is the man of honour who "undertakes self-transforming journeys" as he follows Lucy out of love and genuine concern. He later guides Charles to the Crow camp, where Simon resides with the bote. Custis, though, does not fully conform to the genre's conventions. Bandy and Stoehr define the "classic westerner" as "a southerner who fought in the Civil War on the losing side and who has no choice but to become a westerner" (190). Custis fought for the Union, not the Confederacy, and he is a man who opposes class, gender, and racial divisions.

Both men are haunted by their experiences in the army, yet Addington puts the recurring nightmare of his military mount transforming into a scabrous nag (24) down to the effects of his illness rather than seeing a representation of his own moral and physical corruption, while Custis consciously bears the burden of his participation in the Civil War; feelings of complicity and guilt weigh heavily upon him. Wyile notes—with reference to Anne McClintock's *Imperial Leather*—that Vanderhaeghe "turns the tables on … the Victorian paranoia over contagion, a biological image for a largely social anxiety about 'boundary order'" by "revers[ing] the course of contagion and figur[ing] imperialism as a migration of the ills of Victorian society outward to the margins of empire, subverting the trope of the genteel Victorian being confronted with the lawless, depraved Wild West." Addington is certainly a carrier of moral and physical contagion. Custis, by contrast, is a man whose sense of honour, as Wyile aptly puts it, "excludes the sexual competition and assumption of masculine superiority" and stands apart from "the rugged, individualistic culture of the frontier." Custis has only two friends in town—Aloysius and the town doctor—and is considered eccentric because he chooses not to exploit others. He deals fairly with First Nations traders, and Aloysius recalls Custis's argument that former slaves should be paid "'back wages owed for a couple hundred years of labour'" (91). In the words of Dr. Bengough, Custis "'does his best to harm no one but himself'" (163). When a young man, his mother's friend tells him, "'[y]ou like women, Custis. But you behave towards them just as you do towards men you like. You must recognize the distinctions that separate the sexes'" (123). Custis takes this to mean he should "[d]ance attendance instead of trying to plumb their real and lasting qualities" (123). Part of the appeal of Custis to Vanderhaeghe's twenty-first-century audience is his refusal to "recognize the distinctions" present in nineteenth-century notions of gender, race, and class. Custis's best suit is made of broadcloth (121), a fabric that Brian P. Luskey claims was "democratic as well as respectable" (148) in nineteenth-century America.[4]

Straw knows nothing of the history of the belt when he removes it from the young girl's body and decides to become its "keeper" (66). He walks out of the jail, not realizing he is still wearing it, and the leather cinch that first is "clammy as the dead flesh [he] just touched" (42) inside the jail becomes a "girdle of fire" (65) once he becomes aware of its presence outside of the building. Removing the "burning belt" (66), he rolls it and puts it in his pocket, determined that he at least will not forget the girl as Sheriff Hinckey and Justice Daniels will. (It is pretty clear that the forces of the law will do nothing.) "Memento" seems hardly the right term for the belt once it has become a murder weapon, but it may be useful to think of Andrew Jones's description of the act of "remembrance as a dialogic encounter between the experiencing person and the artefact" (25-26).

As a piece of evidence, the belt, which Custis describes as "[a] working man's belt, cinch for a roustabout, trapper, muleskinner, saddle tramp" (92), does not, as he puts it, "narrow things down. You could fit Fort Benton's quality in a canoe; the ordinary folk would fill a couple of steamboats" (92). It is the sort of thing one of the Kelso brothers could very well own. To echo Jones and Stallybrass, "[the belt] is detachable ... [and it] can move from body to body. That is precisely [its] danger and [its] value" (5). As the only material tie to the murderer, it takes on a new value; outside of its original context, the belt is a dangerously misleading clue. Its metonymic power transforms the length of leather into a type of fetish object for Custis.

Feldman employs the term "metonymic contact point" in a discussion of museum objects, in particular, clothing confiscated in the concentration camps of World War II.

> [M]etonymic contact points are often created through acts of violence wholly disconnected from museums, only to enter museum discourse after an intervening period of time. Metonymic contact points, therefore, are often given meaning within discourses of memory and relics, as opposed to discourses of science and types. What distinguishes the metonymic contact point from an ordinary object, however, is the physical, sensory experience of the body that it symbolizes. A shoe may stand as an example for one or many categories of shoes. As a metonymic contact point, however, it stands for the relations between persons and objects in the contact point. (259)

Custis, of course, is not a museum-goer, nor is he "wholly disconnected" from the violent act employing the belt. Nevertheless, the belt is a contact point with the unidentified killer as well as with the fatal subjugation and objectification of Marjorie, the girl whom Custis vows to remember. What Elaine Freedgood calls the "powerful properties" (14) of metonymy, a "figure of contiguity" (52), are evident both within the framework of the narrative and outside of it. Freedgood observes that "[r]eaders of metonymy routinely and unconsciously recuperate all kinds of relationships between the thing in the text and those things outside the text with which it can be connected, and argues that the "strong, ... materializing, metonymic reading" (11) of objects in Victorian fiction may offer access to the "cultural archives ... preserved, unsuspected, in the things of realism" (1). Custis keeps the cinch used to murder Madge, learning "every inch of it by heart" (92), and under its associative influence, he is taken back through a personal archive of his experiences during the American Civil War, a journey that affects both mind and body. For readers, the "working man's belt" that functions as a memento for both Addington and Custis—though in very different ways—is arguably a metonym that "creates ... a proliferating semiotic chain" (Freedgood 102).

As a fetish (in the anthropological sense), the belt is connected to previous wearers and specific events. In *A Sense of Things: The Object Matter of American Literature*, Bill Brown cites Herbert Spencer's *The Principles of Sociology* (1897) and calls attention to Spencer's "overarching point that in the 'fetichistic conception' of the world ... each 'person's nature inheres not only in all parts of his body, but in his dress and the things he has used,' to the point where such things could assume lives of their own" (qtd. in Brown 116). According to Jones and Boivin, "fetishes concentrate or localize human experience and belief in the power of objects" (344). Andrew Jones builds upon Peter Pels's observation that the fetish "'foregrounds materiality because it is the most aggressive expression of the social life of things. Fetishism is animism with a vengeance. Its matter strikes back'" (Pels qtd. in A. Jones 33). Jones claims that fetishism "can both subjugate and dominate persons.... [W]hereas animist belief proposes that spirit resides *in* matter, fetishism posits an assumption of the spirit *of* matter: objects have spirit and are able to act of their own volition to attract or repel people" (*Memory* 33). As soon as the belt enters Custis's possession, the relationship between subject and object blurs. Custis claims, "I owned the belt, or it owned me" (323) and compares himself to Aloysius's "old Mam [who] was always clicking her rosary and when she wasn't, she was always thinking she ought to be" (92). "A length of wide, thick leather, black, stained, nicked, scarred. Ordinary, clumsy brass buckle" becomes Custis's "dusky rosary" (92). He describes the "[t]hree brass studs on the tip of it as if they'd been put there to add sting to a whipping. The sight of them stings [him] …" (92). The threat of punishment from Caitlin is manifest in the belt for Addington, but Custis carries a complex burden of memories for which he punishes himself. Though Aloysius warns him that the belt "'ain't a keepsake no sane man clings to'" (93), Custis cannot stop touching it or thinking about it: "I see it in my sleep, can't escape it waking" (92). Jones and Stallybrass remark on "a surprising overlap between … so-called 'fetishes' and the Catholic rosary [as] [b]oth focus power in a worn object" (9). Given his early life in Indiana, Custis's influences would more likely have been Methodist than Catholic, and he is not a believer in a conventional sense, having "lost [his] faith" (261) as a result of his battlefield experience. Nevertheless, his tactile response to the belt is suggestive of his enacting a kind of penance.[5] His idea of the belt is drastically different from Addington's.

The movement of the belt from one man to the other by way of the fatally silenced female has implications for what Wyile sees as the novel's contribution to a "reconceptualisation of masculinity and femininity" ("Doing the Honourable Thing"). The American girl in the "homespun dress" does not fit into Addington's usual social categories, but then the mentally and physically ill Englishman simply may not see a human agent before him in the teenager; rather, he wants to believe she is a treatment or a cure, for he recalls a Sergeant Carlyle, who "'swore … that the surest remedy for a blood disease was congress with a virgin. A fresh young girl drew the poison right out of your system'" (Vanderhaeghe 295), rather like a poultice. Having travelled away from the constraints of his social milieu in Britain to Fort Benton—which has been called "the Sagebrush Sodom" (Schneider 67; Touchie 151)—Addington moves beyond the pale, conflating human and non-human prey, killing the girl with his memento of the gamekeeper. When Custis takes ownership of the murder weapon and tool of male aggression, he finds himself in a position of identification with both male murderer and female victim before he rids himself of the belt.

Custis shamefully recounts an erotic dream he has after Marjorie's funeral, which he blames on the "bad combination" of "[t]wo pipes of opium and that belt before bed" (93). In the dream Madge is on top of him, so he is not in an immediate position of dominance, and he does try to "lift her off" (93). However, Custis confesses, "my pleasure rose up in me too fierce and I gave way to it." As his "pleasure" grows, Madge shrinks to the size of "a doll" (93). Custis is aware that "a dream isn't a thought," but in adding that "it surely is a close cousin to one" (93-94), he suggests his complicity in a society that condones male dominance and the objectification of women, even as he is set up in opposition to a man like Addington.

From the time Custis learns of Marjorie's murder, he associates her fate with that of the young soldiers he saw killed and injured in the Civil War. Both contexts feature the killing of innocent or naive youth—deeply troubling to the middle-aged Custis—and both point to a social and political acceptance of the violent assertion of male authority and superiority. As Lucy says, "'It's clear the law can't keep a woman safe in this town, and it's no use outside it'" (59). Custis's battlefield experiences lead him to deny the honour and glory of war. When he is drawn into a situation in which he has to kill Titus Kelso—to engage in the violent competition he had renounced—he is struck by an ailment that Fort Benton's doctor is never able identify. In a classic scene of psychological trauma manifesting itself in physical fever and delirium, Custis "thrash[es] about, bellowing, his mind seemingly enmeshed in the bloody snares of former battlefields" (254). Burning with fever, Custis relives the Battle of the Wilderness (Virginia, May 1864) and his disastrous attempt to rescue a friend taken prisoner. Custis barely escapes being burned alive as a forest fire rages, his injured legs useless. His memory of begging another soldier (his "man-horse" [271]) to carry him out is coloured by the shame of what he perceives as his own cowardice and by his failure to save Hoagy. Clearly, the trauma and guilt associated with Marjorie's murder and then Titus's death merge with that engendered by Hoagy Pinsen's perishing in the flames; the gamekeeper's belt becomes the "girdle of fire" of personal and social responsibility and the survivor guilt that encompasses Custis.[6]

During an encounter with Joel Kelso and Danny Rand (a saddle tramp with a nasty temper), Custis suffers humiliation and experiences a final identification with both victim and murderer that leads to his purposeful severing of his ties to the belt. Just after Joel testifies that he has never seen the belt before, confirming that Titus was not the murderer, Rand grabs the belt and cinches it around Custis's neck, and suddenly "the belt that choked Madge Dray is around [his] throat" (322), placing him in the position of the female victim. Custis, still ill, loses control of his bowels, and he is left alone, "soaked in shit and blood and shame" (322). Through the presence of the belt, Custis experiences something of the horror and degradation felt at the time of violent subjugation. With the disgrace and humiliation, however, comes an epiphany for Custis. He tries the belt on once again to find that he has lost so much weight that "the tongue fits in the punch hole perfectly." At the moment the cinch fits as it would have around the murderer's waist, however, Custis is able to let it go. "A bad conscience, the guilt of all the dead I left behind me," he says, "had to attach itself to something" (323). While it is Charles who makes reference to "sitting like the ship becalmed in *The Rime of the Ancient Mariner*" (177), as Addington decides sport is more important than the search for Simon, it is Custis who, like the Mariner, has experienced the agony of watching those around him die and who wears his guilt around his neck, if briefly. The Mariner, however, shoots the albatross for no apparent reason and so "Instead of the cross, the Albatross / About [his] neck was hung" (141-42); Custis commits no real crime in surviving. Nevertheless, once the belt completes its circle from Addington's waist to Madge's neck, to Custis's neck and then to Custis's waist, Custis understands that his "spirit has wanted to die" (323). The Mariner has to learn to respect all life; Custis has to learn to respect and forgive himself. He decides it is finally time to let go of the "dusky rosary" and "to stop fingering Madge Dray's death, turning it over and over in [his] hands, carrying it around in [his] pocket" (359). According to William Pietz, "[t]he fetish is always a meaningful fixation of a singular event; it is above all a 'historical' object, the enduring form and force of a singular event" (qtd. in Jones and Boivin 344), and here, the belt that is first compared to Madge's skin becomes equated with the event of her death.

Whereas Addington is plagued by an incurable disease, Custis, purged of his guilt, recovers from his ailment and begins to move forward, saying, "[m]y body has to put one foot in front of the other, haul my spirit past the faces in the lighted windows, the gapers in the street, the whispers" (323). Perhaps a sign of the belt's continued life, though, is the fact that Custis does not simply throw the strip of leather away: he chops it up and burns the pieces (359). This reads almost as an exorcism, or if the belt is linked to the contagion of violently perverse notions of masculinity, then Custis takes decisive measures to prevent the spread of the disease. Custis destroys the belt physically, renouncing both his ownership of it and its ownership of him. When Charles mentions after Addington's death that a belt is missing from his brother's things, Custis becomes the only person to know the probable identity of the killer. He opts not to pursue the matter, thinking to himself, "if it was the Captain's belt, would he have left his luck on a young girl's neck? I could ask Gaunt whether he remembers studs. But I won't. Because, God willing, here's where I make an end to it" (359).

In severing the tie and burning the belt, Custis destroys the metonymic contact point to the horrifying event of the Marjorie's murder and to the murderer, breaking the semiotic chain and preventing the repetition of this narrative of violence. A belt can suggest both linearity and circularity, and given that this cinch is also compared to a serpent—when Custis tosses the belt to Joel, Joel "jumps like [he] threw him a snake" (321)—it brings to mind the *ouroboros*. As H. B. de Groot has illustrated, the *ouroboros* has been used as both "an emblem of eternity" and of "the temporal process" (561), but for Coleridge, it "expresses the unity of the successful work of art" (562). As Coleridge writes in a letter to Joseph Cottle: "The common end of all *narrative,* nay, of *all,* Poems is to convert a *series* into a *Whole*: to make those events, which in real or imagined History move on in a *strait* [sic] Line, assume to our Understandings a *circular* motion—the snake with it's [sic] Tail in it's [sic] Mouth" (Coleridge, *Collected Letters*). The story of the belt for Addington does not necessarily move only in a straight line from Caitlin's gift to Addington's theft of Madge's life. The "awful carrion stench" (Vanderhaeghe 309) associated with that formative moment of conflict in his allegiance to Caitlin and to his mother is present as "carrion fetor ... oozing from his own body" (310) just prior to his death by grizzly. The man who thought he would find the "virgin cure" in the open landscape of the prairies and in the body of Madge smells his own corruption before he strips himself naked for the "crisp morning air [to rinse] him spotless" (310). Addington indeed leaves "his luck" on Madge's neck if the luck in question is that of successfully dominating everyone around him. When Bear Child, whom Addington has tried to commission to find him a grizzly, hears that Addington has tried to buy a Blackfoot girl, he decides that the "'Englishman needs to meet his bear quickly'" (304). Subsequently, the boy who helped the gamekeeper mount a macabre collection of "offenders" by handing him the spikes becomes a man "stabbing at the grizzly with an arrow in his fist" (312). In the grasp of the grizzly's jaws, Addington, who once played out his fantasy of angling for a woman—his "'Dearest trout'" (27)—now "flops limp ... legs thrashing back and forth like a trout's tail" (312). (No one carries him from danger as in the case of Custis when his leg is "flopping like a fish" [269].) Subject becomes object; predator becomes the prey—and then so much "pulp" (312). Watching the spectacle, Bear Child counts coup, and then: "It is finished" (312). Together, the Indigenous human and non-human agents put an end to the danger posed by Addington. They may not be able to put an end to all that he represents, in terms of imperialism and moral corruption, but there is a measure of poetic justice that reflects postcolonial issues contemporary with the writing of the novel. Custis's active "here's where I make an end to it" marks his decision to let go of the guilt and to let Marjorie live in his memory rather than continue to obsess over the event of her death. The Civil War veteran furthers his distance from what Wyile terms the "dominant codes of masculine behaviour and honour ... that reinforce uneven and exploitative relations of power—power over women, power over animals, power over other men—instead of empathetic, mutually respectful, and equitable co-existence with others"—the codes that shape Addington's life and death in the novel, but also codes that still threaten to form a noose around the neck of Western society in general. Afterward, Custis does not ride off into the sunset; he accepts Lucy's proposal of marriage.[7]

The "transformational properties" of things (Jones and Boivin 337) in *The Last Crossing* have a role in the destabilization of a "world of social relations" informed by hierarchies of gender, class, and ethnicity. The novel itself subverts what Jerome de Groot calls the "problematic gendering" of genre fiction. De Groot notes that historical fiction for men commonly features "journeys, quests or adventures," while that for women focuses on "social, personal and cultural development and crises" (79). Custis's story is but one part of the collective narrative that refuses such generic distinctions within the frameworks of the historical novel and of the Western in particular. Vanderhaeghe, who grew up when "the Western was a staple of television and the movies" (Vanderhaeghe, "Making History" 29), crosses such divides, painting not only a much more complex portrait of the forces shaping the American and Canadian West than that found in much popular culture but also one that champions "honour and dignity" while "eschewing violence for violence's sake as a stepping stone to prove that you're masculine [and] fighting ... a generalised contempt for women" ("Making History" 50). We may be "creatures of context," says Vanderhaeghe, but "there's the notion of personal acts, personal decisions, and the ability to make moral choices, ethical choices, and different ways of thinking.... [E]xistence precedes essence. We're in the process of making ourselves, and in making ourselves as individuals we're also making history" (51). To step back from the Western to the "intergeneric hybridity" (de Groot 2) of the historical novel, Vanderhaeghe's notion of "making" speaks to the many connections of historical fiction to the *Bildungsroman* and the formation of individuals and nations. A man chops a belt into pieces and burns them. A man and woman from disparate backgrounds, each possessed of painful memories, choose to move north of the Medicine Line in hopes of healing old wounds and creating a new life for themselves and their daughter. Woven in with these narrative threads are questions of relevance to our realities as readers. In what narratives of oppression or exploitation are we complicit? Have we the ability and the means to "make an end" to them? Can Canada be that place that accommodates difference, even as it struggles with the legacy of a colonial past? De Groot observes that for theorists such as Georg Lukàcs, "the historical novel creates a living empathy, a live connection between then and now" (27). I see this connection come to life for students, along with an equally vital connection between here and there, in the case of the Canadian historical fiction that I teach. Spanning both temporal and geographical distances, novels such as *The Last Crossing* tell great stories, but they also perform important work. Like Simon with his "powers of suggestion," authors such as Vanderhaeghe make us feel the bones of history "pulse with living blood and marrow," allowing us to trace the presence of the past and reminding us of our own agency in shaping our society and influencing its future.

NOTES

1 Wyile observes, "Speculative fiction [in the usual sense of science fiction] is not an objective, detached, authentic glimpse into the future, but rather usually a very purposeful, subjective, and rhetorical extrapolation from present circumstances, and the same might be said of historical fiction. Except, of course, that it faces in the opposite direction" (xii). With reference to Brian McHale's *Postmodernist Fiction*, Wyile writes that "[t]he notion that historical discourse is essentially speculative rather than mimetic has certainly given novelists the elbow room to develop their own speculative fictions, probing the gap or 'dark areas' of received history, 'those aspects about which the "*official*" record has nothing to report'" (13).

2 An issue of the *British Medical Journal* from 1903 does promote "[t]he open-air treatment of syphilis," as E. H. Douty writes, "Open air ... rest, high feeding, graduated exercise, and if possible, a bright, dry, bracing climate, are our means for enabling an individual ... to escape the eventual horrors of syphilis" (487).

3 According to Joan Nunn, "In 1857 trousers gathered into a narrow waistband with a strap and buckle at the back were introduced; known as American trousers, they could be worn without braces, and led to the waistcoat being discarded for informal wear in the 1890s, particularly in America, and to the wearing of belts with trousers" (142).

4 Luskey, with reference to an 1853 article by Horace Greeley, notes, "By mid-century, manufacturers and labourers took the lead in 'mechanical invention,' which led to improvements in production and a steep decline in the price of ... high-quality suits. Now "[e]very sober mechanic' ... had the opportunity to own 'one or two suits of broadcloth'" (148).

5 While it is Matthew Arnold's "The Scholar-Gipsy" that Charles cites in the novel, "Dover Beach" and the "girdle" of faith come to mind in the contemplation of Custis.

> The Sea of Faith
> Was once, too, at the full, and round earth's shore
> Lay like the folds of a bright girdle furled.
> But now I only hear
> Its melancholy, long, withdrawing roar,
> Retreating, to the breath
> Of the night-wind, down the vast edges drear
> And naked shingles of the world. (21-28)

Custis loses that "bright girdle" of faith, and his tenure as the "keeper" of the "girdle of fire" is physically and emotionally fraught.

6 The number fourteen figures in the descriptions of Custis's ailment, as in his "deep insensibility for fourteen hours" (253) after receiving treatment. Given that Madge is first described by Justice Daniels as "'thirteen, fourteen year old'" (43), the number seems significant.

7 Unbeknownst to her lover, Lucy is pregnant when Charles returns to England. When she proposes to Custis, he accepts the offer of marriage and becomes a loving father to the child—who is named Marjorie. The family leaves the United States for a ranch near Calgary.

WORKS CITED

Arnold, Matthew. "Dover Beach." *The Broadview Anthology of British Literature: The Victorian Era*. Eds. Joseph Black et al. Peterborough, ON: Broadview, 2006. 446. Print.

———. "The Scholar-Gipsy." Black et al. 439-42. Print.

Bandy, Mary Lea, and Kevin Stoehr. *Ride, Boldly Ride: The Evolution of the American Western*. Berkeley: U of California P, 2012. Print.

Benjamin, Walter. "Unpacking My Library." *Illuminations*. Ed. Hannah Arendt. Trans. Harry Zohn. London: Fontana/Collins, 1973. 59-67. Print.

Brown, Bill. *A Sense of Things: The Object Matter of American Literature*. Chicago: U of Chicago P, 2003. Print.

———. "Thing Theory." *Critical Inquiry* 28.1 (Autumn 2001): 1-22. *JSTOR*. Web. 29 July 2010.

Bryson, Michael. "*A Good Man* by Guy Vanderhaeghe." Review. *Quill and Quire*. Oct. 2011. Web. 26 Sept. 2011.

"cinch." *Oxford English Dictionary Online*. Oxford UP, 2011. Web. 29 Sept. 2011.

Coleridge, Samuel Taylor. *The Collected Letters of Samuel Taylor Coleridge*. Vol. 4 (1815-1819). Ed. Earl Leslie Griggs. Oxford: Clarendon, 1959. InteLex Corporation, 2002. Web.

———. *The Rime of the Ancient Mariner*. Black et al. 415-24. Print.

Comeau-Vasilopoulos, Gayle M. "Oronhyatekha." *Dictionary of Canadian Biography*. Vol. 13. U of Toronto. Web. 12 July 2014.

de Groot, H. B. "The Ouroboros and the Romantic Poets: A Renaissance Emblem in Blake, Coleridge, and Shelley." *English Studies* 50 (1969): 553-64. Print.

de Groot, Jerome. *The Historical Novel*. London: Routledge, 2010. Print.

Douty, E. H. "The Open-Air Treatment of Syphilis." *British Medical Journal* 1.2200 (1903): 487-89. *J-STOR*. Web. 11 July 2014.

Feldman, Jeffrey David. "Contact Points: Museums and the Lost Body Problem." *Sensible Objects: Colonialism, Museums and Material Culture*. Ed. Elizabeth Edwards, Chris Gosden, and Ruth B. Phillips. Oxford: Berg, 2006. 245-67. Print.

Freedgood, Elaine. *The Ideas in Things: Fugitive Meaning in the Victorian Novel*. Chicago: U of Chicago P, 2006. Print.

Jefferies, Richard. *The Gamekeeper at Home* (1878). *The Amateur Poacher* (1879). London: Oxford UP, 1960. Print.

Johnson, Barbara. *Persons and Things*. Cambridge, MA: Harvard UP, 2008. Print.

Jones, Andrew. *Memory and Material Culture*. Cambridge: Cambridge UP, 2007. Print.

Jones, Andrew M., and Nicole Boivin. "The Malice of Inanimate Objects: Material Agency." *The Oxford Handbook of Material Culture Studies*. Eds. Dan Hicks and Mary C. Beaudry. Oxford: Oxford UP, 2010. 333-51. Print.

Jones, Ann, and Peter Stallybrass. *Renaissance Clothing and the Materials of Memory*. Cambridge: Cambridge UP, 2000. Print.

Jones, D. J. V. "The Poacher: A Study in Victorian Crime and Protest." *Historical Journal* 22.4 (Dec. 1979): 825-60. *J-STOR*. Web. 29 Apr. 2011.

Luskey, Brian P. *On the Make: Clerks and the Quest for Capital in Nineteenth-Century America*. New York: New York UP, 2010. Print.

Nunn, Joan. *Fashion in Costume: 1200-2000*. 2nd ed. Lanham: New Amsterdam Books, 2000. Print.

Patten, Robert L. "The Contemporaneity of *The Last Tournament*." *Victorian Poetry* 47.1 (Spring 2009): 259-83. *Project Muse*. Web. 11 July 2014.

Schatz, Thomas. *Hollywood Genres: Formulas, Filmmaking, and the Studio System*. New York: McGraw-Hill, 1981. Print.

Schneider, Stephen. *Iced: The Story of Organized Crime in Canada*. Mississauga, ON: John Wiley and Sons Canada, 2009. Print.

Staines, David. *Tennyson's Camelot: The Idylls of the King and Its Medieval Sources*. Waterloo: Wilfrid Laurier UP, 1982. Print.

Steele, Valerie. *Fetish: Fashion, Sex, and Power*. New York: Oxford UP, 1996. Print.

Tennyson, Alfred Lord. "The Last Tournament." *The Idylls of the King: Victorian Poetry and Poetics*. 2nd ed. Ed. Walter E. Houghton and G. Robert Stange. Boston: Houghton Mifflin, 1968. 137-46. Print.

Touchie, Rodger D. *Bear Child: The Life and Times of Jerry Potts*. Victoria, BC: Heritage House, 2005. *E-Books@Carleton*. Web. 2 Oct. 2011.

Vanderhaeghe, Guy. *The Last Crossing*. Toronto: McClelland and Stewart, 2002. Print.

———. Interview by Herb Wyile. "Making History." *Speaking in the Past Tense: Canadian Novelists on Writing Historical Fiction*. Waterloo: Wilfrid Laurier UP, 2007. 25-51. Print.

Wyile, Herb. "Doing the Honourable Thing: Guy Vanderhaeghe's *The Last Crossing*." *Canadian Literature* 185 (Summer 2005): 59-74. *Proquest*. Web. 23 Aug. 2010.

———. *Speculative Fictions: Contemporary Canadian Novelists and the Writing of History*. Montreal and Kingston: McGill-Queen's UP, 2002. Print.

PART II
Immaterialities

CHAPTER 6

Obama's Playlist
Materializing Transnational Desire at the CBC

Mark Simpson

> The capacity of falsity to produce truth is what mediators are all about.
> —Gilles Deleuze

In early January 2009, CBC Radio 2 announced a new contest on its website:

> Beginning Monday, January 5, CBC Radio 2 invites Canadians to help select the top 49 songs from north of the 49th parallel that would best define our country to incoming U.S. President Barack Obama. An avid music fan, Obama is known for his eclectic tastes ranging from old-school R&B to blues to classical. His playlist could definitely benefit from some Canadian content, especially given the depth of our musical offerings spanning a wide variety of genres and representing our culture from coast to coast. That's why we're asking you to help compile the list of our most definitive Canadian songs!

The terms of this invitation clearly aim to strike a nationalist chord. As imagined here, "Canadian content" offers depth alongside breadth, and affords cultural representativeness "from coast to coast." Its scope and tone, in other words, are capacious—making it a perfect match for Obama's "eclectic tastes" (and thereby making Obama secretly, intuitively Canadian). Playlistnumerology itself—"49 songs from north of the 49th parallel"—will drive home the integrity of Canada's cultural identity by evoking, so as to reinforce, Canada's latitudinal demarcation from the United States.

At the same time, however, the announcement goes beyond purely or narrowly nationalist modes of feeling. It presupposes two musical relations: specificity, in which musical selection showcases national character and divines national identity; yet also universality, in which musical fandom supplies the tissue that connects any radio listener to the incoming leader of the global hegemon. In combining these relations, the ritual on offer works to *fuse* nationalist promotion with transnational adoration: Obama's universal appeal—the attributes making him so lovable to people around the globe in the months surrounding his election—triggers (and merits) an upsurge in nationalist as well as cross-border affection and desire among listeners to the CBC. Obama-love inspires us-love; we embrace ourselves in embracing him.

Premised on this fusion of national pride and transnational desire, the discourse of voting central to Radio 2's contest will indicate the force yet also the irony of pervasive fantasies about democratic life and culture in the contemporary moment. Increasingly, the act of merely venturing opinion in the virtual public sphere comes to demarcate the normal—and normative—terms of political as well as cultural possibility; yet the proliferation of such opportunities to vote or vent arguably constitutes a symptom, not at all of intensive publicity, but instead of the privatization of culture and social life and the total subsumption of the bios. Jodi Dean names the conjuncture at issue "communicative capitalism"—"an ideological formation wherein capitalism and democracy converge in networked communication technologies" (123). By means of such convergence, Dean continues, "[c]ommunicative capitalism seizes, privatizes, and attempts to monetize the social substance. It doesn't depend on the commodity-thing. It directly exploits the social relation at the heart of value" (129). Such are the disquieting coordinates within which the CBC mounted its contest, encouraging listeners to embrace a fantasy of *prosthetic franchise* inextricable from yet irreducible to nationalist sentiment—and thereby to participate, vicariously and retrospectively, in electing Obama by helping to choose a playlist for him.

What structures of feeling, at once national and transnational, does this radio event presuppose—or indeed help to materialize? This chapter will advance some provisional answers to that question. Doing so will require some clarification of "prosthetic franchise" as a concept along with some comment on the role and condition of CBC Radio 2, as a state-sponsored broadcaster, within the Canadian iteration of contemporary neoliberal culture. At issue are not least the vicissitudes of national culture in what we have come to understand—or indeed to presuppose—as an era of globalization. I take up some of these vicissitudes below with respect to radio culture and radio form, past and present, as well as to communicative capitalism's attention economy, and I conclude by contemplating an alternate kind of playlist, one attuned to the challenges of counter-public broadcast. First, though, a brief account of the contest, its outcomes, and the debate it inspired.

1. PLAYLIST FOR A PRESIDENT

Unveiled on 5 January 2009, sixteen days before Obama's inauguration, under the tag line "Building a Playlist Fit for a President," Radio 2's contest marked an effort to capitalize on mounting excitement and enthusiasm about Obama's formal ascension to presidential office. The idea, ironically enough, reportedly issued from a gap in Obama's knowledge, a failure of cross-cultural imagination (Wheeler). In a July 2008 interview with *Rolling Stone*, the then-Democratic presidential nominee enthusiastically described his iPod's musical highlights—none of them Canadian (Wenner). Quick to see opportunity in this oversight, programmers at Radio 2 devised "49 Songs from North of the 49th Parallel" as a playful way to enrich Obama's knowledge about the culture of the country to the north, promoting Canadian music alongside the nation's national broadcaster. This origin story demonstrates a measure of cultural savvy on the part of the CBC, yet it intimates as well the inextricability of the contest from a lingering concern among Canadians about their culture—that it is unremarkable, indistinct, easily overlooked, readily neglected. Presumably, then, the contest aimed to dispel such concern in the process of repairing presidential ignorance about Canadian song.

The contest did another kind of cultural work "at home": it epitomized the comprehensive shift in format and programming implemented in September 2008 at CBC Radio 2 in order to transform the broadcaster's "brand" ("CBC Radio 2 to Revamp Daytime Programming"; "Music at the CBC"; "To save"; Eatock; Robinson; Wells). Moving away from classical music toward a kind of middle-brow pop, Radio 2 cultivated an intimate difference vis-à-vis commercial FM: a comparable format featuring consonant musical styles in regular rotation yet unencumbered by advertising.[1] Anxiety shadowed such innovation: worries about the CBC's financial security percolated through 2008, spiking in the autumn with rumours of a $45 million budget shortfall—one that, by spring 2009, would metastasize toward $200 million, triggering plans by the CBC to lay off up to eight hundred employees ("Conservative Agenda Would Damage CBC"; "CBC to Cut Up to 800 Jobs, Sell Assets"; Vlessing). Arguably the budgetary crisis was politically motivated and manufactured—a happy accident devised by the governing Conservatives to materialize their philosophical antipathy toward state-funded broadcasting.[2] In this budgetary context, the claims routinely made in 2008 about format and programming changes at Radio 2—that they concerned musical diversity and relevance ("CBC Radio 2 to Revamp Daytime Programming"; Wells)—inevitably bore traces of neoliberal common sense about the unviability and unaccountability of public broadcasting. And precisely because of this context, the absent presence of Prime Minister Stephen Harper, President Obama's political counterpart but *affective* antithesis, haunted from the outset (in ways I consider more fully below) the adoration of Obama manifest in the playlist contest.

The contest's format involved a two-part sequence: a seven-day nomination period, in which listeners could propose musical works for inclusion on the playlist, followed by a five-day voting period, in which listeners could determine the final forty-nine choices from a one-hundred-work shortlist compiled by the CBC from all the nominations. The quick turnaround for both parts of the sequence presumably signalled the freshness of the contest—a new start for the CBC, honouring Obama's new start for America and the world—yet also, and more darkly, the urgency in confirming the viability of the CBC's retooled format. "Don't reflect, just vote!" was this contest's implicit imperative—an aesthetic of the gut reaction through which to consolidate political alongside cultural instinctualism as the proper mode of contemporary media subjectivity. Nominations were grouped according to four broadly predictable (if also somewhat incoherent) rubrics: "English Pop Folk etc.," "Jazz," "Classical," "French Pop Folk etc." While listeners could nominate as many entries as often as they liked during the contest's first phase, they could vote for only one entry per category per day during its second phase.

The playlist that emerged from this process features twenty-nine of the fifty-nine "English Pop Folk etc." works on the shortlist, five of ten "Jazz" works on the shortlist, five of eleven "Classical" works on the shortlist, and ten of twenty "French Pop Folk etc." works on the shortlist.[3] The resulting version of "our most definitive Canadian songs"—if tending more toward the iconic than the iconoclastic, with a centre of gravity geographically Ontarian and racially white—is largely uncontroversial, gesturing as it does toward historical breadth, regional coverage, and aesthetic diversity. Listeners evidently embraced the principles of variety and representativeness embedded in the contest's initial announcement. For every classic act such as The Guess Who, the list offers unexpected entries such as Karkwa. Maritime artists such as Great Big Sea rub elbows with West Coast artists such as Diana Krall, while Québécois stalwarts such as Daniel Lanois counterbalance Anglo staples such as Joni Mitchell. Long been a fan of Neil Young? Then check out his indie inheritors The Weakerthans. Nostalgic for the old-school grandeur of Rush? Then embrace the new-school grandeur of Arcade Fire. Put off by the populist charm of The Tragically Hip? Then marvel at the rigorous virtuosity of James Ehnes. Left cold by the mildly avant-garde drone of Marjan Mozetich? Then settle into the novelty-song comfort of The Barenaked Ladies. The playlist is part musical genealogy, where every work offers some kind of anticipation of or inheritance from another, and part musical pharmacy, where one listener's poison is another listener's cure.

What measure can allow genealogy and pharmacy to cohere? What test determines the superlative credentials of these "most definitive Canadian songs"? Such questions will highlight the diverse character of the final playlist—yet also, and more importantly, the institutional common sense latent in and presupposed by the contest itself. At stake is what, colloquially, Canadian audiences call "Can Con": a kind of cultural protectionism designed to ensure the broadcast circulation (by quota or percentage) of recognizably Canadian creative content. In the music industry—and so in radio more specifically—"Can Con" achieves its practical articulation through the MAPL system. Devised by the Canadian Radio-television and Telecommunications Commission (CRTC) to "assist the development of all aspects of the Canadian music industry" (Armstrong 98)—as against the supposed cultural threat posed to Canada by US-based mass-media broadcast—MAPL (its acronym designating music, artist, performance, and lyrics while evoking the maple leaf as nationalist symbol) aims "to increase exposure of Canadian musical performers, lyricists, and composers to Canadian audiences" and "to strengthen the Canadian music industry, including the creative and production components," thereby stimulating "all components of the Canadian music industry."[4] MAPL's test sounds simple enough: meet two of the four conditions encoded in the acronym (M: Canadian-composed music; A: Canadian artist–performed music; P: performance recorded or occurring and broadcast live in Canada; L: Canadian-composed lyrics).[5] Yet the system notoriously entangles aesthetic with economic objectives: where sometimes it fosters the musical creativity of Canadian artists, other times it instead promotes the commercial viability of Canadian recording studios and programs. The objectives are not necessarily incompatible, but their coexistence will make for a complicated, even incoherent understanding of the definitional character or identity of "Canadian song" (a difficulty all the more ironic in view of the MAPL system's evident legislative ambit to protect and consolidate a *normative* musical culture for Canadians).[6]

The guidelines to CBC's playlist contest presuppose MAPL's system for determining Canadian content, a fact that only intensifies the troubling sense, when browsing the selections, that competing templates struggle for primacy.[7] The logic governing definitiveness, the contest's rationale, can seem almost dizzyingly heterogeneous. True, every entry meets the MAPL standard; what's more, a generic understanding of national identity determined geographically can account for every one of the list's selected artists. But beyond these conceptions, Canadian-ness starts to oscillate. Some selections—as, for instance, "American Woman" by The Guess Who—are militant yet also only metaphorical in their nationalism. Other selections—as, for instance, "Bobcaygeon" by The Tragically Hip—are Canadian by gesture, in the sidelong evocation of an atmosphere, a texture, an implicit cultural state. Still others—as, for instance, "Mon Pays" by Gilles Vigneault—confound hegemonic nationalism, encapsulating a vexed history of national identification and dis-identification all at once. And still others—as, for instance, Glenn Gould's 1955 recording of Bach's "Goldberg Variations"—are Canadian most of all in the mythic aura attached to their performers. Canadian-ness, at least as derived from MAPL, may well be a policy condition but, judging from these songs, as a structure of feeling it remains opaque. Pity Obama (largely ignorant about Canadian music, and presumably tone-deaf to the vexed histories of Canadian content) when given the challenge of parsing these distinctions within "Canadian song"!

2. AT HOME AT RISK IN THE WORLD

From the outset, the contest inspired vigorous debate among listeners of CBC Radio 2. They frequented its website to express their views and concerns during the nomination and voting stages, and then to dissect the outcome once the playlist was announced. Numerous perspectives emerge in retrospect, with four distinctive modalities most palpable: (1) enthusiasm about Obama; (2) frustration with enthusiasm about Obama; (3) support for CBC Radio 2's change in format; (4) worry or anger at this change in format. Not surprisingly, the interplay of these modalities produced a series of positions instructive for my argument here.[8]

For listeners channelling a combination of modalities 1 and 3, the contest supplied the occasion to affirm cultural change alongside political change, and to celebrate cultural possibility alongside political possibility. Excited by the Obama phenomenon, these listeners tended in that spirit to promote particular songs for their prophetic political resonance and to welcome the fresh start coming to Radio 2 as to the White House. Listeners channelling a combination of modalities 1 and 4, by contrast, tended to be quite defensive in their cultural nationalism. Even as the playlist contest filled these listeners with excitement at the diversity and vigour of contemporary Canadian music and at the political renaissance south of the 49th parallel, it also inspired them—precisely in the name of cultural diversity and vigour—to advocate interest in Canadian alongside or indeed above American politics: in those political decisions afoot in Ottawa that would seem to jeopardize the CBC as an institution of national culture. Meanwhile, listeners channelling modality 2—usually in combination with modality 4, but sometimes with modality 3—typically espoused a far more dyspeptic national outlook. For them, the contest seemed to signify the confusion of politics with culture, a confusion serving to pervert homegrown cultural forms with predatory (read: American) ones. Whether enthused or affronted by changes to the CBC, these listeners tended to mourn the putative damage done to Canadian cultural integrity either by the rapacious imperialism of foreign cultural paradigms (the prevailing view of the 2/3s) or, closer to home, by institutional politics at the CBC held to admit and encourage such colonization (the prevailing view of the 2/4s). The context for these perspectives involved, explicitly or implicitly, the 2008 program changes connected (as noted above) to ongoing budget volatility at the CBC. For 2/4 listeners in particular, the move on Radio 2 from an intensively classical emphasis to a more disparate selection of pop musical styles evidently entailed betrayal both because it compromised the aesthetic integrity of classical musical tradition and because it undermined the institutional independence of Canadian cultural broadcast. To the ears of these listeners, the new format of Radio 2, displacing classical with pop, signalled nothing less than an "Americanization" of the CBC, in which aesthetic shifts encoded a loss of cultural and national autonomy. At issue for these listeners was a form of symbolic violence that, dovetailing in the case of the playlist contest with a fixation on Obama, also rendered such fixation effectively redundant. Viewed through this lens, Obama's playlist was a prime symptom of the ongoing colonization of Canadian culture by American styles and forms.[9]

These varied responses to the playlist contest all interweave specifically aesthetic with more broadly cultural and institutional political fears and desires. They bear, most immediately, on the problematics of public or (perhaps more accurately) consumer opinion: what above I termed pervasive fantasies about democratic life and culture in the contemporary moment. The playlist contest exemplifies a tendency in online culture to cultivate and record opinion-making as a proxy or synecdoche for democratic debate—a tendency that, in this instance, arguably manages to conflate and confuse nationalist investment with democratic will. It is worth asking whether this tendency (the widespread media practice of soliciting opinion online) opens up new possibilities within democracy, or whether it tends to direct popular attention toward the content of culture, thereby occluding—and helping to sustain—the formal, even systemic, conditions of contemporary life.[10] Either way, the debate surrounding Obama's playlist will reflect, while also recasting, the ambivalent take on democratic expression running through the institutional history of national public broadcasting in Canada.[11]

The matter of public opinion or sentiment—the ways in which and ends to which Canadians think and feel about national broadcast—bears in turn on the function and outcome of national culture as object and idea within the CBC's enterprise. From the outset, nationalist promotion has preoccupied advocates of public broadcasting in Canada: 1929's Report of the Royal Commission on Canadian Broadcasting—the inspiration, in policy, for the founding, in 1932, of the Canadian Radio Broadcast Commission (CRBC) and, in 1936, of its effective replacement, the CBC—envisions radio's potential to "become a great force in fostering a national spirit and interpreting national citizenship" (qtd. in Eaman 19); the most current legislation, 1991's Broadcasting Act, meanwhile, requires CBC programming to "be predominantly and distinctively Canadian" and "contribute to shared national consciousness and identity" (3.1.m.i and vi; qtd. in Armstrong 248-49).[12] The long-standing materialization of such ideals in the institutional form of the CRTC and in regulatory policies such as MAPL will only amplify the extent to which investments in "Canadian content" have historically tended to reflect anxieties about the encroaching power (and perceived threat) of US mass media and, indeed, of an "American style" of privatized broadcast— what Mary Vipond calls "the overwhelming penetration of American popular culture into Canadian lives and, in the case of radio, Canadian homes" (61).[13] Across this history, the positive project of Canadian content (*for* national culture) remains inextricable from its negative supplement (*as against* US impositions). What seems striking, with respect to the playlist contest, is the way its concomitant debate recapitulated such anxieties as the default idiom—the cultural common sense—for imagining the matter of Canadian national radio today.

The two dynamics just discussed—public opinion or popular will; the promotion of national culture—converge in the matter of consecration at stake in the playlist contest. The endeavour to select "49 songs from north of the 49th parallel" trades on the promise of canonicity, in which the playlist stands in, synecdochically, for a national musical whole. The contest's rhetoric stages this canonizing project in terms of representation ("representing our culture from coast to coast"), but as John Guillory has taught us with regard to the literary field, it is a mistake to understand canons as representative: their production and reproduction, power and utility have instead to do with the distribution of cultural capital, and so with institutional form more than cultural content.[14] In this respect the playlist contest, despite its apparent admission of popular will in crafting a pop canon "from below," will underscore the deeper motives at Radio 2 in entering the canonization business: to leverage cultural capital for the broadcaster's new format at a moment of significant institutional change and vulnerability. In effect, it's the *prospect* of canon formation—the conspicuous broadcast of the ability to orchestrate canonically consequential debate about Canadian musical culture—that, institutionally speaking, proves decisive in choosing a presidential playlist.[15] By attempting to consolidate a specific canon of "Canadian song," Radio 2 ventures to secure and assert its cultural capital—to demonstrate (for radio listeners, but in particular for the budgeting ears of administrators and government ministers) its continuing authority and practical ability to oversee acts of nationally relevant canonization, to consecrate *itself* in consecrating definitive Canadian content.[16]

3. LIQUID CULTURE?

In the very process of venturing such compound consecration, CBC Radio 2 also solicits transnational fantasy, promoting transnational narrative—a kind of cross-border cultural traffic—in order to foster transnational desire. Why? One answer will point toward the vexed state of national culture in an epoch notable, as Zygmunt Bauman has argued, for its liquidity.[17] The condition, process, or dynamic popularly termed *globalization* discombobulates long-standing boundaries between nations as between cultures, reconfiguring and recombining—to often dizzying effect—the relations among spaces, peoples, and practices. "[G]lobalization," observes Fredric Jameson, "means the export and import of culture" as "a matter of business" that "also … foretells the contact and interpenetration of national cultures at an intensity scarcely conceivable in older, slower epochs" (58). Arjun Appadurai figures this intense interpenetration in terms of "disjunctive global flows" across a series of "scapes" (ethnoscapes, finanscapes, technoscapes, mediascapes, and ideoscapes) that emerge and interact athwart the given boundaries of nation and state (20); for John Tomlinson, "the 'deterritorializing' character of the globalization process—its property of diminishing the significance of social-geographical location to the mundane flow of cultural experience" means that "the very dynamic which established national identity as the most powerful cultural-political binding force of modernity may now be unravelling some of the skeins that tie us in securely to our national 'home'" (273, 274).

Yet such processes, however transformative to the modern nation, do not simply leave it behind, obsolete and superfluous: indeed, the nation in its state form persists as a key (if also fraught) aspect of the global conjuncture. "[T]he neoliberal state needs nationalism of a certain sort to survive," David Harvey trenchantly remarks (85). "[I]n the old global order," notes Simon Gikandi, "the nation was the reality and category that enabled the socialization of subjects, and hence the structuralization of cultures; now, in transnationality, the nation has become an absent structure" (635). Eric Cazdyn and Imre Szeman suggest that, in the wake of the international financial meltdown in 2008, this absent structure seems poised for some sort of return, becoming fully present again: "In what was imagined to be the post-national era, the nation is stronger than ever" (7). The point I would make in synthesizing these arguments is that the nation, in its very resurgence, has not simply reverted to its twentieth-century form—it materializes instead in deregulatory guise, as a kind of geopolitical switch-point requisite to the tendencies of neoliberal capitalism. As Cazdyn and Szeman make clear, although globalization, with its eclipse of the nation, was always already a fiction, a narrative, it thereby performed—and arguably continues to perform—important ideological work in occluding and normalizing the worldwide predations of post-Fordist capital. And it's in this context that cultural institutions of twentieth-century nationalism such as the CBC struggle to retain their existing cultural office—or else scramble to recast their cultural service toward newly transnational nationalist ends.

Viewed in light of such dynamics, the playlist debates, while illuminating facets of contemporary Canadian-ness, fundamentally misrecognize the underlying problematic. Demanding versions of an *either/or*—America redeemed! Canada undone! Cultural possibility affirmed! Cultural integrity polluted!—voices on the CBC website miss the intimate inextricability of national and transnational modes in the current moment. Being for or against a presidential playlist is immaterial because the geopolitical phenomenon it exemplifies is symptomatic of the neoliberal double-bind. As Cazdyn and Szeman argue, and as the Radio 2 contest shows, the process commonly understood—or at least narrated—in terms of globalization has routinely coupled national fantasy with transnational desire. Neoliberalism's disarticulation of nation from state, as I noted above, does not simply eclipse national discourse; instead, it advances global futurity not least by tapping strategically into nationalist legacies. Hence the potent force of what I'm calling "prosthetic franchise": at a moment when participation in a virtual public sphere contributes in increasingly consequential ways to the manufacture of hegemony, and under the deregulatory pressures of a revamping nationalism, voting for a presidential playlist—or even articulating an opinion about such voting—can intimate the tendencies alongside the constraints of contemporary democratic life.

The virtual, prosthetic affirmation of Obama's presidency was in some sense parodic of his actual election, but it's insufficient to *dismiss* such affirmation as only parody. The president-elect's intense future promise for so many in January 2009 proved potent not least because it seemed belated: a lagging correction for the two terms of Bushism that, in the experience of most non-Americans, felt like perpetual and grotesque misgovernance by a sovereign they neither elected nor could un-elect. With Obama's ascension, finally non-Americans could tolerate rather than despair of their inability to vote for the sovereign symbolically (and in many respects materially) in charge of their lives.[18] This perception distorts—yet also issues from—a larger, longer belatedness: what I would call the neoliberal arc, in which a series of charismatic world leaders have retooled the conditions of governance, admitting corporatized control while also deregulating state accountability. No wonder, then, that the gesture afforded by prosthetic franchise is at once national and transnational—fusing national content (in this case, "distinctive Canadian songs") to deregulatory global form. On offer is a powerful fantasy: no less than the renewed plausibility and desirability lent by Obama to a globalizing narrative jeopardized by eight years of Bush. Vote now for your favourite songs, the Radio 2 contest urges, because at long last you have the emperor's ear. In this way the effort to harmonize nationalist and transnationalist desire occludes jarring contradictions in neoliberal capitalism, precisely by showcasing national cultures in the transnational boutique.

4. AT WORK IN THE RADIO FACTORY

The idea and material fact of radio is worth contemplating in this context. Radio, after all, today carries its own kind of belatedness: in an era of iPods and webcasts, the medium and its technology can seem residual at best. Yet if, technologically, radio now appears outmoded, as a condition it remains surprisingly obdurate. The persistence of radio is arguably a function of its characteristic presence—what scholars term liveness, intimacy, or sociability. Radio fosters the sense of immediate connection through the perceived simultaneity of listening. At stake, many commentators maintain, is what in the context of print culture Benedict Anderson famously calls "imagined community": an imaginary, horizontal connection with dispersed strangers through the shared encounter with media. Whether we understand such dynamics to be intrinsic to the radio form or contingent on its historical deployment, they can help to explain why, through much of the twentieth century, radio—most obviously in state-run manifestations such as the BBC and the CBC, but in commercial incarnations as well—played a key role in producing and reproducing modes of national feeling and styles of national subjectivity. (Hence, too, the significance of the rebranding of public broadcast in a moment of revamped nationalism.)

Yet radio presence becomes precarious in an era of personalized digital media, as the CBC's playlist contest will intimate. Hugh Chignell frames the problem in near-dystopian terms:

> The invention of the portable MP3 player and its ability to play music from a huge cache of songs has been widely described as potentially fatal for commercial music radio and other music formats as well. What pre-recorded music lacks, no matter how wide the choice and how convenient and stylish the technology, are the qualities of co-presence, liveness, and intimacy.... But digital media may so undermine collective forms of consumption that the pleasures of imagined communities and the experience of listening live may themselves become an irrelevance. (78)

Under the shadow of such potential irrelevance, Radio 2's decision to assemble "49 songs from north of the 49th parallel" in playlist form entails a bid to cross-pollinate radio with the style and aesthetics of digital media. The future of radio, in this version, means collaborating with the digital rival that threatens to displace radio's technology. At the same time, as the playlist contest will indicate, such collaboration just might open up ways of revitalizing the threatened content of the state-radio broadcast: a national musical culture or structure of feeling. In this regard, the forty-nine-song playlist constitutes a True North mix-tape directed not just to everybody's latest political crush, but also and crucially to an abstract and idealized Canadian listener who continues, with ardent nationalist feeling, to embrace the CBC.

The interpellative incitement evident here works to hail fans of national radio broadcast in the service of an ulterior objective: to get listeners to visit—or, more accurately, to leave evidence of having visited—the CBC website, a crucial aspect of the contest's bid to maximize cultural capital for Radio 2. For the contest behind the contest to compile a presidential playlist had less to do with musical nationalism or cross-cultural understanding than with the increasingly dire condition of state-funded radio in Canada. Recall the budget uncertainty mentioned above. The substantial changes in format at Radio 2 materialize that uncertainty, but they must also reflect an attempt (largely unsuccessful in retrospect) to forestall and minimize budget cuts by amplifying the competitiveness and currency of the CBC "brand." The argument helps to clarify the gambit of playlist politics: capitalize on an inter-implication of nationalist sentiment and transnational desire—love of Canadian song; infatuation with Obama—in order to intensify traffic on the CBC website and thereby confirm that program changes at Radio 2 are indeed working. In this way, "prosthetic franchise" becomes prophylactic—a means of protecting the CBC from further damage. Voting on Obama's playlist affirms not just Obama's presidency but the CBC itself, precisely through the performative traffic that visiting its website entails.

The narrative here advanced underscores crisis—looming threats to the CBC—but does it not just as readily describe business as usual in the contemporary moment? A contest to choose a presidential playlist will typify culture's current tendency to encourage users to generate content. On Facebook and YouTube, on Pinterest and Instagram, on Twitter and Tumblr, on endlessly proliferating versions of reality TV: consumers produce, producers consume. Analyzing the arc of twentieth-century cinema, Jonathan Beller has theorized the deployment of attention to explain these dynamics. He proposes what he calls an "attention theory of value" that "finds in the notion of 'labor' ... the prototype of the newest source of value production under capitalism today: value-producing human attention" (4). While Beller focuses on the image, his theory is capacious, explicating the breadth and depth of attentiveness—and listening as readily as looking. Judging at least from Radio 2's playlist contest, the auditory relation is every bit as potent in putting the human sensorium to work. And notwithstanding the contest's intensive nationalism, content provision knows no nationality: we are all content providers now.[19]

In a 2005 essay entitled "Nation, Globe, Hegemony: Post-Fordist Preconditions of the Transnational Turn in American Studies," Leerom Medovoi provides a searching analysis of the contemporary cultural moment that can productively reframe the claims I have been making. Medovoi attends to American studies as a trans-disciplinary formation and the US academy as an institution, but for me, his arguments speak to pressing questions of culture and knowledge writ large. Seeking to dispel the view "that post-Fordism is a post-ideological form of capital" (168), Medovoi argues instead "that we have to start thinking of globalization itself as a meta-narrative, one that aims to convert the 'national narrative' of the Fordist era into its own supplement.... 'Globalization' offers a story in which the new world order will culminate, not in an undifferentiated whole, but in an endlessly differentiated circuit of exchangeability. It tells a story, not about our sameness, but about our fungeablity [sic]" (168-69). This proposition captures exactly the dynamic of CBC's playlist politics, where the national content of Canadian song supplements the transnational form—and imperative—of prosthetic franchise, and where the fusion of national with transnational desire requires the inevitability, while provoking the deep anxiety, of fungible subjectivity.

Half a decade on, even as Radio 2 continues to develop contests that generate content and increase Web traffic,[20] the playlist contest itself seems unimaginable. The global excitement attending Obama's first election has since given way to melancholic resignation at his indifference—his unremarkableness as a leader and his indistinction from other leaders, qualities only amplified in the wake of his 2012 re-election. "Obama" now names unrealized hope, and the president himself embodies failure. Viewed in this retrospective light, the playlist contest hinged (as it strove desperately to capitalize) on Obama's incipience—on his prospect as potentiality—that which could only (and necessarily) fail, upon materializing, to materialize. The issue, I would stress, is incidental, and in that sense immaterial, to Obama himself (as to any elected leader): instead, a structuring, systemic condition of market democracy as a mode of capitalism's political operation. Put another way, Obama's playlist contributes to the soundtrack that accompanies the capitalist impasse confronting global society today.

CODA: A TO THE G FLAT

> If a mask is to reveal something, is it necessary for it to perform its own capacity for destruction? Do the eyeholes and mouthholes need to be gouged out? Must we insist on the antimusicality of "Punk Prayer" in order to see its political potential? Or is the interest, maybe, in recognizing the speciousness of such a division—between theatricality and antitheatricality, masking and unmasking, musicality and antimusicality?
>
> —Barbara Browning

Early in 2012, listeners attuned to contemporary music, politics, and protest would find themselves riveted as a very different sort of presidential playlist emerged in the global mediascape. On 21 February of that year, five members from the punk feminist collective Pussy Riot—striking yet anonymous in vividly coloured dresses, leggings, and balaclavas—stormed the altar of the Russian Orthodox Cathedral of Christ the Savior in Moscow to perform "Virgin Mary, Put Putin Away (Punk Prayer)" until church security intervened to stop them.[21] Three of the five, Maria Alyokhina, Yekaterina Samutsevich, and Nadezhda Tolokonnikova, were arrested that March "on charges of 'hooliganism motivated by religious hatred'" (Bernstein 221). At the ensuing trial in August, all three were found guilty and sentenced to two years in prison, although Samutsevich was subsequently acquitted on the grounds that the church guards had detained her before she could take part in the performance. Alyokhina and Tolokonnikova did time in different women's labour colonies before gaining early release in December 2013—a so-called amnesty widely decried as a publicity bid by the Russian government in the lead-up to the Sochi Olympics.[22]

The case of Pussy Riot certainly offers another version of playlist politics—one in which a president, neither ignorant nor indifferent but attentive and all too knowing, hears music and throws its makers in jail. The charges levelled against the three protestors served to frame the case in terms of a violation of religious space, not an attack on Putin's government, yet the very effort to depoliticize "Punk Prayer" entailed in such framing only underscores the deeply fraught political stakes at issue in the case.[23] What's more, "Punk Prayer"—decrying the conspiracy between religious and sovereign power in Russia—was only the most notorious among a number of anti-Putin performances delivered by Pussy Riot. In the months leading up to the February cathedral action, the collective's presidential playlist also featured such blunt, high-octane assaults as "Release the Cobblestones," "Kropotkin-Vodka," and "Putin Has Pissed Himself," performed on Moscow subway platforms and the top of trolley buses, in luxury boutiques, and in Red Square itself. Add to this narrative the fact that the collective formed in response to governmental theatrics in September 2011—with Dmitry Medvedev's decision not to seek re-election effectively signalling Putin's stranglehold on federal sovereignty (Tochka 305)—and the categorically political valence of Pussy Riot's musical intervention becomes undeniable.[24]

Yet while, most immediately, the playlist sought the ears of the Russian despot and of those who would support him, the political horizon for Pussy Riot's address extended far beyond Russia. Despite the tendency of many commentators—whether condemning or supporting the activists behind "Punk Prayer"—to contrast Russian religious orthodoxy with Western secular liberalism, the "political potential" in Pussy Riot's aesthetic activities holds, as Barbara Browning suggests in the epigraph above, not least to the refusal of simplistic, divisional antitheses (143). The Pussy Riot playlist is not at all a simple counterpart to Obama's playlist, condemning totalitarian terror in the name of some liberalizing hope. Rather, Pussy Riot's activist intervention offers a scathing critique of the global present by insisting on the inextricability among autocracy, neoliberalism, and the social relations produced by capital's value-form—an inextricability taking diverse shape in distinct global locales, to be sure, yet nonetheless articulating systemic links across the global conjuncture. In this sense, Pussy Riot works expressly to confront and to reckon the sort of political dynamics occluded—and thereby symptomatized—by the CBC contest itself.[25]

The problem encapsulated in the case (and the playlist) of Pussy Riot is one of public—or more properly counter-public—broadcast: how to venture unrelentingly strident protest of the dominant soundtrack so as to find some other, as-yet unheard tonality, and thereby enable new collectivities to emerge?[26] Corresponding with Slavoj Žižek from prison, Nadezhda Tolokonnikova takes up a figure already invoked in a previous letter by the Slovenian philosopher in order to frame the problem in starkly musical terms: "Two years of prison for Pussy Riot is our tribute to a destiny that gave us sharp ears, allowing us to sound the note A when everyone else is used to hearing G flat" ("Prison Letters" n.p.). At stake here is a question of what Jonathan Flatley calls mood or attunement: "the emergence of revolutionary counter-moods, those world-altering moments where new alliances, new enemies, and new fields of action become visible and urgently compelling" (504). Given the impasse—or what Endnotes terms "the holding pattern"—endemic to contemporary capitalism, the prospect of such attunement, such counter-mood, can seem a long way off ("The Holding Pattern" n.p.).[27] Yet against the panicky strains of a discordant nationalism and a tuneless globalism together on offer in CBC's style of playlist politics, the Pussy Riot version provokes us with a sense of the collective challenge. Stay tuned.

NOTES

1. Writing in 1990 about commercial radio, Jody Berland advances an insight resonant with respect to the recent format changes at the CBC: "[t]hrough format regulation, commercial radio is supposed to be balanced between viable market conditions, on the one hand, and non-market cultural objectives, on the other. Such scrupulous management of the market offers a bureaucratically dense trace of the government's representation of 'public interest,' which used to be defined by the public system" (182). "Used to be": Berland's larger argument in this article could easily be read as a prescient allegory about the deregulating pantomime now underway at Radio 2. And the differences between public and commercial radio continue to disappear, as ads now air on CBC Radio.
2. As Conservative leader Stephen Harper had remarked in 2004, when his party was the official opposition to the then-governing Liberals: "'I've suggested that government subsidies in support of CBC's services should be to those things that [... d]o not have commercial alternatives'" ("Conservative Agenda Would Damage CBC").
3. For the forty-nine songs selected for the playlist, see "Obama's Playlist Revealed!"
4. See the CRTC's policy on MAPL at <http://www.crtc.gc.ca/eng/info_sht/r1.htm>.
5. The guidelines read as follows:

    To qualify as Canadian content, a musical selection must generally fulfill at least two of the following conditions:

       M (music): the music is composed entirely by a Canadian
       A (artist): the music is, or the lyrics are, performed principally by a Canadian
       P (performance): the musical selection consists of a live performance that is
          recorded wholly in Canada, or
          performed wholly in Canada and broadcast live in Canada
       L (lyrics): the lyrics are written entirely by a Canadian. (http://www.crtc.gc
       .ca/eng/info_sht/r1.htm)

6. For a fuller sense of the history and mandate of the CRTC, as of the issue of Canadian content regulation, see Armstrong (76-111) as well as the CRTC website.

7. I accessed the guidelines governing the contest on the CBC website in May 2009; they have since been removed.

8. As with the contest guidelines, I accessed Web-based postings debating the playlist in May 2009; and as with the guidelines, these postings have since been removed.

9. Motti Regev's theory of "rockization" situates such dynamics in a more global framework: "a large part of popular music produced and consumed in the world today is made under the influence and inspiration of Anglo-American pop/rock—or, to be more precise, it is based on the implementation of what I call the *rock aesthetic*. Popular music thus epitomizes the new forms of cultural diversity associated with the globalization of culture—diversities based on cores of shared practices and technologies, and on logics of eclecticism and hybridity" ("Rockization" 222).

10. Ted Friedman puts the issue this way: "[t]oday, it really is possible for any citizen with Web access to publish and distribute her views instantly around the world. The question remains, however, to what extent individual voices can build audiences to rival the distribution power of the mass media" (214)—and to what extent, I would add, those voices get solicited and channelled in ways that, capitalizing on their apparently spontaneous authenticity, only intensify the powers of established institutional mediations.

11. As Sue Ferguson argues, such ambivalence folds into antipathy as "the goal of [public service broadcast] becomes one of *representation* rather than *participation*"—a dichotomy finessed, but not at all overturned, by the playlist contest (196).

12. The compound concern for national distinction and national consciousness will recollect the historical role of cultural education within the modern liberal state: to educe citizen subjectivity. In *Culture and the State*, David Lloyd and Paul Thomas offer a compelling theory—and a trenchant critique—of this ideological process (1-30). The 1991 Broadcasting Act inscribes this tradition (while also marking its adaptation) when it mandates that "the Canadian Broadcasting Corporation, as the national public broadcaster, should provide radio and television services incorporating a wide range of programming that *informs, enlightens, and entertains*" (3.1.1; quoted in Armstrong 218; emphasis added). The language of this mandate renders information, enlightenment, and entertainment as conjoined nodes within a process designed to *fuse* the subjectivities of citizen and consumer. The adaptive persistence of this process is a chief reason why I am unconvinced by arguments attempting to juxtapose state-sponsored public media, on the one hand, and privately funded corporate media, on the other—typically in order to celebrate the first while lamenting the second. In view of the ideological process I am describing, these alternatives seem more aptly understood as distinct but *coordinate* modes of interpellation within capitalist modernity: both educing the sort of possessive and acquisitive individualism requisite to market economics as to liberal sociability.

13. As Vipond makes clear, many participants in the formative debates about public broadcasting in Canada took modes of broadcast to materialize distinct, competing nationalities—a conception catching Canada affectively as well as geopolitically

between the nominally rival (though ideological and materially inter-implicated) styles of British (read: "public") and American (read: "private") broadcast (63-66).

14 See Guillory (55-82). The synecdochic relation at issue in the argument I am making resembles the one theorized by Guillory with respect to the literary institution, where syllabus approximates the (ungraspable) canon (29-38). Lloyd and Thomas warn of the dangers of such mechanisms in modern liberal culture, arguing by way of a theory of supplementation that representatives displace those persons or things for which they purport to stand (46ff). Also pertinent—not least because it was the theoretical and methodological inspiration for Guillory's project—is Pierre Bourdieu's work on the field of cultural production; see the essay of that name as well as "Classes and Classification" in *Distinction*.

15 The ambiguity of the idea of a "pop canon" is worth remarking upon here. Even as the CBC's contest participates in the list-mania evident across the field of popular musical institutions (think of the endless stream of "greatest songs of x" lists in the music press), it also marks, in the very intimacy and ephemerality of the playlist concept and format, the ambivalence these same institutions have about the prospect of canonizing popular song. For Regev, this ambivalence means that "as much as such lists became common practice in popular music journalism, the cultural power of the popular music canon—just like any artistic canon—resides in its unofficial status. There is no formal mechanism of canonization" ("Introduction" 2). The claim is too categorical, and too simplistic: the cultural power of "any artistic canon" has, as Guillory demonstrates, rather to do with its distribution of cultural capital. In the case of popular music, such capital has tended to follow the performance or attribution of social and musical dissidence, such that apparent non- or anti-canonicity has itself achieved canonical status. Hence the widespread consecration over the last two decades of so-called "alternative" rock.

16 In terms of Bourdieu's theory, the coordinates of CBC's struggle for cultural capital will indicate the broadcaster's heteronomous, not autonomous, position in relation to the field of power. See "The Field of Cultural Production," 40ff.

17 See in particular *Liquid Modernity*, *Liquid Times*, and *Culture in a Liquid Modern World*.

18 Cazdyn and Szeman make the point more forcefully: "There has never been a moment in modern history when non-citizens were so interested and instrumental in a national electoral race. Everyone the world over knows that what happened in the US election would profoundly affect their everyday lives—perhaps even more profoundly than their own local and national elections" (29).

19 For a compelling account of this development, see the working papers compiled by Susie O'Brien and Imre Szeman under the provocative title *Content Providers of the World Unite! The Cultural Politics of Globalization*. Dean's account of "communicative capitalism" certainly complements Beller's "attention theory of value": "[p]erpetually engaged," she writes, "we search and link, making the paths we follow—even as Google claims the traces as its own. We constitute the practices that constitute us. We collectively determine our collective conditions, but not yet as the people, still as populations" (122).

20 A memorable one, "Raised on Radio," celebrated the CBC's seventy-fifth anniversary in fall 2011 by upping the stakes, making public radio broadcast the prime source of national nurture—and so the elemental technology in nationalist ontology.

21 The full lyrics appear in Scholder (9).

22 An avalanche of journalism and critical commentary has tracked the events in the Pussy Riot affair. In addition to the chronological narrative offered on Wikipedia, see "Pussy Riot Members Reunited"; Scholder's edited collection of source materials and

tributes; and articles and essays by Bernstein, Bird, Browning, Elder, Etkind, Schuler, and Tochka.

23 As Slavoj Žižek writes: "Pussy Riot members accused of blasphemy and hatred of religion? The answer is easy: the true blasphemy is the state accusation itself, formulating as a crime of religious hatred something which was clearly a political act of protest against the ruling clique" ("The True Blasphemy" n.p.). Browning's account of "aesthetic objections" to Pussy Riot's protests can intimate the inextricability of the political and the aesthetic in the collective's case—precisely in view of the coordinate efforts to depoliticize and de-aestheticize their interventions (139).

24 The full lyrics to "Kropotkin-Vodka" and "Putin Has Pissed Himself" appear in Scholder (22, 26). As "Putin Lights Up the Fires" and "Putin Will Teach You How to Love," songs released after the trial, make clear, state attempts at juridical intimidation have not dulled the pointedness of Pussy Riot's political message. On the matter of politics, see also the Pussy Riot communiqué "Pussy Riot: Art or Politics?" issued 23 March 2012 and reprinted in Scholder (10).

25 Notable, here, are two passages in the Žižek-Tolokonnikova correspondence that explicitly address the problem of global capitalism ("Prison Letters"). In the first, from a letter dated 2 January 2013, Žižek writes: "All hearts were beating for you as long as you were perceived as just another version of the liberal-democratic protest against the authoritarian state. The moment it became clear that you rejected global capitalism, reporting on Pussy Riot became much more ambiguous. What is so disturbing about Pussy Riot to the liberal gaze is that you make visible the hidden continuity between Stalinism and contemporary global capitalism." In the second, from a letter dated 16 April 2013, Tolokonnikova writes: "The anti-hierarchical structures and rhizomes of late capitalism are its successful ad campaign. Modern capitalism has to manifest itself as flexible and even eccentric. Everything is geared towards gripping the emotion of the consumer. Modern capitalism seeks to assure us that it operates according to the principles of free creativity, endless development and diversity. It glosses over its other side in order to hide the reality that millions of people are enslaved by an all-powerful and fantastically stable norm of production. We want to reveal this lie." In a compelling account of the dichotomous common sense underpinning much commentary on the Pussy Riot case and challenged by the sort of arguments made by Žižek and Tolokonnikova here, Nicholas Tochka argues that "[t]wo domains of knowledge underpinned commentators' strategies for representing and explaining the aesthetic and political significance of Pussy Riot"—one that "assumed a global order organised into distinct and mutually antagonistic spheres," free West and unfree non-West, and one that "posited a normative understanding of the popular musician as a rights-bearing expressive agent, and of the utility of popular music ... in speaking 'truth to power'" (307). Given the power of these two domains of knowledge, Tochka continues, "[u]nderstandings of what Western popular music is and does, how it accomplishes cultural work in the name of the political, and musicians' political agency, should thus be understood as having been shaped by, even imbued with, a Cold War ideology that posited an essentialist distinction between 'free' and 'unfree' geopolitical spheres" (308).

26 In works such as *The Letters of the Republic* and *Publics and Counterpublics*, Michael Warner advances a capacious, incisive theory of the modern dynamics of publicity and counter-publicity, as of the entanglements of visibility and anonymity crucial to both—entanglements that Pussy Riot, with their signifying as well as tactical adherence to masking, call upon quite relentlessly.

27 Beginning with a speculative query, Endnotes launches a grim yet compelling account of the contemporary impasse: "What comes next? It is impossible to say in advance.

What we know is that, at least for the moment, we live and fight within the holding pattern. The crisis has been stalled. In order to make the crisis stall, the state has been forced to undertake extraordinary actions. It is hard to deny that state interventions, over the past few years, have seemed like a last ditch effort. Interest rates are bottoming out at zero percent. The government is spending billions of dollars, every month, just in order to convince capital to invest in a trickle. For how long? And yet, for this long, at least, state interventions have worked. The crisis has been petrified. And its petrification has been the petrification of the struggle" (n.p.).

WORKS CITED

Anderson, Benedict. *Imagined Communities*. London: Verso, 1983. Print.
Appadurai, Arjun. "Disjuncture and Difference in the Global Cultural Economy." *Public Culture* 2.2 (Spring 1990): 1-24. Print.
Armstrong, Robert. *Broadcasting Policy in Canada*. Toronto: U of Toronto P, 2010. Print.
Bauman, Zygmunt. *Culture in a Liquid Modern World*. Cambridge: Polity, 2011. Print.
———. *Liquid Modernity*. Cambridge: Polity, 2000. Print.
———. *Liquid Times: Living in an Age of Uncertainty*. Cambridge: Polity, 2006. Print.
Beller, Jonathan. *The Cinematic Mode of Production: Attention Economy and the Society of the Spectacle*. Hanover: Dartmouth College P, 2006. Print.
Berland, Jody. "Radio Space and Industrial Time: Music Formats, Local Narratives, and Technological Mediation." *Popular Music* 9.2 (1990): 179-92. Print.
Bernstein, Anya. "An Inadvertent Sacrifice: Body Politics and Sovereign Power in the Pussy Riot Affair." *Critical Inquiry* 40 (Autumn 2013): 220-41. Print.
Bird, Robert. "Occupy Orthodoxy: Pussy Riot on Liturgy and Spectacle." MS.
Bourdieu, Pierre. *Distinction: A Social Critique of the Judgement of Taste*. Trans. Richard Nice. Cambridge: Harvard UP, 1984. Print.
———. "The Field of Cultural Production, or: The Economic World Reversed." Trans. Richard Nice. *The Field of Cultural Production*. Ed. Randall Johnson. New York: Columbia UP, 1993. 29-73. Print.
Browning, Barbara. "This Balaclava Is Too Hot." *Social Text* 116/31.3 (Fall 2013): 137-45. Print.
Cazdyn, Eric, and Imre Szeman. *After Globalization*. Chichester: Wiley-Blackwell, 2011. Print.
"CBC to Cut Up to 800 Jobs, Sell Assets." *CBC News*. 25 Mar. 2009. <http://www.cbc.ca/news/arts/media/story/2009/03/25/cbc-layoffs.html>. 22 July 2014.
"CBC Radio 2 to Revamp Daytime Programming." *CBC News*. 4 Mar. 2008. <http://www.cbc.ca/news/arts/cbc-radio-2-to-revamp-daytime-programming-1.720872>. 22 July 2014.
Chignell, Hugh. *Key Concepts in Radio*. London: Sage, 2009. Print.
"Conservative Agenda Would Damage CBC." *Friends of Canadian Broadcasting*. 28 Feb. 2008. <http://www.friends.ca/press-release/96>. 22 July 2014.
CRTC. < http://www.crtc.gc.ca/eng/home-accueil.htm>. 22 July 2014.
Dean, Jodi. *The Communist Horizon*. London: Verso, 2012. Print.
Deleuze, Gilles. "Mediators." Trans. Martin Joughin. *Incorporations*. Ed. Jonathan Crary and Sanford Kwinter. New York: Zone, 1992. 280-94. Print.

Eaman, Ross A. *Channels of Influence: CBC Audience Research and the Canadian Public*. Toronto: U of Toronto P, 1994.

Eatock, Colin. "Culture Wars at the CBC." *Queen's Quarterly* 115.2 (Summer 2008): 260-74. Print.

Elder, Miriam. "Pussy Riot Trial: 'We Are Representatives of Our Generation.'" *Guardian* 17 Aug. 2012. <http://www.theguardian.com/world/2012/aug/17/pussy-riot-trial-representatives-generation>. 22 July 2014.

Endnotes. "The Holding Pattern." *Endnotes 3: Race, Gender, Class, and Other Misfortunes*. <http://endnotes.org.uk/en/endnotes-the-holding-pattern>. 22 July 2014.

Etkind, Alexander. "Post-Soviet Russia: The Land of the Oil Curse, Pussy Riot, and Magical Historicism." *Boundary 2* 41.1 (2014): 153-70. Print.

Ferguson, Sue. "Locking Out the Mother Corp: Nationalism and Popular Imaginings of Public Service Broadcasting in the Print News Media." *Canadian Journal of Communication* 32 (2007): 181-200. Print.

Flatley, Jonathan. "How a Revolutionary Counter-Mood Is Made." *New Literary History* 43.3 (2012): 503-25. Print.

Friedman, Ted. *Electric Dreams: Computers in American Culture*. New York: NYUP, 2005. Print.

Friends of Canadian Broadcasting. "Conservative Agenda Would Damage CBC." 28 Feb. 2008. <http://www.friends.ca/press-release/96>. 22 July 2014.

Gikandi, Simon. "Globalization and the Claims of Postcoloniality." *South Atlantic Quarterly* 100.3 (2001): 627-58. Print.

Guillory, John. *Cultural Capital: The Problem of Literary Canon Formation*. Chicago: U of Chicago P, 1993. Print.

Harvey, David. *A Brief History of Neoliberalism*. Oxford: Oxford UP, 2005, 2007. Print.

Jameson, Fredric. "Notes on Globalization as a Philosophical Issue." *The Cultures of Globalization*. Ed. Fredric Jameson and Masao Miyoshi. Durham: Duke UP, 1998. 54-77. Print.

Lloyd, David, and Paul Thomas. *Culture and the State*. New York: Routledge, 1998. Print.

Medovoi, Leerom. "Nation, Globe, Hegemony: Post-Fordist Preconditions of the Transnational Turn in American Studies." *interventions* 7.2 (2005): 162-79. Print.

"Music at the CBC." *The Canadian Encyclopedia*. <http://www.thecanadianencyclopedia.ca/en/article/cbc-emc/>. 22 July 2014.

"Obama's Playlist Revealed!" *CBC News*. 20 Jan. 2009. <http://archive.today/ZePvl>. 22 July 2014.

O'Brien, Susie, and Imre Szeman, eds. *Content Providers of the World Unite! The Cultural Politics of Globalization*. Working Paper Series. Ed. William Coleman. Institute on Globalization and the Human Condition, McMaster University, May 2003. <http://www.economics.mcmaster.ca/institute-on-globalization-and-the-human-condition/documents/IGHC-WPS_03-3_ObrienSzeman.pdf>. 22 July 2014.

Pussy Riot. "Kropotkin-Vodka." <http://www.youtube.com/watch?v=CZUhkWiiv7M>. 22 July 2014.

———. "Putin Has Pissed Himself." <http://www.youtube.com/watch?v=7kVMADLm3js&feature=plcp>. 22 July 2014.

———. "Putin Lights Up the Fires." < https://vimeo.com/67931502>. 22 July 2014.
———. "Putin Will Teach You How to Love." <http://www.youtube.com/watch?v=gjI0KYl9gWs>. 22 July 2014.
———. "Release the Cobblestones." <http://www.youtube.com/watch?v=qEiB1RYuYXw>. 22 July 2014.
———. "Virgin Mary, Put Putin Away." <http://www.youtube.com/watch?v=GCasuaAczKY>. 22 July 2014.
"Pussy Riot." *Wikipedia.* < http://en.wikipedia.org/wiki/Pussy_Riot>. 22 July 2014.
"Pussy Riot Members Reunited After Early Release from Russian Prison." *Guardian* 24 Dec. 2013. <http://www.theguardian.com/world/2013/dec/24/pussy-riot-members-reunited-release-russia>. 22 July 2014.
Regev, Motti. "Introduction." *Popular Music* 25.1 (2006): 1-2. Print.
———. "'Rockization': Diversity within Similarity in World Popular Music." *Global America? The Cultural Consequences of Globalization.* Ed. Ulrich Beck et al. Liverpool: Liverpool UP, 2003. 222-34. Print.
Robinson, Paul E. "CBC Radio 2 Introduces: New Unlikable Format." *La Scena Musicale* 14.2 (Oct. 2008). <http://www.scena.org/lsm/sm14-2/sm14-2_cbcradio2_en.html.> 22 July 2014.
Scholder, Amy, ed. *Pussy Riot!: A Punk Prayer for Freedom.* New York: Feminist, 2012. Print.
Schuler, Catherine. "Reinventing the Show Trial: Putin and Pussy Riot." *TDR: The Drama Review* 57.1/T217 (Spring 2013): 7-17. Print.
Tochka, Nicholas. "Pussy Riot, Freedom of Expression, and Popular Music Studies After the Cold War." *Popular Music* 32.2 (May 2013): 303-11. Print.
"To Save CBC Radio 2, We Must Destroy It." *This Magazine* (2 Sept. 2008). <http://this.org/blog/2008/09/02/to-save-cbc-radio-2-we-must-destroy-it/>. 22 July 2014.
Tolokonnikova, Nadezhda, and Slavoj Žižek. "Nadezhda Tolokonnikova of Pussy Riot's Prison Letters to Slavoj Žižek." *Guardian* 15 Nov. 2013. <http://www.theguardian.com/music/2013/nov/15/pussy-riot-nadezhda-tolokonnikova-slavoj-zizek>. 22 July 2014.
Tomlinson, John. "Globalization and Cultural Identity." *The Globalization Transformations Reader: An Introduction to the Globalization Debate* (2nd ed.). Ed. David Held and Anthony McGrew. Cambridge: Polity, 2003. 269-77. Print.
Vipond, Mary. "Cultural Authority and Canadian Public Broadcasting in the 1930s: Hector Charlesworth and the CRBC." *Journal of Canadian Studies* 42.1 (Winter 2008): 59-83. Print.
Vlessing, Etan. "Belts Tightening at CBC." *Friends of Canadian Broadcasting.* 21 Nov. 2008. <http://www.friends.ca/news-item/7491>. 22 July 2014.
Warner, Michael. *Publics and Counterpublics.* Brooklyn: Zone, 2002. Print.
———. *The Letters of the Republic.* Cambridge: Harvard UP, 1990. Print.
Wells, Paul. "Radio 2: It's CBC for 'Whatevah." *Maclean's.* 19 Aug. 2008. <http://www.macleans.ca/authors/paul-wells/radio-2-its-cbc-for-whatevah/>. 22 July 2014.
Wenner, Jann S. "A Conversation with Barack Obama." *Rolling Stone* 1056-7 (10-24 July 2008): 70-74, 76. Print.

Wheeler, Brad. "Download These Canadian Songs, Mr. President." *Globe and Mail* 20 Jan. 2009; updated 9 Apr. 2009. N.p. <http://www.theglobeandmail.com/arts/download-these-canadian-songs-mr-president/article1146791/>. 22 July 2014.

Žižek, Slavoj. "The True Blasphemy." *Art Leaks*. <http://art-leaks.org/2012/08/07/slavoj-zizek-on-pussy-riot-the-true-blashphemy/>. 22 July 2014.

CHAPTER 7

Grinning Things
Object Lessons in Violent Labour

Michael Epp

The materialist is always ruled by the love of the thing, and true thought is only nominal thought, part of the thing, concrete like the thing. In this sense, critique does not divide concepts but cuts into the thing.

—Michael Hardt and Antonio Negri, *Labor of Dionysus* (19)

A new materialism will investigate how the literary helps to identify the cultural illogic that exposes history's noninevitability. This does not mean displaying the shards of the past as so many bits and pieces; rather it entails testing the limits of those shards to assume recognizable form.

—Bill Brown, *The Material Unconscious* (18)

FACES FOR WAR

In March 2009, members of Glass Tiger, the Canadian rock band known mainly for their hit singles in the 1980s, travelled to Afghanistan to take part in their country's war on terror. Part of Team Canada, a group of over sixty musicians and National Hockey League players, their "mission was to lift the soldiers' spirits for even a few brief moments, to show them Canada still cares, and to learn firsthand about what they are trying to accomplish in Afghanistan." Their work and experiences were marked by the basic material conditions of fighting and entertaining in Afghanistan, such as the difficulty of getting a keyboard to a forward operating base, or finding Tim Horton's coffee in Kandahar when the water ran dry. Their work was also marked by the materiality of relating to soldiers face to face, what we might consider the material dimension of "lifting" spirits, and how that lifting registers, legibly, in the face. For instance, when travelling to a forward operating base, the band learned that "in the case of having some musical equipment, you want light, portable music equipment that you can slug over your back." And they also learned that such practical ingenuity, mixed with courage and determination, could do some of the lifting before a note was played. As Sam Reid, the band's keyboardist explains, "Once you get on the ground, you realize that it's a completely different vibe from the main base. You're looking at these soliders [sic] and they have this look of disbelief on their face. One of the soldiers approached and said 'I can't believe you guys are here.'" This face-work turns out to be one of the main purposes of making the dangerous trip to the tight spaces of the forward operating bases: "when we get to play for them, of course we're working close quarters, and there's a real face time."[1]

The work going on between Glass Tiger and the Canadian soldiers in this morale-building exercise is made up of multiple forms of emotional labour, including courage, caring, determination, a willingness to go without daily comforts, surprise, and pleasure. This emotional labour, in turn, is itself contained within a form of violent labour specific to soldiering (especially soldiering in a foreign country). Here, making music and listening to it, performing music and watching it, making things work on the front lines, and face time, are the assembled parts and products of a tactical military mission that is calculated to contribute to a victorious war effort.

I raise the story of Glass Tiger's trip, and the forms of violent labour that the story brings into focus, because it serves as an object lesson for the productive and messy relationships that obtain between war, emotional labour, and material culture. Moreover, the story suggests, in plain terms, how immaterial things like emotions become material things like facial expressions, which as instances of violent labour, become material things like weapons for defeating an enemy. Thinking through war's relationship to material culture, in the specific form of violent labour, puts pressure on the way we think about the relationship between objects and ourselves by strikingly converting otherwise everyday things (like music and facial expressions) into weapons. Such radical conversion underscores how much we are bound to objects, and at the same time reveals precisely the extent to which the *meaning* of that binding is non-inevitable. This radical conversion is accomplished materially through labour, to which we are similarly bound. Together, war, labour, and materials (and materiality) produce material cultures, and each such culture is recognizable in its specificity by reckoning how it turns practices we don't think of as anything but quotidian behaviours, like smiling or other forms of facial emotional practice, into things like weapons. The overdetermined moment in which a smile becomes an act of labour and a weapon reveals the tensions between how we relate to things and how we relate to ourselves as feeling, labouring, violent creatures, living in specific material cultures, who can turn anything into weaponry, and make any act violent.

I first came to think about these relations belatedly in my work on humour, when I discovered that, during World War II, in an effort to entertain and educate troops, the US Army circulated copies of American humour scholar Walter Blair's *Horse Sense in American Humor* among soldiers and even gave it a place of honour in the US president's White House library. At the time, I saw the link between humour practice, scholarship, literature, and war as bound up in discourses of national character that have always been articulated to violent imperialism, and also to white supremacy. But these relationships became more thorny when I stumbled on the startling 1921 YMCA publication, *Entertaining the American Army: The American Stage and Lyceum in the World War*. Though the book positions itself as simply a history of lyceum lecturing during World War I, and a testament to the contribution of the YMCA to the war effort, it is in fact a detailed argument for the productivity of emotional labour in modern warfare. The book depicts on its cover the articulation of humour to war with the engraved phrase "Thalia Mars," which is dramatically pierced by a majestic and ominous sword. The violent joining of the god of war to the muse of comedy is intended to work as a celebratory effort to commemorate the conversion of smiles into weapons, into the materials of violent labour. This celebration is the main theme of the book, which always emphasizes the serious contribution entertainers made to the war effort; for instance, a staff sergeant is cited as considering an entertainment called "The Shamrock Show" as being "vital" to divisional success on the battlefield as "a regiment of infantry" (Evans and Harding 129). If such work is vital, then so too is it vital that we think through these practices not only as forms of emotional labour, but also as forms of violent labour.

The question I pose, then, is: What does it mean for critiques of feelings, of literature and entertainment, of violence, and of material culture more broadly, when violent labour can convert smiles into weapons? In the course of things, answering this question involves engaging a vertiginous array of critical dimensions, including theories of labour, emotion, entertainment, materiality, and the historical development of the articulation of all of these things to war and violence broadly conceived. To provide a kind of centre for these issues, I ground this chapter in *Entertaining the American Army* and its precocious, manifestly modern joining of emotional management to the prosecution of war. In the end, I argue that a critique of modern violence must account for the material culture, and the violent labour, that makes that violence possible.[2]

VIOLENT LABOUR ON THE CIRCUIT

Entertaining the American Army was written in 1921 for the YMCA by James W. Evans, "Dramatic Producer and Coach," and Captain Gardner L. Harding, "Attached to General Pershing's Staff at Chaumont Intelligence Division of the War Department." The book is, first, an effort to praise the war contribution of the YMCA; second, an effort to praise the war contribution of entertainers; and third, an effort to highlight the key role of emotional labour in motivating mass groups of people to form cohesive publics, and, of course, to kill their enemies. What makes the book precocious is that it recounts, sixty years before Arlie Hochschild's groundbreaking work on emotional labour in *The Managed Heart*, the value of such labour for bringing people together, granting them identity, and encouraging them to perform specific tasks. Like the flight attendants in Hochschild's study, the soldiers and performers in *Entertaining the American Army* are both *alienated from themselves* through emotional labour and *produced as themselves*—as people collectively practising destructive and deadly combat—through their emotional practice, which is indexed materially in their smiles. The process by which emotional labour becomes violent labour is stressed again and again in the YMCA celebration in order to ascribe value to the work of entertainment, which is taken to both produce and manage emotion. Such production and management is perceived to turn on the symbiotic relationship between performances on stage and the performance of identity off stage, a circuit in which the success of the performers, manifested materially in smiles, validates their nationalism, even as the performers themselves deliberately reinforce and construct national identity in their audiences. What distinguishes entertainment, especially in this context, from the emotional labour of the service industry is that it relies less on the modern business mantra "service with a smile" than on the need of emotional labour in the violence industry to produce smiling servicemen (though of course what really makes such labours uncanny is not that they are different, but that they are not as different as they should be).[3]

The joining of emotion to violent labour in the Great War was considered to be culturally transformative. While the YMCA and its bands of entertainers certainly had a stake in overstating their significance, nonetheless their investment in the value of emotion for violent labour seems to have been borne out by subsequent military commitments to managing troop morale through entertainment. "The dean of American dramatists," Augustus

Thomas, identified the value of emotional labour during a typically stirring propaganda speech directed at performers:

> The war has done a great deal to turn over old opinions.... It has brought a great many changes in our social fabric, and is bringing a great one to the theatre and the status of the theatre. We of the theatre come into the field with our contribution as one of the most effective in the whole push behind the drive. We are not renowned as business men, and a lot of us make bad contracts. The world does not call upon us when it wants to revise its philosophy, but business and logic are not the only things in this life. The great thing is the spiritual effect and nothing is done at all where the emotions are not stirred. Now in that field of emotional stir, we do not take off our bonnet to anybody. That is our reason for being. (Evans and Harding 46-47)

Thomas's exaggerated rhetoric is generically representative of the kind of speech that sought support for the war (and specifically one that sought support from entertainers), but while the theatre was probably not one of the top contributors to the war effort, it still was positioned uniquely to produce "spiritual effects" and to "stir" the melting pot of emotions into a coherent, singular form useful for military action and home-front support for that action.

Another speaker, Ames, explains in a similar vein that "we of the theatre can personally help to speed the victory, because our men will fight better if we keep them happy and contented in their exile, and because in addition to entertainment we can bring the unspoken message that America is with them and behind them every day and every hour" (59). Though decidedly self-interested and perhaps pertinently histrionic, such investments in the power of theatre professionals to contribute to the war effort underscored an emerging form of modern subjectivity that increasingly saw emotional management as a form of labour itself that could make other forms of labour more efficient and effective. The circuit of emotions and labours that results in battlefield violence included (among many other activities) the use of stage performance, and it is by virtue of acting in this circuit that Thalia and Mars become one, that smiles and the production of smiles become violent labours and violent things.

An additional point of interest is the book's investment in the *professional* management of emotion, in the assertion that the theatre was uniquely positioned to provide emotional labour in order to produce a specific, targeted product (in this case, the proper emotional labour of soldiers). Although Ames disavows the theatre's ability to conduct business in order to rhetorically stress its other ability, even this disavowal in fact constructs a chain that connects business to emotional management by virtue of linking the two together in a process that produces good wartime activity. Eva Illouz, in *Cold Intimacies: The Making of Emotional Capitalism*, has provided a brief history of how twentieth-century professionalism emerged in tandem with discourses of emotional management (i.e., labour) in order to respond to new demands from capital. Describing "emotional capitalism" as the "progressive fusion of the market repertoires and languages of the self during the twentieth century," Illouz builds a chain that links together processes that are just as good at producing war as they are at producing profit:

> In conjunction with the language of productivity and the commodification of selfhood in the field of mental health, the psychological persuasion has made the emotional self into a public text and performance in a variety of social sites such as the family, the corporation, support groups, television talk shows, and the Internet. The transformation of the public sphere into an arena for the exposition of private life, emotions, and intimacies which has characterized it for the last twenty years cannot be understood without acknowledging the role of psychology in converting private experiences into public discussion. (108)

Illouz follows this by claiming that the problem of this process of publicization of the self is "precisely how to convert that public psychological performance back into a private emotional relationship" (108). But such a problem does not obtain for professional entertainers of the Army, whose goal is, precisely, to convert public performances into the emotional lives of privates in the Army. War mobilization, which is usually approached as an exceptional form of culture building, is not burdened by long-term worries about selfness, and can simply measure its success by witnessing the productive levels and types of morale it creates by virtue of imagining it is engaged not really in a commodification of the self but in a temporary martializing of the self.

And yet, Illouz is right to claim that the conversion of the emotional self into a public text is a problem, and even a problem for the self-congratulatory account of entertainment produced by the YMCA. In principle, post-enlightenment publics are understood to be characterized by the substitution of reasoned debate for violence as a way of solving problems. Propaganda and emotional manipulation, in this way of thinking, contradict the proper, modern resolution of conflict. Such theory, in fact, informs most dominant liberal understandings of the relationships between politics and modernity, insofar as political violence is perceived as a failure to be properly and fully modern. Moreover, manipulating publics through emotional rhetoric and performance is seen in this light as a retreat from modernity, a perversely dialectical step backward. This, indeed, is precisely the perversion critiqued so famously by Horkheimer and Adorno in *The Dialectic of Enlightenment*, in which modern forms of public persuasion (such as mass entertainment) are seen to emerge only because of modernity, even as they simultaneously turn modernity into something greatly resembling what are imagined as pre-modern forms of subject formation and political manipulation of opinion. Basically, the problem here is that liberal enlightenment versions of modern subjectivity and politics object to manipulation, but embrace management (both of the self and of others). The distinction between the two in practice is, of course, obscure, and this obscurity is most obvious in the strange figure of the modern soldier. The successful professional, emotional management of soldiers as "public texts," then, embraces new forms of labour emerging with modernity, producing new forms of killing that are distinctly modern, even as it mobilizes a new kind of violent labour on what might be seen as classically anti-modern or "old" grounds of political subjectivity. It is in this sense that "violent labour" is in the twentieth century a contradiction whose truth is precisely this ugly (and effective), manifestly overdetermined blending of old and new ways of getting violent things done.

But such contradictions, apparently, did not weigh heavily on the minds of the World War I entertainers of the Army, who loved the new material role that dramatic entertainment was to play in the production and circulation of violent labour. In fact, it is their love for their work that makes them such good sources for understanding the emergence of new forms of this labour.[4] It was not only theatre professionals, however, who loved and understood the relationship between capital, emotion, and war in the early-twentieth-century form of modernity. Sergeant Arthur Guy Empey, during a recruitment event, performed this embrace when he "point[ed] his aggressive finger at the audience and shouted: "The biggest job in the War is to send the boys over the top with a smile. It is the men who go over the top with a song in their hearts who keep their wits about them and come back—and you've got to provide them with songs" (61). Empey's rhetorical exaggeration notwithstanding, it is clear that officers, too, believed in the power of professional entertainers to manage violent labour. General Pershing put the case more clinically, stating simply that "morale is a state of mind upheld by entertainment" (88), but the position is essentially the same, that feelings and "states of mind" had to be accounted for in the material organization of war, occupying a position perhaps not as significant, but at least in the same dimension, as the production and circulation of more conventional forms of war materiel.

Crucially, these assessments of the function of theatre and entertainment, and of smiles, were, according to the YMCA anyway, proven on the front. As one humorist explained:

> But at that, there is not money enough in all America to make one of us quit our job. Oh, if you could see what we can do for these boys! We are now playing to men who have been up in the front line trenches in the midst of such hell as you cannot imagine—hungry, dying, seeing their best friends die at their sides—for weeks and are now back before going at it again. When I start in to talk ... [t]heir faces are drawn and tense. But gradually they begin to relax, the lines go, the smiles begin to come, and then, when I think the time has come, I go after a real, man-sized laugh. I may not get it the first time, but by the time I hand them over to [the next entertainer] they are feeling better, and from then on the laughter and applause and cheers are such pay as no living player ever received in America. And then, at the end, to see the changed men that go out of the YMCA huts—well, God has been good to us to let us have this opportunity. (114-15)

This appreciation of the function of emotional labour was apparently shared by performers and soldiers alike. As our writers note, "in the areas where German bombs and long range artillery—and an occasional leakage of gas—penetrated, 'The Shamrock Show' continued its work, as vital to the success of the division, as one staff captain put it, 'as a regiment of infantry'" (129). This measuring of success is also articulated precisely as a point of labour, such as when we hear that "the lecturers did a big work; they deserve great credit. They kept the boys inspired from start to finish. After an invigorating address the soldiers felt like going out into the front line and whipping the whole German Army single-handed" (222). Sometimes measurement became specific and detailed, as in the case of a soldier who praised a lecture, exclaiming "that talk was worth a dozen bayonet drills!" (222). That the YMCA would list anecdotal evidence of its success is not particularly surprising in a book written as a celebration; what is interesting is the language of transformation (changed men), value (pay, worth, vital, great credit), emotion (smiles, laughs, inspiration, feeling better, invigoration), and labour (not quitting, big work) that becomes articulated to a language of violent actions and things (bayonets, drills, whipping). Indeed, the detailed narrative of facial transformation cited above, in which drawn, tense faces have their "lines go" to be replaced by "smiles" and "man-size[d]" laughs, traces with precision the materiality of faces and the production of smiles, and their transformation into weapons. Though the materiality of faces and emotional labour may sometimes be counterintuitive to theorists and historians of material culture, such materiality is manifest here. Moreover, recognizing such forms of materiality bridges the conceptual gap that obtains (for some) between the two terms "material" and "culture."[5]

There are other dimensions to violent labour, of course, that inform the value of the work of these wartime entertainers. The book contains many references to entertainers keeping the soldiers feeling "normal" (237) and reminding them of what "honest-to-goodness American comedy" (67) sounds like, and, just as importantly, what a "regular American girl" looks like (79). The work here is to form the soldiers into a collective, masculine public of privates based on particular notions of identity and sexuality, all usually contained within a concept of the national subject and the bizarre, usually white supremacist concept of national character that is tied to claims about "real American humour," a most paradoxical and contradictory blending (especially in this context) of violence, race, nationalism, imperialism, patriarchy, and emotional practice. But though the writers often claim that the work of the entertainers was to remind the soldiers of home (58), it seems more likely that they were actually *forming* the soldiers' collective identity by "reminding" them of what they desired to have and desired to be.[6] To put it another way, the entertainers were producing "American" subjectivity as they were apparently recalling it. And while they were doing violent labour by building new (and simultaneously reinforcing old) practices of masculinity, sexuality, and nationalism, they were also doing it through relatively new concepts of emotional labour and of emotional subjectivity. Most significantly, perhaps, they were doing it to kill people, and bring the boys back home, by putting smiles on their faces, and by turning those smiles into war materiel, thereby accomplishing "the biggest job in the war ... to send the boys over the top with a smile" (61).

QUESTIONS FOR A CRITIQUE OF VIOLENT LABOUR

In his famous critique of violence, Walter Benjamin argues that "the task of a critique of violence can be summarized as that of expounding its relation to law and justice" (277). To make a similar rhetorical gesture, it would seem reasonable to claim that the task of a critique of twentieth-century violent labour can be summarized as that of querying, among other things, its relation to commodification within a specific mode of capitalist production. Clearly, such a discussion could, and probably should, engage concepts of reification and commodity culture. For instance, when smiles become weapons, do we imagine them fetishistically as relating only to other weapons and not to the people who make them, wear them, and use them to kill? But such questions are famously limiting to discussions of material culture broadly understood. As Bill Brown contends in *A Sense of Things*, "the human interaction with the nonhuman world of objects, however mediated by the advance of consumer culture, must be recognized as irreducible to that culture" (13). Recognition of such irreducibility keeps open the possibility that we can critique a "modernity which insists on an ontological distinction, arbitrary and artificial, between inanimate objects and human subjects" (187). Clearly, the process by which smiles become things—and specifically violent things—is in part a process of reification, a kind of martial commodification, but there is also something eerie and uncanny about seeing smiles as things, uncanny because when smiles become things, they are different from what we expect, but not as different as they should be. Another way of putting this would be to say that while "thingness" is an experience of the interruption of objectness, that interruption is never total. How, then, can modernity—which necessarily includes modern forms of making war—continue to insist on ontological distinctions between objects and subjects when it turns even smiles into war materiel?

We might begin to answer this question by engaging a classically political and economic set of stakes for critiquing violent labour and the transformation of a smile into a weapon. As Hardt and Negri argue in *Commonwealth*, liberal subjectivity equates the individual with the property owner; we might even go so far as to say, as they do, that while for some man is the thinking animal, the political animal, or even the dangerous animal, for liberal thought man is the property-owning animal: "in the dominant line of European political thought from Locke to Hegel, the absolute rights of people to appropriate things becomes the basis and substantive end of the legally defined free individual" (12-13). If this analysis of liberal political and economic philosophy is correct, then is the state in a contradiction when it appropriates the smiles of individuals as weapons, as things of war? Is such appropriation consistent with liberal logic, given the modern state's joining of war to exceptionality? Or, perhaps more appropriately to a discussion of smiles as violent things and violent labour, does a system of rights that grounds the definition of the free individual in the right to appropriate things also necessarily imply the right to *convert* any matter or practice into a thing, including something as personal, and as public, as a smile? This is a terrible alchemy indeed, but then the pursuit of alchemy is one of the founding practices that brought modern political economy and its weird philosophies into being.

In any case, if emotional labour, such as smiling, turns soldiers' emotional practices into things, this is more than a simple extension of the general view that one's labour is owned by whomever it is sold to, and that such labour under such conditions is alienating on the level of the personal, the social, and even of the species. The twentieth-century emphasis on emotional management of ourselves, which has come under substantial critique by Arlie Hochschild and Eva Illouz as I have mentioned, traces the dramatic and productive forms of subjectivity that emerge from what is precisely a regime of control, even if it often includes forms of self-control. Managed desire, managed hearts, and managed anxieties bring into being the very desires, hearts, and anxieties that they supposedly respond to, and invest our emotional landscape with new interests, new stakes, and new potentials. Managed happiness, too, as Hochschild, Žižek, and Illouz (among others) have written, brings into being one of the foundations of modern political subjectivity, even if happiness is typically not understood (in terms of rights) as something we own, but something we pursue, its realization perpetually deferred in modern economic and political life. The formation and transformation of our emotional lives into labour, and then into commodities, produces indeed a special form of alienation, and perhaps even a special form of fetishization that has yet to be substantially theorized.

Violent labour itself, when sold, involves many of the forms of value and alienation associated with more familiar forms of labour. But unlike many other forms of labour, violent labour specifically seeks to produce domination over others, perhaps even over oneself, and thus it often takes the form, as it does with the boys of *Entertaining the American Army*, of permitting one's own domination by superiors in order to secure dominance over others for one's superiors. A violent labourer in war can only imagine sharing in that dominance in the long term ("victory") through concepts like the nation. This is one of the ways in which violent labour is indeed paid, with the promise that one can secure imagined domination through participation in a fantastic nationalized discourse, and this is of course one of the reasons that militarism and nationalism seem so inseparably bound in modernity. Is this imaginative dimension to the value of violent labour in war its great weakness? Its great strength? Or both?

Such tough questions raised by a critique of violent labour carry significant implications for our understanding of material culture because they reinforce the problem, identified by Bill Brown, that the conditions that make such questions urgent are founded on "artificial and arbitrary" ontological distinctions, and on a non-inevitable political and economic context that situates the practice of making ontological distinctions as the dominant mode for determining the ethics of how and what we do in modernity. This problem, of course, is not something to be dismissed simply as contradictory, but to be understood as the truth or motor of our way of doing things. In *Multitude*, Hardt and Negri pinpoint the truth of this problem when (in deliberately problematical fashion) they define immaterial labour, and specifically when they identify one form of such labour "affective." This latter form of labour they define in these terms:

> Unlike emotions, which are mental phenomena, affects refer equally to body and mind. In fact, affects such as joy and sadness, reveal the present state of life in the entire organism, expressing a certain state of the body along with a certain mode of thinking. Affective labor, then, is labor that produces or manipulates affects such as a feeling of ease, well-being, satisfaction, excitement, or passion. One can recognize affective labor, for example, in the work of legal assistants, flight attendants, and fast food workers (service with a smile). One indication of the rising importance of affective labor, at least in the dominant countries, is the tendency for employers to highlight education, attitude, character, and "prosocial" behaviour as the primary skills employers need. A worker with a good attitude and social skills is another way of saying a worker adept at affective labor. (108)

Such labour is indeed immaterial in the sense that it is not productive of materials (in the way we might see traditional factory labour), but of course in practice what it produces cannot be separated from material culture. This relationship is manifest in the work of entertainers who turn smiles into weapons that will produce dead and wounded bodies, among many other things. The questions for a critique of violent labour this implies raise the stakes of inquiry: Does the specific productivity of violent labour *pervert* modernity's insistence on ontological distinctions between inanimate objects and human subjects, so that a critique of this labour has the potential to undermine those distinctions? Or does violent labour *complete* modernity's work through a dreadful, not arbitrary, but precisely ambivalent form of distinction that permits one to be an inanimate object or a human subject depending on the interests of whoever gets to make the distinction?

FACIAL CONFRONTATIONS

In a charged reading of the surprising materiality of certain forms of expression, Bill Brown discusses scenes of "facial confrontation" in his chapter on "Monstrosity" in *The Material Unconscious*. One of the most memorable is an account drawn from Theodore Dreiser's journalism on the 1893 Chicago World's Fair, in which people who were supposed to remain exotic foreigners in the city, subject to the grinning gaze of American fairgoers, are found smiling *back* at the Americans touring the fair, Americans who were innocently expecting to do the simple emotional labour of asserting their emerging desire for global empire. The "smirks and grins" of the foreigners, Brown writes, "transform[ed] the city itself into a spectacle without a stage, which is to say a kind of carnival" (230-32). It is important to these scenes that the weapons of this confrontation are smiles in the specific forms of smirks and grins, and the smiles, as they are practised, register not as signs of submission but as assertions of spectatorial agency. The smiles render their objects—which is to say their targets—as subject to a violent regime of entertainment, and because everyone is firing back at each other the same kind of smile to the same purpose, these facial confrontations become more properly facial conflicts, little battles of violent and emotional labour fought over the stakes of empire. Such facial conflicts may have indeed turned the city into a kind of carnival, but they also turned it into a battleground.[7]

So perhaps it isn't that histrionic after all to say that "the biggest job in the war is to send the boys over the top with a smile." But there's a catch—the deadly smiles of the boys, once sent out over the top, threaten to return. A boy's face that is smiling while running away from you toward an enemy might be reassuring, but a boy running back to you, after battle, still grinning, is something else entirely, for it is exactly the spectacle you wish to present to the enemy. Indeed, the emotional dimension of violent labour actually requires, at some point, the very emotional problems the entertainers of Thalia Mars are so eager to fix—that is to say, you have to get depressed at some point so that you can be made happy. But what would happen if the entertainers failed to reproduce the problem when they fixed it? This is the contradiction that is the strength of modern emotional labour and, at the same time, that which might make it useless to modernity. A face that is smiling in the right direction is a useful object, a properly deployed weapon, but a face that keeps on smiling, that smiles back at you when it is supposed to be busy pursuing other forms of emotional labour, is more like a thing without any use at all, and with all kinds of unimagined potential.

NOTES

1. <http://www.glasstiger.ca/2009/03/glass-tiger-return-from-their-musical-mission-to-afghanistan/> and <http://www.roland.ca/default.asp?c=285>.
2. In *Frames of War*, Judith Butler calls for another kind of new materialism to understand the transformation of things into weapons, asking "that we rethink the received terms of materialism in order to understand, for instance, how cameras work as instruments of war" (x). Insofar as this approach implicitly involves "how war waging acts upon the senses" (ix), such a materialism must also reckon, I argue, how senses *act upon war*, where things, objects, feelings, and feeling practices (like smiles) become weapons (this is a far superior approach to, say, the universalizing theory that smiles, since they often bare teeth, are inherently aggressive). My wager is that the kind of new materialism we need might be achieved if we recognize labour as a

necessary dimension of violence. So, in addition to seeing a smile as a form of emotional labour, as Arlie Hochschild argues, we might also see it as a form of violent labour. With these terms in place, we might then reckon not only how a camera works as an instrument of war, but also how our smiles work as weapons.

3 For a good history of lyceum lecturing, see Angela G. Ray's *The Lyceum and Public Culture in the Nineteenth-Century United States*. Although claiming a premature death for lyceum lecturing, Ray's history usefully identifies the practice of travel and "circuits" associated with lecturing, a tiring but often joyful form of mobility that the authors of *Army* draw upon to emphasize the fun and romance, and social relevance, of the work of entertainers.

4 Hardt and Negri, drawing on Marx, eloquently summarize the value for critique of working with those who love the object under critique, noting that "the reactionaries tell the truth about the object they love" (19).

5 In his essay "Attackability," Mark Simpson discusses facialization in related terms. Commenting on the famous moment when a US Marine covered the face of Saddam Hussein's statue with an American flag during a stage-managed celebration of US victory in Iraq, only to have it removed for its excessive imperial symbolism, Simpson notes the connection between "facialization," war, and politics (302-3).

6 Slavoj Žižek makes a similar claim about desire in *The Parallax View*. For instance, he claims that we desire "reminders" of what we love back home "to learn again" what we love. Love is therefore "performative in the sense that it changes its object…. [I]t is only because of my love for you that your features appear to me as worthy of love" (355). Ultimately, Žižek sees love (insofar as it is performative) as violent labour, adding that "finding oneself in the position of the beloved is … violent, even traumatic: being loved makes me tangibly aware of the gap between what I am as a determinate being and the unfathomable X in me which stimulates love" (355).

7 In *Frames of War*, Judith Butler notes that such "uncontrollability is not a sufficient basis for utopian excitement," since it can "scatter the effects of war, undermine our ability to focus on its costs, and even naturalize the effects of war as a supposed background of everyday life" (xiv-xv). This is indeed so, and while discussion of "uncontrollability" ought to avoid precisely this kind of abstract utopianism, it is nonetheless the case that uncontrollability indexes the productive contradiction of weapons, insofar as they exist as weapons (specific kinds of objects) only by design and use. Because the possibilities for use are never fixed, weapons, like other objects, always promise multiple possible futures.

WORKS CITED

Arendt, Hannah. *On Violence*. Orlando: Harcourt, 1969. Print.

Benjamin, Walter. "A Critique of Violence." *Reflections: Essays, Aphorisms, Autobiographical Writings*. Ed. Peter Demetz. New York: Schocken Books, 1978. 277-300. Print.

Blair, Walter. *Horse Sense in American Humour from Benjamin Franklin to Ogden Nash*. Chicago: U of Chicago P, 1942. Print.

Brown, Bill. *The Material Unconscious: American Amusement, Stephen Crane & the Economies of Play*. Cambridge, MA: Harvard UP, 1996. Print.

———. *A Sense of Things: The Object Matter of American Literature*. Chicago: U of Chicago P, 2003. Print.

Butler, Judith. *Frames of War: When Is Life Grievable?* London: Verso, 2009. Print.

Evans, James W., and Captain Gardner L. Harding. *Entertaining the American Army: The American Stage and Lyceum in the World War*. New York: Association, 1921. Print.
Hardt, Michael, and Antonio Negri. *Commonwealth*. Cambridge, MA: Belknap P of Harvard UP, 2009. Print.
———. *Labor of Dionysus: A Critique of the State-Form*. Minneapolis: U of Minnesota P, 1994. Print.
———. *Multitude: War and Democracy in the Age of Empire*. New York: Penguin, 2004. Print.
Horkheimer, Max, and Theodor W. Adorno. *The Dialectic of Enlightenment: Philosophical Fragments*. [1944 and 1947] Ed. Gunzelin Schmid Noerr. Trans. Edmund Jephcott. Palo Alto: Stanford UP, 2002. Print.
Hochschild, Arlie Russell. *The Managed Heart: Commercialization of Human Feeling*. 2nd ed. Berkeley: U of California P, 2003. Print.
Illouz, Eva. *Cold Intimacies: The Making of Emotional Capitalism*. Cambridge: Polity, 2007. Print.
Ray, Angela G. *The Lyceum and Public Culture in the Nineteenth-Century United States*. East Lansing: Michigan State UP, 2005. Print.
Simpson, Mark. "Attackability." *Canadian Review of American Studies* 39:3 2009. 299-320. Print.
"thing." *Oxford English Dictionary Online*. Oxford UP, 2011. 1 June 2012.
Žižek, Slavoj. *The Parallax View*. Cambridge, MA: MIT P, 2009. Print.

CHAPTER 8

Moses Cotsworth and the Authenticity of Time

Thomas Allen

"It is a strange urge," Samuel Grafton wrote in the *North American Review* in 1929, "this one which makes us want to alter the calendar" (179).[1] The subject of Grafton's essay, provocatively entitled "Chains for the Years," was the calendar reform movement promoted by Moses Bruine Cotsworth, a retired railway statistician, accountant, and civil servant.[2] Cotsworth's International Fixed Calendar promised to ameliorate a number of logistical problems posed to businesses by the irregular lengths of months and quarters in the Gregorian Calendar. Cotsworth had begun his career in Britain analyzing railway schedules and rates before moving to British Columbia in 1910 to pursue a career as a public servant and accountant, and he thus possessed a detailed knowledge of the inconveniences brought to various business enterprises by the idiosyncrasies of the calendar. He hoped to rationalize calendrical time in much the same way that the railways had helped to rationalize clock time in Britain through the adoption of a uniform "Railway Time" in 1840, and in North America through the creation of five standard time zones in 1883. But though the promised benefits of the proposed new calendar were pragmatic, Cotsworth's rhetoric in his many books and pamphlets evinced an ideological conception of an authentic time that could be recovered and possessed through materiality. As Grafton perceived, Cotsworth sought to enchain time by locating it within material objects.

The International Fixed Calendar promised to rationalize time by ensuring that every month of the year would consist of twenty-eight days, and that 1 January of every year would fall on a Sunday. Thus, Mondays would always be days 2, 9, 16, and 23 of each month, in perpetuity, Tuesdays would be days 3, 10, 17, and 24, and so on with the other days of the week (see Figure

8.1). In order to secure this orderly system, Cotsworth proposed adding a thirteenth month, "Sol," to the middle of the year. Since thirteen months of twenty-eight days add up to 364 days, Cotsworth also proposed adding a holiday to the end of the year, to be called "Year Day," that would fall outside the progression of the days of the week. Similarly, the "Leap Day" that would be added to the end of June every fourth year would also not bear the name of any of the seven days of the week. The resulting calendar would be "perpetual," unchanging from one year to the next, and thus ameliorating, in Cotsworth's view, countless inconveniences and economic inefficiencies resulting from the prevailing system of uneven months and shifting dates. By making months and quarters identical, the fixed calendar would allow for meaningful comparison of revenue across different periods, for predictability of payroll and interest, and for easier management of household and business affairs around the dates of major religious holidays. As he wrote in one of his numerous pamphlets, "[a] calendar simplified to meet these requirements will help continuous employment, circulate money, stabilize business, prosper home life, and promote scientific investigations; to benefit all humanity."[3]

While ultimately Quixotic, Cotsworth's campaign for calendar reform was neither unprecedented nor without powerful adherents. The Gregorian Calendar had superseded the Julian Calendar in most of continental Europe

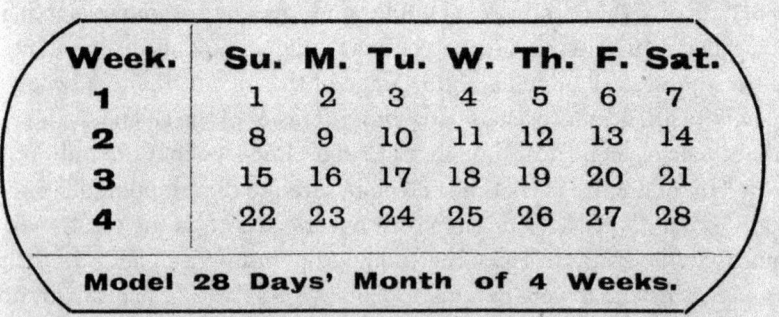

Figure 8.1 Detail from title page of *The Rational Almanac* (1905 ed.)

in the sixteenth century, and in Britain and its colonies in 1752. A variety of other calendar reforms had been proposed in the ensuing century and a half, and in the case of the French Republican Calendar even implemented for a brief period, but all had failed to achieve the widespread acceptance of the Gregorian reform. In large part, this was because any effort at calendar reform required fairly large disruptions in everyday life. As historian Robert Poole observes, "[t]he English calendar as it appeared in the mid-eighteenth century was a great reef of religious, economic, social, ritual, customary, and natural elements, the by-product of centuries of cultural accretion; it could not simply be reformed by a stroke of the legislator's pen . . ." (98). Nevertheless, the Gregorian reform had ultimately met with success that inspired later calendar reformers. Poole disproves the legend that the adoption of the new calendar in the eighteenth century led to riots in England, and, in a study focusing on North America, Mark Smith describes how "the changeover was instituted in the colonies with little difficulty" (561). The Gregorian reform thus provided precedent for the notion that major changes to the calendar could gain political support and broad public acceptance.

It is therefore not entirely surprising that Cotsworth's ideas not only drew enough attention to receive notice (however ambivalent) from major periodicals such as the *North American Review*, but that his campaign attracted powerful backers as well. As Eviatar Zerubavel explains, Cotsworth's reform was promoted by George Eastman, founder of the Eastman Kodak Company, whose "National Committee of Calendar Simplification for the United States . . . included such prestigious and influential members as Henry Ford, the Secretary of Labor, the publisher of the New York Times, the chief of the United States Weather Bureau, the directors of the Bureau of Standards and the *Nautical Almanac*, and the presidents of Yale University, Cornell University, the Massachusetts Institute of Technology, General Motors, General Electric, the National Geographic Society, the American Museum of Natural History, and the American Bar Association" (79-80). In her biography of Eastman, Elizabeth Brayer recounts that Eastman "decided to take Cotsworth under his wing," providing him with financial support and promotional assistance, and even leading Eastman Kodak to adopt the thirteen-month calendar for internal use, a practice that it maintained until the 1980s (499). The proposal for a fixed calendar also attracted significant support within Canada, as Sir Sandford Fleming promoted Cotsworth's ideas to the Royal Society of Canada, and wrote to Cotsworth, "I can do no more at present and it remains for me to congratulate you on being the father of the reform which will be of much benefit to the human family in the future years of the world" (qtd. in Cotsworth, "The Rational Almanak," 540). As Fleming informed Cotsworth in his letter, the Royal Society formally endorsed Cotsworth's proposal in 1912, and recommended that it be brought to the attention of the governor general of Canada. Fleming confidently predicted that the reform would ultimately be adopted by an international conference of nations.

Cotsworth attracted such impressive support for his proposed reform by engaging in a long campaign of education and propaganda. He published a book entitled *The Rational Almanac* in a first edition around 1900, and then republished this book many times over the ensuing years, along with a number of other books and pamphlets (see Figure 8.2). He delivered a paper on calendar reform before the Royal Society of Canada in 1909, founded the

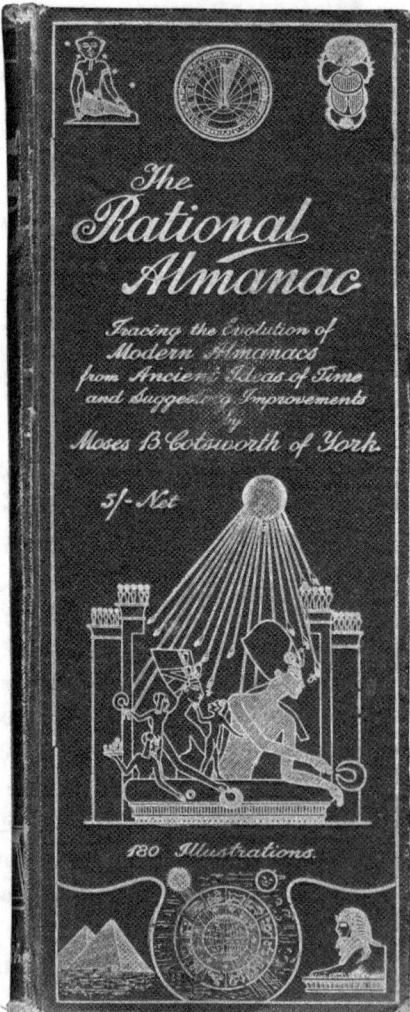

Figure 8.2 Front cover of *The Rational Almanac* (1905 ed.)

International Fixed Calendar League in 1922, and provided expert advice to the Committee on Calendar Reform of the League of Nations.[4] His archived papers include a variety of posters suggesting a regular program of public lectures on the topic. In his *North American Review* article, Grafton observed that Cotsworth's "International Fixed Calendar . . . has received more attention, and rightly, than all of the other plans put together" (180). Cotsworth's best chance to see his ideas put into practice came in 1931, when the League of Nations held a conference on calendar reform in Geneva. The proposal for a perpetual calendar was defeated by the assembled international delegates, mostly on the grounds that it would result in movement of the Sabbath off of its seven-day cycle. Perhaps surprisingly, opposition to calendar reform came primarily from religious groups. Zerubavel notes that it was "the prospect of the interruption of the continuous flow of the week by the introduction of 'blank' days that Sabbatarians found objectionable" about the fixed calendar (80). Christi Davies, Eugene Trivizas, and Roy Wolfe point out that this episode calls into question our presumption that methods of marking and organizing time exemplify the Weberian tendency "to create a rational secular world" (251). In fact, the religious opposition to calendar reform exemplifies the way that modern society is often marked by conflicts between arguments in favour of greater rationalization of everyday life, typically couched in economic terms, and equally vigorous polemics in defence of various forms of tradition. The fact that these traditions are often themselves modern inventions reveals the complexity and ambiguity of the positions and stakes in such cultural debates.

While the International Fixed Calendar failed before a coalition of religious traditionalists, Cotsworth represented himself as a traditionalist as well, albeit one with a different perspective on the history of the calendar. He insistently couched his arguments in studies and interpretations of historical artifacts and records of timekeeping. He portrayed his own scheme for a reformed calendar as both modern and rational but also rooted in antiquity, the restoration of insights into the nature of time that had been gleaned in previous ages and then lost. As he wrote in *The Rational Almanac*: "The Egyptians seem to have first discovered the true length of the year by studying Pyramid Shadows, as shown on the pyramid pages hereof. By rationally instituting equal months of 30 days each, they appear to have used much better common-sense, and studied the convenience of their people, far more than did the Roman originators of our erratic Almanac" (1907 ed., 20). In Cotsworth's view, the calendar had been corrupted by human venality, and a truly rational calendar would restore a more authentic and even moral relationship to time (see Figure 8.3). This authentic time could be recovered

Plate 12
AUGUSTUS CAESAR (1940 years ago) RIGGING UP and MUDDLING our MONTHS
THE PRESUMPTUOUS PRIDE AND ARROGANCE OF AUGUSTUS WAS THE ENTIRE CAUSE OF THE LENGTH OF
FEBRUARY, AUGUST, SEPTEMBER, OCTOBER AND NOVEMBER BEING ARBITRARILY
FIXED BY THOSE THREE STROKES OF HIS PEN—SEE PAR. 6

Figure 8.3 Illustration from *The Fixed Yearal* (1914 ed.). Courtesy of the Library Archives and Special Collections, University of Ottawa.

through the material traces of the past, the objects that human beings had created to measure and record time.

Cotsworth's papers are replete with photographs and newspaper clippings describing objects and relics associated with the history of timekeeping. A typical example of this interest is a note card on which he jotted down: "The obelisks erected throughout Egypt are standing testimony to the fact that the Egyptians recorded their time by shadows."[5] He kept voluminous notes of similar observations, especially regarding pyramids, obelisks, and calendar stones of ancient Egypt, Europe, Mexico, and other places, along with drawings and photographs of such objects, an archive that reflects years of devotion to the study of the physical relics and artifacts of timekeeping methods. Cotsworth applied his professional understanding of mathematics to learning how measurements of time could be taken by observing the relationship between constructed objects and the Sun and stars. He then tested his historical research in the field, making use of more contemporary monuments. According to a handwritten draft of a letter dated 24 September 1922, Cotsworth conducted an experiment in which he measured the shadow cast by the Washington Monument in order to demonstrate how the "Pyramid Priests of Egypt" had discovered the "365.242 days' length of the Year."[6] This note reveals the characteristic way in which Cotsworth sought to link the past to the present by associating materiality, religious history, and science, the "Pyramid Priests" being praised for their mathematical acuity.

Cotsworth also travelled to Egypt himself (a trip he described as "a serious tax upon my limited means") to test the mathematics of the pyramids first-hand: "When I examined the Pyramid's Local conditions, and investigated the shadows . . . in Nov., 1900, they fully confirmed my expectations" (*Rational Almanac*, 1914 ed., 10). By drawing these connections to an ancient world defined by science and industry, in which priests were mathematicians and astronomers, he sought to restore a more authentic relationship to true time, a time both scientific and godly. Cotsworth's sanguine confidence in the inevitable outcome of his observations may raise questions about the rigour of his methods, but the intention of these activities on his part was to establish his credibility as an authority on the subject of time through expert knowledge of the object world of timekeeping.

As Arjun Appadurai has argued, the link between materiality and authenticity has to do with commodification, the circulation of goods through the market within a capitalist system. Indeed, Cotsworth's ideas about calendar reform came in an era when time itself was increasingly viewed as a commodity. Historians such as Ian Bartky and Carlene Stephens have documented the many ways in which time could be bought and sold within the market economy that developed over the course of the nineteenth century: not only as abstract labour time but in the material form of ever more precise clocks for workplaces and time signals sent from observatories.[7] While some versions of the buying and selling of time existed before the rise of capitalism, the circulation of time within market exchange represented a qualitatively different process, a process in which the nature of time itself was fundamentally altered. By the point at which Cotsworth's movement for calendar reform got under way in the early twentieth century, time had assumed the reified characteristics of a commodity within the capitalist system of exchange.

As Appadurai explains, the evolution of the commodity form of objects brings with it "a particular set of issues concerning authenticity and expertise that plagues the modern West" (45). The putative authenticity of a small number of special objects serves a palliative role for a culture in which mass production makes the object world in general more fungible. It is the very threat to the notion of authenticity posed by commodity circulation that calls forth the desire to fix the authenticity of specific objects. Thus, Appadurai notes that the concern with authenticity emerges most vigorously around objects of art. A class of experts is called upon to attest to the authenticity of artworks, and this relatively minor fragment of the market for goods comes to function as a repository for ideas about authenticity as a category. The existence of a small bastion of special objects, designated as genuine in ways defined by experts, helps to enable the fungibility of goods within the larger market.

In a manner akin to that adopted by the arbiters of legitimate works of art, Cotsworth positioned himself as an expert on the authenticity of time. Of course, there are many differences between material objects such as paintings or sculptures, and immaterialities such as time. However, the distinction between material and immaterial is fluid, and our understanding of time is always mediated by the material world. We experience the passage of time through motion and change, physical processes we can sense with our bodies. Indeed, cultural historians have pointed out that different forms of time emerge from the very practices that seek to measure it. Thus, objects such as clocks and watches *produce* forms of time through their particular technologies of measurement, just as the movements of the Earth around the Sun and the Moon around the Earth produce distinctive experiences of temporal change. Far from a purely abstract concept, time is immanent in the material world: the most precise measurements of public time are now taken from the vibrations of cesium atoms, while the aging of our own bodies constitutes the most profoundly intimate experience of time, one that resolutely reminds us of our own materiality.

While Cotsworth did not possess exactly our contemporary understanding of the materiality of time (there were no atomic clocks in his day), the material qualities of temporal experience that Cotsworth discovered in his research provided the foundation for his rhetoric of temporal authenticity. Although he was a contemporary of Einstein, Cotsworth did not at all embrace the kind of relativistic conception of time that we usually associate with the cultural milieu of the early twentieth century. Unlike modernist philosophers such as Henri Bergson, Cotsworth maintained that a single, authentic time had been given to the world by God. Stephen Kern notes that the theories of Bergson and Einstein influenced a generation of cultural workers—artists, writers, and philosophers—who promulgated a notion of time as subjective and relative. Nevertheless, as Kern also describes, these proponents of time's multiplicity and fluidity were opposed by powerful individuals and institutions seeking to homogenize and rationalize public time.[8] In a study of public timekeeping in American cities, historian Alexis McCrossen points out that the proliferation of large numbers of objects such as grand public clocks in urban spaces beginning in the late nineteenth century supported a particular understanding of modern life as synchronized and highly regulated: "Of course all these clocks, time balls, and bells signified the time; but no less they invoked cultural meaning and social values swirling through American cities. The timepieces that went up across the nation were integral to the rhythms, processes, and values associated with a modernity in which time was minutely divided, closely monitored, and constantly accelerating" (218-19). This observation could apply to urban life in the same period in Europe and Canada as well. Monumental objects devoted to public timekeeping promoted a homogenized, universal understanding of time even while scientific theory and philosophy pushed ideas about relativism and subjectivity into popular culture.

Cotsworth's understanding of the calendar as a medium for authentic time thus situates him on one side of a cultural debate over the nature of modernity. His writings suggest a kind of moral imperative in the correct measurement of true time, and as a progressive thinker he believed that scientific and technical progress should lend itself to ameliorating the fallen condition of imperfect timekeeping. Often referring overtly to biblical sources, Cotsworth suggested that the most ancient astronomers had known the most precise ways of measuring time, but that these methods had been compromised over the course of secular history by the corrupting influences of politics, vanity, and irrationality. *The Rational Almanac* promised to show how "Almanacs increased in usefulness as Human Needs developed, until the Roman Cæsars arbitrarily fixed the present Erratic, Uneven Months to suit their Time" (1907 ed., 447). In Cotsworth's view, the various human efforts to measure time represented imperfect attempts to capture a singular, correct time. In a pamphlet entitled "Moses, the Greatest of Calendar Reformers," he asserted, "Only in the 20th century are we beginning to learn from the patient researches of several able and earnest students of Ancient Scriptures that during the later centuries of the Jewish nation's vicissitudes, the nearly perfect Mosaic solar-calendar of the Exodus was lost, forgotten or misunderstood." While Cotsworth identified himself as a Christian, he sought to reach out to members of other religious traditions by casting biblical history in universal terms: "Jews, Christians and Mohammedans unitedly revere the ancient authority and personality of Moses as their great religious leader and law-giver."[9] Cotsworth's studies of artifacts such as pyramids and obelisks were thus situated within a messianic rhetoric of recovery of this foundational and universal state of timekeeping.

The Rational Almanac, the various editions of which each run to hundreds of pages, contains the most complete exposition of Cotsworth's theories. In a

1907 edition, the almanac's title page promises "180 Illustrations explaining the Mystery of the Pyramids, Sphinx, Obelisks, Druidical Circles, Mounds, Vertical Stones, etc., Erected to Record Yearly Almanac Times." Dozens of pages in each edition trace the history of time measurement through such objects. A 1914 edition recounts how the ancient Romans, before the advent of the Julian Calendar, would keep track of the progression of years by "publicly driving the Annual Nail into the wall of the temple of Minerva, Goddess of Wisdom and Science" (2). Cotsworth recurred often to images of such tactile practices of timekeeping, the driving of nails or the insertion of pegs into holes on calendar boards, and discussed the physical makeup of ancient almanacs, such as the wooden clog almanacs used in medieval Europe (see Figure 8.4). He described the construction of the pyramids in Egypt and Mexico, which he believed had led to the discovery of the true length of the year, as a muscular, tactile engineering feat:

> Surely we cannot but admit that such a glorious result as the birth of the Calendar for the welfare of the Egyptian and the furtherance of Civilization, was well worth the vast efforts and stupendous labours expended in building even the vast series of Egyptian Pyramids, to bring forth the knowledge of the true year, which is the greatest permanent and most practically valuable factor ever made known to humanity. (1914 ed., 5)

Cotsworth's descriptions recall Marx's phrase "sensuous human activity"; while Cotsworth was no Marxist in his political orientation, his understanding of time measurement echoes Marx's arguments about how culture and ideas emerge from human activity that transforms nature into a usable object world.[10]

In Cotsworth's representations and interpretations of historical timekeeping objects, authentic time emerges from the intersection between human creation and the true time that such creative acts apprehend. In other words, Cotsworth's time is at once both a product of human activity and a measurement of a pre-existing absolute. To Cotsworth, the very ability of human beings, or at least some groups of human beings, to produce such authentic time through labour signified a closer relationship with God and nature. In *The Fixed Yearal* [sic], another book-length publication, Cotsworth elaborated on the benefits of this sensuously achieved connection to temporal authenticity:

> The Zodiacal record of passing Seasons is the best means by which the mightiest efforts of mankind have established permanent prosperity for all nations. It required the strenuous labors of multitudes of Egyptians during

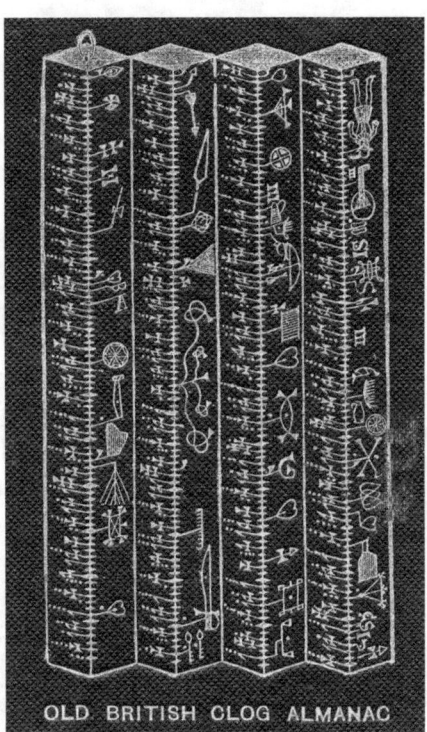

Figure 8.4 Illustration of wooden almanac, detail of back cover of *The Rational Almanac* (1905 ed.)

thousands of years to derive that final pyramid slope by which the 365 day sectors of that Celestial circle were precisely registered to tally the yearly progress of the sun around the star-studded sky. (facing title page)

The illustration on the same page shows a bearded old man, a clock face and gears, and a sphinx with a thirteen-month calendar dangling from its neck (see Figure 8.5). A caption reads, "Plate A—The Length of the Year first sought by the Sphinx Method, was found by the Pyramid-Builders who later developed Star Astronomy, as here depicted. 'Father Time' is Re-gearing the Year to record 13 equal Months of 4 Weeks at his original 'year works,' the Sphinx and Great Pyramid, in Egypt, where the basis of the Calendar and World's Time were evolved, as the most useful knowledge." By representing the monuments of ancient Egypt as a "year works" in which authentic time is produced, Cotsworth connects the present to the past through the continuity of engineering as a human activity. The word "original" attests to this authenticity, while the figure of Father Time evokes the conceptual confusion that underlies much of Cotsworth's thinking: Is Father Time a personification of time itself, or a mythic superman who measures the true time? In fact, he seems to occupy both roles at once.

This conceptual confusion perhaps explains Cotsworth's apparently strange juxtaposition of modern rationalism and economic arguments with an idea that his proposal would represent a restoration of the "mosaic" calendar. If time is both a product of human activity and an attribute of nature that humans seek to measure, then time is perfectly embodied in the figure of Father Time, who is both time itself as well as an engineer seeking to measure time.

This figuration of time within the productive human body also appears in Cotsworth's commentaries on the temporal rhythms of the reproductive cycle. Many of his writings make reference to the periods of gestation and of the menstrual cycle, which he described as another form of authentic, natural timekeeping rooted in the material world. "We all need the equal 4-week month indicated by Nature's life-producing periods of 28 days," he wrote in a pamphlet on the subject. He theorized that the lengths of reproductive cycles had led to the creation of the seven-day week in agricultural societies, writing: "The hen's one week difference from the duck's and from the 28-day

Figure 8.5   Illustration facing title page of *The Fixed Yearal* (1914). Courtesy of the Library Archives and Special Collections, University of Ottawa.

period for farmer's wives, with the 7-days difference between the gestation periods for cats and dogs, helped to establish Nature's 7-day week."[11] Cotsworth elaborated on the connection between the mechanics of timekeeping and animal husbandry in a 1913 article for *British Columbia Magazine*, in which he praised scientists at the government's Experimental Farm in Agassiz, British Columbia, for using precise seasonal measurements to produce a double crop of lambs in the same year. Cotsworth connected their methods to his own interpretation of the biblical story of Jacob. According to Cotsworth, Jacob had enriched himself by doubling lamb production through the use of wooden stakes to mark the position of the Sun on the horizon:

> The vital point of observation he had to watch for was the central distant stake in line from the central sighting stake, to see when the sun rose due east on March 21 and September 23, in order to guide him to the right dates for driving the rams and the goats to their respective flocks for breeding, as Syrian farmers now locate by means of printed calendars Jacob lacked. Jacob had only the sun and his own powers of observation to guide him by means of those stakes he erected each six months. . . .
>
> The main point is that, by using Jacob's method in British Columbia, we can reduce the cost of living. . . . ("Double Crops," 706)

This passage reflects Cotsworth's typical mélange of creative religious historiography, economic utopianism, and the material practices of timekeeping, here intersecting in the analysis of the reproductive potential of the sheep.

While Cotsworth's theories about the biological origins of traditional units of time such as the week were perhaps not as well grounded in fact as his mathematical analyses of the angles of shadows cast by objects, what is of interest in these writings is his perception of a connection between the materiality of human and animal bodies, and the structure of units of time measurement such as the seven-day week. His opponents in various religious communities argued that the seven days of the week had been ordained by God, in order to ensure the observation of the Sabbath every seventh day. For them, the seven-day week was associated with textualism and the Word and signified the elevation of human beings, created in God's image, over the material world. Cotsworth also believed in the importance of the Sabbath, but linked scriptural text to embodiment: "For *women*, the 28-day-month is Nature's regulating unit, which constantly times their physical periods of 28-days, and the 280 days during which all humanity develops to birth."[12] Drawing on quasi-scientific theories circulating at the time, he argued that assigning all months a uniform length of twenty-eight days would enable parents to select the sex of their children and enable women to control reproduction without contraceptives.[13] "Half of humanity is composed of women," he helpfully observed, "everyone of whom will be greatly benefited by the 28-days per month calendar in their personal reckonings of exactly one month and 10-months."[14] While Cotsworth's writings about women and time will strike most readers as a superficial and condescending effort to pander to women for their support of the calendar reform scheme, they are also consonant with Cotsworth's general sense of the immanence of time in the material world. By linking time with biology, and especially the biology of the human body, Cotsworth engaged in the kind of post-Darwinian theorizing that scholars such as Kern and Elizabeth Grosz have associated with Bergson.[15] But while Bergson's "creative evolution" emphasized the potential of biological organisms to create different futures through the indeterminacy of volition within time, Cotsworth sought to fix time by treating not just the object world in general but the organic world, including the human body, as a repository of stability and predictability.

In so doing, Cotsworth produced a notion of authentic time that contrasted with the apparent fluidity of time within modernity chronicled by his contemporaries such as Bergson. This authentic time served an important role in mediating the human relationship to the object world in the first half of the twentieth century. During a period in which capitalist exchange seemed poised to render all temporal contexts merely pragmatic—the coincidental meeting of actors traversing a perpetually shifting marketplace of rootless goods and desires—Cotsworth offered a stable foundation of time as a transcendent context rooted in the object world and the human body itself. Another of Cotsworth's contemporaries, sociologist Georg Simmel, characterized the modern age in terms of "acceleration in the pace of life" in which time itself had become "a very expensive commodity" that was also a symbol and regulator of the market as a whole (549). For Simmel, modern life was characterized by the chaotic incursion of the new, sweeping aside tradition. For Cotsworth, in contrast, modernity could be organized and regulated by experts whose activities would infuse commodified time with the materials of the real.

The calendar itself thus served the role of authentic object that stood outside of but in complementary relationship to the fungible time of market exchange. Quoting a phrase from Baudrillard, Appadurai observes that the authentic object came to be viewed as the "mirror of production" in the nineteenth century. "Authenticity," Appadurai explains, "in this early industrial framework, is no longer a matter of connoisseurship, but of objectively given production methods" (47). Cotsworth thus emphasized the nature of the authentic calendar as a creation of certain specific methods of ancient but quasi-industrial production: sensuous, mathematical, and precise. The calendar itself, as a physical object, represented the mastery (or enchainment, as Grafton intuited in the *North American Review*) of time, abstract, fungible, commodified, and debased in the market. By enchaining time within this material form, Cotsworth, the railway statistician, efficiency expert, and accountant, sought to redeem time from the world he had himself helped to create. Within the accelerating modern world described by social thinkers such as Simmel, Cotsworth made the pages of the perpetual calendar the bastion of material authenticity for that most fungible of abstract commodities, time itself.

NOTES

I would like to thank Véronique Paris and Roxanne Lafleur of the University of Ottawa Libraries for their assistance with the preparation of the images for this chapter.

1 Samuel Grafton would become one of the best-known journalists in the United States, but at the time this article was published he was only twenty-two years of age. See his obituary in the *New York Times*.
2 Cotsworth's biography is not well documented, but the available information is summarized by Francesca Rossetti in "Moses Bruine Cotsworth Fonds: An inventory in The Library of the University of British Columbia Special Collections and University Archives Division" (March 2000). The Moses Bruine Cotsworth Fonds at the Library of the University of British Columbia (MBC Fonds hereafter) are the major repository of Cotsworth's papers. The fonds contains not only pamphlets published by Cotsworth during his lifetime, but also his handwritten notes and a variety of other items he collected such as photographs, postcards, and newspaper clippings attesting to Cotsworth's interest in objects and structures associated with timekeeping.
3 Pamphlet A, p. 1, MBC Fonds, box 2, folder 1.
4 John Ingham's 1931 article on calendar reform in *Popular Astronomy* provides a useful contemporary summary of some of the partial successes of Cotsworth's proposals, including the introduction of a calendar reform bill to the United States House of Representatives in 1918 (199).
5 MBC Fonds, box 1, folder 2. This note is undated.
6 MBC fonds, box 1, folder 1.
7 Bartky focuses mainly on the creation of standard time zones by the railways and on the sale of telegraphic time signals by observatories, while Stephens presents a more comprehensive social history of timekeeping in the United States.
8 While Kern discusses these issues throughout *The Culture of Time and Space*, the most relevant sections of his discussion may be found on pp. 10-35.
9 "Moses, the Greatest of Calendar Reformers," pamphlet C in MBC Fonds, box 2, folder 1.
10 The phrase "sensuous human activity" appears in the first of the "Theses on Feuerbach," where Marx argues against both idealism and mechanistic materialism. "Sensuous human activity" attributes agency to human beings acting within material contexts.
11 MBC fonds, box 2, pamphlet 28, p. 1.

12   MBC fonds, box 2, pamphlet 28, p. 3.
13   MBC fonds, box 2, pamphlet F, "Women's Cause in Calendar Reform."
14   MBC fonds, box 2, pamphlet 28, p. 3.
15   A caution offered by Grosz in her study of time and biological theory seems to apply well to Cotsworth: "there is clearly much that is problematic about many of the assumptions, methods, and criteria used in some cases of biological analysis, which have been actively if unconsciously used by those with various paternalistic, patriarchal, racist, and class commitments to rationalize their various positions" (13). The linking of biology, especially that of the human body, with ideas about culture, politics, and society, has often produced disastrous results. Nevertheless, Grosz points out that such misuse of biological theory does not mean that the topic as a whole lacks more salutary possibilities.

WORKS CITED

Anon. "Samuel Grafton, Newspaper Columnist." Obituary. *New York Times* 16 Dec. 1997: B5. Print.

Appadurai, Arjun. "Introduction: Commodities and the Politics of Value." *The Social Life of Things: Commodities in Cultural Perspective* Ed. Arjun Appadurai. Cambridge: Cambridge UP, 1986. 3-63. Print.

Bartky, Ian. *Selling the True Time: Nineteenth-Century Timekeeping in America*. Stanford: Stanford UP, 2000. Print.

Brayer, Elizabeth. *George Eastman: A Biography*. Baltimore: Johns Hopkins UP, 1996. Rpt. Rochester: Rochester UP, 2006. Print.

Cotsworth, Moses Bruine. "Double Crops of Lambs in British Columbia." *British Columbia Magazine* 9.12 (Dec. 1913): 705-6. Print.

———. *The Fixed "Yearal" Proposed to Replace Changing Almanaks and Calendars*. New Westminster, BC: International Almanak Reform League, 1914. Print.

———. *The Rational Almanac: Tracing the Evolution of Modern Almanacs from Ancient Ideas of Time, and Suggesting Improvements*. Acomb, UK: M. B. Cotsworth, 1907, 1914. Print.

———. "The Rational Almanak." *British Columbia Magazine* 8.7 (July 1912): 532-41. Print.

Davies, Christie, Eugene Trivizas, and Roy Wolfe. "The Failure of Calendar Reform (1922-1931): Religious Minorities, Businessmen, Scientists, and Bureaucrats." *Journal of Historical Sociology* 12.3 (Sept. 1999): 251-70. Print.

Grafton, Samuel. "Chains for the Years." *The North American Review* 227.2 (Feb. 1929): 178-84. Print.

Grosz, Elizabeth. *Time Travels: Feminism, Nature, Power*. 2nd ed. Durham, NC: Duke UP, 2005. Print.

Ingham, John A. "The Thirteen Month Calendar." *Popular Astronomy* 39 (1931): 199-204. Print.

Kern, Stephen. *The Culture of Time and Space: 1880-1918*. Cambridge: Harvard UP, 1983. Print.

McCrossen, Alexis. "'Conventions of Simultaneity': Time Standards, Public Clocks, and Nationalism in American Cities and Towns, 1871–1905." *Journal of Urban History* 33.2 (Jan. 2007): 217-53. Print.

Poole, Robert. "'Give Us Our Eleven Days!': Calendar Reform in Eighteenth-Century England." *Past and Present* 149.1 (Nov. 1995), 95-139. Print.

Rossetti, Francesca. "Biographical Sketch." *Moses Bruin Cotsworth Fonds: An Inventory.* The Library of the University of British Columbia, Special Collections and University Archives Division. March 2000. Print.

Scaff, Lawrence A. "The Mind of the Modernist: Simmel on Time." *Time & Society* 14.1 (Mar. 2005): 5-23. Print.

Simmel, Georg. *The Philosophy of Money.* Trans. Tom Bottomore and David Frisby. London: Routledge, 2011. Print.

Smith, Mark M. "Culture, Commerce, and Calendar Reform in Colonial America." *The William and Mary Quarterly,* Third Series, 55.4 (Oct. 1998): 557-84. Print.

Stephens, Carlene. *On Time: How America Has Learned to Live Life by the Clock.* Boston: Bullfinch/Little, Brown, 2002. Print.

Zerubavel, Eviatar. *The Seven Day Circle: The History and Meaning of the Week.* Chicago: U of Chicago P, 1985. Print.

CHAPTER 9

Materializing Climate Change
Images of Exposure, States of Exception

Nicole Shukin

INTRODUCTION

In *The Material Unconscious: American Amusement, Stephen Crane, and the Economics of Play* (1996), Bill Brown seizes upon the seemingly superfluous mention of a barometer in Flaubert's description of Mme. Aubain's parlour in his short story "Un coeur simple." More than a mimetic detail whose inclusion generates a textual reality effect for readers, Flaubert's mention of an instrument used to measure atmospheric pressure and to forecast weather becomes, for Brown, one site where a material history of things pokes through the surface of the literary text like the tip of an otherwise submerged iceberg.

In what follows I draw attention to two very different barometers, if I can call them that, two cultural instruments designed not so much to generate a barometrics of current atmospheric pressures as to produce moving, material images of a historical crisis that is globally diffuse and staggering in the sheer complexity of its ramifying effects: climate change. The first so-called barometer consists of a series of photographic "ice slides" produced in 2005 by Heather Ackroyd and Dan Harvey, British artists who generated the slides on a Cape Farewell expedition to the Arctic. The Cape Farewell project, founded in 2003 by British artist-educator David Buckland, has launched a string of Arctic expeditions with the aim of directly exposing its mixed crews of artists and scientists to the impacts of climate change upon polar environments. The second barometer is a documentary film co-produced in 2010 by Zacharias Kunuk and Ian Mauro, *Qapirangajuq: Inuit Knowledge and Climate Change*. *Qapirangajuq* is an Inuktituk-language film that relays the observations of Inuit elders and "weathermen" who notice material signs of climate change in the ice, wind, snow, and animals of the North.

Both "ice slides" and *Qapirangajuq* represent unique collaborations between art and science. The Cape Farewell project intentionally invites both scientists and artists to join its series of Arctic expeditions in order to spark exchange between these two forms of knowledge. *Qapirangajuq* brings Kunuk's creative practice, as an Inuk filmmaker best known for his 2001 feature film *Atanarjuat (the Fast Runner)*, together with Mauro's scientific training. In the age of the Anthropocene—the current era in which, as the postcolonial historian Dipesh Chakrabarty argues, "humans have become geological agents" and a veritable force of nature on a planetary scale—it's not just old lines between art and science that become irrelevant; an "age-old humanist distinction between natural history and human history" has itself irrevocably collapsed (207, 201).

I call these photographic and filmic productions cultural barometers even though it is a world-historical climate condition, rather than fluctuations in the weather, that they seek to materialize. The distinction between weather and climate is drawn along temporal lines by meteorologists as well as by authoritative agencies like NASA. According to NASA, "the difference between weather and climate is a measure of time. Weather is what conditions of an atmosphere are over a short period of time, and climate is how the atmosphere 'behaves' over relatively long periods of time."[1] The temporal distinction between weather and climate will take on an enlarged significance as I comparatively assess the cultural interventions posed by these two so-called barometers. For in crystallizing climate change as a crisis-event within the short time frame of an Arctic excursion, the ice slides of Ackroyd and Harvey inadvertently bring something else into view as well: a state of exception excited by a sense of ecological emergency, one that justifies dramatic efforts to avert a global catastrophe. By contrast, *Qapirangajuq*'s engagement with the crisis of climate change complicates the Western cultural and political habit of pronouncing states of emergency as exceptional time-spaces in which a strong state or individual exercises licence to suspend the rule of ordinary life.

The association of the state of exception with a European model of sovereign power traces back to the German political theorist Carl Schmitt's theory of the state and his renowned assertion, "[s]overeign is he who decides on the exception" (7). Schmitt's statement has catalyzed numerous conceptualizations of the state of exception, including Walter Benjamin's counter that "[t]he tradition of the oppressed teaches us that the 'state of emergency' in which we live is not the exception but the rule" (259) as well as numerous reflections by contemporary theorists such as Giorgio Agamben and Judith Butler. The state of exception is usually understood in relation to the state's political or juridical power to suspend the law, and relatively little attention has been paid to how ecological crises condition new states of exception in the late twentieth and early twenty-first centuries.[2] More work calls to be done, in particular, tracking how a state of exception may be culturally declared by ecological subjects who feel justified in mobilizing a set of "emergency powers" that, while obviously different from those politically executed by a sovereign state, nonetheless replicate its model of sovereignty through an exercise of strong subjectivity. Paradoxically, as I'll suggest in my reading of "ice slides," such emergency powers are in this instance expressed in the cultural agency and even hyper-responsibility of the ecological expedition. It may be tempting to view the Cape Farewell expedition as responding to the call made by Benjamin, who proposes that when the state of emergency becomes the rule, the task then becomes "to bring about a *real* state of emergency" (259; emphasis added). However, I am concerned that the opposite may be the case: that under the shadow of climate change there arise ecological citizens who dangerously act as sovereign in relation to a precarious planet that they territorially undertake to defend. And while territory, or space, matters in relation to the Arctic expedition that launches in the South, time will emerge as even more crucial to the ecological state of exception that it passionately pronounces.

By contrast, *Qapirangajuq* visualizes global climate change in a manner that challenges both the model of sovereignty exercised by European nation-states and its mimicry in those forms of ecological subjectivity that mobilize emergency powers through extreme cultural missions. In materializing images of a very different time and duration of both exposure and observation—that is, in placing climate change within a longer history of Arctic incursions and exercises of sovereign power, as well as within a long practice of Inuit environmental attention and adaptability—Kunuk and Mauro's documentary refuses to excite the affect of ecological emergency. Or to put it another way, in contrast with the Cape Farewell project, *Qapirangajuq* refuses to culturally declare a state of exception, even as the film presents moving images of the especially profound impact that climate change is having on the Inuit. By virtue of living in unspectacular, everyday exposure to the environmental and social effects of global warming on the North, the Inuit in the film offer a kind of ecological knowledge and responsibility that makes visible the incongruity of exceptional exercises of environmental witnessing by liberal-minded, well-intentioned Southerners. As such, the documentary can be viewed as contributing to Indigenous critiques of sovereignty as a Eurocentric concept and model of governance—one that is "inappropriate as a political objective for indigenous peoples," as Taiaiake Alfred puts it (38)—by throwing into relief a model of ecological subjectivity that is equally "inappropriate" for those whose conditions of life are most immediately affected by climate change (38).

The different images of climate change materialized by these two collaborative projects is a biopolitical matter of considerable significance when one considers that the signs of melting ice in the Arctic are actively being read not only as a *crisis* justifying eco-cultural incursions into the North to witness its effects first-hand, but as an *opportunity* for Canada and other nation-states to capitalize upon warming Arctic waters. As melting ice formations physically open up new passages for global trade, countries like Canada are making increasingly aggressive assertions of sovereignty over the North. However, it's not only political claims to Arctic sovereignty that are excited by the effects of climate change in the North, but cultural acts of environmental witness that risk reanimating an imperial model of European expeditionizing—and what Lauren Berlant terms a "melodrama" of sovereign subjectivity—as global Southerners seek to actively respond with "the heroic agency a crisis seems already to have called for" ("Slow" 760). That these political, economic, and cultural dramas can function as supplementary or complicit territorializations is suggested by the Canadian government's recent revival of interest, under the conservative leadership of Stephen Harper, in Captain John Franklin's infamous and ill-fated Arctic expedition of 1845 in search of the Northwest Passage. The Harper government's investment in this fetishized fragment of its national history through the funding of archaeological searches for Franklin's lost ships, the HMS *Erebus* and the HMS *Terror*, coincides with its geopolitical interest in control over Arctic waters, bringing into view the long relationship between the spell of the expedition and the extensions of sovereignty.[3]

In an essay on endemic obesity, Berlant works to interrupt what she terms the "mimetic" resemblance between a Schmittian model of the state whose sovereignty is seen to lie in events of decision making (i.e., declaring a state of emergency) and a model of the subject who heroically exercises the decisional agency to improve their situation ("Slow" 757). For Berlant, a "crisis rhetoric" that frames the epidemic of obesity in terms of social urgency and personal agency fails to grasp—even occludes from view—the endemic temporality or "scene of slow death" within which it makes little sense to speak of sovereign subjects, events, and decisions ("Slow" 761). "Slow death" is Berlant's term for a biopolitical time or "zone of temporality" (758) in which "life building and the attrition of human life are indistinguishable" (754). While she specifically theorizes slow death in relation to the structural conditions and everyday, wearing effects of endemic obesity, the concept is arguably relevant to the time of climate crisis. As will come into focus in what follows, the moving images of climate change given in "ice slides" and *Qapirangajuq* are underpinned by a biopolitics that involves stark differences in the duration and intensity of a body's or population's exposure to the most punishing effects of global warming. These incommensurate exposure times are intimately bound up with questions of sovereign subjects and states that invoke ecological emergency as an "exceptional" occasion for melodramatic or militaristic action. The stakes, finally, are whether climate change will be understood within the long historical time frames and structural depredations of imperialist expansion and colonial capitalism, or whether it will be declared a crisis-event justifying new exercises of sovereign power and new states of exception.

THE CLIMATE EXPEDITION AND STATE OF ECOLOGICAL EXCEPTION

In Flaubert's modernity, environment was arguably perceived as existing in homeostatic equilibrium, allowing barometers to measure fluctuations or changes in pressure off a background of atmospheric stability.[4] By contrast, toward the turn of the twenty-first century the "figure of the environment shifts," as Brian Massumi contends, "from the harmony of a natural balance to a churning seed-bed of crisis in the perpetual making" (154). Beyond the techniques of governmentality and biopower that Foucault traced to the management of populations and their milieus, Massumi proposes that environmentality is now the form of power co-extensive with what he calls "the figure of today's threat: [namely a] form of threat [that] is not only indiscriminate, coming anywhere, as out of nowhere, at any time, [but that] is also indiscrimin*able*" (154). Massumi describes, for instance, how the strike of Hurricane Katrina in 2005 and the US occupation of Iraq bled together in the political speech of leaders like George Bush, effectively rendering the indiscriminate threats posed by the weather and by the US-led war on terrorism *indiscriminable*. If the collapse of weather and war into a continuum of threat represents its indiscriminable character, Massumi sees climate change and swine flu as exemplary of threat's new form, given that the etiology of both are so complex as to be "ultimately untraceable" (160). In a similar vein, Timothy Morton theorizes global warming as a "hyperobject." Hyperobjects are "things that are so massively distributed in time and space" they can only be glimpsed or grasped in pieces (1); according to Morton, the world-historical appearance of hyperobjects like global warming actually spells the end of the world as we know it by causing a profound "quake" in the epistemological and ontological footings of (Western) humanity (19).[5]

In this section I look closely at one of Heather Ackroyd and Dan Harvey's ice slides in order to ask how it is possible to square the time of slow death and indiscriminable threat posed by climate change with an artwork that materializes climate change in the tiny time frames of a photographic slide, a slide that crystallizes it as a crisis-event. Behind the time frames of this particular slide there lies the even more exclusive time-space of the Cape Farewell excursion itself, the melodramatic expedition on which the two British artists were invited to materialize moving images of climate change.

Since the 1990s, Ackroyd and Harvey have been involved in numerous time-based green art projects that foreground urban political ecologies, for instance, "large-scale architectural interventions where they grow landmark buildings with seedling grass."[6] While their series of photographic ice slides represents only a small portion of a rich and heterogeneous body of work, because they were produced over the duration of a two-week Cape Farewell expedition that the artists joined in 2005, the slides are implicated in its logic of crisis adventure. In the words of the founder of Cape Farewell, David Buckland, the project "pioneers the cultural response to climate change" by inviting a small group of high-profile artists and scientists on ship expeditions to the "High Arctic."[7] The expeditions are designed to turn cultural producers into ecological witnesses who, through raw exposure to the polar landscapes most vulnerable to climate change, will return motivated to use art as a means of raising crisis consciousness.

In 2008 the national geography of Canada was stitched into Cape Farewell's cultural mission when it served as base camp for the project's second youth expedition to the Arctic. Several Canadian musicians, writers, and artists (including Feist and Yann Martel) have participated in its ongoing series of expeditions. Among the exhibits organized to feature the work of Cape Farewell artists was "Unfold" (on display in New York from September to December 2011), an exhibit accompanied by an artist statement that was again supplied by Buckland: "We intend to communicate through art works our understanding of the changing climate on a human scale, so that our individual lives can have meaning in what is a global problem."[8] Both the authority of first-hand experience and an ecological messianism permeate Cape Farewell's disparate initiatives, as relayed by the description of the "Unfold" exhibit appearing on its website: "Each artist witnessed firsthand the dramatic and fragile environmental tipping points of climate change. Their innovative, independent and collective responses explore the physical, emotional and political dimensions of our complex and changing world stressed by profligate human activity."

As one might imagine, ice calls out as the material of choice for Cape Farewell artists who travel to the Arctic to be affected by climate change. Their time in the North is largely spent photographing, sculpting, sounding, painting, and otherwise artifactualizing ice. In the single photographic slide that I'll zoom in on by way of bringing the cultural project of Cape Farewell under closer scrutiny, Ackroyd and Harvey present ice as the iconic material signifier of climate crisis, reinforcing a popular sense that climate change is most legible in the thinning and melting of Arctic ice sheets and glaciers (see Figure 9.1). Yet in this case ice isn't being photographed, exactly. Instead, ice imprints itself, auto-crystallizing its angel-wing patterns on the celluloid surface of the square film slide that the artists have merely exposed to the Arctic cold. The Arctic cold appears as an animate subject that self-materializes, leaving a trace of its powerful presence in the film-coating of ice covering a slide that was held out as a passive surface of inscription. Only afterwards do the fingers of a human hand hold the ice slide up to be photographed, the act of representation secondary to the powerful visitation. The ice slide in this sense enacts the submission of human image-making to nature's greater art of auto-photography, dramatizing an ecological humility that could be read as the Janus face of the ecological messianism ignited by the expedition.

While powerful, the visitation of ice imaged by Ackroyd and Harvey's slide is nonetheless deeply nostalgic. After all, Arctic cold and ice have been dramatically reduced, the small surface of the slide suggests, to a ghost trace of their former glory. These vanishing formations—the loss or "slide" of polar ice into warming ocean waters—is an ecological trope with tremendous affective traction, making this material image of climate change singularly moving. However, by testifying to and materializing climate change within the time-space of an at once emotionally heightened and strenuous expedition, the biopolitical scene of slow death that Berlant associates with "the temporalities of the endemic" is occluded ("Slow" 756). The ship expedition arguably allows its predominantly Euro-American crew to prolong a fantasy of sovereignty—in the shape of the bourgeois melodrama of personhood described by Berlant, here featuring the heroic witness to eco-crisis—at a moment in which few can still afford to performatively occupy old models of political, cultural, and human sovereignty.

Although the ice slide shown in Figure 9.1 specifies its precise latitude and longitude—78°30N,16°10E—and thus appears to privilege geographic location in its framing of climate crisis, a biopolitics of time is even more at stake in this performance. How can ice slide be pressured to speak to the temporal biopolitics of the expedition in terms of uneven exposure times

Figure 9.1 Ice Slides 2005/78°30N,16°10E. Heather Ackroyd and Dan Harvey. Reprinted with the permission of the artists.

to climate change? Can the peculiarly ecological expression of sovereign subjectivity mobilized by Cape Farewell expeditions be said to constitute an exercise and state of temporal exception? Inspired by Berlant's rumination on scenes of slow death, my question concerns how sovereign power—which in this instance is exemplified by the power to declare a global state of ecological emergency—paradoxically comes to operate through cultural discourses and practices of ecological responsibility. How might sovereign decision-making power get affectively diffused or distributed through a culture of ecological emergency that calls for exceptional acts by enterprising individuals and communities of interest who share a powerful feeling that the time for securing human species survival is now, if not already past?

A refrain that runs through cultural and scientific discourses of climate change—that "time is running out"—operates with perhaps the greatest force in the genre of the chronological countdown. Consider, for example, political countdowns to the Copenhagen climate change conference in 2009 that clocked its arrival down to the minute and second. Or think of scientific calculations of the time remaining before an ecological system reaches its irreversible "tipping points" or before polar ice caps have disappeared. Such countdowns are one illustration of the unprecedented temporalizing of affect that comes to excite a global culture of ecological emergency. Buckland and the crews who are invited to participate in Cape Farewell expeditions act upon a sense of urgency that justifies exceptional excursions from the rule or norm, which in the cultural expression of sovereign power that I'm exploring comes to equal the ordinariness of everyday life and the complacency that ordinary time seems to represent in view of the unprecedented threats facing humans as a species. The high Arctic stands for another time than the ordinary in this expanded sense and practice of exception. Yet what is elided by Cape Farewell's enterprising culture of urgency (or what I've also been calling its logic of crisis adventure) is that the Arctic is the space of the ordinary rather than the exception for those who live there, and that climate change is lived within much longer time frames for Arctic inhabitants than it is for members of the expedition. Also eclipsed is the paradox that climate change is not only the object of its concern, but one of the material conditions of possibility of the expedition. The melting of polar ice sheets not only opens Arctic waters to increased global traffic and excites nation-states like Canada to assert their political sovereignty over polar regions, it simultaneously allows the ships used on Cape Farewell expeditions to penetrate polar regions previously impassable due to ice.

Is Ackroyd and Harvey's ice slide being asked to carry too heavy a burden of responsibility for the ecological state of exception enacted by Cape Farewell expeditions? As I've suggested, the slide seeks to focalize the indiscriminate threat of climate change by dramatizing polar ice as a vestigial presence. I've already noted the incongruity of trying to channel "a generalized crisis environment," in Massumi's words (or a "hyperobject," in Morton's terms) into the small square of a celluloid slide exposed to Arctic cold. However, in trying to reify indiscriminate threat, might the ice slide nonetheless produce some defamiliarizing effects? In his seminal essay "Thing Theory," Brown describes a character in an A. S. Byatt novel whose "interruption of the habit of looking *through* windows as transparencies enables the protagonist to look *at* a window itself in its opacity (4). Something similar could be said of Ackroyd and Harvey's ice slide: against the tendency to look through or past the material stuff of photographic film by seeing only the image, their slide brings the materiality of the celluloid frame back into view. It resists offering a filmic *representation* of climate crisis in favour of staging a physical encounter between celluloid and ice. In this reading, the ice slide could be said to obstruct a metaphysics of nature that would likewise take *it* as given, as the transparent container or timeless envelope of human history. Instead, ice obtrudes as a historically contingent and precarious nature that can no longer be taken for granted as a given.

While it's possible to read ice slide as interrupting naturalized images of both culture and nature in this way, what nonetheless remains transparent is the biopolitical effect it has of crystallizing climate as a crisis-event and of temporalizing affect. Yet the messianic collection of an ice specimen at the moment of ice's traumatic disappearance, far from marking off the present as an historical exception, catches Ackroyd and Harvey in the act of inadvertently repeating a colonial practice of salvage ethnography that turns on tropes of vanishing Natives and vanishing wildlife, and that justifies their collection and museumization.[9] If climate change is being delineated as historically exceptional within the short time frame of the expedition, the tropes of salvage that permeate the Cape Farewell discourse suggest the opposite: that there is a long colonial history of turning vanishing culture and nature into a justification for preservationist interventions by a dominant Euro-American culture.

A temporalizing of affect is also at work in the artists' decision to use old film slides on the expedition, an anachronistic medium associated with an earlier era of photographic capture. Supplied with this anachronistic surface on which to sculpt its dying breath, ice is nostalgized as a thing of the past even as it makes its presence felt. A resemblance or analogy between film and ice is also evoked, a likeness between two material media. If film arrests life and preserves its image for posterity, ice likewise arrests or fixes biological life in a frozen state, and comes to appear as film's double in nature, even film's original. In other words, the ice slide can be read as nostalgic not just for a world of ice before it vanishes into warming ocean waters, but more ambivalently for the loss of a *mastery* over biological life and death represented by the freezing powers of film and ice as twin life preservers.

Again, the anachronistic use of an old film slide helps to bring the larger sentimental trappings of Cape Farewell expeditions into view. The expeditions revive what Renato Rosaldo calls "imperialist nostalgia" in their chartering of ships that look distinctly nineteenth century, evoking earlier naturalist voyages of discovery such as Darwin's expedition on the HMS *Beagle*.[10] Indeed, the ecological rationale for choosing both the Arctic and the Andes as destinations for Cape Farewell voyages—ostensibly because signs of climate change are most visible in both geographies—seems to thinly veil the neo-imperialist imagination that is at play. When Cape Farewell first included the Andes in its itinerary in 2009, it rhetorically posed the question "Why the Andes?" on its website. The answer it supplies: "The ambition of Cape Farewell's first expedition to the Andes was to extend our expedition programme and invite artists to witness the impact of climate change in another climate tipping point: the rainforests."[11] Yet a more critical retort to "Why the Andes?" might challenge the imperialist nostalgia that operates in and through the project's discourse of ecological emergency. In his analysis of imperialist nostalgia, Rosaldo traces how agents of colonialism "often display nostalgia for the colonized culture as it was 'traditionally' (that is, when they first encountered it). The peculiarity of their yearning, of course, is that agents of colonialism long for the very forms of life they intentionally altered or destroyed" (107-8). Beyond the yearning for other cultures that accompanies an intention to civilize them, Rosaldo notes that imperialist nostalgia encompasses an "attitude of reverence toward the natural [that] developed at the same time that North Americans intensified the destruction of their human and natural environment" (109). Cape Farewell utters this paradox by waxing nostalgic for an Arctic and an Andes untouched by anthropogenic climate change, even while it reproduces the anthropological rights of an imperial culture to turn other places into ecological object lessons.

In view of the imperialist nostalgia excited by Cape Farewell expeditions, it is therefore crucial that its temporal assumptions be antagonized. To this end, I put critical pressure, finally, on the trope of exposure, which is pivotal to the powerful affect generated by Ackroyd and Harvey's ice slide. Of course, exposure signifies both the light conditions of photography *and* the vulnerability of a body that cannot protect itself against the elements, potentially leading to death by weather. Photographic exposure slides into environmental exposure and vice versa in the tropic exchange staged by Ackroyd and Harvey: the celluloid frame is literally exposed to the Arctic cold while the Arctic weather, conversely, is captured as an image of filmic overexposure. However, when this slide of signification is transposed to the larger politics of living under the shadow of climate change, it can be made to speak to biopower as a differential time of environmental exposure. Consider again the time window of the Cape Farewell expedition—two weeks—and even more narrowly, the time of the film slide's exposure to Arctic cold. These temporalities carve out a time of exception from the ordinary, endemic time of exposure occupied by those for whom the Arctic is not a temporary excursion. A profound disparity arises between the time of the Cape Farewell crew's exposure to climate crisis and the chronic exposure and attrition lived by Arctic inhabitants. "The phrase *slow death*," writes Berlant, "refers to the physical wearing out of a population and the deterioration of people in that population that is very nearly a defining condition of their experience and historical existence" (754). The gradual, wearing effects that climate change has on bodies and environments cannot be captured or materialized within the urgent time frames of Cape Farewell expeditions, or within a search for tipping points. For this reason, Berlant differentiates between events and environments as temporal frameworks for tracking the destructive effects of global capitalism. "Slow death," she writes, prospers not in traumatic events, as discrete time-framed phenomena like military encounters and genocides can appear to do, but in temporal environments whose qualities and contours in time and space are often identified with the presentness of ordinariness itself, that domain of living on.... (759)

Berlant's work helps to show how the exceptional expedition—indeed, the urgency that is normally understood to propel people to action and to politics—remains within a heroic genre of sovereign agency that is incongruous and inappropriate in relation to the unspectacular labour of life-building that many people pursue amidst structural forces of attrition (763). In relation to climate change, then, the concept of slow death can shift our attention to scenes in the North in which people are absorbed with "living on" in environments that are themselves absorbing the hardest impacts of climate change. This life-buffering is a mundane, biopolitical condition of the (thinning) good life that Southerners are largely content to accept.

INUIT PREDICTION TECHNIQUES

In their documentary *Qapirangajuq*, Kunuk and Mauro can be read as refusing the genres that temporally frame climate change as a discrete event; instead of crystallizing crisis, the film can be read as culturally working to materialize scenes of slow death. To complicate the genre of sovereign subjectivity and heroic agency dramatized by Cape Farewell expeditions is not to pathologize slow death and cast the Inuit as victims of global warming. *Qapirangajuq* generates a very different ensemble of affects in the mixed images it gives of both the large-scale impacts of climate change and the keen techniques of observation and adaptability that the Inuit are disseminating with the help of new technological media.

Possibly the most striking difference between the ice slide examined above and *Qapirangajuq* consists in their producers' choice of cultural media. Ackroyd and Harvey use a photographic slide associated with a now-outmoded age of image-making, a slide transported on board a ship expedition to the Arctic, where it was dramatically exposed to the elements. Kunuk and Mauro's documentary, by contrast, is an Igloolik Isuma TV production that uses Inuit and Indigenous Web-based interactive media to globally distribute the keen observations of Arctic inhabitants. If the former suggests that climate change becomes an occasion for a select crew to indulge in imperialist nostalgia, trying to avert the future by travelling through space back in time, the latter indicates that climate change is an opportunity for life-building as well as a pressing threat for the Inuit. By virtue of inhabiting the threat in the time of the everyday, Inuit people are able to contribute their situated knowledges to global discussions that are at risk of being monopolized by the expert testimonies of scientists or artists for whom the Arctic is a crisis-event rather than a daily environment. And rather than depicting the Inuit as locked in traditions that would appear, under the shadow of climate change, doomed, the documentary itself exemplifies a culture that is adapting its traditional knowledges to new media in order to relay Inuit "thinking" on the politics of climate change. Berlant's definition of "thinking" is instructive here, given that she describes it as "a general opening for cultivating attentiveness and an ethics of mindfulness for a public intimate because they're experiencing together a shift in the atmosphere" ("Thinking" 5). Several of the individuals who appear in *Qapirangajuq* address a global community that has in no uncertain terms been made "intimate" by the threat of climate change, initiating a public sphere in which a particular environmental vulnerability stops thinking, if only briefly, from sliding back into sovereign frames and habits of thought.

Kunuk and Mauro's co-production premiered in 2010 at the imagineNative film festival in Toronto. Through the long historical frames of elders and the "prediction techniques" of Inuk weathermen, the film offers very different time-images and affects than those supporting the dominant genre of ecological emergency. English subtitles translate the words of the Inuktituk speakers who appear in the documentary, one of whom gives voice to the "temporality of the endemic" that contours the Inuit perspective (Berlant, "Slow" 756): "It's a reality for us. It's hot here every year now." A national Inuit leader appearing in the documentary, Mary Simon, similarly shifts the framework from extraordinary crisis-time to ordinary time: "Scientists talk about climate change with studies on pollution and toxins, whereas Inuit discuss the effects as they occur within our lives." The documentary presents Inuit individuals talking in the domestic spaces of their living rooms or kitchens, interspersed with shots of their work and play outside. The at-homeness relayed by the unpretentious settings of Inuit knowledge could not be more at odds with the mobile space of exceptional knowledge contrived by Cape Farewell expeditions.

The film could itself be described as a collection of everyday environmental observations by Inuit from various communities. One motif—in fact, one word—recurs throughout the numerous reflections the film relays on the effects of climate change in the North: "noticing." One elder remarks, "Inuit notice how the sea is thinning the ice." Inuit hunters, who observe the effects that climate change is having on Arctic animals—particularly seals, who have begun appearing with summer fur in the dead of winter—say, "This got my attention" or "That was noticeable." Through a long practice of environmental attention, the Inuit are able to take a measure of changes in snowdrifts and wind directions, in the thickness of ice at floe edges or fishing holes at different times of the year, in the quality of sealskins and caribou meat, in the number and behaviours of polar bears, in the comings and goings of multi-year ice. Moreover, the film corroborates independent observations by showing Inuit from disparate locations making uncannily similar observations about their Arctic environment, and linking them together into a consistent and reliable body of knowledge.

One particularly startling sign of climate change that the film corroborates in this fashion involves a shift that numerous elders and hunters have noticed in the setting Sun. By virtue of a long history of environmental attention, they are able to compare the seasonal location of the setting Sun and stars in the past with their very different location in the present, causing several Inuit to speculate that "perhaps the Earth has tilted on its axis." Western science has interpreted this Inuit perception by noting that greenhouse gases in the atmosphere would indeed optically distort the view of the Sun and other celestial bodies from polar locations, making it seem as though the Earth had tilted on its axis. But against the tendency to translate the Inuits' speculation that the Earth has tilted on its axis into the proper reason of Western science, isn't it equally possible to read the Western science of "tipping points" as itself a genre of knowledge that might appear culturally fantastic—temporally strange—from another epistemological point of view?[12]

Qapirangajuq in fact offers its own correctives to Western climate sciences as it relays the Inuit's close observations of polar bear populations and activities. Against the popular imagination of climate crisis in the West, in which polar bears are mourned in the future anterior tense as animals that soon will have disappeared along with vanishing ice formations, numerous Inuit in the film insist that the polar bear population in the North is in fact increasing. As if resisting a salvage paradigm that frames both Indigenous peoples and wildlife as doomed to disappear in the face of technological modernity—a paradigm at risk of being revived by discourses of climate crisis, as I suggested in my analysis of the Cape Farewell project—several Inuit comment that polar bears are superb swimmers more than capable of surviving warming oceans and thinning ice sheets. This is not to say, however, that the Inuit don't observe climate change having an impact on polar bears. But ironically, they trace the source of these impacts to the methods of wildlife biologists, who tag, radio-collar, and "manhandle" bears in the cause of monitoring how they are affected by large-scale disruptions such as climate change. "It's not climate change that's affecting polar bears," declares one hunter, "but wildlife biologists." His words are corroborated by other Inuit, who note that polar bears "are constantly tampered with by Southerners" and that "these issues [of misbehaving or starving bears] are caused by wildlife biologists."

The ability of the Inuit to read environmental conditions has, however, been destabilized by the environment's unprecedented volatility. "Our ancestors were brilliant on the environment," one individual in the film states. "In the fall, with no ice formed, they could predict and would say: 'The ice will be late' or 'The ice will be early.'" Joanasie Karpik, an elder, affirms that the skills of the ancestors continue to be practised: "I also know these prediction techniques." However, Inuk weathermen are finding it harder and harder to predict the weather due, among many other things, to unusually erratic winds that cause tongue drifts in the snow to point in different directions. "I can't forecast the weather anymore," says David Kalluk, an elder living in Resolute Bay. Prediction techniques are certainly not understood to be ammunition for sovereign subjects in possession of authoritative knowledges; Inuit knowledge of climate change is, instead, a mode of attention that the Inuit continue practising while confronting forces of attrition that slowly wear on the environment of life. It is one means of "inhabiting agency differently" (Berlant, "Slow" 779).

Non-sovereign knowledges of climate change are, finally, what *Qapirangajuq* broadcasts as a matter of global survival. Such non-sovereign knowledges, as I've been approaching them through a comparison of two cultural interventions, are knowledges belonging to subjects who live climate change not as a crisis-event but as an everyday, wearing environment that has been continuously subject to a long history of colonial depredations. They are knowledges that reveal the sovereign subject—a figure of strong will, decision and heroic agency (based on a European model of political sovereignty and the state's power to declare a state of exception)—to be incommensurable with many people's struggles over conditions of life in the twenty-first century.

One final feature of non-sovereign knowledges can be drawn out from the rich visual and aural text of *Qapirangajuq*: a distributed agency that involves the non-human world. Ice, wind, and animals are attributed a kind of agency that, again, counters modern liberal-humanist traditions that reify agency in the willing, autonomous subject. Such attributions problematize categorical assumptions about the human that undergird those traditions. For instance, several Inuit in Kunuk and Mauro's documentary talk about multi-year ice as a lively actor with a mind of its own, a being that exercises volition. As Inusiq

Nashalik, a Pangnirtung man, relays his observations about multi-year ice (icebergs) in the film, he speaks of non-human agency in an idiom that confounds the enlightenment doxa that only humans properly exercise choice:

> Multi-year ice is not just ordinary ice. In the past, they would always appear. They behave like living beings. They came inside Cumberland Sound.... Icebergs, they seem to have a mind of their own. If the ice chooses to, they [sic] can travel against the wind. But now, there seems to be less and less icebergs coming.

Numerous contemporary scholars have sought to reanimate the dead, passive body of nature that Western culture has inherited from the Enlightenment: thing theorists like Bill Brown, political theorists like Bruno Latour, new materialists like Jane Bennett, and anthropologists like Julie Cruikshank have been at the forefront of efforts to decentre the human as the privileged subject of agency. Cruikshank's work in *Do Glaciers Listen: Local Knowledge, Colonial Encounters, and Social Imagination* (2005) is especially relevant, bringing into view Indigenous understandings of distributed agency long before such a concept gained currency in the academy, and challenging Western epistemologies that have treated glaciers as natural rather than social, "inert" rather than active, and timeless rather than historical (6). (Ackroyd and Harvey's work, in dramatizing the visitation of ice, could also be read as part of this post-Enlightenment movement to restore a vision of vital nature.) However, the words of Inusiq Nashalik can also temper the new surge of interest in non-human agency. Although Nashalik speaks of icebergs as social and volitional entities, he also understands that global warming is wearing down the very possibility of their historical comings and goings. Even as his words revive the lively powers of non-humans, then, the non-sovereign knowledge voiced by Nashalik prompts awareness of the contexts of slow death within which vitalism (awakened by many recent formulations of non-human agency) may be as historically inappropriate as the dramas of sovereignty that I've been tracing.

Through Isuma TV's interactive digital network, *Qapirangajuq* can be accessed by Inuit living in remote communities as well as by global publics who are receptive to Indigenous independent media. If local reception of Inuit observations is a priority for many in the North, Southerners also have much to learn from modes of attention that bring climate change into view as an uneven global environment rather than as a spectacular event demanding exceptional responses from sovereign actors. The particularity of Inuit peoples' exposure to the most punishing effects of climate change may, in fact, have the potential to establish an alternate "universal" to the models of European sovereignty (state and self) that have been globally dominant for the past several centuries, and that persist in liberal, well-meaning modes of reckoning with ecological crisis. The Cape Farewell project is illustrative of such a well-intentioned attempt to culturally intervene in the crisis, and I've tried to throw its sovereign trappings into critical relief by comparing it with Kunuk and Mauro's documentary. The sobering words of Mary Simon spoken in *Qapirangajuq* travel laterally through Inuit new media, contesting the "Southern" habits of thinking that obstruct a global politics of climate change based in a non-sovereign vulnerability: "Our whole world is changing.... On the topic of the environment, Southerners focus on borders, which prevents them from getting connected. When Inuit talk environment, we are one."

NOTES

A special thanks to Dan Harvey, who provided me with a scan of "Ice Slide" so that I could reprint it here. His generosity caused me pause in view of my perhaps overly critical reading of the photograph (a failure of generosity that is implicated in the far-from-humble conventions of academic critique).

1. See NASA's website at: <http://www.nasa/gov/mission_pages/noaan/climate/climate_weather.html>. NASA's current involvement in what it calls "Operation IceBridge" is pertinent to my discussion of contemporary efforts to materialize climate change. Operation IceBridge is an "airborne expedition over Antarctica" that aims to measure the change in glaciers vital to sea level rise projections. "Operation IceBridge ... is the largest airborne campaign ever flown over the world's polar regions. Bridging a gap between two ice elevation mapping satellites, and breaking new scientific ground on its own, IceBridge this fall has charted the continued rapid acceleration and mass loss of Pine Island Glacier." The militaristic character of NASA's project to measure ice loss is one expression of what I elaborate as a "sovereign" response to climate change.
2. Among the recent work that does turn in this direction, see Mick Smith's "Against Ecological Sovereignty: Agamben, Politics, and Globalization." *Environmental Politics* 18.1 (2009): 99-116.
3. Others have also made this connection, including John Geiger in "Arctic Sovereignty and Franklin's Lost Ships," *Globe and Mail* 15 Aug. 2008. <http://www.theglobeandmail.com/news/opinions/article703053.ece>. Since the time this article was written, one of Franklin's ships was in fact found on the ocean floor. HMS *Erebus* was located in 2014.
4. To historicize climate-change consciousness somewhat, it was only a few decades after Flaubert's death that there emerged the science of global warming that would lead to today's perception of an environment that is immanent to human history and changeable (rather than a transcendent container of history). However, as Dipesh Chakrabarty notes, "[s]cientific studies of global warming are often said to have originated with the discoveries of the Swedish scientist Svante Arrhenius in the 1890s, but self-conscious discussions of global warming in the public realm began in the late 1980s and early 1990s, the same period in which social scientists and humanists began to discuss globalization" (198-99).
5. Interestingly, Morton metaphorizes the quake in being caused by hyperobjects as a Titanic collision with an iceberg: "[t]he Titanic of modernity hits the iceberg of

hyperobjects" (19). He describes this collision with hyperobjects as taking place in "the Arctic mist" (20), a description that risks floating the Arctic as an exotic signifier in the philosophy of hyperobjects rather than as an inhabited cultural and historical geography.

6 See Ackroyd and Harvey's website: <http://www.ackroydandharvey.com>.
7 Cape Farewell website: <http://www.capefarewell.com/about.html>.
8 A link to the Unfold exhibit is supplied on the main Cape Farewell website: <http://capefarewell.co.k/art/exhibitions/unfold.html>.
9 For a critical interrogation of practices of salvage ethnography and its combined myths of the "vanishing native" and vanishing wildlife, see Pauline Wakeham's *Taxidermic Signs: Reconstructing Aboriginality*.
10 Renato Rosaldo, "Imperialist Nostalgia."
11 See the Cape Farewell website: <http://capefarewell.co.uk/expeditions/2009>.
12 I refer here to Donna Haraway's well-known argument in "Situated Knowledges."

WORKS CITED

Ackroyd, Heather, and Dan Harvey. "Ice Slides." *Burning Ice: Art & Climate Change*. Ed. David Buckland. London: Cape Farewell, 2006. 114-21. Print.

Alfred, Taiaiake. "Sovereignty." *Sovereignty Matters: Locations of Contestation and Possibility in Indigenous Struggles for Self-Determination*. Ed. Joanne Barker. Lincoln: U of Nebraska P, 2005. Print.

Benjamin, Walter. "Theses on the Philosophy of History." *Illuminations: Essays and Reflections*. Ed. Hannah Arendt. New York: Schocken Books, 1969. 253-64. Print.

Berlant, Lauren. "Slow Death (Sovereignty, Obesity, Lateral Agency)." *Critical Inquiry* 33 (Summer 2007): 754-80. Print.

———. "Thinking about Feeling Historical." *Emotion, Space and Society* 1 (2008): 4-9. Print.

Brown, Bill. *The Material Unconscious: American Amusement, Stephen Crane, and the Economics of Play*. Cambridge, MA: Harvard UP, 1996. Print.

———. "Thing Theory." *Critical Inquiry* 28.1 (Autumn 2001): 1-22. Print.

Chakrabarty, Dipesh. "The Climate of History: Four Theses." *Critical Inquiry* (Winter 2009): 197-222. Print.

Cruikshank, Julie. *Do Glaciers Listen: Local Knowledge, Colonial Encounters, and Social Imagination*. Vancouver: UBC P, 2005. Print.

Haraway, Donna. "Situated Knowledges: The Science Question in Feminism and the Privilege of the Partial Perspective." *Simians, Cyborgs, and Women: The Reinvention of Nature*. New York: Routledge, 1991. 183-203. Print.

Kunuk, Zacharias, and Ian Mauro. *Qapirangajuq: Inuit Knowledge and Climate Change*. Igloolik Isuma Productions and Kunuk Cohn Productions, 2010. Film.

Massumi, Brian. "National Enterprise Emergency: Steps Toward an Ecology of Powers." *Theory, Culture & Society* 26.6 (2009): 153-85. Print.

Morton, Timothy. *Hyperobjects: Philosophy and Ecology after the End of the World*. Minneapolis: U of Minnesota P, 2013. Print.

Rosaldo, Renato. "Imperialist Nostalgia." *Representations* 26 (Spring 1989): 107-22. Print.

Schmitt, Carl. *Political Theology: Four Chapters on the Concept of Sovereignty*. Trans. Georges Schwab. Cambridge, MA: MIT P, 1985. Print.

Smith, Mick. "Against Ecological Sovereignty: Agamben, Politics, and Globalization." *Environmental Politics* 18.1 (2009): 99-116. Print.

Wakeham, Pauline. *Taxidermic Signs: Reconstructing Aboriginality*. Minneapolis: U of Minnesota P, 2008. Print.

CHAPTER 10

Waters as Potential Paths to Peace

Rita Wong

We embody the hydrological cycle, but this is not a cycle of mere addition and subtraction. Rather, it is a cycle of continuous becoming and transformation.
—Astrida Neimanis, "We Are All Bodies of Water"

This, I submit, is the freedom of real education, of learning how to be well-adjusted: You get to consciously decide what has meaning and what doesn't.
—David Foster Wallace, *This Is Water*

In his book *What Is Water?* Jamie Linton describes how pre-modern waters were multiple and specific to their locations. Some waters were known for their spirit of place, their genius loci, and writers like Pliny the Elder (23-79 CE) describe certain waters having healing qualities, while others were known to be corrosive or dangerous (Linton 82-85). Today, we might think of the muddy, silt-burdened Fraser River by the time it reaches Vancouver after its 1375 km journey, or the polluted, broken-mouthed Don River in Toronto,[1] versus the rejuvenating qualities of the Radium Hot Springs near Banff. We haven't totally lost an ability to distinguish between different kinds of water, but we simultaneously live with the normative assumption of what Linton calls "modern water," which has been reduced and essentialized into the abstraction, H_2O. For many of us, it is modern water that we drink when we turn on our taps, modern water that is taken for granted without regard for where it comes from and where it goes.

Yet the sociality and materiality of specific waters can teach us a lot about ourselves and our relations to the world in which we live, so it's worth reflecting on how we perceive and interact with the daily waters in our lives. By discussing some questions that arise from water's sociality, I will explore why a participatory water ethics offers an inviting path to peace, a way to rethink and address the conflicts and injustices that logically arise when water is conceptualized as an object and commodity to be transported and sold to whichever customer can afford to pay. Former World Bank Vice President Ismail Serageldin has famously said that future wars will be fought over water (qtd. in Wolf et al.) in the way they're being fought over oil today. It has also been suggested that wars are already being fought over water, in that water scarcity substantially contributes to and exacerbates existing tensions that we might primarily perceive as political or religious from an androcentric lens. But water also presents both an opportunity and a requirement for communities to work together to protect it; as such, it forms a critical nexus through which to reimagine ourselves and our cultures.

Approaching diverse waters as what Jane Bennett calls "vibrant matter," "quasi agents or forces with trajectories, propensities, or tendencies of their own" (viii), it is possible to draw on the capacities of both a material cultures approach as well as ecological studies in order to reframe human relations in terms of reciprocity with the fluids that perpetually move through us, animating and revitalizing us both individually and as a collectivity of living beings. If we start by examining the quantity and distribution of waters in Canada, we will realize that roughly 60 percent of the surface waters flow north toward the Arctic regions, whereas most of the nation's human populations are scattered along the south (Sprague 25). There are five large watersheds that constitute Canada, as the rivers and tributaries flow to either the Pacific Ocean, the Arctic Ocean, Hudson's Bay, the Atlantic Ocean, or the Gulf of Mexico. One could argue that each time we drink water from one of these five watersheds, we become part of that watershed, part of its flows. If I were to imagine my identity as part of the Pacific Ocean watershed, or part of the Hudson's Bay watershed, this could help to attune my sensory apparatus to the larger scale necessitated by global warming, offering a way to imagine community that is spacious enough for both human and non-human members by acknowledging my ecological interdependence with the northern reaches of Canada. A participatory water ethics acknowledges how these waters are not merely outside of us, but help to constitute our bodies, and also how they are, in turn, affected and shaped by our presence and by what our society does to the waterways.

Introducing the concept of hydrolectics, Linton suggests that "[f]rom a relational-dialectical perspective, we can argue that people and water are also *internally* related in the sense that water can change the very nature of human society, while human society can change the nature and disposition of water" (197). The societies in which we live have had an enormous impact on the waterways around the world in the past century; today in the Northern hemisphere, roughly "80% of river discharge is regulated, or controlled by dams" (Linton 229). Hydrolectics describes an approach that redefines water in terms of its social relations and circumstances; it is not merely abstract water to be moved to wherever there is more money, but situated water that is already embedded within communities, generative in its existent flows. Tracing the perpetual movements of these flows, we can follow how watersheds inevitably scale up from specific communities into a larger hydrocommons, where an understanding of our interdependency points to the possibility of shared, long-term stewardship as a wiser alternative to destructive, short-sighted practices of polluting and wasting the waters that keep our planet alive and dynamic.

Whether we organize our cultures and social systems around water in ways that reduce it to a material to be dominated and objectified, or ways that acknowledge how it is constitutive of our own animated materiality and our sociality, has implications for the kinds of futures we enable. How we imagine our relationship to water can cultivate tendencies toward peaceful coexistence, or toward competitive conflict and exclusionary practices, in our daily lives. Linton writes:

> Questions involving whose understanding of water—and whose mode of relating and gaining access to it—attains dominance is what we want to highlight here. As Vandana Shiva has argued, the way water is conceptualized and represented is instrumental in determining who gains access to it and on what terms. This necessarily produces conflict over the meaning and definition of water, a kind of conflict that she describes as "water wars"—paradigm wars—conflicts over how we perceive and experience water. (69)

These paradigm wars are playing out all over the country, and one of the largest conflicts is to be found in the Alberta tar sands, where producing one barrel of oil poisons roughly four barrels of fresh water,[2] and the poisoned waters are stored in huge toxic waste reservoirs euphemistically known as "tailings ponds." These poisoned waters are destroying the traditional hunting and gathering grounds of the Mikisew Cree and the Athabasca Chipewyan First Nations, turning their watershed unsustainable and uninhabitable. And what happens in Alberta does not stay in Alberta. Acid rain migrates east to northern Saskatchewan, the threat of pipeline expansion endangers British Columbia's forests and rivers, and the carcinogenic pollution (such as polycyclic aromatic hydrocarbons, PAHS) released by the tar sands flows north into the Arctic Ocean. The poster for the film *H2Oil*, asks, "What's more important, water or oil?" Tracking people's relations with the Athabasca rivershed, the film raises the question of what would happen if people more wisely prioritized water first. What is at stake is not only water quality but also quantity, as the tar sands have substantially reduced the flow of the glacier-fed Athabasca River. An enormous inequity exists between the massive withdrawals of millions of cubic metres of water by the oil industry and the modest water usage of local Indigenous communities; as Melina Laboucan-Massimo, a member of the Lubicon Cree Nation, points out, her family and First Nations community in northern Alberta still do not even have running water. The impact of the tar sands is immediate upon Indigenous communities, a prominent example of environmental racism and contemporary colonization, but it does not stop with these communities, as the flow of water continues, and the massive contribution to global warming knows no borders. When the Lubicon Cree and other First Nations speak up to protect their lands and waters, they are doing so not only for themselves, but for all of us, if we understand our relationships to be constructed through both a shared hydrocommons and global climate change.

Many of Canada's biggest water struggles are to be found up North on the still inhabited traditional lands of Indigenous communities. From the Chipewyan and Cree courageously speaking out to protect the Athabasca River's watershed in northern Alberta ("Intervention") to the Kitchenuhmaykoosib Inninuwug's dramatic ethical stand against platinum mining ("KI") to the Dehcho First Nations' efforts to protect the South Nahanni River watershed, many Indigenous peoples and their allies are trying to protect watersheds for future generations of living creatures, human and non-human. If we are thinking about specific waters, we also need to recognize specific First Nations with a long history of coexistence with those waters. In speculating on water as a lens for peacemaking, it is necessary to address this country's history of violence and colonialism against Indigenous peoples. John Ralston Saul has argued that most non-Aboriginal people want change and reconciliation with Indigenous peoples but "have no idea of how to go about it" (281). One of the barriers he identifies is the lack of a plan for change. I would like to suggest that one way to move forward together, in peace and with respect, is to co-operatively focus on the health of the waters that give us all life.

There are examples of successful attempts to do so that are important to acknowledge and build from. Notably, in 2010 the Tsilhqot'in Nation,

Esketemc Nation, Canoe Creek Band and the Northern Shuswap Tribal Council made a major gain in their struggle to protect the life of Teztan Biny, or Fish Lake, up near Williams Lake in central British Columbia. While there was clearly hostility from settlers near Williams Lake who wanted the temporary jobs brought by a mine, and were not concerned about the permanent damage it would bring, there were also many settlers working in alliance with the First Nations who sought to protect the lake, such as the Council of Canadians and groups like RAVEN (Respecting Aboriginal Values and Environmental Needs). Following a federal environmental assessment finding that Taseko Mines' proposed gold-copper mine would "result in significant adverse environmental effects" on the water and the land that gives life to these First Nations (Canadian Environmental Assessment Agency), the mine was stopped in November 2010, although the company later submitted a new proposal that would do even more damage, which was subsequently rejected in 2014, resulting in a legal battle as Taseko Mines has now sued the federal government. It is important to remember that Teztan Biny was endangered because of a 2002 amendment to the Fisheries Act, a loophole known as Schedule 2, which allows for freshwater bodies (lakes) to be reclassified as "tailings impoundment areas" for mining. Since fifteen other freshwater bodies across Canada continue to be threatened with becoming toxic waste-water dumps, Schedule 2 still urgently needs to be revoked ("Why?").

And while this victory for Teztan Biny is important to celebrate and defend, we should not underestimate the ongoing impact of mining, which continues to poison immense amounts of water around the world. As James Lyon points out, water has been called "mining's most common casualty" (qtd. by Mining Watch Canada 1). Over 70 percent of the world's mining companies are based in Canada (Deneault), and the global damage these companies have done to specific watersheds urgently deserves more study. For now I'll just briefly sketch a few critical threats to the watersheds of Turtle Island, or North America, with the caveat that many more remain.

Saskatchewan, for instance, is one of the world's largest exporters of uranium (along with Kazakstan and Australia). Uranium mining releases heavy metals, acids, and radioactive particles that pollute the groundwater. Earlier uranium mining in the United States has had such devastating impacts that the Navajo and the Hopi have declared a moratorium on uranium mining, perhaps too late as they are already living with increased cancers and birth defects in their communities. In places like Uranium City in northern Saskatchewan, the toxic waste rock from nearby mines has never been cleaned up. Despite this, and many other abandoned mines across the continent, it is estimated that uranium production will double because of Cameco and

AREVA's investments in Cigar Lake, which is expected to become the second largest high-grade uranium mine in the world, second only to Saskatchewan's McArthur River mine. These corporations have been successful in persuading some Aboriginal leaders to accept the long-term costs of mining, but not all, and it remains to be seen how uranium mining will play out in northern Saskatchewan. What I can say is that uranium mining poses a serious, long-term threat to the health of water, as demonstrated by how mining by-products—namely, radioactive contaminants—have materialized as deadly cancers in communities from as far north as the Sahtu Dene of Great Bear Lake (Northwest Territories) to the Acoma Pueblo (New Mexico) and the Navajo Nation (the largest Indian reservation in the United States, with 1,300 abandoned toxic mines that need to be cleaned up) (Pino).[3] Saskatchewan has over a hundred thousand lakes, and it would be foolhardy and shortsighted to think that it's possible to stop the flow of poisoned water.

What does Canadian culture offer in response to this situation? While there is a broad range of possibilities for critical inquiry, engagement, and the building of more ecologically literate actions for society, three books offer valuable entry points to start with: *Wollaston* by Miles Goldstick (focused specifically on Saskatchewan), *The Highway of the Atom* by Peter Van Wyck, and *Burning Vision* by Marie Clements.[4] Given the urgency of the situations that we face, *Village of Widows*, a film by Peter Blow, should also be necessary viewing for all Canadians who depend on clean air and water for their health. Blow's film traces the experiences of the Sahtu Dene of Great Bear Lake, who have suffered deaths and cancers caused by the mining of uranium on their traditional homelands, uranium that was used without their knowledge or consent to make the atomic bombs that detonated over Hiroshima and Nagasaki, killing hundreds of thousands of people. Upon belatedly learning of this war violence, the Dene decided to send a delegation to Hiroshima in 1998 "to convey their apologies for having been involved, and to acknowledge their responsibility" (Van Wyck 45). The transnational path of a material (uranium) led to relationships not chosen but enacted nonetheless through a shared experience of uranium's destructive effects on the Dene and the Japanese; this is powerfully explored in "Waterways,"[5] the third movement of Clements's play, *Burning Vision*, where the Dene See-er asks:

> Can you read the air? The face of the water? Can you look through time and see the future?
>
> Can you hear through the walls of the world? Maybe we are all talking at the same time because we are answering each other over time and space. Like a wave that washes over everything and doesn't care how long it takes to get there because it always ends up on the same shore. (75)

Through both the global economy and the planet's atmospheric, wind, and ocean currents, we are interrelated by a shared experience of substances both life-sustaining and increasingly toxic, however long it takes for those poisons to circulate around the globe. Industrial mining increases the rate and scale of distribution in ways that call for much more scrutiny and reflection.

Another mining battle that's heating up is near Oka or Kanesatake, an effort to prevent the reopening of a Niobium mine by the company Niocan. In contrast to the Oka Crisis in 1990, which was a conflict over whether to acknowledge traditional, sacred burial grounds, or to redefine them through a colonial lens as a golf course, this time the shared goal of protecting the watershed from toxic pollution is bringing together Mohawk and non-Indigenous local communities. When Niocan launched this project late in 1990, it immediately provoked opposition from people who feared it would lower groundwater and discharge radioactive waste. In 2010, both the Mohawk Council of Kanesatake and the Union des producteurs agricoles of Deux Montagnes publically voiced their strong opposition to the mine, supported by a petition that over 5,600 local citizens signed (Robb). Where disagreements over land caused armed conflict, now the recognition of shared waters and the need to work toward a mutually beneficial future could bring these communities closer together.

An inspiring example of water-related alliance building is the successful struggle to protect the groundwater at Site 41, in Tiny Township, Simcoe County, north of Elmvale, Ontario. This time the threat was not a mine but a proposed garbage dump that brought together both Indigenous and non-Indigenous communities who wanted to protect the Alliston Aquifer from being poisoned by the landfill. That aquifer was the first one to be mapped by the Ontario Ministry of the Environment in 1976, and it provides fresh water to many municipalities, communities, farms, and nature reserves as it discharges into creeks and rivers that drain into Georgian Bay, Lake Simcoe, Lake Scugog, and Lake Ontario. At the same time that this struggle became symbolic of national pride, in that the Council of Canadians helped to mobilize support for local efforts at watershed protection, it also remained specific to the communities who rely on that water for their lives. Five women from the nearby Beausoleil First Nation set up camp near the gates of Site 41, vowing to stay to protect the water. Signs at their camp "welcome[d] all visitors and proclaim[ed] the importance of water to Anishnabe culture" (Calzavara 9). They also put up a sign declining donations of bottled water because they already have the best water in the world. In refusing the commodification of water, they enact what we could call a hydrocommons perspective.

A hydrocommons may be described as that which we share through a water-based ecology, including plants, plankton, rivers, even the moist breath that we exhale or transpire into the environment. From this perspective, water is no longer a singular, external object, but rather a material that animates us, and that we in turn animate. In tracing its transformative flows, our conceptions of internal/external, object/subject, singular/plural become complicated because water is no longer just something out there, but is very much the majority of what is in here, perpetually moving in a temporal flux. In the way that rivers are always different, yet also constant, so might we consider our own bodies as water constantly flows in and out of us. What is notable about descriptions of the Site 41 struggle is that it is not merely a political struggle, but a paradigm shift that is at work, one that expresses a reverence for local waters, and a long-term understanding of their role in both the local ecosystem and human communities. After years of struggle, the Simcoe County council that had earlier approved the dump shifted—in 2009, twenty-two councilors voted against it, while only ten voted in support of it. As of March 2011, there was a proposal for a water innovation centre of excellence in Simcoe County because of extremely clean artesian well water that was tested by Dr. William Shotyk (Harries). The hydrocommons paradigm provides a way to acknowledge both specificity (be they delicious artesian well waters or the fish-abundant waters of Teztan Biny) and commonality through interdependence.

In taking a hydrocommons approach, we might reframe a number of struggles, such as the effort to protect habitat for wild salmon along British Columbia's coast, which has also brought together many communities. Though this movement is discursively framed in terms of salmon, it is equally a water-quality issue if we understand that salmon require clean, healthy waters in order to live, and that they constitute a hydrocommons flow of nourishment that mammals, birds, and forests rely on. Because the sockeye salmon runs collapsed in 2009, when millions of expected fish did not appear, 2010 saw the organizing of Alexandra Morton's long walk for salmon, the Get Out Migration, with over 5,000 people rallying outside the BC legislature on May 8, 2010, in support of wild salmon and in protest of the salmon farms that are contributing to the destruction of wild salmon runs through sea lice infestations. Alexandra Morton is well known for her efforts, but it is important to remember that she is working with many communities, and the role of First Nations is prominent in the rallies and events organized around this issue. Morton has written on her blog:

The Get Out Migration has been protected, blessed, gifted and honored by the First Nations who know best what has been lost. Everyday more people are joining our trek—weathering storms in tents, waving at a thousand honking motorists on the road to Victoria. Our ranks swell as we enter the towns, white doves have been released, First Nation canoes parallel us, songs have been written, feasts laid out, flotillas surround us, people are awakening.

Or as the Haida Gwaii carver Jim Hart has phrased it: "Bears, eagles, trees, and humans all rely on salmon. The BC Coast is here because of the salmon, and people forget that. Salmon have been saving our lives for thousands of years" (qtd. in Wong "Disrupting"). Indeed, when salmon runs suddenly rebounded, with the highest run in ninety-seven years happening in the fall of 2010, it did feel like humans had been given another chance to respect the salmon, and in so doing, our own relationship to healthy waters.

With regard to quality, water is transformative, mobile, and wondrous in how it expands rather than contracts with freezing, unlike almost any other substance we might think of. In considering water's qualities, I find it helpful to contemplate where the water I drink comes from, and where it goes. Where I make my home, in the Coast Salish territories also known as Vancouver, we drink the accumulation of West Coast rain and lake water gathered in one of three large reservoirs: the Capilano, Seymour, or Coquitlam watersheds. While there is a huge amount of water on this planet, whose surface is over two-thirds water, the way human bodies are also roughly two-thirds water, this water is finite. The same water keeps circulating for millennia, for eons; what we drink might have flowed through the bladders of woolly mammoths, or might end up eventually dousing one of the Fukushima nuclear reactors. The water is both plural, moving through planetary paths, but also singular—I'm not drinking just abstract water, H_2O, but the Bow River when I'm in Calgary, or the Ottawa River when I'm in Ottawa.

When we start to visualize and materially track the flows of water that we are part of, we quickly realize how related we are to lives we don't see, and to places we've never been. When we understand our bodies' watery matter as consisting of, say, the Alliston Aquifer, or the juicy salmon we eat from the Fraser River, or the groundwater fed by the Lake of Two Mountains at the Ottawa River in Quebec, this offers us a way to conceptualize and rearticulate what we have in common with the watersheds that give us life, and it gives us energy and incentive to work together to protect that specific watershed. Abstract water, when we don't know where it comes from, or where it goes, perpetuates a disconnection that allows one to passively ignore the damage inflicted on watersheds until it is too late.

A substantial and compelling body of work exists in film, literature, and art that increasingly calls for attending to the value of water. In March 2012, a public event called World Water Night was held in Vancouver, bringing together Lee Maracle, Michael Blackstock, and Jeff Bear to share stories, poems, and films voicing Indigenous perspectives of water's cultural importance. Maracle shared part of her story, "Goodbye, Snauq," reminding us of how what is now known as False Creek in Vancouver was the home of Tsleil Watuth, Squamish, and Musqueam communities before her ancestors were forcibly expelled from the village of Snauq, where the Vanier Park and the Vancouver planetarium now sit—or squat—instead. Michael Blackstock shared his work on "Blue Ecology," a merging of traditional Indigenous knowledge with Western science, including poems from his books of poetry, *Salmon Run* and *Oceaness*. Jeff Bear screened an episode of *Samaqan: Water Stories*, focused on the Mother Earth Water Walk with Josephine Mendamin, an Anishinabe elder who has walked the entire circumference of the Great Lakes as an assertion of the urgent need to protect and respect water. This was presented as part of the Downstream research workshop, a gathering of scholars, artists, writers, environmentalists, elders, and scientists concerned with the question of reimagining water as the centre of our cultures, not merely as a convenience or a commodity, but the main legacy that we pass to future generations.

In his poem "Blue Ecology," Blackstock writes, "Rivers erode and make a deposit. You can bank on it" (*Salmon Run* 28). While the pun is playful, it is also apt; how we attribute value has consequences, as does neglecting or cultivating watershed literacy. The start of Blackstock's poem asks: "Water, where did it come from? / Where is it going? / The power to heal. The power to kill. / Oh, which will it be?" (28). His tone is respectful, affectionate, and humble as he explores water's many facets in his writing. Blackstock reframes weather as "water's mood" (*Oceaness* iv), reminding us that we are dependent on water's mutability, its rhythms, its ongoing circulation. He also draws attention to the differences between a First Nations perspective that attributes spiritual and biotic qualities to water in contrast to Western science, which tends to frame water as secular and abiotic; his methodology is that of a peacemaker: to look for possible convergences and to value what can be learned from both perspectives, rather than to assume that they are mutually exclusive.

Another participant in the Downstream workshop, Astrida Neimanis, has written that "[w]ater facilitates the stretching and expanding of not only our physical bodies, but of our thoughtful, emotional, and imaginative selves as well" (84). Drawing on Deleuze and Guattari's distinction between "the *molar*, as a measure of the stability of chemical concentration, and the *molecular*, as a measure of the unstable collision and reaction of multiple entities" (84), Neimanis suggests that, "[a]s molecular bodies, we are dispersed, expanding, uncontainable. We live simultaneously as stratified and destratifying, holding on to the shape of a body as a necessary convenience, but also extending out into a constantly reconfiguring web of watery bodies" (85). In "We Are All Bodies of Water," an article that enacts inter-being by strategically interspersing one stream of thinking (in black text) with another, more embodied stream in blue text, Neimanis asserts that "we have power not only to contaminate and contain, but to nourish and proliferate as well" (91). Like Neimanis, I see the power of the hydrocommons as one that supports long-term renewal. If we perceive ourselves as part of a constantly reconfiguring Athabasca River, or Fraser River, or Pacific Ocean, how would we act and organize our communities differently? The Save the Fraser Declaration, signed in 2010 by sixty-one Indigenous Nations in opposition to the dangers posed to their watersheds by the Enbridge pipeline, is one prominent instance of how such coordinated reconfiguring has materialized in order to respect and protect threatened waters.

The examples I've mentioned hold a promise that, in this late moment of Canada's colonial history, it might still be possible to work to respect the Indigenous peoples and cultures of this continent. It is very late, but not too late, to find a focus for solidarity and peacemaking through the water-based ecology that connects, not just humans, but animals, plants, and life at the micro and macro scales. We inhabit a historical moment where it is increasingly urgent to reconsider the implications of water's materiality; if we adapt our ways of knowing to learn from and respect the fluidity that constitutes us both individually and socially, a humble, joyful, meaningful future-in-commons could still be generated together. Perhaps the path to peace is wide and moist, welcoming to all.

NOTES

1. "I think of Toronto as haunted by water it hardly knows about" (Harris 12).
2. There is a large body of literature and news articles documenting the effects of the tar sands. A sampling would include: Marty Klinkenberg, "Oilsands Development Linked to Cancer, First Nations Say," *Edmonton Journal*, 6 July 2013, <http://www.edmontonjournal.com/Oilsands+development+linked+cancer+First+Nations/10005985/story.html>; Greenpeace, "Tar Sands and Water," <http://www.greenpeace.org/canada/Global/canada/report/2010/4/Watershed_FS_footnote_rev_5.pdf>; Canadian Association of Petroleum Producers, "Water Use in Canada's Oil Sands," June 2012, <http://www.capp.ca/getdoc.aspx?DocId=193756>; Emily Atkin, "Scientists Find 7,300-mile Mercury Contamination 'Bullseye' Around Canadian Tar Sands," 30 Dec. 2013, <http://thinkprogress.org/climate/2013/12/30/3107761/tar-sands-mercury/>.

The averages change over time with technological changes; estimates range from twelve barrels of water to three barrels of water per barrel of oil, with four being within the often acknowledged amount. While the water may get reused many times, the wastewater tailings ponds remain an enormous unsolved problem.

3   Note that in 2012 the US government announced a twenty-year ban on uranium mining near the Grand Canyon. <http://www.navajohopiobserver.com/main.asp?SectionID=1&SubSectionID =794&ArticleID=14194>.

4   I've also discussed Clements's work in another article entitled "Decolonizasian."

5   Incidentally, "Waterways" is the old name for what is now known as Fort McMurray, the epicentre of the tar sands.

WORKS CITED

Bear, Jeff, dir. *Samaqan: Water Stories*. Web. <http://www.samaqan.ca/>. 15 Dec. 2014.

Bennett, Jane. *Vibrant Matter: A Political Ecology of Things*. Durham: Duke UP, 2010. Print.

Blackstock, Michael. *Oceaness*. Kamloops: Wyget Books, 2010. Print.

——. *Salmon Run*. Kamloops: Wyget Books, 2005. Print.

——. "Water: A First Nations' Spiritual and Ecological Perspective." *Perspectives: BC Journal of Ecosystems and Management* 1.1 (2001). <http://www.forrex.org/jem/iss1/vol1_no1_art 7.pdf>.

Calzavara, Mark. "Victory at Site 41 Shows There Is No Water to Waste." *Canadian Perspectives* (Autumn 2009): 8-9. <http://www.canadians.org/publications/CP/2009/ index.html>.

Canadian Environmental Assessment Agency. *Report of the Federal Prosperity Review Panel*. Executive Summary. 2010. 2 July 2010. <http://www.ceaa.gc.ca/050/documents/43937/ 43937E.pdf>.

Clements, Marie. *Burning Vision*. Vancouver: Talonbooks, 2003. Print.

Deneault, Alain. *Imperial Canada Inc*. Trans. Fred Reed and Robin Philpot. Vancouver: Talonbooks, 2012. Print.

Downstream Research Project. 2012. <http://www.downstream.ecuad.ca>.

Goldstick, Miles. *Wollaston: People Resisting Genocide*. Montreal: Black Rose, 1987. Print.

Harries, Kate. "Shotyk's Site 41 Proposal Gets Positive Responses from County Committee." Stop Dump Site 41. 15 Mar. 2011. <http://stopdumpsite41.ca/?p=5840>.

Harris, Maureen. "Broken Mouth: Offerings for the Don River, Toronto." *Wild Times* 35 (Aug. 2009): 11-14. Print.

"Intervention at the United Nations by the Athabasca Chipewyan and Cree First Nations." *Oil Sands Truth*. 29 Apr. 2008. <http://oilsandstruth.org/intervention-united-nations-athabasca-chipewyan-and-mikisew-cree-first-nations>.

"KI Wins Huge Victory Over Ontario Mining Company." *Ecojustice*. 12 Jan. 2010. <http://www.ecojustice.ca/media-centre/press-releases/ki-wins-huge-victory-over-ontario-mining-company>.

Laboucan-Massimo, Melina. "From Our Homelands to the Tar Sands." Downstream Workshop, Vancouver. 22 Mar. 2012. Talk.

Linton, Jamie. *What Is Water?* Vancouver: UBC P, 2010. Print.

Maracle, Lee. "Goodbye Snauq." *First Wives Club: Coast Salish Style*. Penticton: Theytus, 2010. Print.

Milewski, Terry. "Lakes Across Canada Face Being Turned into Mine Dump Sites." *CBC News*. 16 June 2008. <http://www.cbc.ca/news/canada/story/2008/06/16/condemned-lakes.html>.

Mining Watch Canada. *Acid Mine Drainage: Mining and Water Pollution Issues*. 25 Mar. 2006. <http://www.miningwatch.ca/publications/acid-mine-drainage-mining-and-water-pollution-issues>.

Morton, Alexandra. "Powerful Experience Walking." Blog. 4 May 2010. <http://alexandramorton.typepad.com/alexandra_morton/2010/05/powerful-experience-walking.html>.

Neimanis, Astrida. "We Are All Bodies of Water." *Water (Alphabet City No. 14)*. Ed. John Knechtel. Cambridge, MA: MIT P, 2009. 82-91. Print.

"New Uranium Mining Banned on 1 Million Acres Near Grand Canyon." *Navajo-Hopi Observer*. 18 Jan. 2012. <http://www.navajohopiobserver.com/main.asp?SectionID=1&SubSectionID=794&ArticleID=14194>.

Pino, Manuel. Excerpt of talk at Power Shift 2009. <https://www.youtube.com/watch?v=mQyyQxTgMr0>. 15 Dec. 2014.

Robb, Heather. "Un-digging Oka." *Montreal Mirror*. 30 June 2011. <http://solidarite-avec-les-autochtones.org/content/un-digging-oka>.

Saul, John Ralston. "Reconciliation: Four Barriers to Paradigm Shifting." *Response, Responsibility and Renewal: Canada's Truth and Reconciliation Journey*. Ed. Gregory Younging, Jonathan Dewar, and Mike DeGagne. Ottawa: Aboriginal Healing Foundation, 2009. 279-89. Print.

Save the Fraser Declaration. 2010. <http://savethefraser.ca/>.

Sprague, John. "Great Wet North? Canada's Myth of Water Abundance." *Eau Canada: The Future of Canada's Water*. Ed. Karen Bakker. Vancouver: UBC Press, 2007. 23-35. Print.

Van Wyck, Peter. *The Highway of the Atom*. Montreal: McGill-Queen's UP, 2010. Print.

"Victory for Teztan Biny (Fish Lake)!" RAVEN: Respecting Aboriginal Values and Environmental Needs. 2010. 28 Dec. 2010. <http://www.raventrust.com /projects/fishlaketeztanbiny.html>.

Village of Widows. Dir. Peter Blow. Lindum Films, 1999.

Wallace, David Foster. *This Is Water: Some Thoughts, Delivered on a Significant Occasion, About Living a Compassionate Life*. New York: Little, Brown and Company, 2009. Print.

"Why Is the Canadian Government Letting Mining Companies Turn Lakes into Toxic Dumps?" Council of Canadians. 15 Apr. 2012. <http://www.canadians.org/water/issues/TIAs/index.html>.

Wolf, Aaron, et al. "Peace in the Pipeline." *BBC News*. 13 Feb. 2009. <http://news.bbc.co.uk/2/hi/science/nature/7886646.stm>.

Wong, Rita. "Decolonizasian: Reading Asian and First Nations Relations in Literature." *Canadian Literature* 199 (Winter 2008): 158-80. Print.

———. "Disrupting Currents: Catch + Release." *Fuse Magazine* 27 Sept. 2010. <http://fusemagazine.org/2010/09/disrupting-currents-catch-release>.

PART III
Materials of and for Spaces

CHAPTER 11

The Biotopographies of Seth's *George Sprott (1894-1975)*

Candida Rifkind

From its modern beginnings at the turn of the last century, comics have been defined by their materiality. They materialize exterior and interior worlds on the page and have been shaped by the materiality of the page. Comics are objects that objectify; they are collectible artifacts on the one hand and visual externalizations of interior lives, thoughts, and feelings on the other. Consequently, comics both *are* material culture, however ephemeral or denigrated, and *about* material culture, from the representation of everyday objects within panels to the division of the page into a grid structure that reproduces the repetitions of everyday life. The work of Guelph-based cartoonist, illustrator, book designer, and comics advocate Seth exemplifies this relationship between the medium of comics and material culture through its attention to the book as an object and its investigation of the affective resonances of objects in people's lives. Seth's particular interest in the design and aesthetic detail of architecture from the early twentieth century and his narratives of overlooked, forgotten, and peripheral male characters often leads to criticism of his work as melancholic or nostalgic. Yet this is something that the cartoonist himself acknowledges and his comics are quite self-reflexive about this longing for the material culture of the past. As he comments in a 2004 interview:

> I have no illusions about the superiority of the past. People have always been miserable and life has always been difficult.... However, I can honestly say that I don't think much of this present time. Certainly, here in North America, things couldn't be cheaper, uglier or more vulgar than they currently are (well, they could, and probably will be—in the near future).

> I think that the early to middle 20th century was aesthetically more pleasing time period [sic]. While I personally have no desire to live through the Depression or World War II, I do think that culturally, the quality of many things was superior, especially design. Things were created for actual humans (with genuine care and effort). (Miller)

In his recent work, Seth has explored these tensions between the superior aesthetics of early-twentieth-century Canada and that period's experiences of misery, injustice, and alienation for which he is in no way nostalgic. In so doing, he extends comics' basic syntax of representing time as space on the page (through panel breakdowns that fragment moments into units divided by the gutter, or blank space, between panels) to a philosophical contemplation of temporality itself.[1] In his 2009 "picture novella," *George Sprott (1894-1975)*, Seth tells the fictional life story of a rather unlikeable man, about whom no one, including even the narrator, knows the full truth.[2] Comics can and do tell stories differently from prose, most obviously because they visualize in both pictures and words, and the gaps between these two sign systems may point to the gaps in representation itself. This fictional biography is an opportunity for Seth to represent the palimpsestic play of past and present through visual, verbal, and design strategies that slow down the time of reading and call attention to the materiality of the book as object. Through these semiotic and design elements, Seth foregrounds the idea of reverie as a narrative disruption to biographical authority as well as a temporal interruption to the repetitions of the everyday, including the repetitions of the comics page.

George Sprott (1894-1975) is a remastered edition of twenty-five dense full-page comics, each containing between twenty-five to thirty panels, serialized in the *New York Times Sunday Magazine* between September 2006 and March 2007. Each magazine page is a discrete narrative unit that contributes to the overall story of George's life and death, but Seth also designed it so that "the faithful reader who actually followed the strip, [...] would be free to tap into the bigger narrative" (Spurgeon). The book, published by Montreal's Drawn & Quarterly in 2009, expands the original set of panels, breaking up the chronological birth-to-death narrative in numerous ways. There are some external details of George's life on which the biography lingers: he was a Northern adventurer who shot silent film footage of seemingly exotic travels to the Arctic in the 1930s, and who then traded on these adventures for the rest of his life by hosting a small-town Ontario local television program, in which he waxed nostalgic for his glory years between stints of falling asleep on set. This is a fictional biography of a self-mythologizing man, about whom Seth has said:

In a way, George's life story was chosen almost arbitrarily. It didn't matter who George was or the specific details of his life. What was important was that it was *a life* coming to an end. I wanted to create a situation where the reader feels kind of lukewarm about the person who has just died (as we often do unless they are someone we deeply love). I wanted the reader to then decide for himself just how much sympathy they had for George. (Spurgeon)

Few of the characters in the book who knew George found him likeable since he was, as Jimmie Freeze the cartoonist attests, "pompous, vain, selfish ... a real heel."[3] If any empathy can obtain over the series of comic strips, it is from the sepia-toned flashback sequences depicting an unhappy and lonely childhood. However, the gradual exposition of George's childhood traumas hardly justifies his adult repetition of parental neglect and emotional repression. The narrator's ambivalence toward his subject, which becomes its own narrative of the challenges of biography, shapes this story of a life-not-well-lived that is ultimately more sad than exemplary, dominated by regrets and missed opportunities rather than lessons learned.

The initial magazine serialization of full-page comic strips about George Sprott, their expansion into a hardcover oversized book, and the supplementation of these two-dimensional representations with the three-dimensional city model of the narrative setting combine to form what I will call the biotopographies of George Sprott. I use this term to designate Seth's multimedia project, which attempts to map a fictional life across surfaces in ways that invite us to contemplate the very lack of depth, the superficiality, the gaps and absences, of any such endeavour. Thinking across these surfaces, I hope to demonstrate that the material status of the comic book itself, amplified by the images of objects it encloses, challenges biographical conventions when it substitutes diminution for grandness, caricature for authenticity, and reverie for productivity. As much as Seth picks an atypical biographical subject, he also constructs an atypical reading experience of a fictional biography. I believe that Seth's representations of stillness, silences, and gaps constructs a "pensive spectator," to borrow a term from film theorist Laura Mulvey, who experiences moments of reverie that break the reading from beginning to end, as well as the biographical illusion of a life as forward progression.[4]

Sidonie Smith and Julia Watson distinguish biography from self-life writing (or autobiography) in terms of the form of how it narrates a life: "In biography, scholars of other people's lives document and interpret those lives from a point of view external to the subject [... and] the events the subject becomes renowned for determine what the biographer selects to interpret as formative" (6-7). Certainly, Seth adheres to biographic conventions when he creates a narrator who studies the life of George Sprott and relies on multiple forms of evidence, especially interviews and testimonials, to tell the story of this man's life. At the same time, however, Seth plays with these very conventions and offers a comic book version of the "new biography": the story of a subject's life that makes critical interventions into the genre by refusing narrative authority (Smith and Watson 8-9). This self-reflexivity constructs a reader-narrator intersubjectivity as the text works to build a life story out of visual documents and verbal testimonies of a life that has passed and an era that is passing. From the outset, Seth uses narrative boxes to install a first-person narrator speaking in the second person to readers about George in the third person, but this narrator repeatedly expresses doubt and even attempts to retell events "properly." In the sequence "A Fresh Start," for instance, the narrative runs underneath drawings of photographs from George's life while the narrator admits, "I failed to tell you almost anything about the man. I apologize. I think it best if we just start the whole thing all over again. Perhaps a summary is the way to go—a bare-bones account of his life. I could pretend to have all the facts. But truthfully, I have serious gaps in my information." This sequence concludes with an apology because the narrator feels he has "imparted nothing 'real' about the man himself." "I'm so terribly sorry," he says, underneath a drawing of George's tombstone. This narrator is part explainer, part detective seeking a biographical truth he knows is elusive and impossible. He is in this sense a failed narrator, a bad detective, telling the partial story of a seemingly flawed man and his sad, lonely life. In addition to choosing an unlikely and unlikeable subject for the verbal narrative, Seth uses a range of visual techniques to challenge biographical conventions: he breaks up linear chronology verbally and visually, fragmenting the spatial field and disrupting stylistic coherence by interleaving the more conventional full-page cartoon strips with silent flashbacks, full- and double-page illustrations, and photographs of cardboard model buildings.

Typical of Seth's books, *George Sprott (1894-1975)* contains a great deal of para-textual material to control the enclosed comic panels. In this case, the title page is preceded by a double-page sequence, "George is Born," which introduces us to the biographical subject *in utero* and also to a self-doubting narrator. Focusing on the round head of the embryonic George floating in the panel space, narrative boxes tell us that George is just about to be born, but shift quickly to a set of interrogatives about the very nature of existence. The narrator announces George's imminent birth and then asks, "But where is George arriving from? I s'pose it's the same question I will later ask ...

'where did he go after he died?'" Lest we think this is an existential dilemma alone, Seth quickly moves into the self-referential dilemmas of the cartoon biographer when his narrator muses, "I guess it's easy for us to imagine a void before we exist.... Not so easy to picture one after death." That this book is about the task of picturing a life is evident in the next page panels, in which the narrator describes George's epiphany that life itself is like a comic sequence: the floating head, not the narrator, tells us over six panels that "[t]hese boxes in a row—perhaps they're not just a sequence. Perhaps the action in the middle box ... isn't merely determined by the action in the box before it. Maybe it is also influenced by what must occur in the box that follows. It needs to fulfill and anticipate in both directions. Maybe it is in this way that the future determines the present as much as the past." The narrator may apologize that these seem "very naïve questions," but hardly so. Here, Seth uses the spatial rhythms of the panel sequence to offer a philosophy of time that is also a theory of biographical narration based on the grammar of cartooning itself.

As much as this may seem a postmodern game, it is also a thoroughly modern device, as Seth himself admits:

> I took the germ for the narrator's voice from the introduction to *Don Quixote*. Cervantes doesn't have "all the facts about Quixote" and that struck me as so utterly brilliant and modern—especially coming from the "first" novel.... Because of the narrator's uncertainty the reader doesn't have to take anything as the truth. Another attempt to fragment things—put the decisions in the reader's hands. (Spurgeon)

The other thing that Seth puts in the readers' hands is the material object: a very big book (14 by 12 inches) that is awkward to read without a table, to transport in a bag, or to fit onto a standard bookshelf: it is not a book designed for casual and impromptu reading.[5] Instead, it demands attention as a book, its luxurious design perhaps signifying "art book" more than "comic book."[6] It does have at least one notable companion on the alternative comic book shelf, Art Spiegelman's *In the Shadow of No Towers*, a large-scale hardcover autobiographical comic about the World Trade Center attacks on 9/11 that recreates the scale of full newspaper comics from the early twentieth century. Both objects herald the ephemeral aesthetic past of their medium in a more solid form that also recalls, for the reader, what Gillian Whitlock describes as "those first experiences of reading nursery books somatically" (967). It is a shrinking experience to read both of these comic books as they dominate the reader's lap or table or bookshelf. In their very materiality they function as cardboard signs of juvenile reading, so that their material and medial statuses are both caught up in the affects of nostalgia and the assumptions that comic books are only for children. Of course, their narrative content belies such associations, as Spiegelman's book is a graphic testimony of individual and collective trauma while Seth's is a self-reflexive biographical meditation on the narrative foreclosures of a life-not-well-lived. The narrator's uncertainty makes explicit the tensions between truth and fiction that play out in the various games of scale Seth builds into the book-as-object and the story-as-biography. This is a big book about a large man (numerous witnesses comment that Sprott was overweight) fond of tall tales, but whose behaviour reduces him to a small man, lessened by his callous treatment of women in particular, but also made ridiculous by his delusions of grandeur and diminished by his lack of self-awareness.[7]

George Sprott's identity is very much a part of his time-space of mid-century southern Ontario, and in particular the medium of local access television.[8] Seth revels in the weird and eccentric characters who knew George at the station, featuring such local celebrities as Sir Grisly Gruesome—the horror king—giving testimonials about his subject and celebrating their shared community in a group portrait of the CKCK-television pantheon of stars. To return to the para-textual material, the inside covers of the book feature the station's test patterns from different eras to enclose the narrative in the visual history of local television that is the context for this life story. The book itself mimics the end of the local television day when the double page announcing "The End"—of George's life and its narrative—is followed by the double-page spread "Sign Off," which ends with a panel representing the singing of the national anthem, "O Canada." This is as much an elegy for the ephemeral medium that brought George to the public as it is a biography of the man himself. As the narrator laments at the conclusion of the panels that tell "A Brief History of the CKCK Television Station," the station stopped being able to produce local programming in the 1980s and so the shows "evaporated into the ether along with the folks who made them." They do survive, however, in the pages of *George Sprott (1894-1975)*, a sizable print artifact that tells the story of the ephemerality of local television and its disappearance as a viable form.

Visibility and invisibility are important themes to the story of George Sprott's life as his public celebrity fades, and they are also important to the narrative of the life-not-well-lived that accumulates over the series of witness testimonials. As a maker of silent Northern travel and adventure films, George was at the cutting edge of a modern technology used in the early twentieth century for the residual colonial project of documenting

Indigenous peoples as subjects out of time.[9] George travelled to the Northern Arctic to shoot silent films with a cameraman and also the cartoonist, Jimmie Freeze. Jimmie's task was to illustrate the largely fictional "Northern Dispatches" letters George sent south to be printed and mailed out to boys on a subscription basis. As Jimmie recalls with disdain in "The Gentleman Adventurer," George funded his expedition "with the dimes of little boys" and "those letters read great—polar bears, northern lights, contact with primitive peoples …," but "they had everything in them but the truth." George caricatured Indigenous Northern life to gloss over the reality of "waiting around in shabby camps, wormy blubber meat, diarrhea and lots of inferior quality booze" (see Figure 11.1). The films George directed and then screened for decades on his CKCK program, "Northern Hi-Lights," are never "screened" for readers in the book, but their content is clearly that of typical silent-era travel films depicting Western adventurers among Northern Arctic Inuit. Seth's depiction of George in this role alludes to the famous Robert Flaherty ethnographic documentary, *Nanook of the North* (1922), and to an early-twentieth-century desire to use film to preserve a seemingly dying way of "primitive" life. Fatimah Rony uses the term "taxidermy" in her analysis of Flaherty's film, along with many other early-twentieth-century examples of cinematic spectacle, to designate its particular brand of ethnographic romanticism: "Taxidermy seeks to make that which is dead look as if it were still living" (102) and "thus in order to make a visual representation of indigenous peoples, one must believe that they are dying, as well as use artifice to make a picture which appears more true, more pure" (102).

George's dispatches and films perform precisely this kind of taxidermic romanticization of Inuit life, which at once makes him typical of his timespace but also a caricature in himself. As Jimmie Freeze reflects, George

Figure 11.1 "The Gentleman Adventurer" from *George Sprott (1894-1975)* by Seth. N. pag. Used by permission of Drawn & Quarterly. Reproduced in greyscale.

"fancied himself a Junior Byrd or Amundsen," a "Gentleman Adventurer" type in the spectacle of Northern travel he created in print and on screen. Jimmie also admits to the artificiality of their documentary films when he recalls, "[w]e'd roll in and get them to frolic on an ice floe or pretend to hunt seals for George's cameras." In the next panel, Seth draws a flashback of Jimmie, wearing a parka and clutching his cartoon portfolio, standing on the tundra in front of a garbage dump and recalling: "Even then you could see a way of life coming to an end up there." The handmade sign for the dump is at once a literal marker of the cultural and environmental damage of colonialism and a metaphor for filmmaking itself as a kind of violence. The camera that frames the Inuit in fantasies of the natural other is a visual technology of "salvage ethnography" to preserve a people presumed to be disappearing. Ironically, this panel suggests, "salvage ethnography" does little to preserve or protect and much to transform living cultures into waste material. George's taxidermic films that separate surface illusion from authentic experience work to transform the lived present into the dying past for the profit of the filmmaker. As Pauline Wakeham argues through her reading of the "taxidermic semiosis" of another early-twentieth-century salvage ethnographer/photographer, Edward S. Curtis, the moment at which the camera captures the Indigenous subject alive is the precise moment "that marked native bodies for pending death" (94). The endurance of these photographic and cinematic images of the putative vanishing Indian, which continue to circulate today, signals the ongoing colonial stereotyping of "the aboriginal other in an anterior realm discrete from the purportedly dynamic movement of Western society" (126). Seth's cartoon representation of this cinematic taxidermy of the Inuit other ultimately turns the stereotype back on to the white filmmaker, however, as George Sprott becomes a caricature of colonial nostalgia, his very name—to those few who still recognize it—a synonym for stasis.

George's fictions of the North, presented as fact, were popular and profitable in his youth, but, ironically, it is George who ultimately comes to be a subject out of time and out of place in old age. One of the delayed revelations in this fictional biography is that George had a daughter with an Inuit woman, Kullu Kanayuk. Recursive reading of the comic book opens up a visual hint of this in the early panels titled "Merrily We Roll Along" (see Figure 11.2). Here, Seth uses a sequence of visual images of Inuit in the Arctic that bear little relation to the verbal narrative accompanying them, which describes George's early and unrequited love for a woman named Olive. The second and third row of panels on this page mimic 1930s Northern travel films when they depict a smiling Inuit woman welcoming George and then a small child gazing up and out of the panel with the narrative comment that, at the age

The Biotopographies of Seth's *George Sprott (1894-1975)*   233

Figure 11.2 "Merrily We Roll Along" from *George Sprott (1894-1975)* by Seth. N. pag. Used by permission of Drawn & Quarterly. Reproduced in greyscale.

of twenty-two, Olive had dumped him and, "[f]or a year or two after, George hadn't fully known who he was." Seth exploits fully the irony available in comics between disjunctive images and texts: we learn later through a panel echo on the page titled "The Daughter" that this child is indeed his daughter, Elisapee Kanayuk, and that she never fully knew her father. Like the iconic real filmmaker Flaherty, who had Inuit common-law wives and children, George fathered a child with an Inuit woman, but he never acknowledged her as his daughter. In her testimony, dated 2006, an elderly Elisapee recalls that George abandoned her mother, leaving her with the difficult task of raising a mixed-race child. Elisapee describes her biological father as "an awful man" and regrets that her own behaviour, as "a rotten child, an uncaring wife and a bad mother," suggests she has "more of my father in me than I would like to admit." If George's mistakes have, until this panel, seemed largely foolish and innocuous, by including Elisapee's testimonial Seth gestures to the devastating consequences of his subject's participation in cinematic taxidermy: the gap between the fictions of his Northern travels and the facts of his experiences, for both himself and others, is no laughing matter. His caricatures of Inuit life, which in turn make him into a caricature, hinge on fixing images of living people in an imaginary past. This cinematic project so typical of a colonizing modernity serves as a metonym for the overall life-not-well-lived of George Sprott, for not only is this a narrative of one man's arrested development or self-caricature, but it is also a narrative of auto-taxidermy, of a man whose delusions of grandeur leave him dead to the present. There is little justice in it, but there is much irony in George's descent from the handsome gentleman adventurer to the despised father and disregarded relic. His reproduction of inauthentic images and telling of false tales is ultimately exposed and its tragic consequences revealed to readers, if not to George himself.

The narrator's doubt about his knowledge of George Sprott's life, especially his inner life, is matched by Sprott's own repression of traumatic and significant events in his past and an emotional reticence typical of his gender, time, and place. We learn at various points, from multiple witnesses, that George regrets never telling his mother he loved her; that he fathered and abandoned Elisapee; that his wife, Helen, may have committed suicide; and that his devoted niece, Daisy, became a substitute for his neglect of other women in his life. It is only in his final moments before death, in "And So Here We Are," that George himself seems to recognize what the narrator describes as the "ghostly procession" of women who mattered to him: the "distant Olive Mott ... abandoned Kullu Kanayuk ... and disappointed Helen Sprott." Numerous times, people who knew him—including his beloved Daisy—testify that they never really "knew" George Sprott, that his gregarious public persona masked personal anguish repressed deeply inside George and glimpsed only occasionally by those who knew him best. The book itself mimics this dynamic in the one sequence that moves readers into George's interior, even subconscious mind, in a middle gatefold section. Seth explains that "this six-page sequence is composed of over one hundred small comic panels. It's very dense and the main purpose it served was to symbolically provide the only point in the novel where you actually go inside the main character's mind. Thus, you open the gatefold and 'enter' George" ("Creating" 35). As readers unfold the pages, Seth moves us through sequences of George's life punctuated by black panels with the text "wake," since these pages represent George's memory dreams while he is asleep on set. The sequences move between images of the women in his life (mother, wife, child, lovers) and impressions of his environment, including the wildflowers of his childhood, the outdoor smells of his wilderness adventures, the sight of birds flying between city buildings, and a box of trinkets from his childhood. The sequence ends with the imperative, "Wake up, George."

In this gatefold section, Seth relies heavily on the two cartooning techniques Scott McCloud terms "closure" and "aspect-to-aspect transition" to create the illusion of a wandering eye settling on different aspects of a scene, such that the reader must fill in the gaps of the vertical and horizontal gutters with the meaning that connects the panels (McCloud 72). In this sense, the reader is more knowledgeable about George's life than he is, or than he reveals to others, because we have moved inside his dream state, but on the surface of the comics page and not in the sequential trajectory of the dream. The reader can pass over the images as they pass by in sequence, but we are also able to apprehend the total page and read back and forth, as well as up and down. The book dimensions inherited from the magazine format allow

Seth to juxtapose three or four sequences on the same page, and the gatefold design then multiplies this by four so that the length and breadth of George's memory dream appears contiguous and the book expands horizontally in the reader's hands. In this way, Seth plays with page layout and paper folds to create a self-conscious reading experience, demanding physical participation by the reader through a tactile experience of the book. This, in turn, draws attention to what Charles Hatfield identifies as one of the central tensions of comics design, that between sequence and surface, or between the individual panel as a moment-in-time and "as a graphic element in an atemporal design" of the whole page (Hatfield 48). The spatial fragments of the panels, divided by their gutters, are fixed on the flat surface for us to regard and contemplate both individually and holistically before we "wake up" and return to the regular sequential page-turning of standard book design. This gatefold design is therefore the most obvious moment when the book demands the slowed-down reading time of the pensive spectator. The ideal reader's act of unfolding the central pages is a tactile effort rewarded by the kinds of reverie possible when a film stops on one image: "the fascination of time fossilized overwhelms the fascination of narrative progression" (Mulvey 187). The present time of reading stalls and can start to flow forward again only when the reader closes the gatefold or flips past it. The reader's "entry" into George's interior life, with all of the voyeuristic pleasures it may evoke, is therefore an opportunity to gaze at an alternate, even hidden, version of George that ultimately folds the reader into the intersubjective construction of the biographical subject through the materiality of the book.

Just as these pages are an interior topography of George Sprott, they are also connected to the exterior landscapes that punctuate the biographical narrative. As Seth observes, "I don't think you can ever have a gatefold that isn't a landscape metaphor of some kind. Especially in a book with so much Arctic imagery in it. At the very least it's some sort of a dreamscape" ("Creating" 35). The gatefold that constructs a pensive spectator of the biographical subject is part of the larger project Seth undertakes to punctuate the rhythm of the single-page sequences with pauses, thereby using the space of the page to imply the dynamics of time. There are four double-page Arctic panoramas spaced throughout the book that Seth explains in musical terms: "I put them there to provide the reader with an occasional pause (or long note)—to break up the staccato rhythm of the comic pages themselves (which tended toward a relentless monotony in their pacing)" ("Creating" 34). These spreads also function as visual suspensions of narrative time to convey the ongoing impact of George's early Northern experiences on the rest of his life. The landscapes are typical of Seth's fluid line style and demonstrate his theory that there is a vernacular school of Canadian design defined first and foremost by "a distinct connection to our huge landscape" and the transmission of "the idea of open space" ("Creative" 7). Moreover, their visual style recalls the 1920s and 1930s landscapes of Thoreau MacDonald, the Toronto graphic artist (and son of Group of Seven member J. E. H. MacDonald) for whom Seth has a great deal of admiration (See "Creative" 21). Although he worked primarily in the vernacular forms of drawing, woodcuts, and book illustration, MacDonald shares with his father's famous painting school a landscape perspective identified with "scenic value and spiritual renewal" (Jessup 146). Also, like the Group of Seven, MacDonald's more humble and illustrative works are largely depopulated of either Aboriginal peoples or European settlement, repeating the older generation's romantic vision of the Canadian wilderness as a solitary, private, intimate spiritual experience, which was part of their anti-modernist backlash against the perceived ills of modern urban life (Jessup 146-47). Seth repeats some of this ideology in his frozen, depopulated Arctic landscapes that invite the reader to slow down and gaze on beautiful scenery; at the same time, their placement implies that these are scenes from George's memory, and so the reader is a pensive spectator of George's visual memories rather than of the landscape itself. We see the Arctic as George saw it, and George saw it through the romantic gaze brought to national prominence by the Group of Seven and their descendants. The Arctic landscape pages, then, become a topographical dreamscape that interrupts the biographical narrative formally yet coheres it thematically around the idea of the North as the still time-space of reverie.

George sleeps a lot, literally on set and figuratively in his lack of self-knowledge. He is also a daydreamer and appears in both youth and old age in moments of reverie, gazing out windows in panels that resist linear narrative for moments of quiet contemplation by and of the biographical subject.[10] While George's soporific personality, his on-set sleeping, and his daydreaming are all connected, there is a difference between actual sleeping and the state of reverie. Gaston Bachelard's theories of reverie are helpful in reading George Sprott, as he theorizes that "reverie is entirely different from the dream by the very fact that it is always more or less centered upon one object. The dream proceeds on its own way in a linear fashion, forgetting its original path as it hastens along. The reverie works in a star pattern. It returns to its center to shoot out new beams" (*Psychoanalysis of Fire* 14). Whether he is represented in youth or old age, one pictorial repetition throughout *George Sprott (1894-1975)* is of the biographical subject gazing out a window at falling snow. The snowy landscapes of the Arctic panoramas that interrupt the narrative are echoed within George's story as the scene, or object, of his reverie is their urban counterpart: the winter cityscape. The three-page sequence, "January 15, 1927," depicts a young George, working as editor at *Junior Woodsman*, stuck in his office by a snowstorm. The final page shifts into a silent sequence to depict George smoking alone in a darkened office. The sequence mimics a camera panning across the objects in the room, but the page composition places George close to the centre, in a panel that is larger than the rest, gazing out at the snowstorm (see Figure 11.3). The final panel offers us George's point of view out the window and so we substitute gazing at him in reverie with a reverie of our own. This image repeats in the sequence "December 8, 1971," when an aged George slips into dreams of his Inuit family and wakes to stare out the office window at a snowstorm. The final panels of this sequence repeat the earlier shift to George's point of view out the window, but the concluding strip of five panels pulls back from the subject's perspective to represent him in profile, alternating between the old and young George in the first two panels. Time passes and the man ages,

Figure 11.3 "January 15, 1927" from *George Sprott (1894–1975)* by Seth. N. pag. Used by permission of Drawn & Quarterly. Reproduced in greyscale.

suggests Seth, but he has a lifelong tendency toward reverie, inspired by external winter scenes, that transport him back to the Arctic landscape that is the main object of his memoryscape.

In addition to the double-page Arctic panoramas, *George Sprott (1894-1975)* features another set of visual interruptions that break up the rhythm of the narrative sequences in the form of photographs of cardboard model buildings of the story's setting. This miniature city, which has seen several gallery outings, is Seth's ongoing project to build out of cardboard the fictional city of Dominion, the southern Ontario setting of *George Sprott (1894-1975)*, as well as his long-running serial comic, *Clyde Fans* (1997-) (see Figure 11.4).[11] It is the three-dimensional form of his notebook sketches of Dominion, which contain even more detail about this city he says is about the size of Hamilton, Ontario ("Dominion City" 56-57). Seth has downplayed the significance and quality of this cardboard city by explaining how it started as a middle-aged man's basement hobby, noting that the models were made quickly out of old Fed Ex boxes, a glue gun, and house paint, and that they are not to scale; "I never intended them to be precise or precious objects," he says ("Dominion City" 58). This city is a craft project transferred to the gallery, while the book is magazine serials reframed between hard covers; both blur the lines between the quirky and the ephemeral on the one hand and the esteemed and durable on the other but, most of all, they are both objects to be looked at that use space to convey one of Seth's ongoing concerns, "the

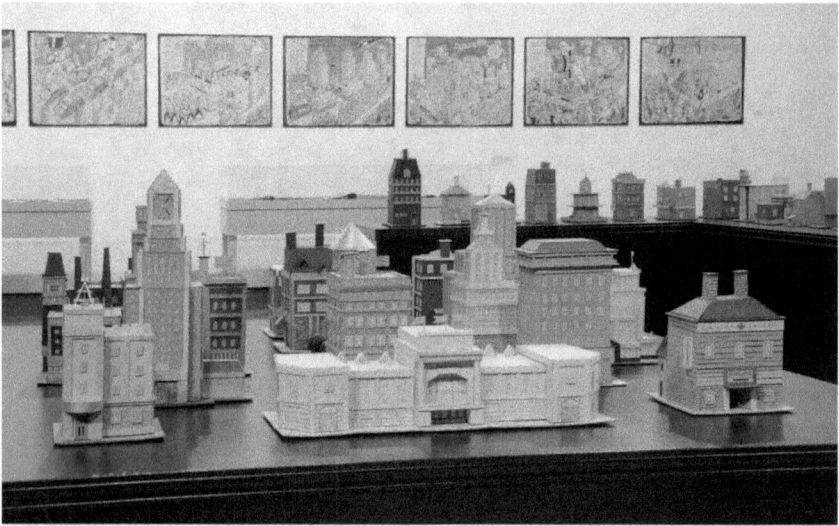

Figure 11.4 Dominion exhibit at Render Gallery, 20 September to 6 December 2008 (photo by Robert McNair, 2009). Seth's *Palookaville 20*, p. 51. Used by permission of Seth and Drawn & Quarterly. Reproduced in greyscale.

feeling of time" ("Dominion City" 58). In *George Sprott (1894-1975)*, photography mediates between the three-dimensional form of the model buildings and the two-dimensional form of the comics sequences (see Figure 11.5). The photograph documents the building in isolation from its miniature cityscape, rendering it as an aesthetic object in white space akin to a pedestal. Instead of the gallery as site of the miniature city, the book becomes the context site for the aesthetic display of individual buildings in documentary photographs that elevate them from rough-hewn objects to art objects. While the architectural model is usually mimetic (a representation of a real building) or projective (a plan for a future real building), Seth's models are retrospective fictions. They are part of a longer European tradition to recreate historical architecture in miniature, as either souvenirs or archival objects, but the buildings they represent never "really" existed.[12]

Seth's cardboard model city of Dominion demands an alternate pace to the forward thrust of so much of contemporary everyday life in urban North America. The miniature city itself uses three dimensions to undermine any reality effect of the two-dimensional comic book, the very medium of which

Figure 11.5 CKCK model reproduced in *George Sprott (1894-1975)* by Seth. N. pag. Used by permission of Drawn & Quarterly. Reproduced in greyscale.

already leans toward caricature and stereotype rather than authenticity and realism. Seth's conception of the relationship between comic strip and cardboard models imagines a biotopography of George Sprott that is all surface, but not necessarily superficial:

> Dominion is an ongoing project and will probably continue, in dribs and drabs, for the rest of my life. I actually included the photos of the buildings as a lark. It just popped into my head and I thought it would be simply fun and "neat" to put the cardboard facsimiles of these places right there next to their comic strip histories and when I thought about it, I liked how it further fragmented the narrative a bit by reminding the reader that the whole thing was "just a story" in my cardboard metropolis. It's funny that showing the 3D model of the building actually makes the place seem less real than the little drawings of it in the strip itself. (Spurgeon)

Seth's biotopographies of George Sprott thus use flat surfaces to represent time spatially, whether it is boxed across the sequential panels of the comics page or drawn onto the cardboard boxes spread across a gallery. To read the book of *George Sprott (1894-1975)* and to contemplate the model city of Dominion as two discrete yet overlapping biotopographies is to raise the question of whether their relationship is one of cross-referencing, supplementation, or correction—to wonder whether the model city needs the comic strips or the comic strips need the model city. On first glance it may appear that Seth compensates for his narrator's uncertainty about the details and truths of his subject's life by offering meticulous notes and detailed models of that subject's urban environment, that buildings and streetscapes are more knowable than people, but I want to argue that there is instead a shared conceptual core between the form of the comic book and the form of the cardboard city. This overlapping terrain is latent at the etymological level since, as Hilary Chute observes, "[t]he word *cartoon* comes from the Italian word *cartone*, which means cardboard, and denotes a drawing for a picture or a design intended to be transferred, historically to tapestries or frescoes. Yet, when the printing press developed, cartoon came to mean any sketch that could be mass-produced" (11). Cartoons and cardboard share a material and linguistic origin, then, but in Seth's work they merge to demand the work of contemplation and regard, performed by both readers of the book and spectators of the exhibit, that slows down time and mediates between present and past, distance and proximity. The narrative and model city need and exceed each other, then, but in their very interdependencies and aporias they call us to reverie as objects that demand a pensive spectator.

Following Susan Stewart's theorization of miniatures in *On Longing*, I believe the cardboard Dominion has a locus of nostalgia, but for what might have been rather than for what was. As Stewart observes of historical miniatures, "the miniature is often a material allusion to a text which is no longer available to us, or which, because of its fictiveness, never *was* available to us except through a second-order fictive world" (60). As a result, Stewart concludes, "the reduction in scale which the miniature presents skews the time and space relations of the everyday lifeworld, and as an object consumed, the miniature finds its 'use value' transformed into the infinite time of reverie" (65). The miniature city is a space of longing, of looking but not touching, a utopian spectacle to be possessed at a glance, a dream space that arrests time. It is a strange and estranging experience; as Sarah Higley observes, "the miniature is power: over the world of things we would like to possess but do not. It is also exclusion: from a space we would like to inhabit but do not" (17). This miniature world is consequently also a dominated world, a cardboard collection of objects that represents a material opportunity for Seth to quote himself. In his discussion of miniatures in the *Poetics of Space*, Bachelard associates the miniature with the daydream, referring to the hours of peace and patience it takes an artisan to produce a miniature world, and then exclaims: "And how restful this exercise on a dominated world can be! For miniature rests us without ever putting us to sleep" (161). Crucial here is Bachelard's understanding of the relay between the dominated world of the miniature and the reverie this object produces in a pensive spectator.

Seth's comic book and cardboard city are representational surfaces that inhabit the time-space of the present in order to send us—readers, gallery goers—into contemplation of what was and, just as importantly, what might have been. This cardboard city is the representation of a lack, since it points to an urban topography that no longer exists, and indeed which never existed except in the artist's imagination, made legible in other media such as the comic book. As much as this medium invites play, it is also serious and even sinister, as the miniature city invites the voyeur's gaze and recalls both Gulliver's and Alice's subject-fracturing disorientations of scale.[13] Seth himself admits,

> I have long had a desire to "gather up" everything I like from the past. Obviously I couldn't bring home an old office tower or a deco apartment house. With old buildings, I had to be satisfied with snapping a photo, but now, through some form of sympathetic magic, I could actually take these places home with me. Not that any of the models are actual recreations of real buildings [...] Yet constructing the city and its past seemed to satisfy that longing to possess. I was collecting buildings—putting them in amber—saving them from the wrecking ball. ("Dominion City" 44)

The collector is a frequent self-reflexive character in alternative comics, which is a subculture often, and perhaps stereotypically, defined by the desire to own rare artifacts. In his 2005 graphic narrative, *Wimbledon Green*, Seth uses a similar narrative structure to *George Sprott (1894-1975)* of testimonials by friends, rivals, and acquaintances to tell the story of the mysterious eponymous comics collector. George Sprott is also about collecting, not least at its structural level of a collection of different visual media (comics sequences, landscape drawings, photographs of models, recreations of television iconography, and so on) but also at its narrative level of multiple perspectives on the same man, and its thematic level of George's attachment to objects from his past.

George lived out his last decades in three rooms of a hotel. The sequence "5th Floor, End of the Hall" is the testimony of Hadrian Dingle, one-time bellhop and now hotel manager, who went into George's rooms after he died "and just stood there and looked around." As he gazes at George's rooms, filled with objects ranging from a gramophone to a bearskin rug, Hadrian wonders, "did those relics make up a record of a man's life?" The ephemerality of human existence opposes the durability of material culture, even those objects never intended for posterity. The sequence ends with fourteen small panel close-ups of individual objects, from a photograph of his long-dead wife, Helen, to Northern souvenirs, to the medical supplies of old age (see Figure 11.6).

This series of objects George leaves behind function as a narrative of the man's biography when they are apprehended as a collection; that is, the comics grammar of panels and gutters at once presents them as unique objects in individual frames and places them in sequence so that we read these objects, from right to left, as a story.

There are different kinds of memory objects represented in this significant sequence: framed photographs of the protagonist in his glory days and a portrait of his deceased wife; mass-produced souvenirs of Inuit culture

Figure 11.6 "5th Floor, End of the Hall" from *George Sprott (1894-1975)* by Seth. N. pag. Used by permission of Drawn & Quarterly. Reproduced in greyscale.

that echo his own role in cinematic taxidermy; a savings bank from the television station that no longer exists because it could not compete financially; a half-read copy of Thoreau's *Walden*; a trophy cup that attests to his public recognition; childhood toys that signal George's attachment to his unhappy past; a naked female figure that recalls his sexual objectification of real women; a birthday card from his beloved niece; and a medical truss and other objects that betray his physical discomfort and old-age ailments. All of the great themes of George's life are here, from his childhood feelings of rejection and their legacy in his treatment of women, to his youthful idea of the North and romantic view of nature as spiritual renewal, to his former celebrity kept alive by his faithful niece. Indeed, Seth implies that George compensates for his failures to achieve intimacy with people through his intimate attachments with objects, some of which are reminders of those failed relationships. In this way, the above sequence depicts George's objects as a collection, the point of which is not so much remembering as forgetting. By including objects from the present that juxtapose George's invented version of his younger virile self with the recent realities of his frail and aging body, Seth envelops the past within the present through signs of material culture. Seth places drawings of George's souvenir objects in a comics sequence that constructs a narrative of George himself and depicts the agency of objects, read in sequence as a collection, beyond the dissolution of the subject. The melancholy of this sequence obtains when the collection itself is dissolved. It ends with a panel of the emptied rooms that suggests a poignant visual response to Hadrian's question: if the relics do indeed represent his life, they are just as disposable as George is forgettable.

This silent sequence demands a pensive spectator in its suspension of narrative description for the visual revelations available in a collection of everyday objects. The inevitable destruction of the collection upon its owner's death seems to suggest that the collection has no external value. Yet, there is some respite from this melancholic message in the Epilogue, which closes the book with Owen Trade, "collector of memorabilia from the CKCK television station." Although he is more "focused on Sir Grisly Gruesome," Owen counts as the centerpiece of his George Sprott collection a "genuine Arctic film reel" he rescued from the CKCK trash can. Like Seth's own project to reclaim the lost past in his model city, Owen values that which others see as detritus. In this detail, Seth coalesces his overlapping investments in collecting, historical ephemera, regional identity, and oddball characters as ways to resist the annihilations of individuality common to contemporary commodity culture and media globalization. And so, rather than the more obvious nostalgia, which only partially explains this complex artist's work,

I believe it is reverie, the possibility of a coherent moment of time in a still moment of space, that is a site of hope within Seth's body of work. In two and three dimensions, Seth rejects the worst of contemporary North American material culture and recreates a world made up of the objects he cherishes from a past now gone. *George Sprott (1894-1975)* is a big book about a little life; its outsized material form sets in relief all of its protagonist's failures and disappointments and expresses the fear that even a life filled with big adventures might be of little consequence. In its self-reflexive work of biotopography, Seth's book invites quiet contemplation about quiet contemplation. As George Sprott reflects on his own life and other characters assess it, the reader, too, is drawn into reverie, asked to think about both a life lived and how that life, or any life, might be represented.

NOTES

1 See Chute's Introduction for an overview of the "time as space" syntax of comics.
2 See Hatfield for a discussion of the term "alternative comics" to describe a literary form that uses comics to tell extended narratives and to which autobiography is central.
3 *George Sprott (1895-1975)* does not include page numbers. Whenever possible, I indicate the location of the panels in my text by page title.
4 See Laura Mulvey, "The Pensive Spectator," for a discussion of this perceptual possibility in relation to avant-garde cinema.
5 The British publisher Jonathan Cape published a smaller paperback edition in 2010.
6 Its mass production notwithstanding, there is an argument to be made that this book is in the tradition of the artist's book, which is self-conscious about its form and interrogates the artistic and conceptual roles of the book itself. Johanna Drucker best summarizes the relationship between artist's books and comic books when she writes: "[r]ather than operate in the one-off mode of fine art production, graphic novels are the realization of the vision of the democratic art form once trumpeted by champions of the artist's book, works of art that circulate widely and freely in consumer culture even as their sensibility keeps open a place for counterculture sensibilities within the mainstream" (39).
7 Throughout much of *George Sprott (1894-1975)*, Seth uses high-angle points of view that minimize George against his background so that we are looking down on him as he is dwarfed by the world around him. There are good examples of this in the sequences "7:01pm, October, 1975" and the final panel of "7:25pm, October 9, 1975."
8 There is a real referent for George Sprott: the Detroit broadcaster George Pierrot, who started his World Adventure Series of lectures at the Detroit Institute of Arts during the Depression. Detroiters paid twenty-five cents each to hear his talks and watch his films about his trips around the world. In the 1950s and 1960s, Seth watched Pierrot's evening travel adventure program broadcast on local Detroit television across the border to Windsor, Ontario. This childhood memory inspires the fictional character, in particular his habit of falling asleep on air, but Seth admits that he mixed the vibrant and eccentric Detroit broadcasting culture with similar material from southern Ontario television (Lorah).
9 See Fabian's landmark discussion of early ethnography's denial of coeval time between Western anthropologists and the Indigenous peoples they study.

10 This is another of Seth's gestures to comics history. From the earliest days of the newspaper funnies, the Freudian possibilities of dream states have shaped the fantastical worlds of the comics. Notably, Winsor McCay's highly innovative *Little Nemo in Slumberland* (1905-14) is organized around the protagonist's dream-world adventures that begin and end with panels of his "real" life in bed. Little Nemo's fantastical adventures form the substance of McCay's narratives, and there is something of both their colonial exoticism and modern cityscapes in the much cleaner visual style of *George Sprott (1894-1975)*. The difference between Little Nemo and George Sprott, however, is that the child dreams at night of participating in grand and surreal adventures outside his bedroom, whereas the man falls into reverie gazing out at the snow-covered world he can no longer conquer.

11 See Seth's essay, "Dominion City," for the exhibition history of this model city (57-58).

12 Mark Morris reviews the different kinds of architectural model traditions, including retrospective models of classical buildings (88-90).

13 See Morris for more on issues of representation and ontology in architectural models.

WORKS CITED

Bachelard, Gaston. *The Poetics of Space*. 1964. Trans. Maria Jola. Boston: Beacon Press, 1994. Print.

———. *The Psychoanalysis of Fire*. Trans. Alan C. Ross. Boston: Beacon Press, 1964. Print.

Chute, Hilary. *Graphic Women: Life Narrative and Contemporary Comics*. New York: Columbia UP, 2010. Print.

Drucker, Johanna. "What Is Graphic about Graphic Novels?" *English Language Notes* 46.2 (2008): 39-55. Web. 21 Sept. 2010.

Fabian, Johannes. *Time and the Other: How Anthropology Makes Its Object*. New York: Columbia UP, 1983. Print.

Hatfield, Charles. *Alternative Comics: An Emerging Literature*. Jackson: UP of Mississippi, 2005. Print.

Higley, Sarah L. "A Taste for Shrinking: Movie Miniatures and the Unreal City." *Camera Obscura* 47 (2001): 1-35. Print.

Jessup, Lynda. "The Group of Seven and the Tourist Landscape in Western Canada, or The More Things Change ... " *Journal of Canadian Studies* 37.1 (Spring 2002): 144-79. Print.

Lorah, Michael C. "The Life of George Sprott: Talking to Seth." *Newsarama.com*. 17 Apr. 2009. Web. 10 Aug. 2011.

McCay, Winsor. *Little Nemo: 1905-1914*. Cologne: Taschen, 2000. Print.

McCloud, Scott. *Understanding Comics: The Invisible Art*. New York: HarperPerennial, 1994. Print.

Miller, Bryan. "An Interview with Seth." *Bookslut* June 2004. Web. 20 Jun 2012.

Morris, Mark. *Models: Architecture and the Miniature*. Chichester, UK: Wiley-Academy, 2006. Print. Architecture in Practice.

Mulvey, Laura. "The Pensive Spectator." *Death 24× a Second: Stillness and the Moving Image*. London: Reaktion, 2006.181-96. Print.

Nanook of the North. Dir. Robert J. Flaherty. Pathé Exchange, 1922. Film.

Rony, Fatimah Tobing. *The Third Eye: Race, Cinema, and Ethnographic Spectacle*. Durham and London: Duke UP, 1996. Print.

Seth. *Clyde Fans Book One*. Montreal: Drawn & Quarterly, 2004. Print.
———. "Creating a Personal Vernacular Canadian Design Style." *DA, A Journal of Printing Arts* 69 (Fall/Winter 2011): 3-60. Print.
———. "Dominion City." *Palookaville 20*. Montreal: Drawn & Quarterly, 2011: 41-58. Print.
———. *George Sprott (1894-1975)*. Montreal: Drawn & Quarterly, 2009. Print.
———. *Wimbledon Green*. Montreal: Drawn & Quarterly, 2005. Print.
Smith, Sidonie, and Julia Watson. *Reading Autobiography: A Guide for Interpreting Life Narratives*. 2nd ed. Minneapolis: U of Minnesota P, 2010. Print.
Spiegelman, Art. *In the Shadow of No Towers*. New York: Pantheon, 2004. Print.
Spurgeon, Tom. "CR Sunday Interview: Seth." *The Comics Reporter*, 7 June 2009. Web. 10 Aug. 2011.
Stewart, Susan. *On Longing: Narratives of the Miniature, the Gigantic, the Souvenir, the Collection*. Durham: Duke UP, 1993. Print.
Wakeham, Pauline. *Taxidermic Signs: Reconstructing Aboriginality*. Minneapolis: U of Minnesota P, 2008. Print.
Whitlock, Gillian. "Autographics: The Seeing 'I' of the Comics." *Modern Fiction Studies* 52.4 (2006): 965-79. Print.

CHAPTER 12

Woodrow
Memory and Nostalgia at Play

Jessa Alston-O'Connor

The decline of the rural community is a difficult and challenging reality in regions all across Canada, especially in the agricultural communities of the prairies, where resource development and farming practices are changing, and where a population exodus to the larger urban centres has nearly emptied rural communities of their residents. The once vibrant small-town service hubs and communities now stand as hollow reminders of a different era. The decay of the physical structures of these towns has been accompanied by a growing sense of loss for a way of life. These buildings as material objects hold meaning and memory, for within them lingers a sense of shared history or mythology that is tied to the small town, even as many Canadians now live in cities. Through his multimedia installation *Woodrow*, artist Graeme Patterson explores these relationships between town buildings, memory, and nostalgia in order to address the disappearance of the small prairie communities. Patterson's sculpture and reimagining of the material structures of his family's small town open up ways in which the memories of these communities and the experiences of past generations may be given life in the present, continuing to live on through art and material culture, even when these small towns and family farms are gone.

Graeme Patterson's sculptural works breathe life into the "ghost town" and the intergenerational memories of Patterson's relatives who had made their lives in Woodrow, Saskatchewan. *Woodrow* is an installation that recreates this family's dying hamlet through animatronic miniatures and large-scale miniature architectural sculptures of landmark buildings in the community. This critically acclaimed exhibition toured across Canada in 2007 and 2008 and was featured at the Montreal Biennale in 2007. It attracted popular and critical success across the country, with major galleries, including the National Gallery of Canada, purchasing works from the series for their permanent collections.

In 2007/08 *Woodrow* was exhibited at the Mendel Art Gallery in Saskatoon to public acclaim.[1] As a program guide with the gallery at the time, I witnessed the response to these works both from residents of urban areas and from those with roots in rural communities. The small-town theme of the exhibition resonated with the experiences of the viewers who lived (or had lived) in small towns. At the same time, many of the urban viewers of the exhibition may have had no personal rural connections, but were already familiar with the mythology of rural farms and small-town life—a mythology distilled through Canadian culture and media, including the popular television shows on prairie life such as *Little Mosque on the Prairie* and *Corner Gas*. These urban gallery viewers, despite not having lived in small towns, still recognized icons of rural life, such as the grain elevator, that are part of the Canadian imaginary. Thus, urban and rural audiences alike were drawn in to the artist's exploration of his family's rural history and the charm of the miniature world Patterson had created. Both haunting and playful, Patterson's works blended feelings of nostalgia with the collective memories of small-town life, capturing these within each large-scale miniature building in the exhibition. Together these works exemplify how the complex entanglement of nostalgia, family history, and memory may be effectively brought to life through the use of miniatures. This chapter frames this exhibition in relation to scholarship on memory and nostalgia in order to consider how the material objects that make up Patterson's *Woodrow* blur the boundary between monument and counter-monument as a means of remembering the dying prairie town.

In order to develop this discussion surrounding memory, miniatures, and materiality in *Woodrow*, I begin with a detailed analysis of the exhibition within the gallery space and highlight the individual works that comprised Patterson's ghost town installation. I then frame this exhibition within theoretical discussions of nostalgia, drawing from literary scholar Svetlana Boym and sociologist Janelle L. Wilson. This analysis also considers Susan Stewart's theories on the important relationships between nostalgia and miniatures, in particular toy-like figures and dollhouse-like structures, in order to critically theorize the larger significance of the miniature elements of *Woodrow* as they relate to memory work. Finally, I will address how the exhibition functions as a marker of memory and loss, and question whether this artistic commemoration of the town of Woodrow may serve as a form of monument or counter-monument to the death of the small town. My discussion will demonstrate how the *Woodrow* exhibition as material culture standing in for the town offers a nostalgic and powerfully engaging alternative approach to remembering and keeping alive such dying communities as Woodrow, Saskatchewan.

Born in Saskatoon, Graeme Patterson developed his practice with a focus on installation works involving stop-motion animation video, sculpture, and animated miniatures that earned him critical attention, including a nomination for the 2009 Sobey Award. While working on his bachelor of fine arts at the Nova Scotia College of Art and Design in 2003, he developed a keen interest in the dying community of Woodrow, Saskatchewan. His father, grandfather, and great-grandfather had all lived in Woodrow, but fewer than fifteen people still remain there today (Cronin 24). Inspired to explore his family's community and to create a series of works surrounding this small prairie town and the memories attached to it, he moved to Woodrow in 2005. While living there over a three-year period, Patterson focused on reconnecting with his grandparents, who still lived in the town. The result of his time in Woodrow is this series of meticulously handcrafted sculptures of the iconic buildings from his family's farm and the larger community, combined with a series of stop-motion animations of the people and memories of the town.

While the original town is not yet a ghost town in real life, Patterson's *Woodrow* is a sculpted town in ruins, a prediction of the inevitable future demise of the real Woodrow. The artist's attention to detail in each sculpture achieves the look of a long-abandoned place, weathered and grey from the passage of time and the harsh prairie elements. The surface of each building has been hand-painted to realistically resemble weathered wood; each structure is dilapidated and empty except for a few eerie lights. Activated by motion sensors, animatronic puppets of creatures, including bats, mice, and other vermin, come to life. Made of wire, rubber, fur, and ink, they scurry past the broken windows whenever a viewer steps closer to one of the works. Video screens are embedded in most of the buildings, featuring short stop-motion animation films of Patterson's grandparents playing horseshoes, farmers with snowmobiles, and the humorous antics of two brothers on a farm. These glimpses of past experiences bring the ruined structures to life with memories or spirits of the people who once inhabited these spaces.

In the exhibition at the Mendel, the physical layout of the exhibition space mirrored the layout of the real town of Woodrow (see Figure 12.1). On the outskirts of the town a group of robotic miniature deer stood clustered together. When a gallery visitor would approach them, motion sensors triggered the animals to turn their heads, their eyes lit as though caught in oncoming headlights. Public buildings in one half of the gallery space included an eight-foot-tall motorized grain elevator with a gaping hole, empty but for the whirring gears in its rafters. A lone church invited gallery viewers to peer in through small double doors to reveal a meticulously detailed interior, complete with a larger-than-life organ that filled the far end of the church (see Figure 12.2). The only three-dimensional animated puppet of a person in the entire exhibition sat within this church; all other people existed only in Patterson's animated videos. This lone puppet sat at the organ and played to the empty pews. She was a tribute to Graeme Patterson's paternal grandmother, who used to play the organ in the family church in Woodrow. Charming stop-motion animation scenes of his grandparents bowling in the "basement" of the church sculpture added a playful surprise to this piece. The community's memory of an epic hockey game in 1972 between teams from Woodrow and Laflèche was brought to life by puppets of players frozen in action on the ice at the local indoor arena (see Figure 12.3). A "Jumbotron" screen presented a stop-motion animation film of the puppets in action, capturing the energy of that memorable game. Together, the grain elevator, the church, and the hockey arena symbolized the public domain of life in this prairie town within the exhibition space. Missing from the town landmarks in the exhibition was a local school—it was closed long before Patterson came to Woodrow (Cronin 28).

Figure 12.1 *Woodrow*, Mendel Art Gallery installation, 2008. Image courtesy of the artist.

Figure 12.2 Graeme Patterson, "The Church," 2005. Wood, foam, foam core, electronics, speakers/headphones, animatronic figure (mixed materials). Animation: *Bowling* 6:42. 9 feet high with stand, 6 feet long, 2.5 feet wide. Collection of The Rooms Provincial Art Gallery. Image courtesy of the artist.

Figure 12.3 Graeme Patterson, "The Hockey Rink," 2005. Wood, metal, foam, foam core, electronics, speakers/headphones, figures (mixed materials), LCD screen, and DVD player. Animation: *Lafleche vs. Woodrow 1972*, 4:03. 8 feet long, 7 feet high, 4 feet wide. Collection of The Art Gallery of Nova Scotia. Image courtesy of the artist.

To complement the decline of the iconic town, the other half of the gallery space mapped out a fantastical, ghostly version of the Patterson family farm. *The Barn* echoed with hurdy-gurdy, carnival-inspired music (see Figure 12.4). Its cavernous interior had been fitted with a grand vaudeville-style stage that displayed an animated film called *Romancing the Farm*, featuring wild and domestic animals, children in snowsuits, a man on a wild snowmobile and even a farmer driving his tractor in his underwear (Cronin 36). The structure of his family home, where the artist lived when he moved to Woodrow, stood crumbling with gaping holes in its roof and walls, and it was overrun by animated puppets and videos of bats and mice (see Figure 12.5). Memories of its former inhabitants flickered on a screen in the "basement" of the house: puppets of his grandparents playing horseshoes.

Four grain silos, each from a different era, featured small animated films inside them, recounting the troublesome antics of two fictional brothers named Pierre and Gerard. In a series of vignettes loosely based on family memories, the characters set off potato guns and mischievously hung stolen undergarments from flagpoles. Against the end wall of the gallery space a giant, larger-than-life pothole stood gaping at the edge of the farm,

Figure 12.4 Graeme Patterson, "The Barn," 2005. Wood, foam, foam core, electronics, speakers/headphones, video projector or LCD, and DVD player. Animation: *Romancing the Farm*, 3:20. 6 feet long, 7 feet high with stand, 3 feet wide. Collection of the Beaver Brook Art Gallery. Image courtesy of the artist.

Figure 12.5 Graeme Patterson, "The House," 2006. Wood, foam core, electronics, speakers/ headphones, LCD screens, DVD players. Animations: *Horseshoes*, 3:13; *Pests*, 1:16; *Monkey and Deer*, 11:40. 5 feet long, 7 feet high, 2.5 feet wide. Collection of the Mendel Art Gallery. Image courtesy of the artist.

reminiscent of the junk piles of the farm in real life. It was filled to the brim with miniature boards of the old house from the first homestead generations ago, the tiny snowmobile from the film in *The Barn*, and other machinery and vehicles of farm life. Beyond the pothole, Patterson constructed a single dirt road that appeared to lead out of Woodrow, beneath a projection of the ever-changing Saskatchewan skies on the wall above.

The only structure that Patterson chose not to recreate in ruin was the *The Shop*, which represented the workshop of his late grandfather, Herbert Patterson. This garage was where Herbert Patterson had worked for most of his life as the town mechanic, metal worker, and fix-it man for the community (Cronin 40). Within the miniature of this building, Patterson had meticulously recreated his grandfather's machinery on one side of the workshop, while a small version of his own studio took up space in the other half, furnished with even smaller, partially completed versions of the buildings he had constructed for *Woodrow*. His grandfather's actual machinery hummed back to life in a small video projected on the back wall of the miniature mechanic's workspace, featuring a stop-motion video that simulated the full-sized machinery operating on its own. The authentic recreation of this space with meticulous attention to detail made it different from the whimsical fantasies of the other buildings in this ghost town, a distinction that will be further addressed later in this discussion.

Graeme Patterson's experience as a newcomer moving to the town and exploring it through this project inspired a twelve-minute film called *Monkey and Deer*, which was not part of a recreated town building but was instead projected on a side wall at the far end of the gallery space. The short stop-motion animated film featured a deer as the spirit of nature in the rural town and a small monkey. Patterson chose a monkey as a semi-autobiographical metaphor for the quirky outsider that he himself was (Ring 10). Just as the monkey is not an animal that is native to Woodrow, Patterson also felt like an outsider when he first came to the small town. As a metaphor for Patterson's own exploration of the spirit of the town, Monkey and Deer meet and give chase through each sculpture of Patterson's ghost town, engaging with each building, interrupting the epic hockey game, and even coming across the puppet of Patterson's grandfather making repairs in the old grain elevator. Through this playful animated depiction of fantasy and friendship, Patterson inserted himself into this fantastic ghost town, weaving together metaphor and whimsy to give viewers a glimpse into these ruins as a living village to be explored in a time and space beyond the gallery.

Patterson infused the material objects and videos throughout the *Woodrow* series of sculptures with layers of memory, nostalgia, and history. Wilson explains that nostalgia is not truly a feeling of longing to go back in time but rather a desire to recapture a mood or spirit of a previous time, to rediscover a former self (26). She suggests that we become nostalgic for those things that symbolize what we wish for in the present. This phenomenon is important in Patterson's work because the impetus for this project was a desire to reconnect with family history and memories of the Patterson generations who had roots in this rural community.

In his artist statement in the exhibition catalogue, Patterson explained this desire to explore his family's ties to Woodrow after the death of his grandfather as follows:

> [M]y childhood was filled with summer vacations, Christmas holidays and Thanksgiving dinners at the farm in Woodrow where his [Patterson's grandfather's] father George Patterson homesteaded and where he and my father were born.... For his entire life he [my grandfather] was a devoted and proud citizen of Woodrow ... not until he passed away did I begin to realize the depth of it.... After two years of living by myself, bowling with my [maternal] grandparents, playing cards at Laflèche café and rediscovering my grandmother at the local nursing home, I felt completely

comfortable and connected to my family's history.... Each piece conveys a sense of my family's and my own characteristics, passions, stories and dreams. (6)

Essentially, Patterson's look to the past was a means of reconnecting with his grandparents and the generations before them who had built lives in Woodrow. In keeping with Wilson's theories about nostalgia, *Woodrow* became a project through which Patterson could rediscover connections with his grandfather and the way of life of the past that had given generations of his family their identity as citizens of Woodrow.

Patterson's work is part of a wider interest among Canadian prairie artists in recent years to grapple with questions of memory work and identity associated with prairie communities. In the same year, Winnipeg-based filmmaker Guy Maddin created the "docu-fantasy" *My Winnipeg*, which dealt with many parallel ideas of family and the collective memories of that prairie city. Maddin's film mixed personal memories of growing up in Winnipeg with reflections on noteworthy historical events in the city's past. Echoing what Patterson achieved with his blending of personal and community memories in *Woodrow*, Maddin explained that "I couldn't separate our family history from the history of Winnipeg" (Persons). In fact, he returned to his childhood apartment to film much of the footage and hired actors to play his family in order to restage key memories of his family's past. Similarly, Patterson moved himself into his family's farmhouse near the town of Woodrow in order to reconnect fully with the community and understand the pull it had over him. Both artists use conventions of nostalgia to form their own mature adult identities by going back to the places of their past that housed so many formative experiences. These works are immensely personal, but at the same time these objects—be they films or sculpture—resonated with those viewers from both rural and urban prairie backgrounds.

In her book *The Future of Nostalgia*, Svetlana Boym explores the history and modern evolution of nostalgia, offering a larger context within which to understand the ways in which nostalgia works as a powerful draw throughout *Woodrow*. The origin of the term "nostalgia" dates back to 1688 with the combining of two Greek roots: *nostos*, meaning "return home," and *algia*, the word for "pain" (3). In the seventeenth century, the concept was understood as an affliction that struck displaced people or servants far from home as well as mercenary soldiers in Europe who longed to die in their homelands instead of in battle in foreign lands. By the nineteenth century any feeling of nostalgia or homesickness at boarding school or in the military was seen as a sign of weak character. Common suggested treatments were to ridicule and bully such nostalgic feelings out of a man, to laugh at him and "question his manhood" until he shed them altogether (6). Modern nostalgia, according to Boym, is the mourning of and longing for a mythical and impossible return home (8). It is fitting, then, that nostalgia's powerful sense of longing for another place or time has shaped nationalist narratives and ideas about heritage, as it does in this exhibition.

Boym goes on to highlight two forms of nostalgia that are both useful in articulating the way nostalgia is experienced in *Woodrow*. These categories do not explain nostalgia, but rather differentiate the ways in which people make sense of the homesickness and their relations to ideas of home and the past. In the case of restorative nostalgia, attempts are made to rebuild or to restore the original state or the "lost home" without signs of decay (49). Boym explains that it is a nostalgia that attempts to reconstruct monuments of and to the past, a form that does not see itself as nostalgic but as a reconstruction of truth and tradition (xviii). This is the type of nostalgia that often forms the foundation of nationalist constructions of shared cultural heritage.

Markedly different from restorative nostalgia, reflective nostalgia dwells in the longing itself. Boym explains that it "lingers in the ruins, the patina of time and history, and accepts the cracks of memory as it dreams of another place and time" (41). Reflective nostalgia allows for decay, and welcomes fragmented memories and details, with an emphasis on individual and collective memory rather than national narratives of heritage, the past, and the future (49). Boym suggests that unlike restorative nostalgia, this form is flexible as it meditates on history and the passage of time rather than attempting to recover a perceived absolute truth of the past. In fact, it questions the truth of the past and values multiplicity of social histories and plots, both individual and collective (xviii). In essence, reflective nostalgia does not look to recreate truth about the past, but to savour the experience of longing and the many layers of memory and experience that may shape one's recollections of the past.

Of the two categories of nostalgia that Boym presents, the majority of Patterson's work in *Woodrow* is most convincingly reflective rather than restorative in nature. The only work that may be considered restorative is *The Shop*, which Patterson intentionally recreated in a lifelike manner. Truth inspired this body of work, but Patterson did not seek to recreate a snapshot of the past in the rest of the series of sculptures. Instead, he played with the past as he expressed the multiple personalities and lives of this small town, finding inspiration without replication. Each stop-motion animation film was inspired by true memories, but the reproductions were never entirely accurate. Horseshoe games never took place in the basement of the family farmhouse, and there was never a bowling alley in the church basement; however, Patterson did recall spending time doing those activities with his grandparents in other places in town. Similarly, the brothers Pierre and Gerard are fictional characters, but their youthful antics and humorous pranks were loosely based on family memories.

While reflective nostalgia provides a useful framework to better understand how Patterson brings the past into his work, it does not go far enough to describe the complexity of time—of the several dimensions of time—evoked in *Woodrow*. Throughout his ghost town, the decay that attends the passage of time that is at the core of reflective nostalgia is an integral part of each work. But Patterson complicates Boym's ideas further by showing the many pasts of this community and simultaneously its future as an eventual ghost town. As curator Dan Ring wrote in his catalogue essay for the exhibition: "it is a simulacrum of a ghost town, a double mirror that reflects backwards to the past and forwards to the future" (14). These layers of time mix with memories of his grandparents or the epic local hockey game, which has still not yet faded from collective memory. Fragments of memory intertwine with carnivalesque music and fantasy throughout his structures and animations. But at the same time, Patterson presents a memory of a ghost town from an eventual future that has not yet happened, for the real town has not yet decayed. *Woodrow* expresses a reflective form of nostalgia, but it is also caught between the past and the future.

Patterson effectively conveys these nostalgic fantasies and memories, from the past and the imagined past of the future, by bringing them into being through his large-scale miniatures. This decision to recreate the town in animated miniature dollhouse-like structures is key, for there is a strong correlation between nostalgia and the fascination many viewers feel when experiencing miniatures. In her book *On Longing*, Susan Stewart writes that the very "locus of the miniature is nostalgia" (60). She further explains that the world of miniatures "is linked to the nostalgic versions of childhood and history" (69). Miniatures create "an 'other' time, a type of transcendent time which negates change and the flux of lived reality" (65). The image produced by the miniature straddles the line between the material world and fantasy because it "not only bears the tangible qualities of material reality but also serves as a representation, an image of a reality which does not exist … the fantastic is in fact 'given life' by its miniaturization" (60).

One of the implications of these strong relationships between nostalgia and miniatures is that Graeme Patterson's sculptures of the iconic buildings function as dollhouses of nostalgia for the viewer. They are edifices to be "consumed by the eye" (62). Stewart argues that miniature buildings and dollhouse structures are the most abstract of miniatures, inaccessible sensually except by the eye (63). This phenomenon is key to the viewing experience of Patterson's ghostly buildings. Drawn to these small houses and puppets, the gallery visitors that I worked with at the Mendel Art Gallery were instantly enchanted by Patterson's childlike world of whimsy and history, mixed with fantasy, as they peered into his miniatures.

This affective element of childhood wonder in *Woodrow* is not surprising as childhood is often associated with nostalgic feelings. Svetlana Boym explains that nostalgia can be "a yearning for a different time—the time of our childhood, the slow rhythms of our dreams" (xv). This perspective is apparent in *Woodrow*. These works were displayed at a height below eye level for most adults, thus requiring the viewers to bend or crouch in order to peer through doors and windows so that they could fully experience the details of the whirring cogs and animated puppets and videos. In order to engage with Patterson's works, viewers were required to experience his world from the vantage point of a child. As a child might explore a dollhouse, adults experienced *Woodrow*. These youthful elements translated into the viewers' exploration of Patterson's *Woodrow*, both through their physical interaction with the space and the toy-like nature of the works. *Woodrow* offers no critique of the economics of rural life, nor a journalistic documentation of the decaying small town. Instead Patterson appeals to childlike wonder and sentimentality to engage the viewer with this world.

In addition to the enduring appeal of their miniature scale, the works in *Woodrow* also captivate because they are animated, building on a long history of animated toys in miniature. Automated toys and puppets date back to the popular automatons in the eighteenth and nineteenth centuries: jigging men, whistling birds, and other automated, wind-up novelties (Daiken 58). Part of the appeal of automated miniature toys, according to Stewart, may be that toys offer a "new, temporal world, parallel to ours, without us but a continuation of life in miniature" (56-57). The public's affinity with the animated miniatures in the ghost town of *Woodrow* might be explained, to use Stewart's argument, by the fact that "we are thrilled and frightened by the mechanical toy because it presents the possibility of a self-invoking fiction which exists independent of human signifying processes" (57). *Woodrow* gives the illusion that this sculpted town has a life of its own, inspired by Patterson's family past and everyday rural experiences but "living" in a temporal realm outside of our own, without us. Stewart goes on to suggest that when our world is miniaturized or giganticized, this transformation tests the relationship between materiality and meaning (57). The miniature town thus has the potential to create meaning above and beyond memory and nostalgia. The miniature *Woodrow* presents a ghostly world that whirrs and lives without inhabitants, but what if the work itself survives after the real town disappears, immortalizing these memories through miniature sculpture and animation? What larger significance might be created by the interplay between these art objects, the town of Woodrow, and the memories and mythologies of rural prairie life?

Part of the answer lies in what has already been demonstrated: that the *Woodrow* series serves as a marker for memory, and speaks to identity in both a personal and collective context. The artist was very close to his grandfather and was inspired to take on this project after his grandfather's death. This project became a way for Patterson to understand him on a deeper level, and he dedicated the exhibition to him (Patterson 6). In returning to the place where his family was born and lived for generations, he rediscovered his past, his family roots, and the lives of the town residents. *Woodrow* effectively embodies both the artist's personal memories and search for his own identity and that of his family who lived there. In addition to marking personal and family memories, *Woodrow* is also a reflection of memories of this community and offers an artistic way to ensure the town lives on and continues to resonate with gallery viewers and residents into the future. Should Patterson's installation art therefore be considered a form of artistic monument to the dying small town and to the residents of Woodrow, Saskatchewan?

In his catalogue essay for the exhibition, curator Ray Cronin does refer to *The Shop* as a "sort of monument" to Patterson's grandfather. Cronin explains the fact that half of the real space remained untouched since the elder Patterson's death as the younger Patterson's way of commemorating the man who had dedicated his life to the town and had been the "fix-it" man for the community (40). The grandfather's metal working machinery was left in place while the artist set up his studio space beside it, and this layout was replicated in *The Shop*.

It can be argued that both nostalgia and monuments are connected with commemoration as ways of remembering the past. In the process, both concepts also have the potential to selectively remember or represent memory, to romanticize or reify the past, and to emphasize particular narratives while erasing others. These concepts differ in the way that people engage with both forms of commemoration. Nostalgia is a deeply personal form of memory recollection, especially when it comes to reflective nostalgia. While feelings of longing and nostalgia may circulate and be collectively or publically expressed, they are still forms of very personal memory work that are closely tied to the emotions and sentimentality felt within.

Moving beyond the personal, however, the monument is an intentionally public form of commemoration. It is often a concrete, tangible object or marker intended to inspire remembrance and recollection in its viewer. Monuments act as places to gather, to congregate and pay homage to loss or to an important event or figure. They are external markers for the internal memories felt by each viewer, expressions of individual recollections or feelings that are also shared, necessitating that they be given material form in a public place. Where does *Woodrow* fit within these two concepts of memory work?

Robert S. Nelson and Margaret Olin define monuments in their book *Monuments and Memory: Made and Unmade* as structures that satisfy "the desire to commemorate, to mark a place, to represent the past to the present, and future, to emphasize one narrative of the past at the expense of others" (2). In a similar vein, Alois Reigl notes in his text "The Modern Cult of Monuments: Its Character and Origins" that a monument is a human creation erected for the specific purpose of keeping "a single human deed or event or combination thereof alive in the minds of future generations" (21). One could make the case that *Woodrow* is a form of intentional monument, commemorating both the individual and the collective memory of this town and other communities like it. It could be further argued that this exhibition strives to preserve the memory of Woodrow for future generations, to keep it alive. However, *Woodrow* complicates the idea of the monument because its material objects are not permanent, nor does Patterson aim to tell a single national narrative or immortalize a grand event for future generations to come. Instead, *Woodrow* reveals a multiplicity of fragmented memories and dreams. Rather than memorialize a hopeful, utopian view of the town, Patterson offers a sentimental and imaginative, but also dystopic representation of the life and the eventual loss of a rural community.

Perhaps *Woodrow* could instead be considered a counter-monument to the death of a prairie hamlet. In his writing on the counter-monuments first created to remember the Holocaust in Germany in the early 1990s, James Young argues that the typical monument acts as "a self-aggrandizing locus for national memory" (270). Monuments offer a way to remember triumphs, or memorials to remember loss, but Young warns that relying on monuments to do our remembering for us might lead us to be more forgetful of the past (270). He goes on to define counter-monuments as being "brazen, painfully self-conscious, challenging the premise of their being" (271). In contrast to most monuments, counter-monuments are humbled, brought down off the pedestal. They challenge everything that monuments stand for, revealing the "possibilities and limitations of all memorials" (277). Counter-monuments address absence or loss by reproducing it, and they do not gloss over painful narratives. Young believes that counter-monuments force memories to disperse, rather than gather in one place. They are not built to last forever but are instead built to disappear with time, and they therefore draw attention to the passing of time, rather than durability and perpetuity. While embracing their own impermanence, they do not challenge the need for memory. Instead, they stimulate memory just as permanent monuments or memorials do, but they also intentionally change over time just as memories change, offering an alternative to the illusion of the permanence of memory that most monuments perpetuate (295).

I would argue that *Woodrow* is not intended to be a monument of either kind, but does incorporate significant characteristics of counter-monuments. Granted, it was not intended as a place to gather to mourn the tragedy of the dying small town of Woodrow or to remember the small town as part of a grand national narrative. Instead, it functions to celebrate community and offers the opportunity to explore the lives of Woodrow's former residents through a multiplicity of narratives and many different personal, familial, and community memories. Given that Patterson created each object out of such materials as foam core, wood, digital media technology, and textiles, the sculptures themselves are by nature impermanent. To create the works in a perpetual state of ruin is to showcase the passage of time, and with it the loss, the absence, and the abandonment that is associated with the depopulation of rural communities. Perhaps most importantly, as with other counter-monuments, the viewer's personal memories are also essential. Norbert Radermacher explained his design for a Holocaust memorial by stating that "the site alone cannot remember ... it is the projection of memory by visitors into a space that makes it a memorial" (quoted in Young 286). *Woodrow* resonates so powerfully because it inspires the viewer to remember his or her own associations with rural pasts, and to bring those memories and understandings into the viewing experience of Patterson's miniature town. In the case of *Woodrow*, the most important connection between the material objects within this exhibition and theories of memory and counter-monuments lies in the active engagement it incites in viewers. Patterson's piece calls to the fore shared memories, memories that arise from the common associations that many Canadians have regarding their own rural roots or rural mythologies, which they then bring to their experience with the works of *Woodrow*.

When it was exhibited at the Mendel Art Gallery, the memories and associations the viewers brought to these material structures deepened the resonance of this exhibition for the patrons. In Saskatoon, the familiar sculptures of the iconic grain elevator, the barn, the rural hockey rink, the farm tractors, and the grain silos struck a chord with audiences. Collective mythologies about farming and rural life, or personal memories of family farms and prairie scenery, coincide with Patterson's own personal narratives. Through experiencing Patterson's adaptation of his family's history, the viewers were called to reflect upon their own rural experience or their understandings of rural life on the prairies. They were prompted to project their own memories alongside Patterson's animation of his family's past in an engaging process that no static stone monument could achieve in quite the same way.

Graeme Patterson's *Woodrow* complicates the conventions of both monument and counter-monument by integrating both personal and collective memories with nostalgia and myth while at the same time embracing the inevitable decay that is to come. Patterson's art brings the act of remembering into the present instead of trying to reconstruct a restorative image of the past. Remembering the town this way essentially reactivates the site of Woodrow as it is being remembered, be it through nostalgic memories, miniature worlds, or commemoration. While this is a project that looks back at disappearing towns like Woodrow, the active ways in which Patterson's work functions to encourage viewers to participate in this reflective, nostalgic and imaginative act of looking back in fact ensures the town and its memories remain alive in the present. Although it is in ruin, *Woodrow* is a ruin that continues to return to life through this sculptural form. It is anything but deserted.

NOTE

1 The Mendel Art Gallery is to close for reconstruction and expansion in June 2015. A new building, with an enlarged collection, is to reopen in 2016 as the Remai Modern Art Gallery of Saskatchewan.

WORKS CITED

Boym, Svetlana. *The Future of Nostalgia*. New York: Basic Books, 2001. Print.
Cronin, Ray. "Welcome to Woodrow." *Woodrow: A Multimedia Installation by Graeme Patterson*. Ed. Ray Cronin and Dan Ring. Halifax: Art Gallery of Nova Scotia; Saskatoon: Mendel Art Gallery, 2007. 22-63. Print.
Daiken, Leslie. *Children's Toys Throughout the Ages*. London: B. T. Batsford, 1953. Print.
Maddin, Guy, dir. *My Winnipeg*. Buffal Gal Pictures. 2007. DVD.
Nelson, Robert S., and Margaret Olin. "Introduction." *Monuments and Memory: Made and Unmade*. Ed. Robert S. Nelson and Margaret Olin. Chicago: U of Chicago P, 2003. 1-10. Print.
Patterson, Graeme. "Introduction." Cronin and Ring 4-5.

Persons, Dan. "Guy Maddin Makes MY WINNIPEG Everyone's Winnipeg." *Cinefantastique Online*. Cinefantastique, 11 June 2008. Web. 20 Apr. 2010.

Riegl, Alois. "The Modern Cult of Monuments: Its Character and Its Origins." 1903. *Oppositions: A Journal for Ideas and Criticism in Architecture* 25 (Fall 1982): 21-51. Print.

Ring, Dan. "Graeme Patterson's Monkey & Deer: An Evolutionary Fable." Cronin and Ring 10-19.

Stewart, Susan. *On Longing: Narratives of the Miniature, the Gigantic, the Souvenir, the Collection*. Baltimore: Johns Hopkins UP, 1984. Print.

Wilson, Janelle L. *Nostalgia: Sanctuary of Meaning*. Lewisburg: Bucknell UP, 2005. Print.

Young, James. "The Counter-Monument: Memory Against Itself in Germany Today." *Critical Inquiry* 18.2 (Winter 1992): 267-96. Print.

CHAPTER 13

Plaques and Persons
Commemorating Canada's Authors

Carole Gerson

There are many ways for fans to connect physically with their favourite writers. The collection of autographs has been a long-standing practice, as has the collection of an author's books. Other dedicated readers like to visit the sites of favourite stories or poems, or view handwritten manuscripts or treasured personal artifacts in museums. Fandom merges with higher levels of significance when governments participate in cultural recognition by designating writers' homes as historic sites, or by formally commemorating authors' achievements with the unveiling of official plaques. Few objects can have a stronger material presence than a historic plaque: a solid brass rectangle, fixed to a building or a sturdy stone cairn, whose words and images will endure through time and weather in a meeting of national and cultural interests that transforms undifferentiated landscapes into places with specific stories to tell (see Ryden 36-40).

Recognition of writers varies tremendously from one country to another, signalling the importance granted to literature and its creators in shaping a nation's self-image. The construction of a historically based national literary identity takes different forms, from the expectation that every citizen will be familiar with a canonical text, such as *Tom Sawyer* or *Hamlet*, to the sanctification of a writer's personal existence and its associated materiality, from birthplaces to gravesites (see Matthews). In Ireland, a good portion of the tourist industry focuses on the country's literary heritage, directing visitors to the Writers' Museum in Dublin and to landmarks such as Yeats's tower in County Galway and Joyce's Martello tower in Sandycove. England's long tradition of literary tourism has produced many published guides to the London of Dickens and of Sherlock Holmes, to Hardy's Wessex and to Brontë country, as well as specialized guidebooks such as A. C. Ward's poignant *A Literary Journey Through Wartime Britain* (1943), with photos of bomb damage to many hallowed sites.[1] In Spain and France, literary tourism is now supported by federal ministries of culture: the website for Spain links fifty writers' houses,[2] while France's Fédération des maisons d'écrivain et des patrimoines littéraires includes 361 literary sites and offers tour itineraries and school programs.[3] In the United States, there are national guidebooks, as well as localized guides to the Midwest, Boston, and New York (including one published in 1903).[4] Evidence of the rise in academic interest includes a recent call for contributions to an anthology on American literary tourism. The topic moved into the realm of parody when Miriam Levine's reverential *Guide to Writers' Homes in New England* (1984, updated 1991, 1997) inspired Brock Clarke's brilliantly titled but otherwise disappointing novel, *An Arsonist's Guide to Writers' Homes in New England* (2007) and Anne Trubek's often sardonic study, *A Skeptic's Guide to Writers' Houses* (2011).

Where does the material commemoration of writers fit into Canada's national sensibility and historical self-definition? While E. J. Hathaway published an article on "Canadian Literary Homes" in 1908, little followed until the nationalism of the 1980s gave us John Robert Colombo's *Canadian Literary Landmarks* (1984) and *The Oxford Illustrated Literary Guide to Canada* (1987) by Albert and Theresa Moritz, along with similar guides to Vancouver (1986), Toronto (1999), Montreal (2000), and Winnipeg (2005).[5] In 1998, Denise Pérusse addressed the francophone side with *Pays littéraires du Québec: Guide des lieux d'écrivains.* All these volumes combine actual and fictional geographies, identifying both the places where writers lived and the settings of their writings. The created landscape is the focus of Amy Lavender Harris's recent book, *Imagining Toronto*, which claims to be "the first full study of the city's literature to appear in print" (14). Literary interest turned literal in the recent campaigns to preserve Al Purdy's legendary A-frame cottage in Ameliasburg and Joy Kogawa's childhood home in Vancouver, both of which have been successfully refurbished and now house writer-in-residence programs. But these efforts seem to be relatively rare blips in an otherwise subdued cultural nationalism, which pays substantial attention to some writers while they're alive, but with the exception of popular figures like L. M. Montgomery, does surprisingly little to remember them in a material fashion once they've gone.

Cultural memorials can be based as much on fabricated literary connections as on the documented sites and spaces of writers' lives. The noted American poet Henry Wadsworth Longfellow offers an opportunity to

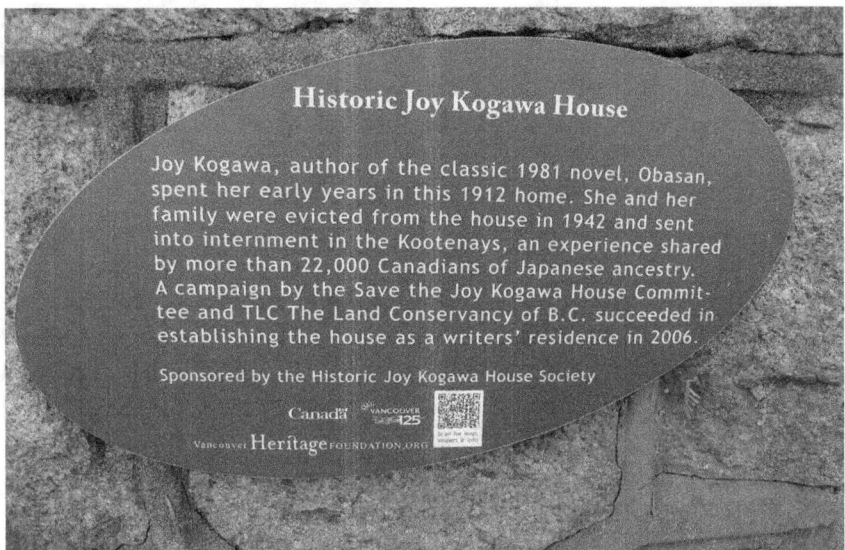

Figure 13.1 Historic Joy Kogawa House, Vancouver, British Columbia. This plaque is on the retaining wall in front of Joy Kogawa's childhood home at 1450 West 64th Avenue, Vancouver. Photograph by Carole Gerson.

differentiate between what David Bentley terms "the literary site piece" (*Mnemographia* 293)—the literary evocation of a specific landscape, in the fashion of the great English romantic poets—and current literary tourism, which is less about the writer's work than about the celebrity of the author. Longfellow's popular long narrative poem "Evangeline" (1847) is a grand literary site piece in the romantic tradition, whose influence in constructing a cultural identity for Nova Scotia led to the "wholesale reorganization of an actual landscape in order to make it conform to a bestselling historical romance" (72), in the words of historians Ian McKay and Robin Bates. Yet Longfellow had no direct connection with the place he wrote about: he heard the story that generated the poem from a visitor, and never set foot in Nova Scotia. As a historical figure, he is commemorated in two American sites with their own accreted layers of significance: the Wadsworth-Longfellow House in Portland, Maine—the home of his grandfather, where he spent most of his childhood—is "the oldest standing structure on the Portland peninsula" (Schmidt and Rendon 54) and has been open to the public since 1901 (Levine 172), and the Longfellow National Historic Site in Cambridge, Massachusetts, the stately house where he resided for forty years, which had previously been "the headquarters for General George Washington during the Siege of Boston in 1775-76" (Schmidt and Rendon 53). In Nova Scotia, there is no such material foundation for Longfellow's sanctification. Since the late nineteenth century, courtesy of Longfellow, the province's tourism has benefited from its invented identity as "the land of Evangeline," but the commemoration of a fictional heroine at the real locale of Long Pré National Historic Site has generated much controversy between proponents of an imagined story and advocates of historical veracity.[6] A recent analysis of this issue appears in *In the Province of History: The Making of the Public Past in Nova Scotia* (2010), where Ian McKay and Robin Bates examine "just how drastically a given place could reinvent itself in the interests of tourism revenues" (20).[7] In the 1960s and 1970s, when Prince Edward Island similarly chose to rescue its economy by focusing on tourism engendered by a fictional character—in this instance, Anne Shirley of Green Gables—the province had the good fortune to possess in L. M. Montgomery a writer whose local connections were indisputable.

In Canada, the creation of public memory through the mounting of commemorative plaques and the preservation of historic sites (including some writers' houses) falls under an assortment of jurisdictions: the Historic Sites and Monuments Board presides at the federal level, while at the provincial level there are various departments of heritage, historical boards, and other organizations, often with shifting titles and mandates. Occasionally, municipal agencies are involved. For example, Benares, the elegant home that served as the model for Mazo de la Roche's Jalna, is now a museum operated by the City of Mississauga; in Ottawa, the Greenspace Alliance is working on the creation of a Poets' Pathway, Poets' Park, and Poets' Hill to mark the city's many historic literary affiliations.[8] In addition to commemorative projects associated with government-based agencies, there are foundations and associations dedicated to specific writers or places, or to a specific style of cultural acknowledgement. A national example is the Writers' Trust of Canada, which maintains Pierre Berton's House in Dawson as a writer's retreat. Focusing largely on recent writers, the charitable foundation of Project Bookmark envisions an ambitious national program of plaques that directly link literary texts with the sites they embody.[9] On a much smaller scale, in Montreal the Writers' Chapel Trust is an independent, non-profit organization dedicated to recognizing the city's literary heritage with plaques mounted on the walls of a small chapel inside a downtown church.[10] It is impossible to identify all such commemorative gestures, although Web resources make it easier to try. Especially noteworthy is the project of a retired school librarian in Ontario, who has created a website for historical plaques in Toronto (citing 831 as of 15 December 2014) and another for historical plaques in Ontario (1,459 as of 15 December 2014), both helpfully indexed.[11]

These different efforts confirm that commemoration is erratic and unpredictable. For example, the long and wide-ranging career of poet Charles Mair, whose name is preserved in the town of Mair, Saskatchewan, has been recognized rather minimally with a federal plaque in the post office of his birthplace of Lanark, Ontario, and an Ontario plaque remembering the "Canada First Movement," of which he was an early member, placed on the National Club on Bay Street in Toronto. Other writers have received more substantial recognition. Isabella Valancy Crawford has been noted in plaques from three levels of government: one mounted by the Toronto Historical Board in 1989 at the entrance to Isabella Valancy Crawford Park near the site of the house where she died, an undated earlier plaque in Paisley (one of her childhood residences) from the provincial Archeological and Historic Sites Board, and a 1983 plaque from the federal Historic Sites and Monuments Board in Peterborough, following her designation as a historically important person in 1947. Each plaque does different cultural work, highlighting Crawford's association with the locale in which it appears: the Peterborough text doesn't mention Paisley, and the Toronto plaque offers the most information about her writing.

Crawford's Toronto plaque, dated 1989 and unveiled in 1992, owes its existence to the confluence of a number of events and concerns. In 1980, journalist Donald Jones discovered that 57 John Street, the house in which Crawford had died, was still standing at the corner of John and King ("Canadian Poetess' Home"). Six years later, he called for an effort to preserve the building and mark the site for the 1987 centenary of the death of Canada's first significant woman poet ("Time"). His *Toronto Star* column sparked responses in a number of quarters, from the literary nationalists in the Writer's Union of Canada to the Women's Canadian Historical Society, who offered to pay for the plaque that was eventually mounted in Isabella Valancy Crawford Park.[12] The old house was doomed to yield to downtown redevelopment (the CBC building is now on the site), but a small nearby park at the intersection of John and Front, adjoining the headquarters of the Royal Bank of Canada, was donated by the bank to the City of Toronto to be named for the poet. While a combination of literary nationalism, feminist historical recuperation, and civic pride culminated in the unveiling of the plaque in 1992, its placement in the park prompts reflection. Marking the entrance of the park are two imposing brick pillars, about twelve feet tall and two feet square. The sides of the pillars facing Front Street each bear plaques: one identifying the park, and the other announcing that "This public park is made available to the residents of the City of Toronto by the Royal Bank of Canada, October 19 1987." Only when one enters the park does one see the Toronto

Historical Board's plaque on the inside of one of the columns, its tiny font requiring the inquisitive visitor to come close in order to read it. While we might query the relative status given to the bank and to the writer, there is a sense of poetic appropriateness in these placements, given that Crawford lived in poverty and died in obscurity.

Similar claims to cultural capital unite the three plaques—again from three different levels of government—identifying L. M. Montgomery's Ontario residences. Her years in Leaskdale (where she wrote eleven books between 1911 and 1926) are noted in plaques from Ontario's Archeological and Historic Sites Board, as well as from the federal Historic Sites and Monuments Board; the latter designated Leaskdale Manse a national historic site in 1996 and gave it a plaque in 2008. Her last home, at 210 Riverside Drive in Toronto, which is currently a private residence, is marked by a plaque from the Toronto Historical Board (1983) placed discreetly in a nearby parkette. As well, a former tourist home in Bala, Muskoka, where Montgomery holidayed in 1922, is now a private Montgomery museum.[13] This Ontario recognition stands apart from the multiple commemorations in Prince Edward Island, where history melds with fiction in an array of designations. Provincially recognized as historic places are several sites where Montgomery resided briefly during her early years as an itinerant teacher: Bideford Parsonage, where she boarded in 1894-95, is now a museum with a reconstructed "Maud's Room," and the school where she taught in Lower Bedeque in 1896-97 has been restored as a typical one-room schoolhouse, now officially named the Lucy Maud Montgomery Lower Bedeque School.[14] More problematic is the canonization of the fictional Anne Shirley at Green Gables National Park in Cavendish (see Gerson), as well as in private sites such as the Anne of Green Gables Museum at Park Corner.

Most of the writers I have mentioned have been recognized by the Historic Sites and Monuments Board of Canada (HSMBC), whose mandate is to designate "national historic persons," defined as "People who have made an outstanding and lasting contribution to Canadian history" ("Persons"). It is both intriguing and illuminating to consider which writers have been included in this magisterial designation and to discern the patterns of recognition that bring some authors into our national narrative and omit others. This project was inspired in part by my own participation in this process, which I shall discuss later. While one can easily get disoriented in the maze of provincial, local, and private recognitions of writers and their associated homes, birthplaces, and other sites, the HSMBC, which is administered through Parks Canada, is relatively easy to navigate via Parks Canada's various websites and some wonderfully helpful Wikipedia entries (which are more user-friendly and more current than the sites emanating from branches of the federal government).[15]

The Historic Sites and Monuments Board was created in 1919 to advise the National Parks Branch and the Minister of the Interior on the "selection, commemoration and preservation of national historic sites" (Taylor 20). Closely associated with the Canadian Historical Association (Strong-Boag 62), most of the board's first members were historians interested in Canada's military and fur-trade past, or advocates of specific causes such as recognition of the Loyalists; most of their selected historic sites were located in Quebec and Ontario. Limited racial and political ideologies prevailed, as board members rejected proposals to commemorate sites important to the history of blacks, Jews, Mennonites, and Ukrainians (Taylor 128).[16] In 1937 the board added a program of secondary plaques, aimed in part at redressing regional and thematic imbalances by including political figures and the arts and letters. In the words of historian C. J. Taylor, author of the only full-length study of the HSMBC, "Anyone of sufficient fame would be considered to be worthy of a secondary tablet including provincial premiers, painters, poets, and popular novelists" (127). The administration of national historic sites remains under the jurisdiction of Parks Canada, whose website informs the public that "The mandate of the Historic Sites and Monuments Board of Canada is to advise the Government of Canada, through the Minister of the Environment, on the commemoration of nationally significant aspects of Canada's history" ("Historic").

A timeline of the commemoration of writers offers an insightful chronology of the Canadian literary canon. The first author to be recognized by the HSMBC was Archibald Lampman, who was declared a nationally significant poet in 1920. He received a plaque in 1930 that was placed on a cairn at his birthplace, the village of Morpeth, Ontario, and marked by a dedication ceremony organized by the Canadian Authors Association and attended by Canada's senior canonical poets (Bentley, *Mnemographia*, 317-23).

Few other writers were thus honoured until the late 1930s. Those canonized between 1936 and 1939 were all men, many of whom were well known for their professional activities as historians, journalists, or educators. This list of English-language writers began with Thomas Chandler Haliburton (1936), followed in 1937 by Charles Mair and James de Mille, who were joined in 1938 by Grant Allen, Wilfred Campbell, Ralph Connor, James Macpherson LeMoine, Gilbert Parker, George Parkin, John Richardson, E. W. Thomson, and J. S. Willison. The first French writers, named in 1937, were Joseph Bouchette, Octave Crémazie, Louis Fréchette, and François-Xavier Garneau. This wave of cultural interest also brought forward the first culturally active

Figure 13.2 Archibald Lampman Memorial Cairn, Morpeth Cemetery, Morpeth, Ontario. Dedication of Lampman's cairn by the Canadian Authors Association, 13 September 1930; Charles G. D. Roberts (*left*) and Duncan Campbell Scott (*right*). Photograph courtesy of the J. J. Talman Regional Collection, D.B. Weldon Library, University of Western Ontario.

woman deemed to be of national historic importance, singer Emma Albani; designated in 1937, she was the second woman to be named a nationally significant person, following Madeleine de Verchères in 1923.[17] The next wave of writers, in the mid-1940s, included the 1943 designations of L. M. Montgomery (the first female writer), Oliver Goldsmith, and Michel Bibaud. They were joined in 1945 and 1946 by Jean Blewett, George Frederick Cameron, Bliss Carman, Pauline Johnson, William Kirby, Stephen Leacock, Peter McArthur, John McCrae, Archibald MacMechan, Charles G. D. Roberts, and Francis Sherman, followed by Marshall Saunders and Isabella Valancy Crawford in 1947. After his death in 1947, Duncan Campbell Scott completed the list of Confederation poets in 1948; this phase concluded with Emily Carr in 1950 and Julia Catherine Beckwith Hart in 1951. This substantial addition of writers during the late 1940s coincided with the interest in fostering Canadian culture that underpinned the Royal Commission on National Development in the Arts, Letters, and Sciences (known as the Massey Commission). During the 1950s and 1960s, in contrast, writers all but vanished from the list of new designations (with the exception of Maritimers Thomas McCulloch and Jonathan Odell in 1959) until the cultural nationalism of the mid-1970s initiated a fresh phase that included Philippe-Joseph Aubert de Gaspé, Mazo de la Roche, Margaret Duley, Susanna Moodie, Émile Nelligan, E. J. Pratt, Goldwin Smith, and Catharine Parr Traill. Recent designations encompass a broad spectrum of English-language writers from Marshall McLuhan to the Labrador-Inuit diarist Lydia Campbell. The first (and still the only) francophone female literary author to be recognized as a national historic person is Gabrielle Roy, designated in 2008.

Some writers' plaques have been placed on the grounds of former residences, while others are in public sites such as schools, churches, libraries, parks, and post offices. Those that are free-standing, such as the plaque on the grounds of The Grange, Goldwin Smith's former Toronto residence, which is now part of the Art Gallery of Ontario, are more eye-catching than those attached to the walls of buildings. Early plaques were unilingually English or French; those installed since the 1980s present parallel texts in French and English. There are occasional exceptions: plaques for both Pauline Johnson and for her childhood home of Chiefswood (separately recognized as a national historic site) are written in three languages, Mohawk, French, and English. A rare multiple plaque, titled Poet's Corner, honours Charles G. D. Roberts, Bliss Carman, and Francis Sherman, who had been students at the University of New Brunswick (albeit not all at the same time). Their plaque is the centrepiece of a recently renovated monument that includes welcoming benches and is strategically placed outside the Harriet Irving Library, at the heart of the UNB campus. Not all national historic persons receive plaques—the best-known example of an unplaqued figure is Sir John Franklin, for whom no specific site has been determined.

While some of these people were long dead when honoured, others (Montgomery, Roberts, Leacock, and D. C. Scott) were recognized within a year or two of their demise. Such immediacy has not been possible since the regulations were changed during the 1980s to limit nominations to those who have been dead for at least twenty-five years. One of the first female writers to be designated a national historic person was Jean McKishnie Blewett (1862-1934), a Scottish-Canadian poet and journalist of modest renown who was recognized in 1946. Yet Sara Jeannette Duncan (1862-1922), a novelist and journalist of the same generation and ethnic background as Blewett and

Figure 13.3 Poets' Corner, University of New Brunswick. At this newly refurbished site outside the Harriet Irving Library, a single plaque honours three national historic persons who studied at the University of New Brunswick before becoming known for their poetry: Bliss Carman, Charles G. D. Roberts, and Francis Sherman. Photograph courtesy of the Harriet Irving Library, University of New Brunswick.

much more significant both during her lifetime and later, was overlooked until 2014. Other absences include Agnes Maule Machar, Marjorie Pickthall, Felicité Angers (Laure Conan), and Laura Goodman Salverson, to cite a few women writers—along with Norman Duncan, Charles Sangster, and William Henry Drummond. Why Jean Blewett and not Sara Jeannette Duncan? Presumably because supporters from Chatham, Ontario, where Blewett died in 1934, were more proactive about their local literary celebrity than were Duncan fans from her hometown of Brantford—or possibly because of the advocacy of long-time board member Fred Landon, from the University of Western Ontario, who researched the history of southwestern Ontario, where Blewett resided. The pattern of recognition accorded to Canadian writers dovetails with the observation of historians Nicole Neatby and Peter Hodgins that "any given act of public remembering is usually the product of a wide variety of often contradictory motivations ranging from the ideological, the pecuniary, and the manipulative to the sincere and heartfelt to the traumatic." Moreover, "there is growing recognition that every memory text or performance is the product of a series of complex negotiations between cultural producers, their patrons, and the communities whose past they are purporting to be commemorating."[18] While the import of maintaining and focusing public memory is often national, scholars continually remind us that the local is the level where sites of memory are selected and developed. In their introduction to a recent collection of articles about memory in Canada, James Opp and John C. Welsh point to the importance of the local as a "centre of meaning" where memorial acts may affirm or resist the national narrative.[19]

Canada now has close to 650 persons of national historical significance, about one hundred of whom can be described as writers. A number of people whom I include in the category of authors are not officially recognized for their literary activity; for example, although Nellie McClung wrote many novels, her citation describes her as a politician, feminist, social activist, and the first female board member of the Canadian Broadcasting Corporation; Jessie Archibald and E. Cora Hind similarly make the list for their work for women's rights rather than for their writing. Even when such women are added to the list of authors, they raise the proportion of female names to barely 20 percent, perhaps not surprising, in view of the paucity of women on the board of the HSMBC.[20] Some ethnocultural imbalances in the representation of Canada's cultural history began to receive correction with the addition of Icelandic poet Stephan G. Stephannson in 1946, of many Aboriginal cultural and historical figures since the 1970s, of early black writers Mary Ann Shadd in 1994 and Mary and Henry Bibb in 2002, and of A. M. Klein, the first Jewish writer, in 2007. But the list of approved literary and cultural figures still favours men who were white, Christian, anglophones or francophones, and based in eastern Canada, thus exemplifying the board's historic representation of "elites who privilege their own storylines," in the words of historian Veronica Strong-Boag (62). My own recent experience with the selection process of the HSMBC shows that its conservative evaluation criteria remain well in place.

I first became involved with the board in 2006, when I was consulted about the nomination of Mary Anne Sadlier, whose lengthy and prolific literary career as a Catholic novelist during the nineteenth century earned her recognition as a national historic person in 2008. Two years later, I was asked to review the wording on her plaque, which is to be placed in Old Montreal at the site once occupied by the Sadlier publishing company. More direct participation ensued when I attended a women's history workshop in Vancouver in February 2008, which was organized by UBC historian Jean Barman and sponsored by Parks Canada. Its purpose was to generate a stronger female presence among the names recognized by the HSMBC, particularly from the West. Subsequently, I nominated five Western women writers: Marie Joussaye, Isabel Ecclestone Mackay, Florence Randal Livesay (mother of poet Dorothy Livesay), Agnes Deans Cameron, and Ethel Wilson; in the end, only Wilson was deemed to "meet the benchmark set by other literary figures recognized for their national historic significance, such as L. M. Montgomery" (HSMBC minutes). Her plaque will be located at the elegant apartment building at 1386 Nicola Street, which was her home from 1943 to 1965 in Vancouver's West End, thus making a significant addition to a cityscape that displays surprisingly few such historical markers.[21]

There are two stages to the board's review process, both involving historians employed by Parks Canada. All nominees receive a preliminary screening; those deemed potential candidates for the designation of national historic person then proceed to more detailed investigation, written up in a report that is presented at a meeting of the board. As nominator, I received signed copies of the board's full reports on the three names recommended for serious consideration (Livesay, Cameron, and Wilson), as well as the anonymously written screening reports rejecting my other two nominees (Joussaye and Mackay). The texts of these reports illuminate the board's criteria and procedures. The task of Parks Canada's historians is to build a case that will meet the board's criteria for significance, a self-referential practice that largely involves noting resemblances to previously designated figures. The evaluation process also includes seeking additional published information about the nominee, and comparing the nominee to canonized figures in the same realms of activity. I knew that Marie Joussaye was a longshot, but hoped that her case would be carried by her identity as Canada's first female labour poet. However, as I am the author of most of the published documentation on Joussaye, little else could be found to substantiate her significance. The report rejecting her nomination directly states the narrow basis of the evaluation process. It notes that "The HSMBC has recommended the designation of a relatively small number of poets," and found recognition of Joussaye lacking in comparison with her selected peers: Lampman, Roberts, Scott, Carman, and Pauline Johnson. On the labour side, she was not nearly as visible as a list of left-wing activists then under consideration, most of whom were born several decades later.

I was more surprised by the rejections of Mackay and Cameron as I naively assumed that any woman writer with an entry in the *Dictionary of Canadian Biography* (*DCB*) was self-evidently worthy of recognition from the HSMBC. Mackay's nomination was turned down because the reviewer could not find sufficient scholarly material to testify to her significance—for example, Mackay has not yet been the subject of a PhD thesis. However, reading between the lines of this report, I inferred that this anonymous historian was suggesting several writers, brought in for comparative purposes (Agnes Maule Machar and Marjorie Pickthall), whose cases for HSMBC recognition would likely be more valid and whom I subsequently nominated, along with Sara Jeannette Duncan. At the end of 2014, I was informed that Duncan and Machar had been officially designated as national historic persons.

In addition to overseeing the approval of national historic persons, the HSMBC designates national historic sites. While writers as a group have received a good share of federal plaques due to their recognition as significant individuals, and the HSMBC has clear policies for approving sites associated with historic persons, the paucity of sites associated with writers is intriguing. There are over 950 national historic sites in Canada, of which 167 are administered by Parks Canada; the remainder are managed and/or owned by other levels of government or by private entities. Yet only eight national historic sites are associated with writers, five of them with women: Chiefswood, the Ontario birthplace of Pauline Johnson; the house in which Emily Carr was born in Victoria, British Columbia; Maison Gabrielle Roy in St. Boniface; and two for L. M. Montgomery—the generalized real and imaginary landscape of "L. M. Montgomery's Cavendish" at Prince Edward Island National Park and the Leaskdale Manse in Ontario, where she lived from 1911 to 1926. Although male writers vastly outnumber women as nationally historic persons, the homes of fewer have been recognized as national historic sites: the birthplace of John McCrae in Guelph, the residence of Ralph Connor in Winnipeg, and Stephen Leacock's mansion in Orillia.[22] Moreover, the patterns of recognition differ somewhat. The women's houses tend to be personal shrines, reconstructing the material conditions in which the writer lived (or her literary creation, in the case of Green Gables). In comparison, while the museum homes of the men contain some artifacts from the author's life and career, the buildings largely function as public sites for events and education. The Ralph Connor House has long been occupied by Winnipeg's University Women's Club (who rescued the house from demolition), and McCrae House displays more artifacts and information about World War I than about the poet and his family. This distinction isn't absolute: Emily Carr house, which contains none of Carr's paintings or manuscripts, follows the masculine pattern, and holds frequent exhibitions of other painters. The Leacock Museum is closer to the feminine model, as it houses the writer's archive of books, manuscripts, and personal papers. Extant furnishings make it possible to keep much of the house looking as it did in 1928, while also offering an attractive site for private functions such as weddings and public events such as exhibitions and children's summer programs.

Given the number of Canadian writers designated as nationally important persons, why have so few of their houses been named as national historic sites? Many of their homes, especially those that were modest urban residences, vanished when old downtown areas of major cities like Ottawa, Montreal, and Toronto were demolished to make way for office towers and commercial facilities. In addition, money and dedication are required to maintain old buildings and turn them into museums. While most extant writers' houses that are identified on provincial and national historical registers have only been noted and have not been restored, it is evident that some writers' advocates are very active—for example, the designation of Gabrielle Roy as a national historic person and her birthplace in St. Boniface as a national historic site both occurred in 2008, the very year they qualified, twenty-five years after her death in 1983.[23] Margaret Laurence (who died in 1989) and her childhood home in Neepawa are similar candidates for recognition. As well, a handful of writers' homes function as provincially supported museums, such as Haliburton House in Windsor, Nova Scotia, which is "A part of the Nova Scotia Museum" (Haliburton House Museum), and Stephansson House in Alberta.[24] In Quebec a few writers' houses are active cultural sites, some of which obtain federal funding without designation as national historic sites.[25]

Museums, houses, and durable brass plaques inflect historical consciousness by extending a writer's material presence from the bookshelf to the landscape. Robert Kroetsch's much-cited dictum about the importance of creativity in constructing Canadians' self-awareness—"In a sense, we haven't got an identity until somebody tells our story. The fiction makes us real" (63)—also applies to those who make the fictions and to the recognition they receive in our local and national historic narratives. Whether prompted by scholars and bureaucrats on the boards of national agencies or by fans clamouring to visit the supposed residence of a fictional heroine, the material commemoration of Canada's writers tells important stories about how we construct and preserve our cultural history in relation to our shifting notions of value and identity.

NOTES

I would like to thank historian Danielle Hamelin for showing me her unpublished paper, delivered to the Canadian Historical Association in 2007, about her experiences as a historian working for the Historic Sites and Monuments Board.

1 Twenty-six museums connected to the residences of British writers (including twenty-four in England, as well as the Keats-Shelley House in Rome and Robert Graves's home in Mallorca) share the private website <www.lithouses.org>. See Watson, *The Literary Tourist: Readers and Places in Romantic & Victorian England*, which examines both biographical and fictive sites; Watson, ed., *Literary Tourism and Nineteenth-Century Culture*; Hendrix, ed., *Writers' Houses and the Making of Memory*. In her book, *Literary Celebrity, Gender, and Victorian Authorship, 1850-1914*, Easley cites a number of nineteenth-century guides to Dickens's London.
2 See <www.acamfe.org>.
3 See <http://www.litterature-lieux.com>. This French website includes one Canadian site—the Maison de la littérature in Quebec City: <http://www.maisondelalitterature.qc.ca/maisonlitterature/mlitterature.php>.
4 Hemstreet, *Literary New York: Its Landmarks and Associations*. Recent titles include Welborn, *Traveling Literary America: A Complete Guide to Literary Landmarks*; Burke, *The Ideals Guide to Literary Places in the US*; Holden, *The Booklovers' Guide to the Midwest: A Literary Tour* and *Literary Chicago*; Morgan, *Literary Landmarks of New York: The Book Lover's Guide to the Homes and Haunts of World Famous Writers*; Wilson, *Literary Trail of Greater Boston*.
5 Twigg, *Vancouver and Its Writers*; Gatenby, *Toronto: A Literary Guide*; Demchinksy and Naves, *Storied Streets: Montreal in the Literary Imagination*; Arnason and Mackintosh, *The Imagined City: A Literary History of Winnipeg*.
6 In the late nineteenth century this connection was fostered by Charles G. D. Roberts, among many others, whose guidebooks forged an alliance between poetry, patriotism, and tourism; see Bentley, "Charles G. D. Roberts and William Wilfred Campbell" 83-89. Most such publications were supported and promoted by the railway companies that profited from American tourism to Canada.
7 The popularity of the French song, "Évangéline," written by Michel Conte in 1971, has also played a role in this touristic reinvention.
8 See <http://greenspace-alliance.ca/poetspath>; my thanks to Cynthia Sugars for drawing this Ottawa effort to my attention.
9 See <http://www.projectbookmarkcanada.ca/>. To date, most of its sites are in Ontario.
10 <http://www.writerschapeltrust.com/home.php>. Thus far John Glassco, Gwethalyn Graham, Louis Hémon, Hugh MacLennan, F. R. Scott, and A. J. M. Smith have been selected for commemoration.
11 See <http://www.torontohistory.org/index.html> and <http://www.ontarioplaques.com/index.html>.
12 "Isabella Valancy Crawford" file, Minutes of the City of Toronto, Historical Parks and Markers Program, seen 13 Feb. 2013, courtesy of Heritage Toronto, at their office at St. Lawrence Hall.
13 See <http://www.bala.net/museum>.
14 See <http://www.bidefordparsonagemuseum.com> and <http://www.gov.pe.ca/hpo/app.php?nav=details&p=2977>. The Community Museums Association of Prince Edward Island includes three Montgomery sites, as well as sites commemorating Mi'kmaq, Acadian, and Scottish communities, the military, lighthouses, fishing, railways, and the potato. The only other writer to appear in this context is Sir Andrew Macphail, whose homestead is maintained by a private foundation.
15 See <http://en.wikipedia.org/wiki/Persons_of_National_Historic_Significance>.
16 Some contentious sites were claimed by both French and English, whose accounts of historical events and their significance differed profoundly.

17 Francophone women are surprisingly sparse: Marguerite Bourgeoys, one of the most important historical figures in New France, wasn't named until 1985.
18 Neatby and Hodgins 6.
19 Opp and Walsh 6. See also Gordon.
20 See Taylor's membership lists for 1918-87 (193-98).
21 In comparison with Fredericton and Toronto, for example, Vancouver seems quite bare of plaques and other markers of its historical geography.
22 In addition, while not a designated national historic site, Grey Owl's cabin in Prince Albert National Park is maintained by Parks Canada; Grey Owl himself (Archie Belaney) was designated a national historic person in 1993.
23 See, for example, the national historic register: <http://www.historicplaces.ca/en/home-accueil.aspx> and the New Brunswick register of historic places: <http://www.gnb.ca/0131/historicplaces/index-e.asp>.
24 See <http://history.alberta.ca/stephansson/default.aspx>.
25 See <http://www.maisonfrechette.com/partenaires/>. The website for Louis Fréchette's birthplace, in Quebec City, lists a score of contributors ranging from the Canada Council and Heritage Canada to a local bingo hall.

WORKS CITED

Arnason, David, and Mhari Mackintosh. *The Imagined City: A Literary History of Winnipeg*. Winnipeg: Turnstone, 2005. Print.

Bentley, D. M. R. "Charles G. D. Roberts and William Wilfred Campbell as Canadian Tour Guides." *Journal of Canadian Studies* 32.2 (Summer 1997): 79-99. Print.

———. *Mnemographia Canadensis*. Vol. 1. London, ON: Canadian Poetry, 1999. Print.

Burke, Michelle Prater. *The Ideals Guide to Literary Places in the U.S.* Nashville: Ideals, 1998. Print.

Clark, Brock. *An Arsonist's Guide to Writers' Homes in New England*. Chapel Hill: Algonquin Books of Chapel Hill, 2007. Print.

Colombo, John Robert. *Canadian Literary Landmarks*. Willowdale: Hounslow, 1984. Print.

Demchinksy, Bryan, and Elaine Kalman Naves. *Storied Streets: Montreal in the Literary Imagination*. Toronto: Macfarlane Walter and Ross, 2000. Print.

Easley, Alexis. *Literary Celebrity, Gender, and Victorian Authorship, 1850-1914*. Newark: U of Delaware P, 2011. Print.

Gatenby, Greg. *Toronto: A Literary Guide*. Toronto: McArthur, 1999. Print.

Gerson, Carole. "Seven Milestones: How *Anne of Green Gables* Became a Canadian Icon." *Anne's World: A New Century of Anne of Green Gables*. Ed. Irene Gammel and Benjamin Lefebvre. Toronto: U of Toronto P, 2010. 17-34. Print.

Gordon, Tammy S. *Private History in Public: Exhibition and the Settings of Everyday Life*. Lanham, MD: AltaMira, 2010. Print.

Haliburton House Museum. <http://museum.gov.ns.ca/hh/en/home/abouthaliburtonhouse/default.aspx>. Web. 18 May 2012.

Harris, Amy Lavender. *Imagining Toronto*. Toronto: Mansfield, 2010. Print.

Hathaway, E. J. "Canadian Literary Homes." *Canadian Magazine* 30 (Jan. 1908): 225-32. Print.

Hemstreet, Charles. *Literary New York: Its Landmarks and Associations*. New York: Putnam, 1903. Print.
Hendrix, Harald, ed. *Writers' Houses and the Making of Memory*. New York: Routledge, 2008. Print.
"Historic Sites and Monuments Board of Canada," Parks Canada. Web. <http://www.pc.gc.ca/eng/clmhc-hsmbc/index.aspx>. 18 May 2012.
Holden, Greg. *The Booklovers' Guide to the Midwest: A Literary Tour*. Cincinnati: Clerisy, 2009. Print.
———. *Literary Chicago*. Chicago: Lake Claremont, 2001. Print.
HSMBC. Excerpt from the minutes of July 2009. Received 29 July 2011.
HSMBC. "Screening Report: Marie Joussaye (c. 1864-1949)." 2008.
Jones, Donald. "Canadian Poetess' Home Discovered on King St." *Toronto Star* 29 Nov. 1980.
———. "Time to Take a Very Fine Poet to Our Hearts." *Toronto Star* 27 Dec. 1986.
Kroetsch, Robert. "A Conversation with Margaret Laurence." *Creation*. Ed. Robert Kroetsch, with James Bacque and Pierre Gravel. Toronto: New P, 1970. 53-63. Print.
Levine, Miriam. *A Guide to Writers' Homes in New England*. Rev. ed. Cambridge, MA: Applewood Books, 1984. Print.
Matthews, Samantha. *Poetical Remains: Poets' Graves, Bodies, and Books in the Nineteenth Century*. Oxford: Oxford UP, 2004. Print.
McKay, Ian, and Robin Bates. *In the Province of History: The Making of the Public Past in Twentieth-Century Nova Scotia*. Montreal and Kingston: McGill-Queen's UP, 2010. Print.
Morgan, Bill. *Literary Landmarks of New York: The Book Lover's Guide to the Homes and Haunts of World Famous Writers*. New York: Universe, 2003. Print.
Moritz, Albert, and Theresa Moritz. *The Oxford Illustrated Literary Guide to Canada*. Toronto: Oxford UP, 1987. Print.
Neatby, Nicole, and Peter Hodgins, eds. *Settling and Unsettling Memories: Essays in Canadian Public History*. Toronto: U of Toronto P, 2012. Print.
Pérusse, Denise. *Pays littéraires du Québec: Guide des lieux d'écrivains*. Montréal: L'Hexagone, 1998. Print.
Opp, James, and John C. Walsh, eds. *Placing Memory and Remembering Place in Canada*. Vancouver: UBC P, 2010. Print.
"Persons of National Historic Significance," Parks Canada. Web. <http://www.pc.gc.ca/eng/docs/r/system-reseau/sec1/sites-lieux11.aspx>. 18 May 2012.
Ryden, Kent C. *Mapping the Invisible Landscape: Folklore, Writing, and the Sense of Place*. Iowa City: U of Iowa P, 1993. Print.
Schmidt, Shannon McKenna, and Joni Rendon. *Novel Destinations: Literary Landmarks from Jane Austen's Bath to Ernest Hemingway's Key West*. Washington: National Geographic, 2009. Print.
Strong-Boag, Veronica. "Experts on Our Own Lives: Commemorating Canada at the Beginning of the 21st Century." *Public Historian* 31.1 (Feb. 2009): 46-68. Print.
Taylor, C. J. *Negotiating the Past: The Making of Canada's National Historic Parks and Sites*. Montreal and Kingston: McGill-Queen's UP, 1990. Print.

Trubek, Anne. *A Skeptic's Guide to Writers' Houses*. Philadelphia: U of Pennsylvania P, 2011. Print.

Twigg, Alan. *Vancouver and Its Writers: A Guide to Vancouver's Literary Landmarks*. Madeira Park: Harbour, 1986. Print.

Ward, A. C. *A Literary Journey Through Wartime Britain*. New York: Oxford UP, 1943. Print.

Watson, Nicola J. *The Literary Tourist: Readers and Places in Romantic & Victorian England*. New York: Palgrave Macmillan, 2006. Print.

———, ed. *Literary Tourism and Nineteenth-Century Culture*. New York: Palgrave Macmillan, 2009. Print.

Welborn, J. B. *Traveling Literary America: A Complete Guide to Literary Landmarks*. Lookout Mountain: Jefferson, 2005. Print.

Wilson, Susan. *Literary Trail of Greater Boston*. Boston: Houghton Mifflin, 2000. Print.

CHAPTER 14

Archaeological Detritus and the Bulging Archive
The Staging of *He Named Her Amber* at the Art Gallery of Ontario

May Chew

When the Art Gallery of Ontario (AGO) reopened its doors in 2008, after a highly touted expansion and renovation project (Transformation AGO), visitors were given a chance to take tours through The Grange, the historic manor attached to the rear of the main gallery that was originally the home of the AGO in the early 1900s.[1] Here, they were told the captivating tale of Mary O'Shea, a young Irish immigrant who in the late 1820s escaped the imminent famine and came to Canada, where she worked as a scullery maid at The Grange household for a number of decades. Visitors were then invited to witness the rather extraordinary archaeological excavation of The Grange property, which had unearthed mysterious waxen objects believed to have been both handcrafted and then surreptitiously hidden by Mary throughout the site, usually behind walls or underneath floorboards. Descending into The Grange's cavernous basement and led through the kitchen, cold cellar, and other restricted pockets of the manor, visitors were shown objects ranging in size from diminutive marble-size globules of rolled-up wax, to a large conical structure formed from wax poured into a hole dug deep in the earth. Even more curious was the fact that Mary's objects all contained within them peculiar fragments, such as the limbs of porcelain dolls, baby teeth, and animal bones, as well as bits of hair, nails, and blood believed to have been shed by Mary herself. Visitors were left to puzzle over who this beguiling Mary O'Shea was. What was the tenor of life she left behind in Ireland? What great tragedy prompted her mysterious and compulsive productions? At the very end of the tour, tiny slips of paper were distributed by the docents; only if the unsuspecting visitors read through a lengthy treatise on the excavation would they have then finally come across the quiet disclosure that the entire thing was in fact a carefully orchestrated fiction, conceived of and manifested by artist Iris Häussler, under the auspices of the AGO.

Drawing upon Häussler's installation, *He Named Her Amber* (2008-10), this chapter considers how the archive is performatively enacted via the choreography of objects and bodies through space, in a process that speaks to how the ontological and juridical archival topography congeals in that interstitial terrain between national narratives, historical f(r)ictions, material residues, and the bodies that engage them. This installation reveals the gallery's subscription to what critics have diagnosed as a "new museology," heralded by institutions eager to rebrand themselves as postcolonial. Even though this supposed paradigm shift is meant to express museums' wide-ranging attempts to adopt more inclusive, participatory, and self-reflexive curatorial mandates that are disencumbered from older tenets of imperial collecting and display (Vergo; Macdonald; Witcomb), it is possible to argue that new museology can also work complicitously alongside these long-standing colonial discourses. This is because "non-traditional," interactive techniques can often be a convenient overlay adopted to help attract new audiences, enhance revenue, and ensure institutional health. In this way, not only do such participatory approaches fail to achieve radical structural transformation, they can even be used to buttress neoliberal-cum-multiculturalist logics. Many of the aesthetic-symbolic strategies used in *Amber* fall easily in line with liberal-multiculturalist tropes, namely the re-crafting of hegemonic subsumption into the national narrative as benevolent inclusion. Emblematic subscription to this new museology is a means through which the AGO is able to capitalize on the circulation of desire and fetish attached to colonial forms of exhibition, while simultaneously diverting the pathology of such practices away from the institution and onto Mary, the body under scrutiny. In this way, the nation's imperial past and multiculturalist present become mutually reinforcing.

Amber speaks to the ways that, within the AGO's multiculturalist paradigm, archival inclusion can in fact function as a strategy of control. The installation capitalizes on the performative gestures of archaeological discourse to produce a self-confessing object while disguising the means through which this confession is incited. The aesthetic-scientific choreographies that construct Mary as an explicitly gendered, racialized, and classed body also present her as an enigmatic spectacle whose secrets are constantly *just* on the verge of being divulged. Crucially, the installation places an onus on Mary to perform her otherness and disclose her compulsions, at the same time that it absolves institutional culpability through a narrative of innocent discovery wherein the AGO stumbles across Mary's objects by pure happenstance. This rendering of Mary's *self-motivated* confession, set alongside the institution's *unmotivated* discovery, works to divert the pathologies of a neocolonial archive whose modus operandi is the active rather than passive ingestion and incorporation of the other. In the case of *Amber*, otherness is compulsively articulated in order to then be collapsed securely back into the folds of a long-standing colonial text. This allows the archive to continue to swell, but with active seizure or pillage conveniently eschewed for a more innocuous program of incidental discovery and benevolent multicultural inclusion.

This chapter also suggests, however, that the incommensurability of materiality as proof comes back to haunt this archive, turning colonial fantasies of accumulation quickly into nightmares of attrition. *Amber* is intriguing because of the evocative way it performs archival vulnerability and lingers on the mercuriality of objects whose tendency to sometimes slip beyond seizure reveals the inherent fissures of the archival framework. In some ways, the installation can also be seen as the sensual manifestation of the gallery's various anxieties, or an uneasy reminder of the ways that the archive unintentionally produces the phantasmagorias or hallucinations that expose the hauntedness of the settler-colonial imaginary.

It bears mentioning that this chapter is not an indictment of artistic intentions, but rather a critical examination of the problematic discourses mobilized in and through the installation narrative. The crux of this argument rests on the notion that, while Häussler's brilliant ploy can be read as contributing a critical lens to issues of representation and difference, this possibility is considerably dampened by the fact that large portions of its audience walk away oblivious to the artist's reveal. Without this denouement, the installation is taken solely at the level of authoritative museological truth, and in this way reinforces the neocolonial encounter between a hegemonic subject and its symbolic marginalized other.

DETRITUS AND DISCOVERY

Material archives deserve theoretical attention because, as Ann Laura Stoler argues, the "aftershocks of empire" persist in their material "debris" ("Imperial" 194). *Amber* reveals the ways in which colonial detritus and the affective residues left on objects continue to produce subjects and others, as well as organize the relations between them. The installation is mobilized through a narrative of fortuitous "discovery" wherein the figuring of historical detritus and the transference of fetish and desire play a central role. Tour participants are told that Mary's waxen artifacts were only uncovered because, unbeknownst to her, Mary had a faithful sentinel who kept track of her movement throughout the house. Henry Whyte, a butler at The Grange during Mary's time, not only kept an eye on Mary, but also diligently recorded her activities on a hand-drawn map, marking with an "x" all the spots where he observed her secreting away her objects. Participants are also given an account of how, almost a century later during Transformation AGO, this very map found its way (back) into the hands of the AGO through one of Whyte's heirs by a stroke of fortune. Guided by the butler's map, the AGO's excavation team went about scavenging The Grange property, eventually stumbling upon Mary's waxen objects. This map functions in many ways like the imperial map of Anne McClintock's description—that technology of knowledge, which guides the colonizing eye through the thicket of dark and wild, translating the unknown into "pure, scientific form" (27-28). Häussler's chronicling of this map's sequence of heirs is also particularly revealing; its lineal passage from Whyte to his nephew, and eventually from the nephew to the AGO, discloses a structuring logic of patriarchal possession and patrimony that begets the *Amber* narrative.

Mary's "discovered" objects are framed in part as archaeological waste—the refuse of time, and perhaps outgrowth of pathology—that merely need to be placed under a museological narrative in order to be reordered with significance. The objects, in Mary's hands, were shorn of meaning; in the gallery's hands (via Henry Whyte), however, they are recovered into narrative. The installation thus enacts the objects' transformation from detritus into valued object and, more importantly, signals the gallery's fundamental role in this procedure. Only when framed within the authority of archaeological discourse, and placed under the institutional gaze, does cultural waste become the valued collection of objects worthy of display and acknowledgement. This performative archaeology operates through a logic of allochronism, which Johannes Fabian describes as the "existential, rhetorical, political" strategies of distancing that place the referents of anthropology outside history, in a time other than that of the anthropologist (31-32). While the *Amber* narrative is constituted exactly through this discourse of spatial-temporal distancing, it centres just as much on Mary's "recovery" through the institution—the process whereby her mute body is dredged up from Fabian's allochronistic time of the other and recuperated into the present where she can be surveilled, and woven into further museological fantasies.

Adding to this patrimonial assertion, tour participants are told that it was Whyte who, on his hand-drawn map, curiously granted Mary with the code name "Amber"—hence the installation title *He Named Her Amber*. No real explanation is given as to why he did this. Participants might surmise that he resorted to the cipher in order to conceal his own voyeuristic fascination with Mary. The naming of *Amber* stands as a gesture of symbolic ownership on behalf of Whyte, who functions as the AGO's discursive surrogate. This secondary moniker also signals Mary's entrance into an economy of desire, whereby her narrative presence is bestowed by Whyte, just as the value of her objects is conferred through the authorial gaze of the AGO. The implication here is that patrimony guides this other (back) into the disciplinary architecture of a dominant narrative, where she is preserved for scopic intervention. Mary thus becomes the object of fascination symbolically embalmed in amber—and literally embalmed in beeswax—preserved at the height of visibility and access, her body disclosed, her secrets divulged.

All the more striking is the AGO's purportedly passive role in the acquisition and unearthing of these objects. Unlike more familiar tales of museum collections wrought through imperialism's exertive venturings to the beyond, this one tells of anthropological plunder miraculously materializing within the museum without any necessary initiating effort on the institution's part. Susan Stewart sheds some light on this myth of serendipitous discovery and *in*active seizure when she writes of how collecting enacts the erasure of labour; "one 'finds' the elements of the collection much as the prelapsarian Adam and Eve could find the satisfaction of their needs without a necessary articulation of desire. The collector constructs a narrative of luck which replaces the narrative of production" (165). One can add that such "narratives of luck" also distract from the violence of active appropriation and seizure. The figuring of artifacts as detritus or waste therefore allows the museum to somewhat effectively dilute the imperial compulsion to actively pursue, seize, and collect, for it posits an innocent model of acquisition through serendipitous discovery. Similar to Stewart, James Clifford writes of the museum as the site where desire and fetish are transformed into "proper" collecting through Western notions of taste, restraint, and property. In the museum, desire becomes appropriately channelled and its excess expunged, so that the subject (upheld by the institution) does not risk cleaving to the object, but remains a distantiated authority for whom collected objects can act as the mediating field of property between self and an ordered universe.

Amber adds something significant to Clifford's thesis: by producing a museological encounter wherein fetish and desire play crucial roles, the installation facilitates not a *renunciation* but in fact a *transference* of fetishistic accumulation onto the body of the other. The compulsion to collect is transferred onto Mary, who is characterized as "obsessed" (Hegert), and "deranged" (MacKay). Meanwhile, the AGO is validated as the neutral site of the archaeological excavation, and the irreproachable scientific-rational vehicle to house its uncovered spoils. Tour participants, gently goaded by the docents, eagerly conjure up a slew of fantastical tales to explain Mary's mysterious activity, including witchcraft and madness derived from heartbreak (Goddard; Hegert).[2] These implied motivations behind Mary's impulse to conceal and collect—tellingly shrouded in gendered discourse and hinting at the abject—are stacked against the AGO's curatorial paradigm, which is cast, through juxtaposition, as comparatively sterile and dispassionate. Thus, Mary's feverish and furtive accumulations, while they provide the canvas through which the participants' scopophilic desires can be invigorated, function at the same time to disguise the institution's own fetish by underscoring the supposed rationality and forthrightness of the latter's own framing device. The installation thus invites the visitor to brush thrillingly close to the pathological and abject, all the while maintaining the inculpability of both visitor and museum.

MATTERS OF LIFE AND DEATH

At play within the installation is an interesting tension between detritus—signalling *end of life*—and institutional transformation and renewal. The reopening of the AGO came in November 2008, when the gallery was just nearing the tail end of Transformation AGO, a major renovation and revitalization project that lasted over seven years, and ambitiously branded itself as both an architectural and curatorial overhaul, promising to offer the public "new art, new building, new future, new ideas" ("Transformation"). When the gallery reopened its doors to the public, the first visitors were ushered unsuspectingly into the *Amber* experience, believing that they were merely partaking in the latest incarnation of the standard historic Grange tour presented throughout the years at the AGO. It is hardly a coincidence that *Amber* was staged for the public at this particular moment in the institution's life, during its full-throttle campaign to pronounce its capacity for economic survival and cultural relevance/continuation. During the Transformation, in fact, Häussler was among a select group of artists commissioned by the AGO's curator of contemporary art, David Moos, to create a work specifically for the auspicious occasion of the gallery's reopening (MacKay). The inclusion of this particular installation in the new AGO discloses the fact that the institution's program of revitalization benefited from, and to a certain extent even necessitated, an auxiliary return to beginnings. This is to say: possessing access to the narrative's point of origin means ensuring the ability to steer its course down the road. The AGO's declaration of institutional futurity and endurance through its "Transformation" project needed to be staged in part through the fabrication of archival topographies—a *fabrication* that, in both senses of the word, concurrently involved production as well as forgery. This spectacle of continuance required not only a return to the exordial chimeras, but to an "actual" archive sensuously materialized and housed within the domestic grounds of The Grange.

The desire to possess the archive—the originary moment—through frenzied production brings to mind Derrida's disclosure of the archive, or *arkhē*, in its double function: to demonstrate the "physical, historical or ontological" beginning (*commencement*), and to indicate the nomological seat of power (*commandment*) (1). In other words, the archive is simultaneously sequential designation as well as utterance of law. As mythic-historical speculation made flesh, *Amber* speaks to how the archive needs to be taken up as material encounter in order to demonstrate the institution's protracted ability to choreograph detritus into an institutional narrative, and to institute law through the revisioning of history. The strategic embedding of the installation within the overarching framework of Transformation AGO elucidates how an institutional makeover hardly requires complete historical jettison; on the contrary, it benefits considerably from archival supplementation and addition *alongside* the dexterously selective insistence on historical integrity and narrative longevity. Architecturally speaking, this is further revealed by the fact that during the renovations, which saw much of the older gallery structure gutted, expanded, and otherwise radically transformed according to the designs of Frank Gehry, only the neo-Georgian shell of The Grange manor remained unaltered. Held up as both the originary locus of the AGO, as well as one of Toronto's oldest buildings, and hence a remnant of the city's earliest colonial settlement, The Grange's granted historical status is particularly useful for the AGO's revisioning of its future in and through its (revealingly colonial) past. Häussler's proficient appropriation of The Grange's ready store of historic ambience allows her to construct a startlingly visceral space of archival intimacy, and allows the gallery an actualized archival topography to which it can compulsively return.

More than just utilizing the "return" to (fictive) archival beginnings, *Amber* also bolsters the institution's own continuing vitality by putting the death of the other on display. Mary's waxen globules, placed under the aegis of the AGO's grand narrative of transformation and revitalization, are similar to the exotic souvenir characterized by Stewart. Rent from its context and reframed as property, the exotic object operates as a "sign of survival"—not of the object, but of the triumphant possessor instead: "its otherness speaks to the possessor's capacity for otherness" (Stewart 148). To effectively function as trophy of survival for the possessing subject, the exotic souvenir must also embody its own death, or the death of the other. Within the installation, Mary is spectacularized as a dead object through the display of her synecdochic waxen objects. The intricate archaeological guise of the *Amber* fiction emphasizes the strategies of allochronistic distancing used to bring her to life/death, strategies that centre on the denial of "coevalness," or the "common, active 'occupation,' or sharing of Time" (Fabian 31). Like devices of salvage ethnography, which execute destruction at the very hand of aesthetic preservation, allochronistic strategies can easily be equated with the putting to death of the other. Furthermore, the installation's justificatory archaeological framework becomes precisely the vehicle to invoke the gallery's and the artist's potent ability to bring this object (back) to life. The display of the exotic object is here employed to project the institution's persevering life, which ultimately belies the fact that this institutional vigour—powered by neoliberal multiculturalist discourses—must necessarily occur alongside the sacrificial death of the other. Through the object-as-souvenir, the subject displays its power to reanimate detritus by reintroducing it back into narrative circulation, and paradoxically enough, in such a way that the *end-of-life* of the other is ultimately used to reanimate the subject.

"BENEVOLENT" INCLUSIONS

Another method by which the archive attempts to divert the notion of seizure and active appropriation is by adopting multiculturalism's well-rehearsed strategies, particularly the seemingly benevolent inclusion of the other within the national archive. A number of criticisms levelled at the official multiculturalism of settler-colonial nations like Canada within recent decades point to its tendency to compensate for the lack of actual political power afforded to these nations' many disenfranchised groups with overabundant symbolic distractions (Ahmed; Gunew; Thobani). As illustrated by Häussler's installation at the AGO, such strategies, more than merely compensatory, also involve the hailing in of otherness for the purposes of surveillance and discipline. By enacting the archaeological extraction of the "hidden" other from darkness into light, the installation reveals a Foucauldian logic of positive power at play; here, otherness is literally mined from its secret recesses—or, more specifically, from beneath the floorboards of a house—and superintended by means of its circulation through the necessary discursive channels. The seemingly benevolent invitations into canonical archives can themselves be technologies of "internment and reservation," especially when they are overly aesthetic subsumptions that succeed in eliding the political (Rickard 87). Colonization via inclusion, argue Classen and Howes, is the "regulation of artifactual bodies by the regimen of the museum," a process whereby displayed objects are forcibly interpellated into Western taxonomic and aesthetic orders of the collector/institution (209). For Classen and Howes, the "model of an ideal colonial empire" (210) is thus manifested in the collection of objects lined up quietly along a shelf or behind a sterile slab of glass in the museum.

Just as multiculturalism functions to mark bodies deemed divergent while simultaneously unmarking those of the unspoken "norm," so too does the *Amber* narrative reveal its inclination in highlighting specific bodies of difference. On display are two bodies in particular: Mary O'Shea and Dr. Chantal Lee, the head archaeologist and "site coordinator," who, like Mary, is a fictional construct. While both subjects are physically absent, their narrative presence is nonetheless lushly filled in through the artifactual and embodied "dressing" of the scene, which participants are made to believe these characters inhabit. Though Mary is the presumed focus of the excavation-tour, there is a crucial parallel tale of archaeologist Dr. Lee, who, as tour participants are made well aware, is herself an immigrant, though of Korean descent. Dr. Lee's abandoned office (participants are informed she conveniently "just" stepped out) is as meticulously crafted as Mary's world and becomes part of the tour, open to participants who eagerly believe they are detouring from the main narrative into another treasure trove of curiosities. It is a dimly lit, windowless, and stuffy room, located in The Grange basement near the kitchen and pantry—the concealed spaces that would have been seen and traversed only by the servants in the manor's early days, but which, during *Amber*, indiscreetly summon the gazes of curious onlookers. Amidst the litter of books, photographs, maps, floor plans, and scientific paraphernalia scattered about the office are also strewn objects made to appear as the archaeologist's personal belongings. These include stained coffee mugs, rumpled pyjamas, and even an unmade cot tucked away in a corner of the room, all meant to suggest to the onlooker, perhaps, that Dr. Lee is so consumed with the mystery of Mary O'Shea that she has decided to permanently encamp herself at the site of the excavation. Perhaps because they are not granted the safe remove of temporal distance, Dr. Lee's discrete objects and their affective geography evoke an ambience of "private" clutter so provocatively as to almost make one avert one's eyes.

But this elaborate *mise en scène* effectively directs the gaze, and Mary and Dr. Lee both become the surfaces upon which the participants' voyeurisms are trained. The members of the audience, for their part, become part of the surveillance technology, a mobile army of free-floating eyes scouring the constructed landscape and the bodies displayed for secrets to uncover. This just begins to suggest how sensuous encounters with archives—in this particular case, through the act of looking—can effectively marshal bodies into what Benedict Anderson elucidates as the *imagined community* of nation. More crucially, such practices also reflect what Sunera Thobani refers to as citizenship through *exaltation*, a process wherein privileged subjects are seduced into reproducing the "master narrative of nation" at the expense of those constructed as immutable outsiders (4). *Amber* reveals the corporeal and emotional rituals that go into *imagining* and *practising* nation. By training their eye upon the splayed body of the other, visitors making their way through this performative narrative of "archival detritus" enter into a scopophilic covenant with the "master narrative," which hails them in as its privileged subjects.

The scrupulously staged archival scene effectively choreographs the gaze, directing the eyes toward narratives they are meant to capture, but just as importantly, directing them away from those they are meant not to. The highly elaborate *mise en scène* marking the spaces into which Mary's and Dr. Lee's bodies are confined work to guilefully obscure the biographies of Häussler and also that of Moos—an especially impressive feat given that this erasure occurs in the gallery, a space otherwise given to venerations of the artist. Although *Amber* contains some self-referential hints that it is an art installation rather than an archaeological excavation, its "haptic conceptual" approach rests on the camouflage of Häussler's and the AGO's authorial tracks, and in the audience's belief that they are entering into a factual, historical diegesis.[3] The installation is very revealing of how, when it comes to the materialization of such archives and the national imaginaries that these archives figure, notions of truth and fiction are of smaller consequence than the affective labour invested in bringing these archives to life. The audience, in other words, is haptically seduced into believing. In this sense, the apparent absence of artist, curator, and institution stands as a testament to their authorial power. Unhindered by biographical culpability or spatial circumscription, Häussler and Moos possess precisely the resources to masterfully divert the gaze upon Mary's and Dr. Lee's bodies. Reminiscent of the ways in which symbolic multiculturalist representation paves over the lack of real agency, Mary and Dr. Lee's absence as agents/authors is enabled by (at the same time that it also enables) their proliferating aesthetic presence within the archive.

Closely allied to multiculturalism's imperative to *come within, allow your difference to be marked*, is Irit Rogoff's notion of plenitude, which commands that the other *come into (or rather, under) the dominant text*. Rogoff describes the Western museum's plenitude or additive model as "the museum's untroubled *ability* to add others without losing a bit of the self" (66). This process, whereby change occurs without loss, and without the institution having to interrupt its drive of endless accumulation, slips easily in line with neoliberal multiculturalism. Through the plenitude paradigm, the archive continues to swell, ingesting the other so that this other can be disciplined by implementations of violent visibility. *He Named Her Amber*, in its perhaps unconscious mobilization of certain tropes, presents one particularly compelling example of how the AGO compulsively articulates otherness in order to enclose it within a dominant text or institutional rubric. The installation's archaeological unfolding is particularly useful in this regard, for it tells a fantasied tale of the institution "discovering" an otherness already snugly tucked within an existing colonial scaffolding, which remains unruptured and is in fact bolstered through the sublimation of otherness.

In the case of neoliberal multiculturalism, self-congratulatory designations of open barriers do not merely cloak the violence of hegemonic enclosure, but in fact become the strategic lynchpins of a carceral structure which understands that the issue at hand is no longer how to keep the other *out*, but instead the specific manner in which the other must be kept *within*. With regard to the *Amber* installation, it is no coincidence that its drama of fabricated intimacies is staged on its particular site. The installation's expedient choreography of multiculturalist inclusion hinges in large part on its doubly fortuitous location within The Grange, an intimate limb of the gallery umbilically connected to the institution in which it is housed. Its setting thus affords the narrative legitimation both on the level of official or public archival "truth," as well as private, domestic authenticity.

That empire and the intimate are faithful bedfellows is hardly a novel supposition. Stoler makes the convincing case that, since the nineteenth century, the consolidation of the "macrodynamics of colonial rule" has crucially depended upon "interventions in the microenvironments of both subjugated and colonizing populations" ("Intimidations" 2). The energy expended by colonial powers in attempts to police affective relationships, penetrate intimate pockets of "darkness," and restructure these domains through social and urban planning, labour regimes, and medical protocols (3) divulges the fact that empire has, to a significant extent, always been secured and/or threatened by what was going on behind closed doors. While in many ways a continuation of these earlier disciplinary practices, what is significant in the multiculturalist institution's "turning-in" to private spaces, as expressed through *Amber*, is that the latter centres on the frenzied *production* and highly elaborate performance of the intimate domain, which becomes the grounds on which to compulsively *exercise* as well as *exorcise* difference. *Amber* illustrates how multiculturalist incursions into intimate domains are about more than just invasion and discipline. These also entail the triumphal production of space, and subsequently the population of this space, and the dressing of the scene—its *mise en scène*. One particularly effective and quixotic aspect of this installation is that it dramatizes the fiction of inclusion as affective and immersive spectacle. Here, private space, like the other's body, is constructed primarily for public access, even while being couched in the seductive language of secrecy and intimacy, which of course merely heightens the pleasure of invasion. In *Amber*, the discrete landscape is narrated into existence to be subsequently yielded.

Aside from its physical expansion, the institutional archive continues to expand both spatially and temporally. Not only does the installation burst forth beyond the "white cube" of the modernist gallery into the domestic space of The Grange, it also attempts chronological annexation by reaching back into a time before the gallery's founding. Further examples of the unabashed spatial and temporal expansion of the overflowing archival container abound elsewhere in the renovated gallery. During Transformation AGO, the J. S. McLean Centre for Canadian Art underwent a massive rehang under the direction of Gerald McMaster, curator of Canadian art, who promulgated the AGO's new interest in decentring established colonial narratives of history and truth, and cracking open the 250-year container of "official" Canadian history traditionally confined to Confederation and Cartier (McMaster, "Our (Inter) Related History"). One example of this curatorial intention is the added exhibit of projectile points in *A Thousand Points for a Thousand Generations*, located in the "Ancient Memory" gallery at the front of the Canadian wing. The inclusion of these "ancient" artifacts not only leaves the colonial narrative intact, but in fact allows its tentaculoid ambit to muscularly unfurl beyond its previous container and lay claim—as the gallery boasts—on an expanded chronology of eleven thousand years (McMaster, "Art and Ideas").

The AGO's newer interest in polyphonic expansions of Canadian Art presents itself as the supposed subversion of the traditional dominant narrative through the insertion of women and First Nations artists, and, in general, the questioning of the commonly understood definitions of art and its reception (McMaster, "Art and Ideas"). One by-product of this ever-expanding archive of Canadian Art is that it finds itself decreasingly bound by historical confinement and representational boundaries. As both the *Thousand Points* and *Amber* examples illustrate, the existing colonial archive, rather than being interrupted by postcolonial critiques into the museological terrain, merely continues its prerogative to accumulate and expand, fervently lapping up those in its wake. Aside from the so-called "benevolent" inclusion of historically silenced minority voices, one must also note the AGO's incorporation of "new ways of seeing" and viewer-friendly means of consuming art, as well as its new prioritizations of more reflexive critiques and interventions, all of which have now become institutionalized and sutured into the brick and mortar of the institution itself. Such seeming curatorial shifts, placed alongside Rogoff's remark on the ways in which dominant Western museological frameworks continue to expand and adapt without undergoing real altercation, affirms how neoliberal paradigms are simply becoming increasingly more flexible, rather than more anemic. By resorting to a ready arsenal of postmodern techniques—including intertextual quotation, interdisciplinarity, self-reflexivity, and the collapsing of past/present—and appropriating oppositional models of interpretation, institutions like the AGO leave little room for counter-narratives to emerge beyond the official dictates of the institution. Under the guise of benign inclusivity, or unity through diversity, previously excluded voices are thus voraciously folded into the bulging archive, their assimilation serving in many ways to bolster neoliberal, neocolonial narratives.

A MERCURIAL ARCHIVE

In order to avoid leaving off with the direful romance of the inexterminably voracious neocolonial archive, it is crucial to account both for the tension between the performative archive and materiality as proof, as well as the work of aporia that threatens perpetually to pry the seemingly coherent threads of the dominant archive apart. Two notions in particular gleaned from the Derridean characterization of the archive help in this regard: first, the implicit archival vulnerability, which must be ameliorated through constant production and, second, the destructive "fever" or annihilative tendency enfolded within the heart of archive itself. In *Archive Fever*, Derrida writes that every archive "is at once *institutive* and *conservative*," "revolutionary and traditional" in the sense that—and here he focuses on the archive's juridical capacity—it "saves" and "puts in reserve" at the same time that it also *makes* the law, and institutes the relationship between law and subject (7). Production and conservation are, of course, neither innocent nor circumstantial auxiliaries within the archive. One could argue that each requires the other, and that the archive is thus structured through and determined by its rather ambivalent proclivities to *make* and to *hold*. This double economy points implicitly to what can be figured as the wavering productive energies through which the inherently irresolute archival project attempts to utter the law while anxiously safeguarding its own authority. Into this already precarious archive, Derrida also asserts the notion of the death drive, or "archive fever," enfolded within every archive or monument, which, he writes, "exposes [an archive] to destruction" and "forgetfulness." As such, "the archive always works, and *a priori*," Derrida claims, "against itself" (12). Taken together, these elucidations offer an archive that is driven to synchronously *make* and to *make last*, if only because it inscribes and, by the very same hand, also obliterates.

Perhaps in spite of itself, the archive's ephemeral economy is rather elaborately revealed through the *Amber* installation, a work that begins to point us toward what follows once the archive's phantasmagoric scaffolding falls away, and we encounter the revelation of—not so much "truth" as history's vivid and cunning hallucinations. This installation might, in the end, belie the archive's fleeting lifespan, and the notion that when its material "proof" dissipates, we are left with only a ghostly trail of corporal gestures and affective residues woven by the bodies that wound their way through The Grange and narrated the exhibit to magnificent life.

But a crucial question remains: What of the objects themselves? There is something about the very materiality of the waxen globules—their uncanny capability to generate "real," bodily affect, their undeniable *thingness*—that somehow manages to escape the chimerical grip of the hegemonic archive, and that hints toward possibilities beyond the stringent Derridean economy of production/conservation. Bill Brown's characterization of *thingness*, as the "before and after an object," a "latency" and an "excess" (Brown 5), is helpful here for its implication that things can subvert the archival container by speaking to that lapse in time before an object's discursive circulation, or before its entrance into an economy of desire. As Brown further explains, "things lie beyond the grid of intelligibility the way mere things lie outside the grid of museal exhibition, outside the order of objects" (5). It is this crucial quality of "latency" that marks the thing's essential incommensurability with objects of discourse. Allowing for the very *thingness* of Mary's artifacts therefore means recognizing that they exist somewhat beyond archival seizure, ever slipping between the fractures and fissures of an exhaustive architecture.

To this end, wax becomes an especially resonant medium for this archival performance, particularly because it is a capricious material given equally to remembrance as well as amnesia, and thus serves as a reminder that even the juridical force of the Derridean archive must ultimately account for—and perhaps even yield to—unassimilable archival *things*. Häussler herself describes why the mercurial quality of wax was important in this work:

What interests me particularly about this material is its process of hardening while it cools, changing from a liquid to a solid substance.... Also, the vulnerability of the material has a symbolic quality that resonates with me—just by leaving a waxen globule on the windowsill on a sunny day, or, as Amber did, hiding it under a brick too close to the fire-place it can be destroyed.

With the right amount of heat, wax bends its form to retain the traces of the hand that meets its skin, but give it too much and it surrenders its anatomic integrity, and thus archival capacity, almost entirely. One the one hand, wax indeed speaks to the flexibility of the multiculturalist archive, which in many ways is able to bend and shift to allow for strategic inclusions and incorporations. The very *thingness* of wax, however, also makes it a material too unpredictable and volatile to be put fully in the service of the archival project. An archive built of wax is an archive forever given to transfigurations, evasions, pauses, and erasures. It is an archive that breathes, an archive structured as much by accumulation as by attrition. Perhaps one might venture to say that the archivist always dreams of the reassuring solidity and lucidity of amber, but ultimately ends up—like Iris Häussler and her Mary O'Shea—carving her elegies out of wax.

It therefore remains possible to conceptualize the installation not merely as the complicit by-product of liberal-multiculturalist discipline or the innocent refuse meeting the jaws of an insatiable archive. This installation *also* becomes empire's symptom—the delirium brought on by the half-conscious awareness that any buoyant excursion led by the drive to expand and accumulate is necessarily imperilled by the possibility of encountering the shadowed entrails of histories severed in the settling/colonizing of the nation. The waxen objects are perhaps this anticipant fear materialized—the fleshy, pounding "tell-tale heart" hovering precariously by the skin of the scaffolding, threatening to emerge at any moment from beneath the floorboards.

NOTES

1. For a more detailed history of The Grange, see Bradley and MacKay; Lownsbrough.
2. I was also privy to similar theories during my own tours through the installation.
3. The installation had its share of self-referential moments such as a display case in The Grange library showcasing a string of beads arranged to spell out the word "ART." Häussler also stated that the exhibit included several referential nods to the work of artists such as Marcel Duchamp and Jeff Wall (Hegert).

WORKS CITED

Ahmed, Sara. *Strange Encounters: Embodied Others in Post-Coloniality*. London: Routledge, 2000. Print.

Anderson, Benedict. *Imagined Communities: Reflections on the Origin and Spread of Nationalism*. 2nd rev. ed. New York: Verso, 2006. Print.

Bradley, Jessica, and Gillian MacKay, eds. *House Guests: The Grange 1817 to Today*. Toronto: Art Gallery of Ontario, 2001. Print.

Brown, Bill. "Thing Theory." *Critical Inquiry* 28.1 (2001): 1-22. Print.

Classen, Constance, and David Howes. "The Museum as Sensescape: Western Sensibilities and Indigenous Artifacts." *Sensible Objects: Colonialism, Museums and Material Culture*. Ed. Elizabeth Edwards, Chris Gosden, and Ruth Phillips. Oxford: Berg, 2006. 199-222. Print.

Clifford, James. "On Collecting Art and Culture." *The Predicament of Culture*. Cambridge, MA: Harvard UP, 1988. 215-29. Print.

Derrida, Jacques. *Archive Fever: A Freudian Impression*. Trans. Eric Prenowitz. Chicago: U of Chicago P, 1995. Print.

Fabian, Johannes. *Time and the Other: How Anthropology Makes Its Object*. New York: Columbia UP, 1983. Print.

Goddard, Peter. "(Dis)Honest Iris." *Toronto Star* 22 Jan. 2009: E1. Print.

Gunew, Sneja. *Haunted Nations: The Colonial Dimensions of Multiculturalisms*. London: Routledge, 2004. Print.

Häussler, Iris. "A Question about Amber." Message to the author. 2 May 2011. Email.

Hegert, Natalie. "The Slant on Iris Haussler." *ArtSlant*. 11 June 2011. Web. 30 Sept. 2011.

Lownsbrough, John. *The Privileged Few: The Grange & Its People in Nineteenth Century Toronto*. Toronto: Art Gallery of Ontario, 1980. Print.

Macdonald, Sharon. "Expanding Museum Studies: An Introduction." *A Companion to Museum Studies*. Ed. Sharon Macdonald. Oxford: Blackwell, 2006. 1-12. Print.

MacKay, Gillian, "Brilliant Disguise: Iris Häussler's Fact-Meets-Fiction Odysseys." *Canadian Art*. 1 Dec. 2009. Web. 26 Sept. 2011.

McClintock, Anne. *Imperial Leather: Race, Gender and Sexuality in the Colonial Contest*. New York: Routledge, 1995. Print.

McMaster, Gerald. "Art and Ideas: The New Canadian Installations." Art Gallery of Ontario, 317 Dundas Street West, Toronto. 18 Feb. 2009. Lecture.

———. "Our (Inter) Related History." *On Aboriginal Representation in the Gallery*. Ed. Lynda Jessup and Shannon Bagg. Hull: Canadian Museum of Civilization, 2002. Print.

Rickard, Jolene. "After Essay—Indigenous Is the Local." *On Aboriginal Representation in the Gallery*. Ed. Lynda Jessup and Shannon Bagg. Hull: Canadian Museum of Civilization, 2002. 115-21. Print.

Rogoff, Irit. "Hit and Run Museums and Cultural Difference." *Art Journal* (2002): 63-73. Print.

Stewart, Susan. *On Longing: Narratives of the Miniature, the Gigantic, the Souvenir, the Collection*. Durham: Duke UP, 1993. Print.

Stoler, Ann Laura. "Imperial Debris: Reflections on Ruins and Ruination." *Cultural Anthropology* 23.2 (2008): 191-219. Print.

———. "Intimidations of Empire: Predicaments of the Tactile and Unseen." *Haunted by Empire: Geographies of Intimacy in North American History*. Ed. Ann Laura Stoler. Durham: Duke UP, 2006. Print.

Thobani, Sunera. *Exalted Subjects: Studies in the Making of Race and Nation in Canada*. Toronto: U of Toronto P, 2007. 1-22. Print.

"Tranformation AGO." *AGO*. Art Gallery of Ontario. Web. 26 Sept. 2011.

Vergo. Peter, ed. *The New Museology*. London: Reaktion Books, 1989. Print.

Witcomb, Andrea. *Re-imagining the Museum: Beyond the Mausoleum*. London and New York: Routledge, 2003. Print.

CHAPTER 15

Poetry and Globalized Cities
A Material Poetics of Canadian Urban Space

Jeff Derksen

Globalization and urbanization have not simply coincided in intensification over the last forty years, but they have heated up together, merging and colliding with one another to an extent that we can neither distinguish them as isolated processes nor cleanly separate them in spatial scale. In this nexus, cities are cast into a new set of cultural, economic, and affective relations. The urban has gained a new dynamism and is taking on pressure in both positive and troubling ways. Positively, cities have become the sites where the contradictions of global capital are most visible and, as a result, they have also become the sites where struggles for rights and claims to common wealth (which was previously figured at a national level) are acted out in more and more intense and creative ways. The negative effect has been the emergence of a competitive cities system with an economic imperative that resembles a rescaled version of the global competitiveness in which states positioned themselves. Through governance, planning, and branding, cities are now globalized in new ways as they vie for the fleeting and nervous capital that is looking for new nesting places after the economic crisis.

This emphasis on cities in globalization has curiously tended to obscure the role of the state. The state is as active in the world system and in our lives, even in our bedrooms, to invoke Pierre Elliott Trudeau, as it ever was, yet globalization may no longer be as "statecentric" as it was in the recent past. Given the relationship of the global, the national, and the urban (which is nonetheless mediated by the state to some degree), it is curious that, as Richard Cavell puts it, "The notion that Canadian literature has a deep and abiding relationship with the land has governed criticism of Canadian literature (generally thematic, but also more avowedly theoretical) for the last half century, largely to the exclusion of critiques relating to literary systems as urban institutions ..." (14). Cavell's carefully accurate statement identifies the belated emergence of an urban-focused criticism of Canadian literature, but it is also crucial to note that this criticism, governed by the occlusion of the urban, developed over the same period of global urbanization. Both Atwood's exemplar *Survival* and D. G. Jones's *Butterfly on Rock* appear in the early 1970s, just at the moment that Canada's urban population begins a climb that continues today, and both appear just prior to the intensification of urbanization globally.[1]

However, this turn to the urban in Canadian criticism does not imply a simple shift down from the nation as the scale of cultural imagination. This national frame has been recently troubled by the critical perspectives driven by globalization and transnationalism, which are understood to have refigured the nation and altered nation-space and its discourses of identity and senses of belonging. This shift is also important in terms of an urban-based criticism in Canadian literature for, while land and place have been the material markers of a *national* criticism, these markers have been troubled by the construction of the nation in relation to the role of the state. The forceful cultural critiques of multiculturalism, of the exclusions of citizenship, and of governance aimed at Aboriginal peoples[2] were necessarily place-based and localized, but they also often bound the nation and the state (and their historical convergence) together in a productive manner. By emphasizing the urban, Canadian literary criticism brings new complexities of scale to the discourses of nation and identity. As well, belonging and exclusion are rescaled and brought into an expanded global space rather than being symptoms of the disintegration of the nation as a cultural and affective construct, or the desiccation of the state as a political actor. Cities are much more than global command posts for finance—or "global cities," as Saskia Sassen defined them—but they have subtly moved into the space that states so centrally occupied.

This critical mistiming of an urban literary criticism, which perhaps reflects our belated modernism, is also exacerbated when we consider that, as cities accumulated a new emphasis globally, a new relationship to the very things that Cavell identifies as central to our literary criticism—nature and land—was also emerging. From Rachel Carson's 1962 warning signal on the relationship of "nature and man" in *Silent Spring* through the ecological movements of the 1960s and the 1970s, nature was no longer figured as the passive backdrop for humans' (or a nation's) life, nor as an endless expanse of resources ready to be extracted and capitalized. More dramatically, geographer Cindi Katz argues that, in the 1970s, "the utilitarian presumptions that undergirded so much of the relationship to nature under capitalism hit their limits" ("Whose Nature, Whose Culture?" 46). Katz traces a shift from a paradigm of "extensive nature" to one of "intensive nature," in which nature ceased to be considered an "open frontier" for expansion and was an accumulation strategy through which capital regrouped to "plumb" nature ("Whose" 46). Within the Canadian cultural industry, the representational presumptions that linked land and identity have been disrupted by critiques of such geographical determinism, from the poststructuralist troubling of thematic criticism to the forceful unsettling that First Nations' land claims have on the legal, ethical, ideological, and cultural entitlements to the land. And once we consider the return to an economy based again on resource extraction and raw export, a *national* relationship to nature may well have shifted *thematically* from a garrison mentality to a pipeline mentality, from an imagined excess of space to an imagined endless supply of tar sand.[3]

But what the related dynamisms of the urban and globalization *and* the relationship to nature (or the "pastoral," to use a term Cavell brings in) demonstrate is that the global, the urban, and nature (or the rural) have become so entwined that they can no longer be thought of separately. Nor can they be thought of outside of the economic forces that link them. A recent real estate listing in Vancouver exemplifies the new intensification of capital, nature, and the urban: the sole remaining urban dairy in the Greater Vancouver region, which has operated since 1906, went on the market ("First time offered to the market in 105 years!" the description from Collier's International listing exclaimed) and was sold last year for $6 million (Nakhelh and Freyvogel 1; see also Ryan). The Avalon Dairy, the heritage-designated emblem of a time when the rural was a productive site outside of the urban, was described as a "Rare 1.26 acre residential development opportunity in east Vancouver" ("Historic"). Aside from yet another sign of the ceaseless euphoria of the real estate market in Vancouver, this shift of a profitable (and much loved) dairy to development lots reflects a shift in the economic emphasis that has intensified pressure on cities and real estate to be economic engines even as we become nostalgic for a localism based on, in this case, food production. This urbanization produces the nostalgia of local food (as food production is pushed farther outside cities) at the same time as it creates a "scarcity" of nature. Nature then is refigured as a limited resource that commands a price and intensifies it as a commodity: the proximity to parks, or the possibility of viewing the ocean or mountains from apartments adds to their price, and Vancouver, as a city branded with natural beauty due to such views, has housing prices among the highest in the world. Nature can never sleep in this figuration—it is always at work, producing beauty and surplus value.

As I have been arguing, together globalization and urbanization have reorganized the global political economy and restructured the very scales at which different kinds of political and economic activities are organized. Yet, this rescaling also poses a cultural problem within Canadian literary criticism. My proposition is therefore twofold. Firstly, *the urban* is not simply a scale, or a designation of a static space defined by density and infrastructure and patterns of living, but can better be understood as a dynamic process. As a process, the urban unleashes a representational problem within any artistic practice: How can city life, with all of its spatial practices and all of its modes of living, be represented? Beyond a question of complexity and difference, it is also an aesthetic, formal, and ideological question. Secondly, we live in the midst of a transformation of forms of the urban that dramatically alters our spatial practices and experience. This too troubles the representation of cities. This is not a demographic argument based on the dramatic growth of cities over the last forty years; rather, cities have changed in ways that reflect the uneven geography of globalization, which has re-spatialized both production *and* consumption globally. But cities have also been changed by a drift in cultural common sense influenced by neoliberal governmentality. As a result, many of the aspects of the "right to the city" and spatial justice that Henri Lefebvre raised in 1968, and which were inserted in the United Nation's *World Charter for the Human Right to the City*, are being recast. Rights to housing, rights to public space, rights to the imagination of the city, all have been fundamentally reopened. Margit Mayer outlines a trajectory of urban movements that provides a narrative for this overlapping of specific urban issues:

> The [urban] movements entered a new phase with the austerity politics of the 1980s. This politics initiated a global shift towards a neoliberal paradigm, which in its initial rollback phase grinded away at Keynesian-welfarist and social-collectivist institutions. This brought the so-called "old" social issues back onto the agenda of urban movements: increasing unemployment and poverty, a "new" housing need, riots in housing estates, and new waves of squatting changed the makeup of the urban movements, while local governments—confronted with intensifying fiscal constraints—became interested in innovative and cheap ways to solve their problems. (21)

To bring this analysis up to the moment, we recognize that not only have these *old* issues remained (and in some cases deepened), but the "creative city" paradigm has emerged as one of the "cheap ways" for cities to *appear* to address structural problems and to make themselves *appear* as a stable site for investment.[4] And the creative city paradigm enables cities to garner a high ranking in the livability rating of cities globally—a ranking that is based on lifestyle rather than social reproduction.[5] As a result, culture as an economic engine and artistic practices have been retooled in the life of the city. Canadian urban literary criticism has the challenge of keeping pace with these processes that trouble the representation of cities and urban life while maintaining an examination of scale in relation to the nation and the state.

TOWARD A MATERIAL URBAN POETICS

What can poetry bring to the complex of financialization, privatization, and governance that is now characteristic of the neoliberalization of the urban? And what role can poetry play in the contestation and renewed calls for the right to the city that have urgently sprung up in reaction? I will indicate several entry points that I hope can lead toward an identification of poetry's relationship to urban space, to spatial practices, and to the right to the city, a right that is spatial and cultural, but that is driven by an insistence on difference. My goal is to propose a schema that links modes of poetic representation to urbanism and urbanization, and to approach poetry as both a form of research and knowledge that can show us something about cities and the challenges they face and the opportunities they produce. To grasp poetry as a form of investigation and knowledge could assist us in getting at the very dynamism of urbanization, understood as a process that is as filled with the moments and events of everyday life, the life of the streets, and the deep levels of affect and engagement of the city, as it is fettered with neoliberal urban governmentality and its new spatial regime.

To lay a groundwork, I will address problems of artistic representation of the city, and of urban *imageability* that I believe arise out of a tension between our present moment of neoliberalism, in which urban space is configured according to the immediate needs of capital, and an earlier modernist spatial regime in which urban space was planned and rationalized. From there, I will turn to the problem and possibilities of the poetic representation of the urban through two recent books of poetry: Barry McKinnon's *In the Millennium*, which features two devastating serial poems that track the tearing of the urban fabric of a northern industrial hub city, Prince George, British Columbia; and *Triage*, by Cecily Nicholson, which mounts a critique of the neoliberal dismantling of modes of social reproduction in Vancouver, as well as raising a claim for the right to the city.

PROBLEMS IN SPATIAL REPRESENTATION

> Thus space participates in the same concrete-abstract tension as the commodity itself. Space is a rich, dialectical relation with both thing and process features.
>
> —Katherine Jones and Jeff Popke (117)

Henri Lefebvre's concept of space as a social product provides a useful and necessary starting point for analyzing spatial representation in poetry. Lefebvre rejected a static theory of absolute space in favour of a concept of social figuration. As Christian Schmid explains:

> (Social) space is a (social) product: in order to understand this fundamental thesis it is necessary, first of all, to break with the widespread understanding of space imagined as an independent material existing "in itself." Against such a view, Lefebvre, using the concept of the *production of space* posits a theory that understands *space* as fundamentally bound with social reality. It follows that space "in itself" can never serve as an epistemological starting point. Space does not exist "in itself"; it is produced. (28)

This social space is also laced into social time, and both are understood as social practices. But perhaps what is more unique, and more neglected, in Lefebvre's schema of space, is the role of language and the creative or poetic act: both are also understood as dialectically tied into the relationship of social thought and social action (Schmid 33). But even this model ties the energy of Lefebvre's thought into a system that does not adequately encounter the ceaseless dialectic of structure and event, of system and contradiction. In a dynamic structuralist movement that takes Roman Jakobson's poetic function of language and materializes it in urban processes—focusing on the life of the street and the possibilities of encounters—Lefebvre embeds the poetic act into the city as a moment both within and in excess of the system of the city. Lefebvre does not romanticize the street as a force and a site not fully tamed by the total administration of capitalism as it rescaled itself to the everyday, but rather he urges: "The urban space of the street is a place for talk, given over as much to the exchange of words and signs as it is to the exchange of things. A place where speech becomes writing. A place where speech can become 'savage' and, by escaping rules and institutions, inscribe itself on walls" (*The Urban* 19). I think we can recognize this statement in the residual analysis of May 68 and an acknowledgement of the Situationists as well as a belief in the lived over the structural. However, it is key that Lefebvre never simply falls on the side of the lived—he champions it, but only in a robust relationship to structural determinates. Language, and particularly poetry, *debanalizes* (to use a term from the Russian Formalists) urban experience: "Language in action and the spoken word are inventive: they restore life to signs and concepts that are worn down like old coins" (Lefebvre, *The Production* 139).⁶

Kevin Lynch's *The Image of the City* is a key conceptualization of the representation of urban space. Like Lefebvre, Lynch is concerned with the relationship of time and space, and how the city is never immediately or completely graspable, but is "a thing perceived only in the course of long spans of time" (1). Drawing some elements from Lefebvre's concept of space, Lynch addresses the temporal aspect of cities—how they evolve in space over time. For Lynch, the city is both a "temporal art" and a process. To catch this unfolding Lynch uses the term "imageability" to provide "a concept ... [that] does not necessarily connote something fixed, limited, precise, unified, or regularly ordered, although it may have these qualities" (1). Lynch's book grappled with the imageability of the urban before cities entered into an explosive period in the late 1960s when the temporal art of the city was shaken apart by the riots of the late sixties (student, anti-war, and race riots) and the state violence that cohered as a response. While Lynch's study developed out of North America's postwar urban expansion, it predates the intensified period of urbanization that globalization catalyzed. However, as Mayer's indication of the uneven temporality of urban issues illustrates, the problem of representing the city that Lynch identified and worked to provide a concrete approach for has been reanimated today. The temporality of cities today, and their image as a temporal art, are shaped by the creative destruction of the urban territory. The originator of the term "creative destruction," Joseph Schumpeter, has been cited by commentators on the left and the right for his description of what he determines as "the essential fact about capitalism" (83). Creative destruction itself is either lauded or critiqued as a process that "incessantly revolutionizes the economic structure *from within*, incessantly destroying the old one, incessantly creating a new one" (83; see also Peck and Tickell). Perhaps what makes this term so compelling is exactly its entanglement of violence and renewal, a process that holds both fear and possibility. But what creative destruction also does is push the economic deeper into all aspects of life, for it sets aside or brackets human agency by putting economic and therefore societal change in the hands of an *essential fact* of capitalism, in the hands of a law internal to an economic system. In this way creative destruction is both utopic and dystopic, as its celebration and critique from the right and the left of the political spectrum shows.

Globalized cities are caught in a series of contradictions that are continually produced from different scales and by the rollovers of creative destruction. These contradictions are a part of what Guy Baeten describes as "the twin processes of dystopianization and utopianization of the city in contemporary society" (45). Baeten dramatically argues that "The neoliberal urban revolution is often presented as a necessity rather than a choice: in a world of limited investment and limited amounts of 'creative people', cities have to do whatever is in their reach to attract a fair share of investment, high-tech industries and a well-educated workforce" (47). Cities therefore develop, on the one hand, "cultures of policy" and the demonization of poor neighbourhoods, and on the other hand, the utopian horizon of the "creative" or the "green" city produced by policy, innovation, and real estate as an eternal engine of the economy. But does not creative destruction prolong the contradictions embedded into the heart of our current models of cities—such as sustainability and a city oriented to a single creative class? And does not a contradiction arise in the city itself as an engine and site of collective human agency when such agency is suspended by economic laws internal to global capitalism?

Lefebvre's work suggests that a potential (if somewhat metaphorical) answer might be found in poetry, in the poetic act refigured as a spatial and social practice. In locating movement at the heart of Lefebvre's dialects, Schmid proposes: "At a general level, the fundamental dialectical figure in Lefebvre's work can be understood as the contradiction between social thought and social action, supplemented by the third factor of the creative, poetic act" (33). Within this framework, the poetic act is neither a resolution nor a sublation of the contradiction. Instead, as Schmid argues, "The contradiction tends toward its resolution, yet since the resolution does not simply negate the old contradiction, it also simultaneously preserves it and brings it to a higher level. Therefore, the resolution bears in it the germ of a new contradiction" (31).[7] In this way, the poetic act opens possibilities that cannot be contained within dialectical thought *and* within the city—it always produces "something else."[8]

An aesthetic or artistic question therefore arises within this relationship of creative destruction, the contradictions it produces, and the city. The question of the imageability of a process that does not reach resolution—or of urban conditions that are not resolved through governmentality or urban movements, to make the question material—shows both the limits of Lynch's proposition and the stakes of the representation of cities today. The limits to Lynch's important work are shown not only in the difficulty of grasping, mapping, or even codifying urbanism today, but in his emphasis on phases of city development rather than the alteration (destruction even) of the textures of urban space. Today, phases of urban change do not slide into one another, disorderly yet overlapping; instead, whole traces of past phases can be removed. A walk along almost any urban waterfront that has been redeveloped, or "revitalized," over the last ten years will reveal this phenomenon.

In place of the cognitive mapping and orderly cataloguing of the city by urban planners, the *imageability* of the city has passed over to artists whose aesthetic practices can grasp the contradictions and competing temporalities of urbanization. This transition suggests that urban planners have no plan for the city other than to strengthen the urban as an accumulation strategy, that their social imagination is limited to managing the inequities of the neoliberal city rather than working toward an equitable city. But on a productive aesthetic side, these questions suggest a shift in the *knowledge* of the city and the social and spatial act of representation.

TYPES OF TIME IN THE SPACE OF MCKINNON'S PRINCE GEORGE

In a detailed reading of Barry McKinnon's "Prince George 1" and "Prince George Core" from *In the Millennium*, time begins to assert itself dialectically in relation to space. For Lefebvre, as Schmid observes, space is always situated in relation to time: "*Space* stands for simultaneity, the synchronic order of social reality; *time* on the other hand, denotes the diachronic order and thus the historic process of social production" (29). The poems map or track, or better *imprint* the spatial reordering of the urban core of Prince George (what we might call its historic downtown) by forces seemingly outside of its influence. The downtown has been emptied of the potential for publicness, the core of the city dumped into disinvestment, and an urban fabric that emerged under another economic and political order torn apart. The poems describe an intersection of temporalities that defies a linear progression, or an urban evolution: the poems react to, document, and angrily point to the uneven temporal development of the city, its creative destruction. The types of diachronic stacking that unite or tie various utterances and images of the poem together do unfold over time in reading the poems, but time as both an effect and as a theme (semantic content) is key to these poems: time is both enacted and thematized.

Moved formally to this serial poem, which traces the unravelling of the fabric of downtown Prince George—the mill town that is in full disinvestment, recast to the point where real estate and a hopeful Starbucks in a hotel lobby cannot compete with the layers of urban poverty, overused social services, and the vacuum created by the loss of industrial jobs—the relationship of space as simultaneity and time as diachronic begins to give us a model of grasping an urban poetics. Time as a social process within capitalism and time as a material social determinate is represented in the poem. This tension *within time* is dramatically detailed in Marx's chapter on "The Working Day," *Capital*'s most affective section: "The worker needs time in which to satisfy his [sic] intellectual and social requirements, and the extent and the number of these requirements is conditioned by the general level of civilization. The length of the working day therefore fluctuates within boundaries both physical and social" (341). However, McKinnon's Prince George poems do not so much show the social contradictions *in* space that sediment over time; rather, the poems build a compelling trace of the social contradiction *of* space (to paraphrase Andy Merrifield on Henri Lefebvre's key concepts [see *MetroMarxism* 88]). Space, conceived in this way, is never neutral. McKinnon's poems are both diachronic and synchronic: they present us with serial images that are synchronic, yet the images accumulate to allow an urban process to cohere. The effects of the images accrue over time. In this way, they grapple with the imageability of urbanization even as they lament the loss of a particular *urbanism* as lived spatial and social practice*:*

>   what do *we* see   so clearly in its lack
>   to see   without image / articulation   — a reason
>   malls fill / downtown empties / history (capital / frontier
>   without   human hope: *this is the end*, we sing (crows peck
>   puke, buckles in the sidewalk / hole of asphalt, piles of blood (104)

And then the effect, spatial and social, of this process:

>   "everything must go".   so the shell is left — its last punch
>   through the wall — broken
>
>   windows
>
>   empty   *for lease* /
>   *for sale*
>   *the city*
>   *core* / (139)

And then McKinnon's poems point toward a cause, one that hinges on a pun between ecology and economy:

> what is left. brooding, landscapes / ravaged. trees — in many
> places gone. logging. bugs. stock piles — sense of world fast
> tracked for the last grab / *this is eco nomics* (142)

McKinnon gives us a dialectics of neoliberalism and urbanization in a material manner similar to Fredrick Engels's dialectics of industrialization and urbanism (Merrifield, *MetroMarxism* 88). If, for Engels, industrialization had produced a certain type of urbanization, now neoliberalism has created a different, equally distinctive form of urbanization and social reproduction. What is striking in this parallel is that Engels poetically sketched the shadows, the depths, the literal hellholes of "the great towns" of England as they were ascending, building themselves into industrial centres, whereas McKinnon is catching a great industrial town and hub city seemingly in its descent (at least from the economic perspective), facing an unsure future as it is caught in a shift in the economic regime of total urbanization.

Lynch's approach to the expanding modernist city cannot be mapped onto the neoliberal city: a tension exists between modernist modes of representation of urban space and emergent modes of representation of the spatial regime of the neoliberalized city. McKinnon sparks off this tension intertextually through references—and ways of seeing—that are in dialogue with the paradigmatic modernist text *Paterson* by William Carlos Williams. Williams provides a history of Paterson, New Jersey, through his rigorous imagist poetics; McKinnon begins "Prince George (Part One)" with the fragment, "a man in himself is a city," from Williams's "Author's note" to *Paterson*, "that a man in himself is a city, beginning, seeking, achieving, and concluding his life in ways which the various aspects of a city may embody—if imaginatively conceived—any city, all the details which may be made to voice his most intimate convictions" (xiv). Yet, the surety of "a man" and "a city," and the metaphor that joins the body and the city are unstable and fragment in McKinnon's text, even as the poem hangs off an autobiographical frame:

> the man, the city — what parts in
> the metaphor, this *way* of dreaming — is the heart a down
> town? ... (104)

The modernist trope of the city as a harmonious, integrated system, exemplified by Le Corbusier's city designs of rationalized spaces hinging on light, air, and greenery or pushed further into a metabolistic relationship by the Japanese Metabolists, is not applicable to the image of the city in *In the Millennium*. Nor does the social body, or a sense of urban collectivity, hold together in McKinnon's text:

>   *the they.*   the *who*, the *us* in the disintegrated
>   disintegration — nothing can be known; its own hopeless
>   statement — *the north / everywhere (but not revealed —*
>
>   in this   what? ... (106)

Whereas Williams could write tightly of "the city / the man, an identity—it can't be / otherwise—an / interpenetration, both ways" (4), the relationship between the "man" and "a city" (or in a less gendered model "a citizen" and "a city") in McKinnon is mediated, even distorted, by the economic: it is not unmediated interpenetration both ways.

But this imbalance is not so much between the city and citizen, for that affective relationship is very strong in these works—and in fact it is this dis-identification that is angrily badgered—but the imbalance between neoliberalism's creative destruction of the city and the actually existing city and the citizen. Neoliberalism gets between the city and the urban dweller, throwing the city into disinvestment and distorting the affective and lived relationship of urban dweller to the city. Williams's modernist model for a representation of the city breaks down through dis-identification with the neoliberalized city in McKinnon. Ironically, this dis-identification was to be the contradiction of modernist urban planning that fuelled the critique of such top-down planning, that the city would be separate from the human, that the rationalized city would allow no humanness. The power of the straight line in modernist planning was later understood as a dividing line that separated design from life, the body from architecture, and split the spheres of urban life. Out of this tendency springs Lefebvre's belief in the streets and everyday life, and his critique of the rationalization of the city and of the spatial determinates on life. This problematic, moved over to McKinnon's poems, makes it possible to consider them as a politicized lyrical counterpoint to the ascendance of the economic theory of value systemic to neoliberalism. Lyrical because the lyric subject is everywhere evident, but in a dialectical relationship to the absence of the human aspect of urban life. In this cold logic, the lived and even human aspect of the city is rationalized economically. Yet, McKinnon's lyricism has always troubled a secure lyric subject, the self-assured Cartesian subject in space. The Prince George poems in *In the Millennium* exteriorize this relationship and trouble the relationship of the citizen-subject and the city via a lyrical form: the poems struggle for a reconnection to *a relationship* with the city, but those spatial, affective, and lived relations are eroded by creative destruction as an essential fact of urbanism in our time.

TRIAGE: SOCIAL REPRODUCTION AND THE RIGHT TO THE CITY

Andy Merrifield, in his extremely engaging *Dialectical Urbanism*, arrives at the speculation that "perhaps, in the last instance, there is no authentic transcendence of the dialectic of urbanization and urbanism, no last instance. Perhaps instead, progressives need to find ways of incorporating struggle, conflict, and contradiction into a passionate and just urban life, secretly acknowledging that the way beyond the contradictions is working through them, not around them" (170). Cecily Nicholson's *Triage* represents such a working though social contradictions and the contradictions of urban space within the neoliberalized city. However, throughout the book, a more compelling and just urban life flashes out from *within*, or despite, the ways that social inequity is spatialized—specifically, while *Triage* moves between the global news of the day and very specific neighbourhood and community issues, the poems locate the ways that community, critique, and a form of social sincerity cohere in domestic and urban spaces. Often these spaces in the book—from rented rooms and apartments to the streets and to the tent village that the community in Vancouver's Downtown Eastside erected, maintained, and protected during the 2010 Winter Olympics. Looked at in relation to past urban movements, in the way proposed by Margit Mayer, "[s]uch places and zones of actual contradictions could be new starting points of formative utopian interventions" (54). While the interventions that populate *Triage* (and *Triage* as an intervention itself) are not utopian in a way that could be called idealist, they do forcefully locate the ways that community, critique, and a form of social sincerity cohere to bring another material alternative to the administered, homogeneous urban life that Lefebvre railed against in his urbanist writing.

> Successive bodies
> contingents of rioting hosts
>
> In the mean volunteer streets
> we need to find cover
> Flicker of a thin discursive film
>
> Unable to sit still multiplies
>
> Beneath hospital and holding cell windows
> parking lot vigils
>
> Warrior song bodies
> hushed in the headlines (Nicholson 20-21)

Alongside the difficulties of representing urban processes and spatial practices, the book troubles a politics of representation at a time when cities actively construct images (along with brands) of themselves that are designed to give the city a "strategic advantage" within the "competitive city" model of global urbanism. But, as Guy Baeten points out, in the neoliberalized city, poor neighbourhoods are figured as dystopic:

> The poor neighbourhood is neoliberalism's Other. It is the spatialized, embodied, and visualized dystopia of moral, economic, and social deviance, inhabited by benefit-addicted victims of social democracy, immersed in a subculture of poverty and violence, and ready for neoliberal experiment. (46)

Sadly this brutal characterization does parallel the characterization of Vancouver's Downtown Eastside in Canada's dominant media—and I'm careful to say *characterization* rather than the actually existing neighbourhood—for nowhere in Vancouver are both urban politics and the politics of representation more fraught and possessed of more human stakes.[9] However, *Triage* confounds a dialectic of dystopia and utopia in terms of representation precisely by resisting the transcendence that Merrifield warns of—there is no "last instance" in *Triage*, but rather a working through of contradictions *of space* and the possibilities of resistance to spatial injustice and social exclusions.

I want to propose *social reproduction* as a theme through which space is socialized in this book—and socialized in a way that thoroughly dislodges the representation of "poor neighbourhoods." Building up, over time, in *Triage*, is both the temporality and spatiality of social reproduction. By focusing on this aspect of social reproduction, *Triage* swerves from a structuralist view and toward a messier, less predictable definition provided by Cindi Katz in her study of globalization and childhood:

> Social reproduction ... encompasses that broad range of practices and social relations that maintain and reproduce particular relations of production along with the material and social grounds in which they take place. It is as much the fleshy, messy, and indeterminate stuff of everyday life as it is a set of structured practices that unfold in dialectical relation to production, with which it is mutually constitutive and in tension. (*Growing* x)

Katz's notion of social reproduction gives the temporal and spatial elements of *Triage* both a spatial materiality and a sense of social time. Katz writes: "If the political-economic aspect of social reproduction takes place in some combination of the household, the market, the workplace, 'civil society', and the state, the relationship and balance among settings varies across time, space, class and nation, amongst other things" (*Growing* 19). The other things that forcefully emerge in *Triage* are race and gender, but these are never separate from spatial struggles.

Reading with the concept of social reproduction in mind, the book takes on a stronger sense of the determinates and struggles embedded into everyday life and into spatial relations. For instance, consider how this cluster (unfairly grabbed out of the serial poem, "Service") negotiates the household (domestic space), the state, and poverty:

> Husband's rent check
> Welfare says it's domestic (prolly a crack thing)
>
> Food bank's a long commercial walk
> past Flowers and fresh meat
> for cardboard boxes re-sealable bags (20)

Or how another poem, "on scale," presses the most necessary and intimate issues—the domestic and housing—through the logic of investment and space as speculation:

> hedge on par to capital
>
> injection recognized as ink
>
> reduced rates with coupons
>
> sanctuary future fade-proof record
> . . . .
>
> carbon bodies hardly warmed
> conditioning predictable
> costs and storms
>
> baseboard heater dash slippery liquor
>
> downturned mouths telling stories
> curved belly wordly
>
> believes her
>
> empty can ash on the rim
>
> increased cost of living decisions
>
> investment attention a portion between (26)

I have been emphasizing how social contradictions are not only reflected spatially in cities, but that social contradictions are *spatial*. This formulation never allows space to be neutral, but it emphasizes that space is a social practice that is shot through with the textures of social relations. In *Triage*, contradiction is worked *through* thematically and viscerally, but also syntactically. In the very linguistic texture of the poems syntax collapses or is compressed so that ideologically competing discourses clash up against each other as if syntax can represent the spatial struggle within the city. For instance, consider the syntactic collapses in the poem, "appropriate":

> Whereas therefore zoning amendments allow for existing development
> to expand uses without it pre-empting overall zones review slate stand
> to protect place ... les murs ont des ailes ... letters proud sponsors online
> intent paper participant fees forfeited in this timely application process
> software dial tones are excise consigning submit neatly and proper files
> for the complete document entry system regard claims when encounter
> information hour body language answer awfully dark employment rebel
> populace downtown blue north metropolis special care string through air
> return with receipts awake wide narrow corridor cold hard construction
>
> take it
> from my mouth (27)

The appropriated "appropriate" language of an administered life (forms, timely applications, etc.) thickens in this poem, but it also hits up against a "rebel populace" and bodies that do not submit neatly.

Lastly, I want to examine how *Triage* makes a claim to the city through notions of social justice, collectivity, and collective action. Writing in 1969, Lefebvre, working out the relationship of agency and structural determinations at the level of the city, arrives at the idea of the "right to the city." This right, which can be universal (indeed it is now picked up by *World Charter for the Human Right to the City*, which declares that "the Human Right to the City is both an individual and a collective right of the city's inhabitants, especially protecting and serving members of vulnerable and disadvantaged groups") migrates as an idea or a claim, and gets picked up and made particular again in a place-based politics.[10] Liette Gilbert and Mustafa Dikec give us this expansive definition:

> The right to the city, or what Lefebvre also referred to as the right to urban life, is a claim upon society rather than a simple claim to territorial affiliation. For Lefebvre, the urban is not limited to the boundaries of a city, but includes the social system of production. Hence the right to the city is a

claim for the recognition of the urban as the (re)producer of social relations of power, and the right to participate in it. (254)[11]

This right to participate politically and imaginatively, and collectively in the city is asserted throughout *Triage*. As moments of social solidarity, as acts of protest and contestation, and as a deep sense of affective alliances based in social justice, this assertion or right counters the neoliberal urban regime, which replaced a shared civic *humanism* (in the larger sense, but also in terms of social welfare) with a form of revanchism that emphasizes ownership as the entry point to rights. It is difficult to express how deeply this idea runs in Vancouver—a city that had a serious discussion across all levels of governmental, civic, and public life about whether renters deserved to live in the Olympic Village—as renters would drive away buyers for the troubled development. The poem, "Today at tent village," gives a visceral sense of the very type of community work that counters such spatial politics:

> We have to take back the land
>
> The Russian Media wants to talk to someone
>
> I love Vancouver
>
> I'm going to the Women's Centre
>
> We need some reading material
> We need some wood
> We need some bricks
>
> Once we unite they cannot bend us
> They're not going to walk over us (61)

Against this new politics of a spatial divide, *Triage* invokes the potential for, or the struggle for, a just city and a city of belonging and dwelling (rather than ownership, "enjoyment," and speculation).

Mustafa Dikeç describes how Lefebvre's right to the city extends beyond the notion of access to the city:

> The right to the city, therefore, is not simply a participatory right but, more importantly, an enabling right, to be defined and refined through political struggle. It is not only a right to urban space, but to a political space as well, constituting the city as a space of politics. Urban citizenship, in this sense, does not refer to a legal status, but to a form of identification with the city, to a political identity. The construction of this identity through political struggle is enabled by another right—the right to difference. (1790)

Can we then rethink poetry's engagement with various forms of difference in terms of the right to the city? This would imagine poetry as a spatial practice and as a form of critique as well as an aesthetic representational tool of the urban.

EPILOGUE

The poetry of both Barry McKinnon and Cecily Nicholson tests the manner in which we look to language to represent space and social relations. Both of these writers reflect an urban poetics that is an act of representation. However, theirs is a poetics that enters into the problematic of the representation of space by language while aiming to ignite a dialectic between space and language. Crucially, both space and language are understood as signifying processes that are social and that are both informed by and productive of social relations and ideological textures. The city, rather than being seen or understood as a totality that one can cognitively map, view with surety, or grasp within a temporal moment, is imagined as a series or ensemble of processes that are instigated and altered across a varied spatial scale. McKinnon's Prince George is born out of an uneven temporality as economic and civic imperatives shift and the textures of urban space alter—a creative destruction of the city is felt materially and lived locally, but the city is inevitably tied into other trajectories. While McKinnon cannot inhabit the position that Williams tries to in relation to Paterson, the two cities may be woven closer together than they were in the 1940s and 1950s when Williams was writing his investigation of the local. Likewise, the space of Vancouver in Nicholson's *Triage* is pushed and pulled by local governance, dreams for the city by the global elite, and by the resistance and imagination of those who fight for a more spatially and socially just city. The rippling of processes, power, and resistance from the streets to speculative finance (or across a "scalar dynamic," as the geographers would say) is what produces urban textures. This dynamic makes the urban wonderfully compelling, dense with power relations, and famously hard to represent. What both of these writers pose, in various ways, is the question: Can we read the production of space and the transformation of cities in the long neoliberal moment through poetic strategies of representation? This question productively places poetry as an urban texture and as a spatial practice.

NOTES

1. David Harvey has located the early 1970s as a moment for the end of modernism and the intensification of urbanism globally (see *The Urban Experience* and *The Condition of Postmodernity*) and the beginning of the neoliberal experiment (see *A Brief History of Neoliberalism*). Henri Lefebvre's *The Urban Revolution*, in which he identifies an integrated system of "total urbanization," is published in French in 1970 (it arrives in English in 2003).
2. Glen Coulthard argues that "prior to 1969 federal Indian policy was unapologetically assimilationist, now it is couched in the vernacular of 'mutual recognition'" (438).
3. In "Hardheaded Socialism Makes Canada Richer Than the U.S.," Stephen Marche identifies resources as one of the major sources of our economic position: "The Alberta tar sands—an environmental catastrophe in waiting—are the third-largest oil reserves in the world, and if America is too squeamish to buy our filthy energy, there's always China. We also have softwood lumber, potash and other natural resources in abundance." The uneven development of capitalism at the present moment has seemingly brought us to the beginning of the twentieth century. From this perspective, at least our "high-tech" future is still on the horizon. Nortel? RIM?
4. See my *How High Is the City, How Deep Is Our Love* for a critique of Richard Florida's creative city model and for a discussion of the ways that affect has become intertwined with urban policy.
5. *The Economist* magazine produces an influential livable cities ranking. In 2012 "Melbourne has been adjudged the world's most livable city, ahead of Vienna and Vancouver" ("Livability Ranking"). While this list is often reported as being a universal ranking of cities (for instance, see "Vancouver, Calgary, Toronto among Most 'Livable' Cities"), *The Economist*'s rankings are only of what they consider "business centres." Dhaka is last, at place 140, "though," they remark, "it would probably come above the likes of Baghdad and Kabul, which were not considered business centres." Also see, The International Making Cities Livable Council (www.livablecities.org), which hands out a series of design awards based on their criteria for livability.
6. Lefebvre is being canny here as well in his use of the coin as a symbol of renewal. For Marx, designated money, and coins in particular, act as slippery signs that carry arbitrary meaning—meaning that can change and can be in need of renewal. Very poetically, Marx notes, "[f]or a coin, the road from the mint is also the path to the melting pot" (222). Marx uses this proverb to point to the split in money, in coins, of their "real content" (i.e., the valuable metal) and their "nominal content" (222-23): from there he devotes the bulk of a page to the wear of coins in the circulation of commodities.
7. Schmid also argues that "[i]n Lefebvre's opinion a contradiction when sublated does not reach its true final state or destination but its transformation—it is overdone, but at the same time also preserved and further developed in keeping with this twofold determination" (31). Lefebvre's work is notable for its alterations, and its plurality of positions, contradictions, one might even say, productively. For example, in *The Production of Space* he writes: "The task confronting us is not to speculate on an ambiguity but rather to demonstrate a contradiction in order to resolve it, or, better, in order to show that space resolves it" (137).
8. For instance, see *The Production of Space*, 129.
9. The neighbourhood, the Downtown Eastside, is not a passive object of representation, but is extremely active in representational politics—a politics that focuses on neighbourhood issues but which are rights-based and which build a critique of both City of Vancouver policies, but also engage and foster a highly informed and acute critique of issues associated with the neoliberal city—particularly gentrification.

Through the Downtown Eastside Neighbourhood Council (DNC), the neighbourhood also demands the right to self-determination and participatory democracy. See, the DNC-sponsored newspaper: <http://dnchome.wordpress.com/dteast/>. For a useful overview of how the dominant media has figured the DTES, see Sommers and Blomley.
10 *The World Charter for the Human Right to the City* has its roots in The Habitat International Coalition, which first met in Vancouver in 1976. See "World Charter."
11 Very productively, the "right to the city" spatializes rights instead of embedding them in the citizen—this has implications for "people without papers"—and it has implications for an understanding of spatial justice.

WORKS CITED

Baeten, Guy. "The Uses and Deprivations of the Neoliberal City." *Urban Politics Now: Re-imagining Democracy in the Neoliberal City*. Rotterdam: NAi, 2008. 44-57. Print.

Cavell, Richard. "An Ordered Absence: Defeated Topologies in Canadian Literature." *Downtown Canada: Writing Canadian Cities*. Ed. Justin D. Evans and Douglas Ivison. Toronto: U of Toronto P, 2005. 14-31. Print.

Coulthard, Glen. "Subjects of Empire: Indigenous People and the 'Politics of Recognition' in Canada." *Contemporary Political Theory* 6 (2007): 437-60. Print.

Derksen, Jeff. *How High Is the City, How Deep Is Our Love*. Vancouver: Fillip, 2010. Print.

Dikec, Mustafa. "Justice and the Spatial Imagination." *Environment and Planning* A 33.10 (2001): 1785-1805. Print.

Gilbert, Liette, and Mustafa Dikec. "Right to the City: Politics of Citizenship." *Space, Difference, Everyday Life: Reading Henri Lefebvre*. Goonewardena et al. 250-63. Print.

Goonewardena, Kanishka, Stephan Kipfer, Richard Milgrom, and Christian Schmid, eds. *Space, Difference, Everyday Life: Reading Henri Lefebvre*. New York: Routledge, 2008. Print.

Harvey, David. *A Brief History of Neoliberalism*. Oxford: Oxford UP, 2005. Print.

———. *The Condition of Postmodernity*. Oxford: Blackwell, 1990. Print.

———. *The Urban Experience* Baltimore. Baltimore: Johns Hopkins UP, 1989. Print.

"Historic Vancouver Dairy Up for Sale." *CBC News British Columbia*. Canadian Broadcasting Corporation. 29 Apr. 2011. <http://www.cbc.ca/news/canada/british-columbia/story/2011/04/29/bc-avalon-dairy-for-sale.html>. 7 July 2012.

Jones, Katherine T., and Jeff Popke. "Re-envisioning the City: Henri Lefebvre, Hope VI, and the Neoliberalization of Urban Space." *Urban Geography* 31.1 (2010): 114-33. Print.

Katz, Cindi. *Growing Up Global: Economic Restructuring and Children's Everyday Lives*. Minneapolis: U of Minnesota P, 2004. Print.

———. "Whose Nature, Whose Culture?" *Remaking Reality: Nature at the Millennium*. Ed. Bruce Braun and Noel Castree, New York: Routledge, 1998. 45-62. Print.

Lefebvre, Henri. *The Production of Space*. Trans. Donald Nicholson-Smith. Oxford: Blackwell, 1991. Print.

———. "The Right to the City." *Writings on Cities*. Ed. and trans. Eleonore Kofman and Elizabeth Lebas. Cambridge, MA: Blackwell, 1996. 147-59. Print.

———. *The Urban Revolution*. Trans. Robert Bononno. Minneapolis: U of Minnesota P, 2003. Print.

"Livability Ranking: Australian Gold." *Economist.com*. *The Economist* 14 Aug. 2012. <www.economist.com/blogs/gulliver/2012/08/liveability-ranking> 12 Dec. 2012.

Lynch, Kevin. *The Image of the City*. Cambridge: MIT P, 1960. Print.

Marche, Stephen. "Hardheaded Socialism Makes Canada Richer than the U.S." *Bloomberg.com*. 15 July 2012. <http://www.bloomberg.com/news/2012-07-15/hardheaded-socialism-makes-canada-richer-than-u-s-.html>. 19 July 2012.

Marx, Karl. *Capital*. Vol. 1. Trans. Ben Fowkes. London: Penguin, 1976. Print.

Mayer, Margit. *Social Movements in the (Post-)Neoliberal City*. Civic City Cahier 1. London: Bedford, 2010. Print.

McKinnon, Barry. *In the Millennium*. Vancouver: New Star Books, 2009. Print.

Merrifield, Andy. *MetroMarxism: A Marxist Tale of the City*. London: Routledge, 2002. Print.

———. *Dialectical Urbanism*. New York: Monthly Review, 2002. Print.

Nakhleh, Sam, and John Freyvogel. "Avalon Dairy Lands." Colliers International. Vancouver, BC. pdf file. Web. 15 Jan. 2013.

Nicholson, Cecily. *Triage*. Vancouver: Talon, 2011. Print.

Peck, Jamie, and Adam Tickell. "Conceptualizing Neoliberalism, Thinking Thatcherism." *Contesting Neoliberalism: Urban Frontiers*. Ed. Helga Leitner, Jamie Peck, and Eric S. Sheppard. New York: Guilford, 2007. 26-50. Print.

Ryan, Denise. "Historic Avalon Dairy in East Vancouver Sold for $6 million." *Vancouver Sun* 23 Dec. 2011. Web. 7 July 2012.

Schmid, Christian. "Henri Lefebvre's Theory of the Production of Space: Towards a Three-Dimensional Dialectic." Goonewardena et al., 27-45. Print.

Schumpeter, Joseph A. *Capitalism, Socialism, and Democracy*. London: Routledge, 1994. Print.

———. "The Worst Block in Vancouver." *Every Building on 100 West Hastings*. Ed. Reid Shier. Vancouver: Vancouver Art Gallery/Arsenal Pulp, 2002. 18-58. Print.

"Vancouver, Calgary, Toronto Among Most 'Livable Cities.'" *CBC News Canada*. Canadian Broadcasting Corporation. 15 Aug. 2012. <www.cbc.ca/news/canada/story/2012/08/15/most-livable-cities-top-ten-economist.html>. 22 Dec. 2012.

Williams, William Carlos. *Paterson*. New York: New Directions, 1992. Print.

"World Charter for the Right to the City." *Hic-net.org*. Habitat International Coalition. 27 June 1995. <http://www.hic-net.org/document.php?pid=2422>. 23 Dec. 2012.

AFTERWORD

Endless Material
The Future of Things in Canada

Thomas Allen and Jennifer Blair

As a "state of the field" look at material culture studies from the perspective of Canadian scholars, *Material Cultures in Canada* explores the question of the limits of the material object—of what counts as an object today and of what it means to conceive of and set about researching a certain object or collection of things. In the Introduction to this book we highlighted the route that contemporary material culture studies has taken from Appadurai's analysis of the role of things in shaping culture (which set this field on its path as a distinct area of critical inquiry) to recent scholarship that focuses on matter as a way of acknowledging the importance and vitality of the non-human world. The past decade has witnessed the confluence of ecocriticism, actor-network theory, new materialist philosophy, and anticolonialism within material culture studies. The effects of this mixing of scholarly concerns and practices through and beyond this field are significant—in fact, many of them are likely yet to be realized. Our book serves as one indication that at the current moment much of what drives material culture studies is this interest in exploring the shifting boundaries of the material world. Many of the chapters in this book also highlight the fact that requisite to this project is an assessment of critique's own limits when it comes to understanding matter and its influence on social life and physical worlds. Rather than present a particular answer to the question: What is material culture studies in Canada now?, this book highlights the dynamic tensions at the heart of the field. Each of the three parts of this book troubles the assumption that material objects are discrete, knowable entities in the world. Even those chapters in Part I that emphasize the persistence of materiality do so in ways that recognize the dissolution of objects into broader social, symbolic, and environmental contexts. The beaver, for example, is less a species of animal than it is a series of humanizations and nationalizations; what's more, as Berland's chapter also points out, the beaver is inseparable from the environment it inhabits. And yet at the same time, beavers are animals—they are non-human beings, despite the many ways in which humans have given meaning to them and organized their own lives (not to mention economic systems and political domains) in relation to them.

If there is an interest in exploring the boundaries of materiality—especially the tendency for things to disaggregate and scatter across different networks, institutions, imaginaries, economies, and sometimes non-human domains—then the impetus for this work seems to be to ascertain the best and most ethical roles that human inquiry, debate, and judgment have to play within (and as part of) material worlds. In other words, the goal of scholarly work in this area is not only to acquire more information, more understanding, about objects. Instead, at stake in this question of whether things are singular or multiple, and in the related question of how much of material culture remains outside of any human capacity to know and affect it, is the potential for humans to do better with the capacity we have to act within and upon matter. Increasingly, topics like democracy, public culture, political expression, and civic engagement arise in material cultures scholarship. Economics, too, has returned with a new kind of vigour and urgency, inspiring scholars to revisit more traditionally Marxist approaches to materialism. All in all, while material culture studies has come to recognize that the future of things is not entirely under the purview of human knowledge and control, it is still the case that the future of some things—things of human value and/or things that have a striking impact on the world of humans—will benefit from the attention of scholars who can present critical arguments about how such things are affected by people and what the outcome of these interactions might be.

This emphasis on the capacity for action within material cultures scholarship in Canada comes in part from the increasingly urgent discussion surrounding the management of natural resources by private companies and governments, especially with regard to Canada's rush to become a "big oil" nation. The widespread concern over Canada's identity that this strategic direction has inspired can be seen in the interdisciplinary Petrocultures conferences that were hosted by the University of Alberta in 2012 and by the McGill Institute for the Study of Canada in 2014. As the conference organizers indicate, Canada's emergence as "an energy superpower" has had far-reaching effects on Canadian life and raised a multitude of political and ethical concerns.[1] Notably, several of the scholars who took part in these conferences are also some of Canada's foremost experts in material culture studies. This includes one of our contributors, Mark Simpson, and also Imre Szeman, who, along with Sheena Wilson, runs the Petrocultures research cluster at the University of Alberta. These scholars, among others, demonstrate the value of a material cultures approach to the critique of resource management.

The urgency of fuel industry–based environmental concerns has been highlighted by recent debates over two proposed oil pipelines: Keystone XL and Northern Gateway. Both of these projects have raised issues of cultural nationalism and Canadian identity in relation to the material environment. In the case of Keystone XL, which would transport material from Canada's tar sands to refineries in the Gulf Coast region of the United States, many Canadians have felt abashed to recognize that, upon comparing the responses generated within the two rival nations, it is American politicians and activists who have raised the most steadfast objections to the pipeline on environmental grounds. Canadians are used to thinking of themselves as more environmentally conscious than their southern neighbours, a theme made clear in classic texts of Canadian literature such as Atwood's *Surfacing*. Keystone XL thus raises Canadian anxieties about national identity on two fronts, first by casting Canadians in the role of despoilers of the environment, and second by reiterating Canada's position as a supplier of raw materials and resources to the economy of the United States, a position historically associated with the dynamic of colonial exploitation.

Enbridge's equally contentious Northern Gateway proposal would run a pipeline from Bruderheim, Alberta, to Kitimat, British Columbia, at which point the material extracted from Canada's tar sands would be loaded onto tankers for export across the Pacific via the Douglas Channel. In some ways, this proposal epitomizes Canadians' desire to escape their historical relationship with the United States by opening routes to new trading partners. The circulation of material substances drawn from the earth and propelled through vast engineering projects and into the networks of the global economy thus exemplifies how our interactions with the object world can become bound up in urgent and competing political agendas, in this case differing visions of cultural nationalism.

News and commentary on both of these projects has appeared frequently in the Canadian media in the past year, and the word "pipeline" can be guaranteed to incite extreme reactions from people on all sides of the political spectrum. Yet, curiously, it has taken a long time for those of us who engage with that media to fully understand what material is to be transferred through these pipelines. Diluted bitumen, or "dilbit," is now considered to be the most accurate of terms for the viscous petroleum substance that is separated from the sand and then dissolved through other products (such as light crude, gas, and synthetic polymers) that are added in order to facilitate the flow of the material in a pipeline. Some of the signifiers that have been used for this product are as euphemistic as "heavy crude," which suggests that the material is "heavy crude oil." Enbridge uses this one in its Line 9 pipeline reversal and expansion project application.[2] In some cases, however, any association with the word "oil" is strategically avoided. For example, following the Pegasus pipeline spill in Mayflower, Arkansas, on 29 May 2013, ExxonMobil was exempted from any obligation to pay into the US Oil Spill Fund because its pipeline was transferring dilbit (from Canada) and not "oil."[3]

Representations of the environment the Northern Gateway pipeline would traverse have also caused some controversy. Enbridge has been widely criticized for its misleading explanations of its Northern Gateway project. In one notorious example, an animated video showing the route of the pipeline erased all of the islands in the Douglas Channel to make it appear as though the tankers carrying the bitumen would have an open water straightaway to the ocean, rather than the complex, meandering route in narrow waterways around large bodies of land that ships must in fact navigate before arriving at the Pacific.[4]

In addition to these debates about accurately understanding the physical materials, territories, and routes that play such a key role in tar sands development, there are other interesting concretizations of immaterial entities. We began writing this Afterword in the spring of 2014 as the Canadian government was about to decide whether or not to approve the Northern Gateway pipeline. According to several articles published at that time, the decision "loomed" as though it was itself a kind of object about to hit us (or some of us). Anticipating the announcement of the decision, we felt as though we should write faster, before the conditional future "woulds" and "coulds" and "possibilities" concretized into "wills" and "cans" and "likelihoods." When is an oil spill a likelihood? What are its material and spatial limits? What material effects does it produce? These are the sorts of questions that have been put to Enbridge in regard to the Northern Gateway project, but of course they are not new questions, and if Canadians feel an increased sense of urgency about them, this is the result of placing national affiliation over other relations that inform resource consumption. There is, of course, a history of political struggle over pipelines, but, curiously, cases like Ken Saro-Wiwa's fight against petroleum development in Nigeria rarely get raised in discussions about the Northern Gateway pipeline, the Keystone XL, or others. Where does Canada fit in this legacy of pipeline development and resistances to it? Rob Nixon discusses the life and work of Saro-Wiwa and his son, Ken Saro-Wiwa Jr., in the "Pipedreams" chapter from his well-known book *Slow Violence and the Environmentalism of the Poor*. Addressing the futurity of the situation in a global context, the chapter ends with a comment made by a Mongolian leader upon the discovery of oil in his territory: "[W]e don't want to become another Nigeria" (127). Nixon's book focuses on "oil minorities," and one wonders about who will count as the "minorities" in the extraction and distribution of material from Canada's tar sands. While First Nations peoples in Canada are often cited as those who experience the adverse effects of tar sands development because it's their land that is immediately affected, Rita Wong reminds us that this "prominent example of environmental racism and contemporary colonization" does "not stop with these communities, as the flow of water [polluted by the tar sands] continues, and the massive contribution to global warming knows no borders" (212). In what ways might it be relevant to ask how Canada might become another Nigeria? The looming decision piqued public interest and perhaps mobilized some increased action around the case. For some stakeholders who have long been involved in fighting Northern Gateway, however, the decision does not qualify as a "crisis event," to use Nicole Shukin's term, in the project's timeline. The Haisla First Nation launched a legal case against the pipeline back in January 2014, electing to take their issues with the project through the court system. Others waited until the Supreme Court decision on the Tsilhqot'in First Nation title claim, which was made at the end of June, before going to the courts.

As expected, the pipeline was given the go-ahead with the recommendation that Enbridge meet the 209 conditions outlined by the Joint Review Panel in its assessment of the project.[5] Soon after, Eden Robinson published an article in the *Globe and Mail* called "How Gateway Stokes a Simmering Fury among B.C. Natives" reminding readers that "If Enbridge has poked the hornet's nest of aboriginal unrest, then the federal Conservatives, Stephen Harper's government, has spent the last few years whacking it like a piñata. Their Omnibus budget bills gutted everything from our education to our sovereignty and (yes, you are reading this correctly) our right to clean drinking water." How, one wonders, does dilbit's material ambiguity compare with the public's lack of knowledge about the omnibus bills? What would a material cultures-based analysis offer an understanding of the Canadian government's new favourite way to make legislation? Robinson concludes her article by suggesting that the government is sidestepping its own obviously central role in land claims negotiations by turning the task of resolving such claims over to Enbridge. "If the Northern Gateway Pipeline fails to be built," she writes, "history will say it was partly because Enbridge failed to lobby the First Nations of British Columbia early or intensely enough. But the Harper government's role in this debacle will not be forgotten, and, whatever the outcome, its legacy will be an entrenched native antipathy to any Conservative agenda." In such examples where the government abdicates its right and responsibility to govern—to make decisions, negotiate, ascertain rights to territory, defend already established constitutional and other legal rights, and legislate accordingly—the necessity of understanding the nature of law, of judgment, in relation to material culture seems ever more pressing.

It is no wonder, then, that material culture studies has moved increasingly toward a discussion of matter in the context of the formation of publics, the nature of debate, and the function of democracy. Every chapter in this collection can be said to ask and respond to the question of what social and cultural critique is, what function it has in society, and what roles people can have in charting material futures—from Wong's consideration of the politics of water (pertinent to our pipeline example, Wong highlights the fact that in the oil sands "producing one barrel of oil poisons roughly four barrels of freshwater") to Shukin's assessment of representations of climate change in the North. What is especially remarkable about such discussions is their turn to consider not just public expression *about* material culture, but also *as* material culture. This approach is evident throughout the book, and it is at the forefront of Michael Epp's analysis of the role of smiles in the theatre of war, Jeff Derksen's exploration of poetry's critique of neoliberal cities, and Simpson's reflections upon a music playlist. These works consider the material qualities and conditions of participating in public spheres alongside their assessments of the materiality of their selected objects.

Another indicator of this future of material culture studies is evident in Catriona Sandilands's recent essay "Acts of Nature: Literature, Excess, and Environmental Politics." This piece considers the potential for action—in this case action in a specifically ecopolitical context—in relation to questions about the ontological nature of human judgment and its position within culture and also the non-human environment. The question for Sandilands (as with Latour's discussion of democracy that we discussed in the Introduction) is not the extent to which objects are material or immaterial, or singular or heterogeneous entities, but instead how so-called "immaterial" things (like debates, decisions, omnibus bills—the word she uses most is "judgment") function ontologically and thus can benefit from a materialist approach. Drawing from Hannah Arendt's notion that works of art (and especially literature) constitute worlds that are separate from the ever-changing processes of nature, and acquire a unique "durability" in this sense, Sandilands makes the case for understanding the role of literature neither as a reflection of the environment nor as an avenue for articulating environmental concerns, but rather as a site of action, specifically of the action of forming opinions as part of a public.[6] Sandilands's essay is just one among several examples of recent scholarship that undertakes what we would call a "material cultures" analysis of public engagement. It insists upon understanding acts like judgment and debate, and the conditions in which they take place, as material things.

Where does this material action take place? Traditionally, any discussion of public culture raises the issue of the nation-state. For each of the things addressed in this Afterword—judgment, dilbit, pipelines, lands, laws—location is crucial. However, as Jeff Derksen writes in the concluding chapter in this collection, the shift in national culture represented by the emergence of a "pipeline mentality" can perhaps be understood and confronted most effectively in localities, which for a majority of Canadians means the city. Canada has become an increasingly urban nation in the twenty-first century. In 1951, 38 percent of Canadians lived in rural areas; by 2011, that number had dwindled to 19 percent.[7] In many respects, despite Canada's historic attachment to the rural landscape and the wilderness as sources of national identity, the city is now where Canadians encounter nature. And nature has been reconfigured by the new urbanism, so that, as Derksen puts it, nature "is refigured as a limited resource that commands a price" (303) whether in the form of organic dairy products or access to green space. Derksen's analysis of the "material urban poetics" that resists neoliberal paradigms such as "the creative city" helps us to see how our resistance to ecological destruction can be enacted through tactics of materialized language, language that affirms our commitment to the vibrancy, agency, and even the rights of the non-human world.

Derksen notes that the pipeline mentality replaces a previous concept of boundless space with a new vision of endless plenitude of energy flowing from the ground into pipelines and the global economy. His account of how a "material urban poetics" resists neoliberalism reveals how making critique material, as Sandilands suggests, can offer a similar plenitude, an endless resource for reasserting Lefebvre's "right to the city" through spatial and temporal practice. These material tactics of representation and memory produce a layered knowledge of the city, in the face of projects of urban "renewal" that erase the past to make way for gleaming new waterfronts and "arts districts" that carefully manage the interactions of citizens of different economic strata. In Derksen's analysis, then, it is poetry's attention to materiality as it extends across both space and time, geography and history, that makes it a resource as essential to critique as the pipeline of oil is to the neoliberal global economy.

As English professors, we are glad to embrace an argument that gives literature such an important role in charting the material interactions between people and their environments, between human and non-human life, between organic and inorganic agents. More broadly, we hope that Derksen's chapter provides a fitting conclusion to a collection of chapters that emphasizes the importance of representation in various media, from literary texts to visual art and music, in the project of rethinking our human relationship to the non-human world. Collectively, these chapters support and extend Derksen's description of representation as a material practice, one that asserts a right not only to the city, but to the nation and the planet. Even more than this, however, the creative materialism on display in these chapters attests to the potential of Canadian thinkers to counter the paradigm of resource extraction with a new material practice of our relation to that planet in which not only our rights, but those of other actors are acknowledged as well. Along with our right to the planet, does the planet have a right to us?

NOTES

1. "Petrocultures 2014," <http://petrocultures.com/?page_id=687>. 25 Aug. 2014.
2. See Martin Laplante's Letter of Comment to the National Energy Board: <https://docs.neb-one.gc.ca/lleng/llisapi.dll/fetch/2000/90464/90552/92263/790736/890819/958044/980216/969806/D71%2D3_%2D_Martin_Laplante_%2D_Letter_of_Comment_%2D_A3I8X9.pdf?nodeid=969807&vernum=-2>. The Line 9 project reverses the flow of crude from Sarnia, Ontario, to Montreal. Part of this project includes a proposal to expand the amount of material flowing through the pipeline from 240,000 to 300,000 barrels per today. See: <http://www.enbridge.com/ECRAI/Line9BReversalProject.aspx>.
3. See "Pegasus." See also the testimony by Rush D. Holt Jr. (representative for 12th District, New Jersey) about the Keystone XL project from the House Energy and Commerce Subcommittee on Commerce, Manufacturing, and Trade Hearing. Holt says:

   > We are talking about a pipeline with the capacity to transport 830,000 barrels per day of tar sands oil—one of the dirtiest energy sources on the planet—from the despoiled Boreal Forests of Alberta, Canada, through the central United States, over one of this country's most valuable underground aquifers, to Gulf Coast refineries where much of the oil and refined product will be exported to overseas markets.
   >
   > The tar sands oil that Keystone XL will transport is unbelievably, not oil for purposes of paying into the Oil Spill Liability Trust Fund, meaning that Canadian tar sands currently gets a free ride through U.S. pipelines. [...]

4 Enbridge's video can be seen here on the older (but still online) version of the website (now called the "legacy" site): <http://www.northerngateway.ca/project-details/route-video/>.

See also this article by Shawn Conner from the *Vancouver Sun* for an alternative depiction of the region by filmmaker Dave Shortt: <http://www.vancouversun.com/This+Enbridge+animation+shows+reality+Northern+Gateway+route+with+video/7114129/story.html>. Another interesting alternative can be found here: <https://www.youtube.com/watch?v=U3vxhnan_ZA>.

5 In 2009 a three-person Joint Review Panel was established by Environment Minister Jim Prentice and the National Energy Board. The panel's mandate was to consult with various stakeholders regarding the proposed Northern Gateway Project. According to the government's press release, "The public and Aboriginal groups are encouraged to bring their views on the Northern Gateway Project forward to the Joint Review Panel (the Panel)" (see Canadian Environmental Assessment Agency and the National Energy Board n. pag.). On 19 Dec. 2013 the Joint Review Panel recommended that the government approve the project provided that the 209 conditions it identified were met.

6 See also Michael Epp's discussions of the concept of "durability" in his special issue of the *Canadian Review of American Studies* (on the topic of "Durable Americas").

7 <http://www.statcan.gc.ca/tables-tableaux/sum-som/l01/cst01/demo62a-eng.htm>. 24 Sept. 2014.

WORKS CITED

Canadian Environmental Assessment Agency and the National Energy Board. "Joint Review Panel Established for the Northern Gateway Pipeline Project." News release. 20 Jan. 2009. Web. 5 July 2014. <http://www.neb-one.gc.ca/clfnsi/archives/rthnb/nws/ nwsrls/2010/nrthrngtwjrpstblshmnt-eng.pdf>.

Epp, Michael, ed. and introd. "Durable Americas." Spec. issue of *Canadian Review of American Studies/Revue Canadienne d'Etudes Américaines* 41.2 (2011): 125-276. Print.

Nixon, Rob. *Slow Violence and the Environmentalism of the Poor*. Cambridge: Harvard UP, 2011. Print.

"Pegasus Pipeline Spill: Unanswered Questions." *Oil Spill Intelligence Report* 36.23 (22 May 2013): 1. ProQuest. Web. 20 July 2014.

Robinson, Eden. "How Gateway Stokes a Simmering Fury among B.C. Natives." *Globe and Mail* 23 June 2014. Web. 20 July 2014.

Sandilands, Catriona. "Acts of Nature: Literature, Excess, and Environmental Politics." *Critical Collaborations: Indigeneity, Diaspora, and Ecology in Canadian Literary Studies*. Ed. Smaro Kamboureli and Christl Verduyn. Waterloo: Wilfrid Laurier UP, 2014. 127-42. Print.

CONTRIBUTORS

THOMAS ALLEN
Thomas Allen, associate professor of English at the University of Ottawa, is the author of *A Republic in Time: Temporality and Social Imagination in Nineteenth-Century America* (University of North Carolina Press, 2008), and has published articles on literary and cultural topics in journals such as *American Literary History* and *Raritan*. His current research project explores time and material culture through the lens of vitalism, with a particular focus on nineteenth-century America.

JESSA ALSTON-O'CONNOR
Jessa Alston-O'Connor holds an MA in art history from Concordia University and is a recipient of the Joseph-Armand Bombardier Canada Graduate Scholarship awarded by SSHRC. Her research focuses on multiculturalism, critical race theory, and cultural identity as they are constructed, addressed, and negotiated through Canadian artists and curatorial practices. Her thesis investigated the negotiation of Asian Canadian identities through Chinese and Japanese food culture in the art practices of Karen Tam and Shié Kasai. Jessa has a professional background as an arts writer and art educator in public art galleries across Canada. She currently works at the Vancouver Art Gallery.

JODY BERLAND
Jody Berland is professor in the Department of Humanities, York University. She is author of *North of Empire: Essays on the Cultural Technologies of Space* (Duke University Press, 2009), awarded the 2009 Canadian Communication Association G. G. Robinson Book Prize, and editor of *TOPIA: Canadian Journal of Cultural Studies* (www.yorku.ca/topia). She is co-editor of the books *Art and Theory; Theory as Art* (1996), *Capital Culture: A Reader on Modernist Legacies, State Institutions, and the Value(s) of Art* (2000), and *Cultures of Militarization* (2010). Recent articles include "The Musicking Machine" (2007); "Cat and Mouse: Iconographies of Nature and Desire" (2008); "Postmusics" (2008); "Animal and/as Medium: Symbolic Work in Communicative Regimes" (2009);

and "The Politics of the Exasperated: Arts and Culture in Canada" (2009). She was awarded the Association of Canadian Studies 2009 Award of Merit. Her current research project, "Virtual Menageries," is funded by SSHRC. See <www.virtualmenageriescom>.

SUSAN BIRKWOOD

Susan Birkwood is a full-time instructor at Carleton University (Ottawa), where she teaches Canadian and British literatures. She has worked extensively on late-eighteenth- and early-nineteenth-century accounts of Canada by British travellers, publishing on writers such as Anna Jameson. Her knowledge of exploration and travel literature informs her current research on Canadian historical fiction that seeks to engage with the colonial past and to bring particular regions, peoples, moments—and things—in this land's history to imaginative expression.

JENNIFER BLAIR

Jennifer Blair is an associate professor in the Department of English at the University of Ottawa. Her recent publications have appeared in *Deleuze and the Postcolonial* (Edinburgh University Press, 2010), *Studies in Canadian Literature*, and *Open Letter*. Jennifer also co-edited the essay collection *ReCalling Early Canada: Reading the Political in Literary and Cultural Production* (University of Alberta Press, 2005) along with Daniel Coleman, Kate Higginson, and Lorraine York. Jennifer's current project examines eighteenth- and nineteenth-century Canadian conversion narratives.

SHELLEY BOYD

Shelley Boyd is the Canadian literature specialist in the English Department at Kwantlen Polytechnic University in Surrey, British Columbia. Prior to moving to Vancouver in 2010, Boyd held a limited-term faculty appointment at McGill University, where she also served as the Max Bell postdoctoral fellow at the McGill Institute for the Study of Canada. Boyd's *Garden Plots: Canadian Women Writers and Their Literary Gardens* (McGill-Queen's University Press, 2013) examines the intersections of gardening and writing by cross-fertilizing garden history and theory with literary analysis. Boyd's previous publications have appeared in *English Studies in Canada*, *Essays on Canadian Writing*, *The Brock Review*, *Her Na-rra-tion: Women's Narratives of the Canadian Nation* (Canadensis Series, France), and in the award-winning edited collection *What's to Eat? Entrées in Canadian Food History* (McGill-Queen's University Press, 2009). Boyd is still searching for the perfect geranium for her balcony.

ALISON CALDER

Alison Calder is an associate professor in the Department of English, Film, and Theatre at the University of Manitoba, where she teaches Canadian literature and creative writing. She has written numerous articles on Canadian prairie literature and culture. She is the editor of critical editions of *Settlers of the Marsh* and *Over Prairie Trails*, both by Frederick Philip Grove, and also of a selection of poetry by Tim Lilburn, *Desire Never Leaves*. Her poetry collection, *Wolf Tree*, won two Manitoba Book Awards and was shortlisted for both the Pat Lowther Award and the Gerald Lampert Award.

MAY CHEW

May Chew is a doctoral candidate in cultural studies at Queen's University. Her SSHRC Joseph-Armand Bombardier-funded dissertation examines the uses of interactive and immersive technologies in Canadian national museums, and specifically how these technologies re-engage the material afterlife or detritus of colonial history. More broadly, her research interests centre on affect, technology, material culture, multiculturalism, and postcolonialism. Chew is also a curator, film lecturer, and filmmaker.

JEFF DERKSEN

Jeff Derksen is a poet and critic who works at Simon Fraser University. His writing on art and culture has appeared in *Springerin, Hunch, Open Letter, Poetics Journal*, and *XCP*, amongst other magazines. His book of essays *Annihilated Time: Poetry and Other Politics* (Talonbooks) was published in 2010, and *After Euphoria* (JPR Ringier) is forthcoming. Derksen's books of poetry include *Down Time, Dwell*, and *Transnational Muscle Cars*. Under the name Urban Subjects he collaborates with Sabine Bitter and Helmut Weber; they recently edited *Autogestion, or Henri Lefebvre in New Belgrade* (Fillip/Sternberg).

MICHAEL EPP

Michael Epp is an associate professor of English literature and public texts at Trent University. His current research focuses on the relations between violence and publics. Co-founder and current director of the public texts graduate program, and a former Winterthur fellow, his thinking works to bridge (or sometimes widen) the gap between the material and the cultural, in order to explore "the public thing" through its public things.

CAROLE GERSON

Carole Gerson is a professor in the Department of English at Simon Fraser University and a member of the Royal Society of Canada. She has published extensively on Canadian literary history and was a co-editor of the multi-volume project *History of the Book in Canada*, issued in both French and English. With Gwendolyn Davies, she co-edited *Canadian Poetry: From the Beginnings Through the First World War* (1994; rpt. 2010). Her ongoing research on early Canadian women writers has yielded two books on Pauline Johnson and many publications about other authors, including Susanna Moodie and L. M. Montgomery. She received the Gabrielle Roy Prize for Canadian criticism for her most recent book, *Canadian Women in Print, 1750-1918* (2010), which examines the work and context of Canadian women writers from a print culture perspective.

TANIS MACDONALD

Tanis MacDonald is the author of *The Daughter's Way: Canadian Women's Paternal Elegies* (Wilfrid Laurier University Press, 2012) and the editor of *Speaking of Power: The Poetry of Di Brandt* (Wilfrid Laurier University Press, 2006). In her work on memory in Canadian poetry, she has published scholarly work on Dennis Lee, Dionne Brand, Kristjana Gunnars, Sarah Klassen, Gregory Scofield, Jay Macpherson, P. K. Page, and Anne Carson; in her work on Canadian film, she has published articles on Terrance Odette's *Heater*, John Fawcett's *Ginger Snaps*, and Bruce McDonald's *The Tracey Fragments*. She is also the author of three books of poetry, most recently *Rue the Day* (Turnstone, 2008), and is associate professor in the Department of English and film studies at Wilfrid Laurier University.

CANDIDA RIFKIND

Candida Rifkind is an associate professor in the Department of English at the University of Winnipeg. She specializes in twentieth-century Canada, popular and leftist writing, and comics and graphic narratives. Her award-winning book, *Comrades and Critics: Women, Literature, and the Left in 1930s Canada*, was published by the University of Toronto Press in 2009. Recent and forthcoming publications include articles on Mazo de la Roche and middlebrow Canada, Mountie serial fiction and kitsch, and cultural memory and Norman Bethune. Her current research focuses on Canadian visual nostalgias and the politics of memory. She is co-editing a collection of essays on Canadian Graphic Life Narratives with Linda Warley.

NICOLE SHUKIN

Nicole Shukin is an associate professor in the Department of English at the University of Victoria in Canada, where she is presently the director of the graduate interdisciplinary program in Cultural, Social, and Political Thought (CSPT). She teaches courses on the politics of nature, cultural animal studies, and contemporary Canadian literature, among other things. The author of *Animal Capital: Rendering Life in Biopolitical Times* (University of Minnesota Press, 2009), she has also recently published articles on "animal touch" and bio-security in *Social Semiotics*, on pastoral power and non-human life in the post-colony in *CR: The New Centennial Review*, and on slaughter and cinematic affect in a volume on animal life and the moving image (forthcoming). She is presently working on a manuscript that examines states of ecological emergency in relation to the production and governing of affect.

MARK SIMPSON

Mark Simpson is an associate professor in the Department of English and film studies at the University of Alberta. His research takes up issues of mobility, circulation, and collectivity in US culture. He has published *Trafficking Subjects: The Politics of Mobility in Nineteenth-Century America* with the University of Minnesota Press (2005), and articles and chapters in *English Studies in Canada, Nineteenth-Century Prose, Cultural Critique,* and the recent Oxford University Press collection *US Popular Print Culture 1860-1920,* among other venues. Current projects include a study of postcard culture circa 1900, and a study of taxidermy and animal conservation.

RITA WONG

Rita Wong is the author of three books of poetry: *sybil unrest* (co-written with Larissa Lai), *forage* (winner of Canada Reads Poetry 2011 and the 2008 Dorothy Livesay Prize), and *monkeypuzzle* (for which she received the Asian Canadian Writers Workshop Emerging Writer Award). Wong is an associate professor in the Faculty of Culture and Community at Emily Carr University of Art and Design. With the support of a fellowship from the Center for Contemplative Mind in Society, she has developed a humanities course focused on water. She is researching the poetics of water with the support of a SSHRC Research/Creation grant: <http://downstream.ecuad.ca/>.

INDEX

Page references followed by *fig* indicate a figure.

Ackroyd, Heather, 16, 189, 194
actor-network theory, 4
Adorno, Theodor W., 161
Agamben, Giorgio, 191
Albani, Emma, 272
Alfred, Taiaiake, 192
Alliston Aquifer, 215, 217
Alyokhina, Maria, 144, 145
Anderson, Benedict, 141, 292
"Anglosaxon Street" (Birney), 88, 89
animality, 26
animals: as commodity, 30; mind of, 46n17; in North America, extinction of, 32; relations with humans, 27, 34-35, 45n4; representations of, 29-30, 45n5; role in spatial ecology, 42; as subjects, 27
Anne of Green Gables, 83, 95, 101n1
Anne Shirley (character), 83-84
Appadurai, Arjun: on globalization and culture, 139; on interpretation of commodity, 6; on life, 2; on materiality and authenticity, 177, 184; as scholar of material culture, 323; *The Social Life of Things*, 2
Archibald, Jessie, 275
archive: as collection of interruptions, 40; concept of installation, 297; as container of history, 40; Derrida's notion of, 38-39, 45n7, 289, 295-96; functions of, 295-96; multiculturalism's strategies, 290; plenitude paradigm, 293; vulnerability of, 295; wax as medium for, 296-97
Arendt, Hannah, 328
Armitage, Allan, 101n3
Arnold, Matthew, 110, 125n5
Art Gallery of Ontario (AGO): articulation of otherness, 293; curatorial shifts in, 295; expansion of Canadian art, 294; The Grange, 18, 283, 289, 297n3; interest in colonial narrative, 294; opening after renovations, 283, 288; *Thousand Points for a Thousand Generations*, 294; Transformation project, 288-89
Atanarjuat (the Fast Runner), 190
Athabasca River, 211, 212
"attention theory of value," 143, 148n19
Atwood, Margaret: "Bad News," 94-95; on beaver, 25-26, 35; *Surfacing*, 25, 36, 325; *Survival*, 302
Augustus Caesar, 176*fig*
authenticity, notion of, 177, 178
Aylmerm Louisa, 102n6

Bachelard, Gaston, 236, 241
"Bad News" (Atwood), 94-95
Baeten, Guy, 308, 314
Bailey, Thomas, 58
Baker, Steve, 28
Bandy, Mary Lea, 108
Bantock, Nick, 56
Barman, Jean, 275
Barthes, Roland, 26

Bartky, Ian, 177, 185n7
Bates, Robin, 267, 268
Baudrillard, Jean, 46n20
Bauman, Zygmunt, 139
Bear, Jeff, 218
Beaudry, Mary C., 5
beaver: in art and life, 43; circulation of image of, 26; circulation significance of, 27; in colonial history of Canada, 28, 29; colonial view of, 38; as commodity, 30, 31, 34; coolness of, 44; decreased population, 32; depiction of, 30, 44-45, 45n10; ecological importance to waterways, 42; economic and cultural significance of, 25, 33; in feminist studies, 41-42; human relationships with, 42-43; images of, 39-40; Indigenous people and, 36, 37; in knowledge economy, 43; as national symbol of Canada, 7, 29, 35; as nature's hydrologist, 42; Northwest Company's pursuit for, 33; representation of, 39, 45n5; as sacrificial subject, 25-26; studies of, 324; symbolism of, 39-40; trade in Europe, 31-32; value of fur, 30-31; virtual archive of, 44
beaver archive, 38, 40-42
Beaver Manifesto, The (Hood), 27, 40-41
Beller, Jonathan, 143
belt: destruction of, 122; detachment from clothing, 109; as fetish object, 118, 119; function of, 109; movement across class lines, 113; as murder weapon, 116, 118, 121; ownership of, 119; as piece of evidence, 118; reference to cinch, 116; as symbol of masculinity, 108
Benjamin, Walter, 112, 163, 190
Bennett, Jane, 4, 210
Bentley, David, 267
Bergson, Henri, 178, 184
Berlant, Lauren, 192, 195, 199, 200, 201
Berman, Marshall, 2
Bibb, Henry, 275
Bibb, Mary, 275
biography *vs.* autobiography, 227, 292
biopolitics, 27, 43, 193; of time, 195
Birney, Earle, 88

Blackstock, Michael, 218
Blair, Walter, 157
Blewett, Jean McKishnie, 273, 274
Blight, Elizabeth, 91
Blow, Peter, 214
Bode, Katherine, 20
Boivin, Nicole, 112
book: history of, 11; materiality of, 20n5
Bouchette, Joseph, 271
Bourgeoys, Marguerite, 280n17
Boym, Svetlana, 248, 255, 256, 258
Braun, Bruce, 14
Brayer, Elizabeth, 173
broadcasting, 147n11, 147n13
Broadcasting Act (1991), 138, 147n12
Brown, Bill: on characterization of thingness, 296; on Chicago World's Fair, 168; on collection and organization of objects, 52; on facial confrontation, 166-67; on human interaction with objects, 164; *The Material Unconscious*, 8, 166, 189; on new materialism, 3, 155; *A Sense of Things*, 62; on Spencer's conception of the world, 119; thing theory of, 3, 197
Browning, Barbara, 144, 145
Bryan-Wilson, Julia, 74
Buckland, David, 189, 194
Burning Vision (Clements), 214
Bush, George W., 193
Butler, Judith, 167n2, 168n7, 191
Butler, Tanya, 103n12

calendar: attempts to reform, 173-74, 175; depiction of, 176*fig*, 182*fig*; history of, 172-73, 175-76
Callon, Michel, 4
Cameron, Jim, 40
Canada: beaver in history and culture of, 25-26; claim to Arctic sovereignty, 192; commemoration of writers in, 269, 271-72, 273, 274, 275; creation of public memory, 268; cultural studies in, 9-10; debates on management of natural resources, 324; historic sites and museums, 268, 277; history of colonization, 32; identity, 7, 28; maps illustrated with animal figures,

33; material culture studies in, 1, 7, 10; national symbols, 28; oil pipeline projects, 325-26; persons of historical significance, 275; popular television shows, 248; tourist guides, 266; as urban nation, 329

Canadian Beaver Book, The (Cameron), 40

Canadian Radio Broadcast Commission (CRBC), 138

Canadian songs, 134-35, 136, 144

canon. *See* literary canon

Cape, Jonathan, 245n5

Cape Farewell project, 189, 194, 195, 196-97, 198-99

capitalism, 43, 140-41, 177, 193, 199, 306-10; neoliberal capitalism, 140-41; emotional capitalism, 160

Carman, Bliss, 274fig

Carr, Emily, 272, 277

Carson, Anne: approach to form, 53; on death, 58, 60; "Decreation," 53; on elegies, 61; fascination with objects, 63; and her brother, 52; on history, 51, 57, 59, 62; *If Not, Winter: Fragments of Sappho*, 62; interviews of, 53, 54, 56; journal of, 52; as literary phenomenon, 52; *Men in the Off Hours*, 59; mixed-media approach to writing, 60-61; *Nox*, 13, 61; *Plainwater*, 59; reputation of, 51-52; on "skating" between perspectives, 63; "The Anthropology of Water," 60

Carson, Rachel, 302

cartoon, definition of, 240

Catullus, 57, 61

Cavell, Richard, 301

Cazdyn, Eric, 140

CBC/Radio-Canada: brand transformation, 133; budget cuts, 133; content provision, 143, 148n19; contests, 131, 134, 136-38, 144; format regulations, 146n1; government support of, 146; mandate of, 147n12; playlist of Canadian songs, 134-36; practice of soliciting opinion online, 137-38, 142; programming, 138; promotion of national culture, 137-38; seventy-fifth anniversary, 148n20; struggle for cultural capital, 148n16; transnational narrative, 139

"Chains for the Years" (Grafton), 171

Chakrabarty, Dipesh, 190, 205n4

Chevalier, Sophie, 83, 84

Chicago World's Fair (1893), 166-67

Chignell, Hugh, 142

Chute, Hilary, 240

city: artistic representation of, 305; contradictions of globalized, 308; "creative destruction" of, 307; creative paradigm, 305; dis-identification with neoliberalized, 312; as ensemble of processes, 318; idea of right to the, 304, 316; metaphor of "a man" and, 311, 312; modernist model for representation, 312; neighbourhoods in neoliberalized, 314; notion of global, 302; phases of urban change, 309; poetics and urban planning, 309; in poetry, 310-11, 312, 313; positive and negative effects of development, 301; problem of representation, 304, 311; ranking of livable, 319n5

Classen, Constance, 291

Clements, Marie, 214

Clifford, James, 287

climate change: as alternative to sovereignty, 205; in Arctic, 197; art and, 194; chronological countdown, 196; concept of slow death and, 200; Copenhagen conference on, 196; effects of, 16; global warming as "hyperobject," 193; non-sovereign knowledge of, 203; origin of scientific study on, 205n4; polar bear and, 202-3; visualization of global, 191

climate *vs.* weather, 190

clothing, 70, 78-79, 107, 118, 125n3, 125n4

Clyde Fans, 238

coin, as symbol of renewal, 319n6

Cold Intimacies: The Making of Emotional Capitalism (Illouz), 160

Coleridge, Samuel Taylor, 123

collection, 111, 286-87; collector 242
Colombo, John Robert, 266
colonization, 77, 87, 137, 212, 291
Colvin, Jeremina, 80
comics, 225, 235, 244n1, 244n2, 244n6
commodity fetishism, 6
communicative capitalism, 132
concealment drama, 56
Conner, Shawn, 331n4
Connor, Ralph, 277
Conte, Michel, 279n7
contradiction, 308, 319n7
cool: definition and culture of, 43, 44
Coole, Diana, 3
Cotsworth, Moses Bruine: on authenticity of time, 171, 178, 184; on biology of human body and time, 184; on calendar reform, 172, 174, 175, 185; on cycles of time, 182; on Egyptian calendar, 180-81; experiments conducted by, 175-76; International Fixed Calendar, 171; life and career of, 171, 185n2; on origin and mechanics of timekeeping, 183; perception of time, 179; on practices of timekeeping, 176-77, 180; travel to Egypt, 177; understanding of time measurement, 179, 180
Coulthard, Glen, 319n2
Cowichan knitting, 71, 72-73, 80n8
craft: conservatism of, 70-71; definition of, 74; emotional experience of, 79-80
craftivism, 79n2, 80n4
Crawford, Isabella Valancy, 269-70, 272
Creative Subversions (Francis), 40
Cronin, Ray, 259
crude oil, 326
Cruikshank, Julie, 204
cultural barometers, 189, 190
cultural materialism, 9
Currie, Robert, 55
Curtis, Edward S., 232

Davies, Christi, 175
Dean, Jodi, 132
Dean, Misao, 10
Deleuze, Gilles, 131
Dempsey, Shawna, 77

Derrida, Jacques, 28, 38-39, 45n7, 289, 295
Dialectic of Enlightenment, The (Horkheimer and Adorno), 161
Dictionary of Canadian Biography (DCB), 276
digital media, 142
Dikec, Mustafa, 316, 317
Dominion model city, 238-39, 238*fig*, 239*fig*
Don River, 209
Doody, Margaret Anne, 101n1
Downtown Eastside Neighbourhood Council (DNC), 320n9
Dreiser, Theodore, 166
Drucker, Johanna, 244n6
Duncan, Sara Jeannette, 273, 274, 277

Eastman, George, 173
Eaton, Nicole, 35
Economist, The, 319n5
Edwards, Elizabeth, 20n6
elegy, 54, 55
Emberley, Julia, 40
emotional labour, 156, 158, 159, 162, 164, 168n2
emotional management, 165
emotions: as commodity, 165
Empey, Arthur Guy, 161
Enbridge, Inc., 326, 327, 328
Engels, Fredrick, 311
Entertaining the American Army, 157, 158, 165
entertainment: power of, 161, 162
environmental racism, 212
epitaph: definition of, 54
Evangeline (character), 268, 279n7
Everson, Ronald, 89, 90
"everyday creativity," 66
Ewing, Juliana Horatia, 86
Expo 67: Not Just a Souvenir, 21n6

Fabian, Johannes, 286
face contact, 156
facial conflicts, 167
facialization, 168n5
Fair Country (Saul), 44
Feldman, Jeffrey David, 108, 118

Ferguson, Sue, 147n11
fetish: as historical object, 122
fetishism, 119
Findley, Timothy, 98-99, 103n15, 103n16, 103n17
Fixed Yearal, The, 176*fig*, 180, 182*fig*
Flaherty, Robert, 231
Flatley, Jonathan, 146
Fleming, Sandford, 173, 174
flowers, 86-88. *See also* geranium
Folkart, Barbara, 104n18
Ford, John, 108
Foucault, Michel, 34
Frames of War (Butler), 168n7
Francis, Margot, 28, 40
Franklin, John, 192, 205n3, 273
Fraser River, 209
Fréchette, Louis, 280n25
Freedgood, Elaine, 6, 119
Freeze, Jimmie, 227, 231, 232
Friedman, Ted, 147n10
Frost, Samantha, 3
Fur Nation (Nadeau), 40
fur trade, 30, 31-32, 34, 38, 40-41
Fur Trader and the Indian, The (Saum), 36
Future of Nostalgia, The (Boym), 255

Gamekeeper at Home, The, 114
gardening, 91, 95, 102n5, 103n11
Gauntlett, David, 19, 66
Gehry, Frank, 289
George Sprott graphic novel: "5th Floor, End of the Hall" sequence, 242, 242*fig*; Arctic landscapes, 235-36; biotopographies of, 239-40; as caricature of colonial nostalgia, 232; characteristic of, 230, 243-44; daughter of George, 232-33; depiction of buildings, 237-38; Dominion city, 238-39, 240; drawing technique, 244n7; as fictional biography, 226-27, 228; "George is Born" sequence, 228; imitation of local television story, 230; "January 15, 1927" sequence, 237; lack of pagination, 244n3; as material object, 229; "Merrily We Roll Along" sequence, 232, 233*fig*; page layout, 235; paperback edition, 244n5; para-textual material, 228; personality of George, 233, 234, 236, 237; plot and design, 226; representation of memory objects, 242-43; romanticization of Inuit life, 231-32; salvage ethnography, 232; "The Gentleman Adventurer" sequence, 231*fig*; travel to Northern Arctic, 230-31; visual style, 235-36
geranium: in American literature, 101n2; association with female characters, 95, 96; in British society, 85, 101n3; in Canadian colonial culture, 84, 85-86, 90, 101, 102n6; cultivation in Europe, 85; cultural significance, 99-101; dark purple zone on leaves, 101n4; endurance of, 101, 102n5; femininity of, 103n12; in fiction, 91, 92-93, 102n10; introduction in North America, 102n7; medical qualities, 102n8; melancholy and, 102n9; in Newfoundland setting, 88; origin of, 84-85, 101n3; as part of domestic interior, 94, 95; vs. pelargonium, 101n3; in photography, 91, 95*fig*; physicality of human experience and, 100; in poetry, 88, 96-98, 99-100, 103-4n18; as popular houseplant, 86; as public display in windows, 92, 103n16; women's domestic lives and, 98-99
"Geranium" (Everson), 89-90
Get Out Migration rally, 216-17
Gibson, Barry, 67
Gikandi, Simon, 140
Gilbert, Liette, 316
Glass Tiger rock band, 155-56
globalization, 139, 140, 143, 301
global warming. *See* climate change
Goldstick, Miles, 214
Gosden, Chris, 20n6
Grafton, Samuel, 171, 185n1
Grange, The, 283-84, 289, 297n3
Grey, Thomas, 54
Grey Owl, 36, 37, 45n10, 280n22
Griffin and Sabine (Bantock), 56
Groot, H. B. de, 123
Groot, Jerome de, 124
Grosz, Elizabeth, 184, 186n15
Guattari, Felix, 42

Guillory, John, 138, 148n14
Gwaii, Haida, 217

H2Oil (film), 212
Haliburton, Thomas Chandler, 271
Hamelin, Danielle, 278n
Harding, Gardner L., 158
Hardt, Michael, 155
Harper, Stephen, 134, 146n2, 192
Harris, Amy Lavender, 266
Harvey, Dan, 16, 189, 194, 205n
Harvey, David, 140, 319n1
Hatfield, Charles, 235
Hathaway, E. J., 266
Häussler, Iris, 18, 284, 288, 292, 296-97
HBC (Hudson Bay Company), 71
Hearne, Samuel, 37
He Named Her Amber installation: allochronistic strategies, 286, 290; benevolent inclusions, 290-91; butler's map, 286; characteristics of, 18, 284-85; conceptual approach, 292; death on display, 289; Dr. Lee's abandoned office, 291; as material archive, 284, 285; multiculturalism's strategies, 290, 291, 293, 294; as new museology, 284; origin of name, 287; presence of bodies, 291; as self-confessing object, 284
Henry Gaunt (protagonist), 115
Hibberd, Shirley, 85
Hicks, Dan, 5
Highway of the Atom, The (Wyck), 214
Higley, Sarah, 241
Hind, E. Cora, 275
historical novel, 124-25
historic sites, 277, 278, 279n16, 280n22
Historic Sites and Monuments Board of Canada (HSMBC): board's review process, 276; designations of historic sites by, 277; history of, 271; mandate, 270; nominations, 276; selection process, 275-76
Hitchcock, Peter, 9
Hochschild, Arlie, 158, 165
Hodgins, Peter, 274
Holdenby, Christopher, 115
holding pattern, 146, 149-50n27

Holt, Rush D., Jr., 330n3
Hood, Glynnis, 27, 40
Horkheimer, Max, 161
Horse Sense in American Humor (Blair), 157
Horwood, Catherine, 84, 85, 86, 101n3, 102n6
Howes, David, 291
Hudson's Bay Company (HBC), 32-33, 34, 35
hydrocommons paradigm, 216, 219
hydrolectics: concept of, 210-11
hydrological cycle, 209
hyperobjects, 193-94, 205-6n5
ice: analogy between film and, 198; artistic representation, 195; Inuit perspective on, 204; vanishing formations of, 195
ice slide: comparison with *Qapirangajuq* film, 200; environmental exposure, 199; geographic location, 195; image of, 196*fig*; materiality of, 197; nostalgic nature of, 198; temporality of, 198, 199
Ideas of Things, The (Freedgood), 6
identity: construction of, 278
Illouz, Eva, 160, 165
imagined communities, 141-42, 292
Imagining Toronto (Harris), 266
imperialism, 6, 90, 109, 117, 137, 157, 287
Indian policy, 319n2
Indigenous people, 231; association with animality, 37; beaver and, 36, 37; colonial view of, 35, 37; critiques of sovereignty, 192; Inuit, 201-2, 203, 205; participation in fur trade, 38; photographs of, 35-36; report on practices and beliefs, 36
industrialization: dialectics of, 311
Ingham, John, 185n4
Innis, Harold, 30, 31, 32, 34, 37, 45n13
intangible cultural heritage, 12, 21n7
International Fixed Calendar, 171-72, 172*fig*, 174-75
In the Shadow of No Towers (Spiegelman), 229
In the Village of Viger (Scott), 93
Isabella Valancy Crawford Park, 269-70

Jakobson, Roman, 306
James, William, 21n8
Jameson, Fredric, 2, 12, 139
Jefferies, Richard, 114, 115
Johnson, Barbara, 5, 112
Johnson, Pauline, 273, 277
Jones, Andrew, 112, 118, 119, 120
Jones, Ann, 107
Jones, D. G., 302
Jones, D. J. V., 115
Jones, Donald, 269
Jones, Katherine, 306
Joussaye, Marie, 276
Joy Kogawa House, 266, 267*fig*

Katz, Cindi, 303, 314
Kelly, Maura, 79n2
Kern, Stephen, 178
Kern, While, 184
Keystone XL pipeline project, 330n3
Kimber, Clarissa T., 91
Klein, A. M., 275
knitting, 66, 73, 74. *See also* Mary Maxim sweaters
knowledge economy, 43-44
Kroetsch, Robert, 278
Kunuk, Zacharias, 16, 189

Laboucan-Massimo, Melina, 212
labour: immaterial, 166; material culture and, 156; war and, 156
Lahontan, Louis Armand de Lom d'Arce, baron de, 36
Lampman, Archibald, 271, 272*fig*
Landon, Fred, 274
Lane, Patrick, 99-100, 104n18
Last Crossing, The (Vanderhaeghe): animism and fetishism in, 111-13; dedication, 109; depiction of Victorian patriarchy, 111; dominant codes of masculine behaviour, 123; encounter between person and artifact, 116, 118; genre, 109, 124; impact on readers, 125; Indigenous people in, 123; main protagonists, 109-10, 111; plot, 9, 107-8, 116; on role of material agency in social interactions, 109; significance of numbers, 125n6

Latour, Bruno, 4, 13-14, 15, 34
Laurence, Margaret, 278
Leacock, Stephen, 272, 273, 277
Lecker, Robert, 20
Lee, Chantal, 291
Lefebvre, Henri: on coin as symbol of renewal, 319n6; on concept of space, 17, 306; dialects of works of, 308; idea of the "right to the city," 304, 316; on spatial justice, 304; *The Urban Revolution*, 319n1
Le Jeune, Paul, 45n9
Linton, Jamie, 209, 210
literary canon, 138-39, 148n14
Literary Journey Through Wartime Britain, A (Ward), 266
literary tourism, 265-66, 267-68
Little Nemo in Slumberland (McCay), 245n10
Liu, Alan, 43, 44
Livesay, Dorothy, 96-97, 103n12, 103n14
Lloyd, David, 147n12, 148n14
Longfellow, Henry Wadsworth, 266, 267-68
Luskey, Brian P., 118, 125n4
lyceum lecturing, 168n3
Lynch, Kevin, 307
Lyon, James, 213
Lyttle, Bethany, 72

Macdonald, Anne L., 66
MacDonald, Thoreau, 236
MacKinnon, Richard, 12, 21n7
Maclean's, 89
Maddin, Guy, 77, 255
Mair, Charles, 269, 271
management *vs.* manipulation, 161
Manzoni, Alessandro, 109
MAPL (music, artist, performance, and lyrics), 135, 146n5
Maracle, Lee, 218
Marche, Stephen, 319n3
Marilla (character), 83, 84
Marx, Karl, 180, 185n9, 310, 319n6
Mary Maxim company: collaboration with Roots, 80n9; Cowichan and, 72, 73; history of, 66; on international market, 67, 79n3; location of, 76; marketing

strategy, 67-68; poetry manuscript on, 74; success in hand-knitting market, 67; tagline, 67
Mary Maxim sweaters: advertisements, 68*fig*, 69*fig*; audience responses to, 79; Canadian identity and, 65, 79; cardigan design, 77, 80n12; Cowichan design, 71, 80n5; description of, 65; design features, 75-76, 77, 78*fig*; experience of knitting, 75-76, 77-78; modification of patterns, 76; museum collection of, 75; as national symbol, 69-70; as Olympic clothing, 71; reindeer motif, 80n6; research project on, 74-75, 79; spirit of, 70; vintage design, 67; Wikipedia on, 79n1; in Winnipeg history, 77
Mary O'Shea (character): activities of, 286, 288; as Amber, 287; artifacts of, 18, 286; as dead object, 290; otherness of, 285; personality of, 283, 287-88
Massey Commission, 273
mass media, 147n12
Massumi, Brian, 193
Material Culture Review, 11, 12
material environment, 21n9
Material History Bulletin, 11
materialism, 155, 167n2
Material Unconscious, The (Brown), 8
material urban poetics, 329
Mauro, Ian, 16, 189
Maximchuck, Mary, 66
Mayer, Margit, 304
Mayer, Sophie, 60
McCay, Winsor, 245n10
McClintock, Anne, 117
McClung, Nellie, 275
McCrae, John, 277
McCrossen, Alexis, 178
McFarlane, Craig, 46n15
McInnis, Nadine, 103n12
McKay, Ian, 267, 268, 277
McKinnon, Barry, 305, 309, 310, 312, 318
J. S. McLean Centre for Canadian Art, 294
McLuhan, Marshall, 273
McMaster, Gerald, 294
McNeilly, Kevin, 52, 53

McPhedrain, Willard, 66
Medovoi, Leerom, 143
Meikle, Margaret, 72
Mendel Art Gallery, 248, 250*fig*, 262n1
Merrifield, Andy, 310, 313
metonymic contact point: notion of, 118
metonymic reading, 6
metonymy, 119
Millan, Lorri, 77
Miller, Daniel, 4
Milton, John, 54, 61
miniatures, 241
Mitchell, W. J. T., 5
Montgomery, L. M.: *Anne of Green Gables*, 83, 84, 101n1; commemoration of, 270, 272, 279n14; national historic sites, 277; plaque dedicated to, 276
monuments: definition and function of, 260-61
Moos, David, 288, 292
Morgan, Lewis Henry, 46n17
Moritz, Albert, 266
Moritz, Theresa, 266
Morris, Mark, 245n12
Morrison, Toni, 54
Morton, Alexandra, 216
Morton, Timothy, 42, 193, 205n5
Multitude (Hardt and Negri), 165
Mulvey, Laura, 227
Munro, Alice, 102n10
museum studies, 20-21n6
music, 97, 131-53, 155-56, 252
myth: concept of, 26, 27
My Winnipeg (film), 77, 255

Nadeau, Chantal, 40
Nanook of the North, 231
NASA, 190, 205n1
Nashalik, Inusiq, 203, 204
national family, 71
national identification, 8
Native people. *See* Indigenous people
nature, 42, 302-3, 329
Neatby, Nicole, 274
Negri, Antonio, 155
Neimanis, Astrida, 218
Nelson, Robert S., 260

neoliberal city, 311
neoliberalism, 140, 312
neoliberal multiculturalism, 290, 293
neoliberal state, 140
New Directions Publishing, 54, 55, 56
new materialism, 3-4, 20n1
new museology, 284
New Voyages to North America (Lahontan), 36
New York Times Sunday Magazine, 226
Nicholson, Cecily, 305, 313, 318
Niobium mine, 215
Niocan company, 215
Nixon, Rob, 327
North American Review, 173
Northern Gateway pipeline project, 326, 327-28, 331n4, 331n5
North of Empire, 28
Northwest Company (NWC), 33, 34, 35
nostalgia, 226, 230; definition of, 255-56; forms of, 256; miniatures and, 257-58
Nox (Carson): as artifact, 56; characteristics of, 51, 55-56, 59, 63; comparison with *Griffin and Sabine*, 56; as elegy, 53, 57; as epitaph, 53; first page of, 57; fragility of, 56; history of publication, 54-55; inclusion of photographs, 58, 60; Latin text in, 57, 61-62; marketing of, 55; as meta-reproduction of scrapbook, 59; motif of lost beloved, 61; public reception of, 52, 55; reviews of, 52
Nunn, Joan, 125n3

Obama, Barack, 7, 131, 133, 141, 148n18
Obama's playlist: as canonizing project, 138-39; as reflection of Canadian identity, 140; responses to, 137
objects: characteristics of, 19; collection and organization of, 52; features of, 19; humans' interaction with, 164; immaterial, 16; materiality of, 15-16, 18, 296, 323; migrant, 8
O'Brian, Susie, 148n19
O'Connor, Flannery, 101n2
oil exploration, 325, 326, 328
oil minorities, 327
Olin, Margaret, 260

Olsen, Sylvia, 73, 80n6
Ondaatje, Michael, 51, 53
online culture, 137-38, 147n10
Operation IceBridge, 205n1
Opp, James, 275
O'Shea, Mary. *See* Mary O'Shea (character)
ouroboros: notion of, 123
Outwater, Alice B., 32, 42
Owen Trade (character), 243
Oxford Handbook of Material Culture Studies, 5

paradigm of control, 43
paradigm wars, 211-12
Pass, John, 99
Paterson (Williams), 311
Patten, Robert L., 111
Patterson, Graeme: artistic career of, 249; art works of, 13, 17, 255; *The Barn*, 252, 252*fig*, 253; childhood memories, 254-55, 257; *The Church*, 251*fig*; family home, 252; *The Hockey Rink*, 251*fig*; *The House*, 253*fig*; *Monkey and Deer* (film), 254; presentation techniques, 257; recreation of grandfather's machinery by, 253; *Romancing the Farm* (film), 252; *The Shop*, 253, 256, 259; *Woodrow* (installation), 247
Peers, Laura, 38
Persons and Things (Johnson), 5
Pérusse, Denise, 266
Phillips, Ruth, 20n6
Picturing the Beast (Baker), 28
Pierrot, George, 244n8
Pietz, William, 122
pipeline, 211, 325
pipeline mentality, 303, 329
Plainwater (Carson), 53
plants: as friends, depiction of, 101n1; imperial history of, 89; personification of, 83-84; in photography, 91
plaques: characteristic of, 265; Joy Kogawa House, 267*fig*; levels of government responsible for, 269; location of, 267*fig*, 269, 273; Poet's Corner, 273; purpose of commemorative, 268; website of historical, 268
plentitude: notion of, 292, 293

Pliny the Elder, 209
Plotz, John, 6
poaching: symbolic meaning of, 115
Pocius, Gerald, 11, 12
poetics, 61, 305, 310, 311, 318
poetry, 19, 53, 80n10, 305, 318
Poets' Corner, 274*fig*
polar bear: climate change impact on, 202-3
Political Unconscious, The (Jameson), 2
Pollan, Michael, 86, 87, 100
Ponting, Clive, 31, 32
Poole, Robert, 173
"pop canon": idea of, 148n15
Popke, Jeff, 306
Portable Property (Plotz), 6
Post-Prairie (poetry anthology), 80n11
Prentice, Jim, 331n5
Prescott, Henrietta, 87-88
Price, Rachel, 40
Prince George (BC), 309-10, 312
property, 33, 85, 164, 287, 289; "portable property," 6
"prosthetic franchise": concept of, 132, 140-41
publicity, 149n26
Pussy Riot (feminist punk group): accusations of, 149n23; arrest and trial, 144-45; counter-public broadcast, 146; critique of global present, 145-46; explanation of political significance, 149n25; media attention to, 148n22; playlist, 145, 149n24; "Punk Prayer," 145; rejection of global capitalism, 149n25

Qapirangajuq: Inuit Knowledge and Climate Change (film): as collection of environmental observations, 201-2; in comparison with ice slide, 200; interactive media, 200; perspective on climate change, 191, 200, 201; premier in Toronto, 201; public perception of, 204; theme, 189-90; visual and aural text of, 203

Radermacher, Norbert, 261
radio: characteristics of, 141-42

Radium Hot Springs, 209
Rae, Ian, 52, 53, 56, 60, 61
Rational Almanac, The (Cotsworth), 174, 179, 180, 181*fig*
Raunio, Anna-Mari, 70, 76
Ray, Angela G., 168n3
Regev, Motti, 147n9
Reigl, Alois, 260
Reilly, Sharon, 66
Richman-Kenneally, Rhona, 20n6
right to the city: idea of, 316, 317, 320n11
Ring, Dan, 257
Roberts, Charles G. D., 272*fig*, 273, 274*fig*, 279n6
Robinson, Eden, 327
rock aesthetic, 147n9
"rockization," theory of, 147n9
Roethke, Theodore, 101n2
Rogers, Linda, 96
Rogoff, Irit, 292, 293
Rolling Stone, 133
Rosaldo, Renato, 198, 199
Ross, Alexander, 37
Ross, Sinclair, 102n10
Rossetti, Francesca, 185n2
Roy, Gabrielle: depiction of prairies, 91; *Enchantment and Sorrow*, 96; historic site, 277; recognition as national historic person, 273, 278; *Street of Riches*, 96; *The Tin Flute*, 92
Rutt, Richard, 67

Sadlier, Mary Anne, 275
Sahtu Dene First Nation people, 214
salvage ethnography, 198, 206n9, 232
Sam, May, 71
Samutsevich, Yekaterina, 144, 145
Sanderson, Heather, 103n15
Sandilands, Catriona, 328
Saro-Wiwa, Ken, 326, 327
Saro-Wiwa, Ken, Jr., 327
Sassen, Saskia, 302
Saul, John Ralston, 44, 212
Saum, Lewis, 36, 37
Save the Fraser Declaration, 219
Sayers, Ivan, 79n
Schmid, Christian, 306, 308, 319n7
Schmitt, Carl, 190

Schumpeter, Joseph, 307
Scott, Duncan Campbell, 93, 272, 272*fig*, 273
Scott, Elizabeth Duncan, 102n9
Scratching the Surface: The Post-Prairie Landscape, 76
Sehgal, Parul, 56
Sense of Things, A (Brown), 62, 119, 164
"sensuous human activity," 180, 185n10
Serageldin, Ismail, 210
Seth (Gregory Gallant): cardboard constructions, 13; on character of George Sprott, 234; on Dominion project, 240, 241; drawing techniques, 234, 244n7; inspiration of, 244n8; "picture novella" *George Sprott*, 17, 226; reflections on life, 229; on superiority of the past, 225-26; use of narrative boxes, 228; *Wimbledon Green*, 242
Sexual Politics of Fur, The (Emberley), 40
Shadd, Mary Ann, 275
Shaw, W. David, 55
Shelley, Percy Bysshe, 54
Sherman, Francis, 274*fig*
Shetland knitting, 72, 80n8
Shields, Carol, 95
Shotyk (Harries), William, 216
Simmel, Georg, 21n9, 184
Simon, Mary, 201, 205
Simon Gaunt (character), 109, 110
Simpson, Mark, 168
Site 41 (Simcoe county), 215, 216
Sloan, Johanne, 21n6
slow death: concept of, 192, 199-200
smiles: as form of emotional labour, 168n2; as things, 16, 164
Smith, Goldwin, 273
Smith, Mark, 173
Smith, Sidonie, 227
Social Life of Things, The (Appadurai), 2
social reproduction, 314-15
Solway, David, 52
Somerset, Mary Capel, 85
sovereignty: Canada's claim to Arctic, 192; climate change as alternative to, 205; concept of, 191, 192
space: characteristic of urban, 306; concept of boundless, 329; concept of urban, 307; language and, 318; social, 17-18, 306; things and, 18-19; time and, 309
spatial justice, 304
spatial representation, 306-9
Spencer, Herbert, 119
Spiegelman, Art, 229, 230
Stagecoach (film), 108
Staines, David, 89
Stallybrass, Peter, 107, 120
Stengers, Isabelle, 14
Stephannson, Stephan G., 275
Stephens, Carlene, 177
Stevens, Peter, 103n13
Stevens, Wallace, 3
Stewart, Susan, 240, 241, 248, 257, 287
Stoehr, Kevin, 108
Stoler, Ann Laura, 285, 293
Strong-Boag, Veronica, 275
stylistic abstraction, 43, 46n20
Surfacing (Atwood), 25
Sutherland, Fraser, 52
syphilis: old views of treatment of, 111, 125n2
Szeman, Imre, 9, 10, 12, 140, 148n19, 325

Taseko Mines, 213
Taylor, C. J., 271
Teicher, Craig Morgan, 51
Tennyson, Alfred, 110, 111
Teztan Biny, 213
"thingness," 56, 164, 296, 297
things: changing nature of, 16-17; meaning of, 5; as objects, 19; space and, 18-19; theories of, 3
Thobani, Sunera, 292
Thomas, Augustus, 159-60
Thomas, Paul, 147n12, 148n14
Thompson, David, 31
Thrift, Nigel, 11, 14, 17
Tilley, Chris, 84, 91-92
time: biological theory and, 186n15; as commodity, 177; conception of authentic, 171; Cotsworth's concept of, 181-82; different forms of, 178; notion of relative, 178; space and, 309; types of, 310; of workers, 310
timekeeping: practices of, 179-80

time zones, 171, 185n7
Tin Flute, The (Roy), 92
Tochka, Nicholas, 149n25
Tolokonnikova, Nadezhda, 144, 145, 146, 149n25
Tomlinson, John, 139
topos: idea of, 33, 45n7
tourist guides, 266
Traill, Catharine Parr, 87, 102n8
Triage (Nicholson): "appropriate" language of, 316; on contradictions of space, 314, 315; race and gender, 315; space of Vancouver, 317, 318; syntax of, 316; themes, 313, 314; "Today at tent village" poem, 317
Trivizas, Eugene, 175
Trudeau, Pierre Elliott, 301

Uexkull, Jakob von, 45n4
uncontrollability, 168n7
"Unfold" exhibit, 194
uranium mining, 213-14, 220n3
urban imageability, 305, 307
urbanism, 310, 319n1
urbanization, 303, 305, 319n1
urban movements, 304
urban planning, 309
urban space: concept of, 307

Vancouver (BC), 303, 313, 314, 317, 319-20n9
Vancouver's Original Costume Museum, 75, 79n
Vancouver's Tish group, 97, 103n13
Vanderhaeghe, Guy, 9, 107, 124
Verchères, Madeleine de, 272
Village of Widows, 214
violent labour: circulation of, 161; as commodity, 165; critique of, 163, 165, 168n4; love as, 168n6; production and circulation of, 161; smile as form of, 168n2; transformation of emotional labour to, 158
Vipond, Mary, 138, 147n13

Wachtel, Eleanor, 54
Wakeham, Pauline, 10, 232
Wallace, David Foster, 209

war: biggest job at, 163, 167; facialization and, 168n5; humour and, 157; labour and, 156; material culture and, 156; over water, 210; role of entertainment at, 157, 161, 163; theatre and, 159; weather and, 193
Warner, Michael, 149n26
Washington, George, 267
water: cultural significance of, 218; efforts to protect, 212-13, 215, 216; in films, 218; First Nations and, 218; future wars over, 210; human relationship to, 211; materiality of, 217; metaphor of bodies of, 219; *vs.* oil, 212, 219-20n2; perception of, 209; in poetry, 218; qualities of, 209, 217; quantity and distribution in Canada, 210; uranium mining and pollution of, 213-14; urgency to reconsider materiality of, 219
water wars, 211-12
"Waterways," 214, 220n5
Watson, Julia, 227
wax: as medium, 296, 297
"Well of Dunrea, The" (Roy), 91-92
Welsh, John C., 275
What Is Water? (Linton), 209
Whatmore, Sarah J., 14
Whitlock, Gillian, 229
Whyte, Henry, 286
Williams, Kristen, 68
Williams, William Carlos, 311, 312, 318
Wilson, Ethel, 276
Wilson, Janelle L., 248
Wilson, Sheena, 325
Winnipeg (MB), 76, 77
"Without Benefit of Tape" (Livesay), 103n13, 103n14
Wolfe, Roy, 175
Wolf Tree (poetry collection), 80n10
Wollaston (Goldstick), 214
wooden almanac, 181*fig*
Woodhead, Eileen, 85
Woodrow exhibition: appeal to miniature scale, 258-59; artist's attention to detail, 249; artist's identity, 259; catalogue essay, 257; characteristics of, 262; as counter-monument, 261;

element of childhood wonder, 258; as form of intentional monument, 260; as material culture, 249; mechanical toys, 258; memories associated with viewers, 261; nostalgia, 254, 256, 259; personal and collective memories, 262; resemblance with real city, 249, 250; theme, 248; tour across Canada, 247-48; use of animation, 249-50
Woodrow *vs.* Laflèche hockey game, 250
Woolf, Virginia, 59

World Charter for the Human Right to the City, 316, 320n10
World Water Night, 218
Writers' Chapel Trust, 268
Wyck, Peter Van, 214
Wyile, Herb, 116, 125n1

Young, James, 260

Zerubavel, Eviatar, 173, 175
Žižek, Slavoj, 146, 149n23, 149n25, 168n6
Zolkewich, Shel, 65, 69

Books in Cultural Studies
Published by Wilfrid Laurier University Press

The Politics of Enchantment: Romanticism, Media, and Cultural Studies | J. David Black | 2002 | ISBN 978-0-88920-400-3

Slippery Pastimes: Reading the Popular in Canadian Culture | Joan Nicks and Jeannette Sloniowski, editors | 2002 | ISBN 978-088920-388-4

Dancing Fear and Desire: Race, Sexuality, and Imperial Politics in Middle Eastern Dance | Stavros Stavrou Karayanni | 2004 | ISBN 978-088920-454-6

Auto/biography in Canada: Critical Directions | Julie Rak, editor | 2005 | ISBN 978-088920-478-2

Canadian Cultural Poesis: Essays on Canadian Culture | Garry Sherbert, Annie Gérin, and Sheila Petty, editors | 2006 | ISBN 978-088920-486-7

Killing Women: The Visual Culture of Gender and Violence | Annette Burfoot and Susan Lord, editors | 2006 | ISBN 978-088920-497-3

Canadian Cultural Exchange / Échanges culturels au Canada: Translation and Transculturation / traduction et transculturation | Norman Cheadle and Lucien Pelletier, editors | 2007 | ISBN 978-088920-519-2

Animal Subjects: An Ethical Reader in a Posthuman World | Jodey Castricano, editor | 2008 | ISBN 978-088920-512-3

Covering Niagara: Studies in Local Popular Culture | Joan Nicks and Barry Keith Grant, editors | 2010 | ISBN 978-155458-221-1

Imagining Resistance: Visual Culture and Activism in Canada | J. Keri Cronin and Kirsty Robertson, editors | 2011 | ISBN 978-155458-257-0

Making It Like a Man: Canadian Masculinities in Practice | Christine Ramsay, editor | 2011 | ISBN 978-155458-327-0

When Technocultures Collide: Innovation from Below and the Struggle for Autonomy | Gary Genosko | 2013 | ISBN 978-155458-897-8

Parallel Encounters: Culture at the Canada-US Border | Gillian Roberts and David Stirrup, editors | 2013 |ISBN 978-155458-984-5

Europe in Its Own Eyes, Europe in the Eyes of the Other | David B. MacDonald and Mary-Michelle DeCoste, editors | 2014 | ISBN 978-155458-840-4

Reclaiming Canadian Bodies: Visual Media and Representation | Lynda Mannik and Karen McGarry, editors | 2014 | ISBN 978-155458-983-8

Material Cultures in Canada | Thomas Allen and Jennifer Blair, editors | 2015 | ISBN 978-177112-014-2

www.ingramcontent.com/pod-product-compliance
Lightning Source LLC
Chambersburg PA
CBHW072143100526
44589CB00015B/2059